THE SHIPWRIGHTS

OTHER BOOKS BY THE SAME AUTHOR:

THE HISTORY OF NORTH EAST SHIPBUILDING

NORTHUMBERLAND AND DURHAM—A SOCIAL MISCELLANY

NEWCASTLE PAST AND PRESENT

THE GREAT GUNMAKER—THE LIFE OF LORD ARMSTRONG

The Shipwrights

THE HISTORY OF THE SHIPCONSTRUCTORS' AND SHIPWRIGHTS' ASSOCIATION
1882–1963

by
DAVID DOUGAN

FRANK GRAHAM
6 Queen's Terrace, Newcastle upon Tyne, 5

First published 1975

Printed in Great Britain by
Northumberland Press Limited
Gateshead

CONTENTS

ILLUSTRATIONS

PREFACE

This history of the Shipwrights' Association represents the third element in a trilogy of histories of the unions which twelve years ago joined forces to become the Amalgamated Society of Boilermakers, Shipwrights, Blacksmiths and Structural Workers. Mr J. E. Mortimer has written the history of the Boilermakers, at least up to 1907, and Miss Angela Tuckett the history of the Blacksmiths. This book completes the story.

In writing it I became indebted to a number of people. Firstly I must mention Mr Dan McGarvey, President of the Amalgamated Society of Boilermakers, Shipwrights, Blacksmiths and Structural Workers, who provided both the opportunity and continuing support and help. Secondly I must thank his colleagues and staff who were always most willing to offer their time and service, and in this regard I must particularly mention Mr Hall and the late Mr John Dennett.

The present Lord Westwood was most helpful in talking to me about his father and in letting me browse through his voluminous collection of press clippings.

As so often in the past I must also thank Miss June Thompson and her colleagues in Newcastle Central Library, and Emeritus Professor Edward Allen of Durham University. And above all I must thank my wife, not only for her enormous help in typing the manuscript, but also for agreeing to be a grass widow for so long.

The main source material were the minutes of the Executive Committee and the Quarterly and Annual Reports. Other published works were also of considerable value, as will be seen from the notes.

David Dougan, Newcastle upon Tyne
May 1975

1

INTRODUCTION

AN ANCIENT CRAFT

With one notorious exception, shipwrights belong to just about the oldest profession in the world. For there have been ships almost from time immemorial and the men who built them, however untrained and unscientific their methods, were essentially carrying out the work we associate with shipwrights from Noah's Ark onwards. And it is no accident that the shipwrights have always used the Ark as their symbol. For it suggests both the vital importance of their work—offering a refuge against the elements—and its long history.

Mythology aside, there is clear evidence that Egypt had properly-constructed boats from about 4000 B.C. There is a well-known picture of Queen Hatshepset's trading ship, dating from about 1500 B.C. indicating that it could probably undertake quite long voyages although no doubt keeping to coastal waters. The Minoans, the Phoenicians, the Greeks, the Romans all found increasing use for ships—for trade, for voyages of discovery and, of course, for war.

Developments in the North Sea probably started a little later than in the Mediterranean. But by the time of Julius Caesar warships had been built there. They put up a good fight against the Roman Navy. By the late eighth century, the Vikings who were great travellers and warriors had developed their famous 'long ships'. With these they could travel great distances. They established a colony in Greenland and discovered America. William the Conquerer's ships were of this type.

These early ships were built by early shipwrights. No doubt their work was unsophisticated but it was certainly not unscientific. The safety of the seamen depended on their skill and so did the success of their missions.

In later centuries, as military warfare was replaced by or complemented by economic competition, ships became more important still. It is no coincidence that Edward III's gold coinage represented him standing armed and crowned in a ship. For his power at least in part derived from the strength of his navy in securing the defence of the country or in expanding its wealth through trade. And with this expanding power the demand for ships—and for shipwrights to build them—continued to grow. Shipbuilding became a speciality and its mysteries became sanctified in a gild.

In writing of shipwrights therefore we are dealing with men who have an incredibly long family tree. We are also dealing with men who have one of the most demanding jobs in the industrial world.

THE NATURE OF SHIPBUILDING

Shipbuilding is a tough business. In recent years there have been some improvements in working conditions, such as the introduction of covered yards, but these improvements have been relatively small and in any case not universal. The ships themselves have become more sophisticated and are often stuffed full of the latest scientific or military equipment. But they are still built—and probably always will be—by sheer, demanding hard work. A shipyard is no place for a weakling. On the contrary, the open-air life, especially in winter, the huge, draughty sheds, the ringing racket of the drills and welding equipment, the sheer size of the vessels and of the component parts, the nature of the materials—all of these provide a stern test of anyone's mettle.

The location of shipyards near the mouths of rivers also increases the harsh conditions. The wind in winter comes bitterly off the Irish or North Seas and is funnelled up the Clyde, the Tyne or Wear, the main shipbuilding rivers in Great Britain. In such conditions no one would stay out of doors if they could avoid it. The men who work in the shipyards cannot avoid it. This is their working environment.

Against all of this, there are a number of consolations. The craftsmen in the industry, the welders, the caulkers, the shipwrights, the electricians, the joiners and others are relatively well paid, well above the industrial average, and always have been. Shipwrights themselves in belonging to one of the oldest crafts in the world have always had the remuneration to match their position.

There must also be the satisfaction that craftsmanship itself can bring. To have a mastery of a trade, both practical and theoretical is, even in this somewhat cynical and slap-dash age, to have a confidence in one's own ability. A craftsman is still a proud man, someone to be envied. And then there is the product itself. To create one of the beautiful cruise liners—such as *Queen Elizabeth II*—or, more prosaically, an oil tanker that is almost a third of a mile long or a missile ship capable of destroying cities and even regions hundreds of miles away, must produce an undeniable sense of achievement. And to think that these ships will probably still be plying the rough seas of the world in all weathers long after the men who built them have gone is to grasp the solid quality of that work.

Ships are a vital part of the modern world, just as they were in ancient times. Indeed it is impossible to conceive how we would fare without them. Even in the jet and motor age they are still essential for many journeys. And they are still one of the most flexible of all forms of transport, ranging as they do from simple little tramp ships to highly sophisticated aircraft carriers. There is still too, even in this programmed, computerized world of advanced technology, a romantic element about ships, a sense of 'flung spray and the blown spume and the seagulls crying'. No doubt a sense of the romance of shipbuilding does not occur very often to the men actually working in the cold and dirty yards but it may still be there at times, if only subconsciously. In the same way, it is said that one of the consolations of coal-mining is the feeling of community among the men.

The element of romance may have been easier to appreciate in the days of wood and sail when the shipwright played a much more important and central part than he does now in the construction of a ship. Then he was the supreme builder, responsible for all aspects of the basic construction. Today he is hemmed in by the metal tradesmen such as the platers or by the joiners who are responsible for fitting out work. The advent of iron and then steel in the construction of ships had a devastating effect upon the shipwright's position. His natural conservatism led him to regard these materials as new-fangled and unlikely to succeed. Indeed at times shipwrights actually refused to work with iron. But, more important, iron shipbuilding led to a fundamental dilemma between two groups of workers. On the one hand, there were the shipwrights, who had traditionally been responsible for the basic construction of ships. While, on the other hand, there were the boilermakers, who claimed the right to any work in metal. In theory, the problem was insoluble. But in practice it was resolved largely in favour of the boilermakers. And it was resolved in their favour largely because since 1834 they were united in an increasingly effective national union while the shipwrights did not form a similar body until 1882, by which time the battle was won and lost. As a result shipwrights were constantly in conflict with platers, who were members of the Boilermakers' Society, and over the years demarcation disputes between these two groups have been a notable feature of industrial relations in the industry. Only in the Naval Dockyards did the supremacy of the shipwrights linger on, largely because the Dockyards, being under Government control, were less open to new ideas and new influences.

By contrast, the shipwrights were unable to turn to the fitting out work done by joiners. They too were a more powerful union than the shipwrights and much less specialized. The majority of their members were involved in housebuilding or factory work, particularly in the furnishing trade. Shipwrights by their nature were dependent on the shipbuilding industry and their power was constrained by the refusal of the joiners to let them share in the fitting out work consequent upon the construction of the hull.

Yet despite these difficulties, the shipwrights have remained a viable and indeed a proud craft, making an important contribution to an important industry.

For almost a hundred years—in the second half of the nineteenth century and the first half of the twentieth—Britain was unquestionably the greatest shipbuilding power in the world, a factor that added appreciably not only to her industrial success but also to her military might. At one time, in the 1880's and 1890's, the United Kingdom was turning out four in every five ships built anywhere in the world. This was a remarkable record. Seldom has any small country equalled, never mind exceeded, that performance in a basic industry although Japan might be getting near it today. Of course one can make all sorts of excuses: that Britain was the first industrialized nation; that her naval and maritime fleets, the main markets for her shipbuilders, were overwhelmingly supreme; that she had been blessed by nature with the physical resources that made economic miracles possible. The fact still remains that this was one of the great industrial records.

Since those days, two major events have reduced British shipbuilding to a shadow of its former self. The severe depressions of the 1920's and 1930's crippled the industry and the strong post-war growth in foreign competition, especially from Japan, prevented it from regaining its former dominance. The causes of the decline have never been fully revealed—and indeed have probably got more to do with the sickness in the British economy than just with the industry itself. What one can say very simply is that U.K. output which at one time exceeded eighty per cent of the world total was by 1966 less than ten per cent and that since then the figure has gone even lower.

Within that general rise and fall, there were shorter-term slumps and booms. In fact, the industry is characterized by an extraordinary pattern of switch-back production, moving from peak to trough and back to peak again within a decade. This in turn led to volatile employment and wages policies and consequently to permanently suspicious relations between managers and men. During periods of rising demand, the employers knew that the unions would press for big wage increases and go on strike if they did not get them. In return, the men knew that as soon as a recession occurred, the employers would first call for a reduction in wages and then start to lay large numbers of them off. If only a more stable level of output could have been achieved, many of the problems in the industry, particularly in labour relations, could have been avoided.

A smaller number of unions would also have helped. Every report on the industry has noted the difficulties that arise from the large number of unions. In all, there are twenty-two unions for an industry that contains only about 150,000 workers. Five of the twelve manual unions combined account for less than two per cent of the workforce. One of the most famous reports on the industry compiled in 1966 by a committee headed by Mr Reay Geddes commented: 'We believe that for the trade unions to consider this matter and to try to effect over a reasonable period of time some simplification in union representation, will be beneficial to the industry and to the workers engaged in it.'

The report also declared: 'The joint failure of both management and unions to tackle the problems of bad industrial relations resulting in the wasteful use of labour has cost the industry dear in money and reputation. The present state of affairs has hampered the work of managers, planners and individual workers alike; has kept costs up and deliveries late; and has in consequence tied the industry's right hand behind its back.'

How this situation arose—and how some of the other themes mentioned here developed—will become clear in the following pages, which attempt to describe the history of the shipwrights' union against the background of what was happening in the industry and in the country at large.

CHAPTER ONE

As an ancient craft, the shipwrights were one of the groups of workers to form themselves into a gild in mediaeval times. Yet, on the other hand, they were among the last of the traditional trades to create a trade union as we would know it today.

THE GILDS

Shipwrights were among the earliest of the craft gilds. These gilds were an essential part of the mediaeval economy. They managed the affairs of the various crafts in the towns, fixing prices, wages and conditions of work. There were strict requirements for entry—as a general rule only sons of craftsmen were admitted—and arduous conditions were imposed on the apprentices. At the expiry of their indentures, however, the apprentices became either masters or journeymen and had a secure and relatively well-paid occupation for life. Outside the gilds there were large pools of unskilled labour, ill-paid, uncared-for and with no prospect of improvement. By the fourteenth century the gilds were altering their nature. They had been noted for the closeness of the masters, journeymen and apprentices. They were all 'small men' together, brother labourers in the shop, sharing the same bench, the same meals and more or less the same rewards. But now a sense of rift was developing. The expansion of trade was bringing an increasing difference of monetary rewards. The master was becoming less the brother craftsman and more the entrepreneur, engaged in organizing the business and selling the goods. The distinction between the employers and the employed was becoming more marked. 'And so we find in the towns of the fourteenth century not only occasional strikes for higher wages inside the gilds but in some cases the formation of permanent "Yeomen Gilds" to champion the interests of the employees and perform the fighting functions of a modern Trade Union.'[1]

The prime purpose of the gilds was to protect the members' interests, either individually through the operation of various benefit schemes or jointly through restrictions on entry or regulation of the quality and the price of the work that was done. Members falling into poverty were supplied out of the common tax. The gilds were also responsible for passing on the 'mysteries of their craft'. This was one of the reasons why entry was always carefully regulated for if too many apprentices were admitted, it would be impossible for the journeymen to give them proper training. Indentures were very strict as the following example from the early eighteenth century illustrates:

'This indenture witnesseth that John Watson of Stockton upon Tees hath of his own free and voluntary will found himself an apprentice under John Headlam ... the said apprentice, his said Master shall well and truly serve; his secrets keep; his lawful commands everywhere do and execute ... taverns or ale houses he shall not frequent ... at Dice, Cards, Tables, Bowls or any other unlawful games he shall not play ... Matrimony during the said term he shall not contract nor from the service of the said Master at any time absent himself.'[2]

The gilds also had political power. In Newcastle a charter from Edward III in 1342 allowed twelve gilds to nominate twenty-four burgesses who would govern the town and appoint the Mayor and officers. This power clearly gave the gilds a most important and influential position in the life of the town. At the beginning of the seventeenth century, a charter from James I widened the local franchise by bringing in other gilds, including the shipwrights to nominate burgesses. This remained the law until the 1835 Municipal Reform Act.

The shipwrights' gild in Newcastle kept alive their symbolic origins in two interesting ways. Firstly, their emblem or 'armorial bearing' as it was then called, incorporated Noah's Ark not once but twice. On top of one of the arks was a silver dove, holding an olive branch in its beak, surely the happiest of symbols. Secondly, the playlet performed by the gild in the annual cycle of Miracle Plays was 'Noah's Ark'. It contained the lines spoken by God:

> 'Bid him go make a ship
> 'Of board stiff and great
> 'Although he be not a wright.'

This play is the only survivor of all the plays performed at that time in Newcastle. A few other early records remain. We know that the Newcastle Shipwrights' Gild met on 8th August 1636 and agreed that on 27th December each year they would choose two wardens and two 'overseers', that they would not work on Sundays or holidays and that they would restrict apprentices from working 'tide work' until they had served three years at the trade. In 1651 ten brethren were fined for working on 30th January, a day of thanksgiving, and on 24th June 1673 a brother was fined for challenging another to a fight. There is also a scrap of evidence from Sunderland at this time. A record from the year 1648 refers to John Forster, who lived in Low Street as a shipwright. Perhaps the most famous shipwright at the beginning of the seventeenth century was Phineas Pett who lived in London. In 1610 he designed and built the large galleon *Prince Royal* which had three decks in the hull as well as those in the forecastle, quarter deck and poop. She was ornately carved and gilded. The carving cost £441 and the gilding £868. As a shipwright Pett was important enough to be able to ask James I to keep his designs secret. In 1639 Pett and his son produced another outstanding ship, *Sovereign of the Seas*.

By this time, State control was taking over from municipal control. 'In the Middle Ages each locality, through its town council or craft gilds, had decided questions of wages and prices; the relations of master, apprentice and journeyman, the right to trade in a place; and the conditions under which trade there should be carried on.'[3] But by Elizabeth's reign, at the beginning of the seventeenth century, this local control was being replaced by a national system. 'The reasons for this great change were various: The decay of many towns and the spread of industry into the country districts where there was no municipal authority; the decline of the craft gilds which had received their coup de grâce in the confiscatory legislation of Edward VI against gild property; the growth of the power of the Crown, working through Privy Council and Parliament; and the joyous sense of nationhood which inspired the Elizabethan English. A man no longer felt his first loyalty owing to his town, his gild, or his "good lord" but to his Queen and country.'[4]

EXPANSION OF TRADE

Shipbuilding, like the economy of the country as a whole, continued to grow through the expansion of trade, especially cloth-making, and more particularly as far as the North of England was concerned through the development of the coal trade. By the start of the eighteenth century there were over a thousand colliers and coastal vessels plying around these coasts and across the channel. This increase stimulated a demand for more shipbuilding and consequently for more shipwrights. Daniel Defoe in his *Tour Through England and Wales* published in 1727 wrote these historic words about the river Tyne: 'They build ships here to perfection. I mean as to strength and to firmness and to bear the sea; and as the coal trade occasions a demand for such strong ships, a great many are built here.' The ships were small, wooden vessels. In 1750 for example the Tyne launched its largest vessel up to that time, which could carry just thirty keels of coal. This was the *Russell*, launched from Headlam's yard. But while they were not very big by today's standards, they were certainly serviceable and essential. Throughout the eighteenth century not only did shipbuilding output expand in the traditional areas such as Newcastle, Liverpool, or Bristol but it also extended to new areas like the Tees. The American War of Independence nurtured shipbuilding there followed by the general stimulus provided by the Napoleonic Wars. In Whitby a contemporary account recorded: 'The skill of our shipbuilders and carpenters has long been generally acknowledged and has brought much business to the town and produced a great influx of property, especially during the first American war and the last French one.'[5]

Other areas were recording a similar advance. In Liverpool there are records of 144 shipwrights between 1700 and 1750. By the end of the century the total had gone up to 600. No doubt they were not continuously employed in shipbuilding but an account of 1804 lists 487 shipwrights in Liverpool.[6] Bristol was still an important shipbuilding centre although it was about to lose its eminence. Shipbuilding had been carried on there for centuries, providing transport for the wealthy merchants and their flourishing businesses. As early as the fourteenth and fifteenth centuries there were well-established shipyards in the town. There is a record from 1645 of William Bullock acting as 'chief builder' of a merchant ship named *Love's Increase*. Around the same time, Francis Bailey was building warships for Charles II.[7] By the end of the eighteenth century, Bristol was a very busy shipbuilding centre. For the Navy alone it built fourteen warships during and just after the American war.

The workers lived near the yards. The Poll Book for 1784 mentions forty-three shipwrights and anchorsmiths in Clifton Parish, thirty-two in Redcliffe and twenty-three in St Augustines. We also find here the first sign of industrial unrest. When the builders tried to reduce wages in 1784 to 2s 6d a day, the men came out on strike and the builders had to retain the wages at 3s.

Glasgow and Sunderland were also developing very rapidly at this time. Clydeside was the first river to develop steampower, first with the *Charlotte Dundas* and then with the *Comet*, the first steamship to brave open waters. That was in 1811. From that point Clydeside shipbuilders made rapid progress and the introduction of iron ships provided another important stimulus.

This continuing impetus to trade encouraged the shipwrights to form modern versions of the mediaeval gilds. Among the first to be formed was the Shipwrights' Association of South Shields. Its 'articles' are dated 16th March 1795 and describe it as 'for the mutual relief of its members'. It was managed by a committee of fifteen. The subscription was 10d in the £, or ½d in the shilling of each member's earnings. Members unfairly contributing or concealing their earnings forfeited a guinea, while they were expelled on failing to pay their contribution for six months. The Association comprised both shore-working and sea-going members, the latter receiving a benefit when shipwrecked of £8, 'or such damage as he has sustained if less than that amount'. Any 'member finding fault with the amount awarded him to be fined £5'. Any member captured by the enemy received £8, with an allowance of 6s per week during his imprisonment, the money presumably being paid to his family. Where any member was 'pressed to serve' (that is, in the Navy), his wife or mother received an allowance of 3s per week. The allowance to sick members was 7s per week, while their widows received £10 per annum, or £15 should the capital fund of the Association reach £1,000. Orphans with both father and mother dead received the same allowance yearly until the youngest was fourteen, while any orphan incapable of getting a livelihood was allowed 1s per week for life.

A similar organization in South Shields was the Amicable Association of Shipwrights for Mutual Relief which was founded on 12th February 1798 at the house of a Mr Grieve. Its benefits were slightly smaller: £6 to shipwrecked members; £6 and 6s a week to those taken by the enemy; 7s a week for sickness or for life to those members unable to work; £8 a year to widows or £12 when the funds exceeded £1,000. According to one commentator, the shipwrights 'were very strongly organized and were exceedingly tenacious of the many and curious customs connected with their craft, of which one was the wearing of tall hats as part of their working dress'.[8]

Another powerful body was the Union Society which was described as 'an exceedingly autocratic body'.[9] It prescribed the maximum output of daily work which no member must exceed. The working rules were also very intricate. Not a few referred to the 'lewance' or allowance of beer given to the workmen at the various stages of the construction of a ship, a custom handed down since the days of Queen Elizabeth. On inspecting a naval dockyard she had apparently commented that the work of shipwrights was so heavy and exhausting that they must be in need of refreshment between ordinary meal hours.

The method of distribution was usually by tin checks, each one representing one, two or three pints which were exchanged for beer at particular public houses. As the tin checks were transferable, it was no uncommon thing for apprentices, who were entitled to half shares, to get more money for the sale of their 'lewance' than they received in wages. Another curious custom was that at a launch every apprentice was expected to plunge into the water with all his clothes on to assist in recovering the floating timbers which had formed the ways. Any who showed reluctance to perform this unpleasant duty were generally thrown in. The Union Society was a wealthy body and in times of depression even employed its funds to build vessels in order to create work for its members. In 1826 when 400 of the town's 630 shipwrights were out of work, Shields Union spent £800 on a 'new ship'. Its annual income at that time was £676.

The Liverpool Society of Shipwrights was equally well organized. It built almshouses for older members and provided substantial benefits of other kinds. It was said to be so powerful that any employer who refused to obey its rules found his business brought to a standstill.[10] There was also the Liverpool Shipwrights' Trade and Friendly Association founded in 1784.

These early signs of organization and power were not without disadvantage. For the Government, fighting the Napoleonic Wars which had sprung out of the French Revolution, became seriously alarmed by the power of these trade groups. They feared that they might harbour revolutionaries whose intentions, far from simply protecting members' interests, might spread to a wish to overthrow the Government. In June 1799, they brought in the Combination Bill which forbade all 'combinations' of masters and workmen. The Bill was hurried through the House and gained the Royal Assent only 21 days after its introduction.

The following year another Bill was introduced to tighten matters still further. This called for 'the prevention of conspiracies among journeymen tradesmen to raise their wages. All benefit clubs and societies are to be immediately suppressed'. This second Bill, coming so quickly after the previous Act, stung the trade clubs and societies into action.

The Liverpool Shipwrights' Society approached their two members of Parliament, General Tarleton and Colonel Gascoyne, and they agreed to unite to bring in an amending Bill. It secured only the most minor of modifications in the face of a very determined Government but it does illustrate the direct political power enjoyed by the shipwrights at that time when the vast majority of people in the country had no political power or influence of any kind.

The Combination Acts of 1799 and 1800 represented a fundamental change in the status of the working man, a change that had numerous causes. Perhaps the most important was the new relationship between the craftsman and his employer. In a feudal economy, the craftsman was largely his own master but with the arrival of a capitalist economy based on the factory, on machinery and on increasingly larger-scale production, the position of the individual decreased. He was no longer the centre of the production process but only a component, along with machinery, raw materials and finance. Secondly, Britain was entering the age of laissez-faire advocated by Adam Smith in his famous book *The Wealth of Nations* produced in 1776. Every restraint to trade was questioned and felt to be against the interest of the country. The division of labour into a multitude of different functions, the organization of mass production and the liberalization of trade were the three principal tenets which would provide the greatest stimulus to manufacture. The Combination Acts, preventing restraint of trade by workmen or employers, was seen to be part of this philosophical framework.

Finally, there was the influence of the Napoleonic Wars and more particularly the French Revolution. There was general alarm that associations of any kind might lead to rebellion and insurrection. It is noticeable that although the Combination Acts outlawed groupings of employers as much as workmen, it was only the latter who were prosecuted. Thousands of tradesmen were convicted for combining. There is no case on record of an employer being punished for the same offence.

But while thousands of workmen were convicted, for many more life went on as normal. This was partly because there was no adequate police system. But, more important, life could hardly exist without a union. A contemporary account stated: 'It would be almost impossible for many of those trades to be carried on without such societies and the roads and parishes would be much pestered with these travelling trades, who travel from want of employment, were it not for their societies who relieve what they call "tramps".'[11]

THE NINETEENTH CENTURY

By 1824 the Napoleonic Wars were long over. The security of the state was no longer in question. Trade could return to normal. A Select

Committee of the House of Commons, enquiring into the state of industry, found that the Combination Laws were no longer necessary. Indeed they were a positive hindrance and tended to 'produce mutual irritation and distrust'. The Committee also came to the conclusion 'that masters and workmen should be freed from such restrictions as regards the rate of wages and the hours of working and be left at perfect liberty to make such agreements as they eventually think proper'. The Government accepted these findings. The result was the Combination Law of 1824 which repealed all previous statutes and declared that the mere act of combination should not be grounds for prosecution.

The immediate outcome was a sudden crop of strikes and a certain amount of violence. The Government, under pressure, set up another committee of enquiry which heard rather more evidence on combinations than its predecessor had and uncovered various apparently undesirable practices. Shipbuilding employers in particular were incensed by the growing power of the men. They told the committee about the Shipwrights' Provident Union Society, which operated in the Thames shipyards. They said that it drew up stringent rules for the employment of members and their conditions of work. The employers felt that their own freedom of action was severely curtailed. Accordingly they wanted to see the original Acts back on the Statute Book. In this bid, they failed. Shipwrights from London and Newcastle joined thousands of their workmen in resisting the re-introduction of the Acts. But they could not deter a compromise Bill which the Government passed into law in the summer of 1825. This reaffirmed the repeal of the previous Acts but tightened up the provisions against violence and intimidation. The purpose of legal combination was also narrowed to exclude such questions as the ratio of apprentices to journeymen which were felt to be for the employers to decide. But although they could deal with wages, hours and conditions of work and little else, combinations of workmen were now legal and could operate openly and freely.

No doubt this compromise Bill reflected at least in part the political influence of some of the traditional craft societies. The master shipwrights, like other powerful tradesmen, being freemen were entitled to vote in Parliamentary elections. In the days before the 1832 Reform of Parliament this privilege was of considerable value. It was general practice for votes to be sold to the highest bidder or to the candidate who made the best offer to look after one's interests. The Liverpool Shipwrights' Society was particularly concerned with this power at its members' disposal and spent a great deal of time on organizing its 'sale'. We have seen how they persuaded their two members of Parliament, General Tarleton and Colonel Gascoyne, to speak on their behalf in the debates on the Combination Bill in 1800.

While the 1825 Act pleased the embryonic trade societies, the year was a bad one economically. The four following years were even worse. Hundreds of thousands of workmen were thrown out of work. Wages were reduced all round. In many areas workmen were kept from starvation only by public subscription.

In these circumstances, many men went 'on tramp' to look for work elsewhere. 'At a time when railways were not yet in existence and when the cycle of boom and slump was more regional than national or international, it was quite practical for a skilled man who was unemployed to set out 'his kit packed on his back and walking stick in hand' in order to seek work in his trade in some other town.'[12] His card would entitle him to hospitality for a few days from the trade club in the town while he looked for work. If he failed he would set out on his travels once more.

The shipwrights were organized in societies in most of the ports of the country. Indeed in many of the ports, as we have seen, there was more than one society. For example, there were two in Sunderland at the beginning of the nineteenth century. 'The shipwrights were a steady and reliable body of men and were excellent workmen.'[13] As an alternative to 'tramping' the Sunderland Societies emulated the South Shields Union Society by shipbuilding 'on spec' in the yard vacated by Thomas Tiffin in a bid to create work for the men. This was a more viable alternative—indeed it has a Keynesian ring to it—of creating work where ordinary demand proved ineffective—if only because the tramping system was unlikely to produce dividends. Local societies were so jealous of their power and privilege that they did not welcome strangers. Sidney and Beatrice Webb in their book *Industrial Democracy* published in 1897, commented that local shipwrights' clubs 'strove with might and main to exclude from any chance of work in the port all but men who had learned their trade within its bounds. These monopoly rules caused incessant friction between the men of the several ports.'

After the mid point of the century, 'the old type of local independence in the trade union movement gradually became obsolete'.[14] The expansion of trade, the widening market for labour and goods, the ironing out of regional differences, the creation of employers' organizations, all these factors tended to emphasize the inadequate nature of the tightly-controlled autonomous local societies. Yet many of them were intensely conservative and felt that any national merger would represent an unacceptable dilution of their power and interests. The problem was particularly acute among shipwrights, as Sidney and Beatrice Webb observed:

'To remedy this disastrous state of things a loose federation was between 1850 and 1860 gradually formed among the local societies for the express purpose of discussing, at annual congresses, how to establish more satisfactory relations between the ports. In the records of these congresses we watch, for nearly thirty years, the struggle of the monopolist societies against the efforts of those, such as Glasgow and Newcastle, whose circumstances had converted them to a belief in complete mobility of labour within a trade.'[15] As we shall see, the struggle became so fierce, with neither side able to convince the other, that a parting of the ways was inevitable. The Associated Shipwrights' Society grew out of the obduracy and obscurantism of the United Kingdom Amalgamation of Shipwrights.

These local societies also demonstrated their backward attitude in their opposition to iron shipbuilding which was starting to come in during the 1840's and 1850s'.

The South Shields Union Society even went so far as to impose a heavy fine on any member who accepted work in an iron shipbuilding yard. This negative attitude, which was typical of other societies around the country, provided a glorious opportunity for boilermakers and others to establish their position in shipbuilding. This in turn laid the basis for many of the demarcation disputes which were to follow in later years.

As early as the 1860's there were frequent disputes. The boilermakers claimed that any work in metal belonged to their members, including shipbuilding, whereas the shipwrights argued that shipbuilding as such, no matter what materials were involved, was their traditional preserve. It was, of course, an insoluble problem. Both sides clearly had right on their side. The disputes reached a particular degree of ferocity in the Admiralty Dockyards where the shipwrights had been established for many years or centuries and where tradition tended to be supplemented by regulations. These regulations provided the safeguard that their industrial strength or weakness could not give them. But in private yards, regulations were not so well set down. The boilermakers who had formed a national union in 1834 were able to make substantial inroads and the weak shipwright societies were almost powerless to stop them.

Another example of the innate and deep-seated conservatism of some societies is again provided by the actions of the South Shields Union Society. A long and bitter strike occurred in 1841 following an attempt by the employers to abolish beer allowance in favour of money payments. The men claimed that abolition would be an interference with one of the oldest regulations in the trade, existing from 'almost beyond the memory of man'. The strike, which also concerned a pay demand, lasted a long time and caused great distress in the town. An old weigh-house in the Market Place had to be fitted out as a soup kitchen. In the end the men returned to work on their old terms. But ten years later the men went on strike again from 31st January to 10th March 1851. This time they were pressing for an advance in wages, a reduction in hours and the right to prohibit the employers asking apprentices for a shorter term than seven years. Although this strike also failed, an indirect outcome was the abolition of beer allowances for which money payments were substituted.

Against the deadening effect of local autonomy we must balance the progress that was made in other directions in the trade union movement. In 1867 the Government modified the severity of the Master and Servant Law which had previously treated the employee as a criminal for any breach of contract. He could be sent to prison whereas the employer was liable only to civil proceedings. The new law allowed criminal action against the employee only in 'aggravated cases'. Secondly the Royal Commission on Trade Unions which sat from 1867-69 came out with a not unfavourable report largely because it thought trade unions were of little value to their members or the public. Its main recommendation was that something should be done to legalize trade unions. Their rules should be registered with the Registrar of Friendly Societies who should have the power to reject 'objectionable' clauses such as restrictions on the employment of apprentices. The Report also recommended that the benefit and strike funds of unions should be separated. 'The publication of the Commission's Reports resulted in a remarkable change in the public attitude to trade unionism. People recognized that the great bulk of the work done by unions was of a character that was entirely beneficial.'[16]

The recommendations were taken up in the Trade Union Act introduced by Gladstone's Government in 1871. It laid down that union members were not liable to prosecution on the ground of being 'in restraint of trade', that unions could register with the Registrar of Friendly Societies which would bring them certain advantages and that internal agreements, such as those concerning the payments of subscriptions and benefits, should be free from legal action. 'Trade unions, in fact, were to have the protection of the law but to be free from its interference in their internal affairs.'[17]

The movement towards national unions was continuing to develop particularly following the example of the Amalgamated Society of Engineers, the 'new model' as it was called by the Webbs. Founded in 1850 it had a high rate of contributions and a generous scale of sickness, superannuation and funeral benefits. While its district committees were allowed a degree of autonomy, the bulk of its funds were centralized at the headquarters in London under a full-time general secretary, supervised by an Executive Committee. By the end of 1851 membership was 12,000 and in 1870 it was 35,000.

By the third quarter of the century unions were banding together to discuss joint action. In 1868 the first meeting was held of what was to become the Trades Union Congress.

This progress towards a national movement had been achieved without necessarily reducing the sense of local independence. 'The apparent reduction of local autonomy was mitigated by the absence of any attempt to dictate "custom and practice". Standard rates and hours, bans on illegal men, limitation of apprentices, and monopolies of materials and machines were left to the branches, to be imposed by withdrawing men from the illegal shops and supporting them by an unemployment benefit rendered all the more secure by centralized finance.'[18]

But while this was true of certain unions such as the Amalgamated Society of Engineers or the Boilermakers' Society, it was not true of the shipwrights. Their only national forum, the United Kingdom Amalgamation of Shipwrights which had been created in 1850, had signally failed to develop into a centralized body of any significance. It was an inefficient and badly-managed institution without any permanent staff, whose main function was to arrange an annual conference. But since the discussions nearly always proved irrelevant or inconclusive, dealing with the shadow and not the substance, and since the conference was in any case dominated by the traditional shipbuilding centres such as London and Bristol rather than the emerging power centres such as the North-East and Scotland, there arose a growing sense of frustration and disillusionment. The shipwrights were being left behind. The new unions were showing the way. And nowhere was this more apparent than in shipbuilding itself where the Boilermakers' Society, which had been founded as long ago as 1834, was making rapid strides under the guidance of its new general secretary, Robert Knight. 'Robert Knight epitomized both the strength and the weakness of trade unionism among the aristocracy of labour in the heyday of British capitalism. He was efficient in administration and was concerned always to protect the funds of the union. His policy was one of conciliation towards the employers ... Nevertheless it did not provide an adequate answer to some of the wider economic and social changes which took place during his period of office, particularly towards the end of the century.'[19] Notwithstanding this criticism, the progress by a rival union as well as the more general progress of other unions alarmed the progressive elements of the shipwrights. If they could not get satisfaction from the U.K. Amalgamation—and they had tried on many occasions—then they must set up something new. To this end they got those representatives who remained unconvinced of the need for change to agree that they should try to transform their dreams into reality. They should try to establish a national body. If they succeeded then the doubters would be willing to consider the question again. But until such a time the independence of the local societies should remain intact and inviolate.

And so at the tail end of 1881 representatives of a few local shipwrights' societies in Scotland and the North-East of England laid their plans for creating a powerful organization out of a rather sickly one. The Associated Shipwrights' Society was about to be born.

CHAPTER TWO

Having tried without success to put some 'ginger' into the Amalgamation, the more determined societies now accepted the challenge of creating a more vigorous organization. It is important to appreciate that at this stage there was no question of a breakaway. The new union grew out of the old and had its blessing. Indeed, it was not necessarily regarded as a new independent union but rather as a strengthening of the old union and an extension of its interests. The societies and members who favoured a more cohesive format remained members of the Amalgamation. The new Society was supplementary to the old one and not necessarily competitive.

THE SOCIETY IS FORMED

Throughout January of 1882 special general meetings were held by those societies which favoured the formation of a national association. The impetus came largely from Scotland and the river Tyne. The Tyne Shipwrights' Provident Society, for example, met in the house of a Mr Bewick in Hebburn on 18th January while the following evening the Glasgow Shipwrights' Society convened a meeting in the schoolroom in Douglas Street, Partick. Ten days later the Leith shipwrights met at 10 Riddle's Close. All these meetings—altogether eleven societies were involved—had a list of identical proposals in front of them which hopefully would form the basis of national schemes and thereby in turn a national trade union organization. To allow the maximum flexibility and to forestall criticisms which had been raised so often before, the proposals concerning benefits were divided into three sections. A prospective member could then decide which sections to join. If he did not feel the need to pay for a particular kind of benefit then he could elect not to subscribe to that particular section, while still finding it advantageous to join the Society for the other benefits it had to offer.

Furthermore, the proposals offered a gesture towards appeasing the autonomy of the local societies. For while the first two sections covering benefits for trade protection and unemployment were to be common to every port or district that adopted them, the third section covering what were called 'Friendly Benefits' were to be left under the control of the local societies.

As the circulars giving details of the proposals said: 'The object of dividing into sections is to endeavour, as far as possible, to meet every objection urged by non-members against joining our Society. Some object because it is too much of a Friendly Society; and as they are members of other Friendly Societies they don't require it but would join it if it was a "Trade Protection Association". Well, the first section is purely Trade Protection and we thus meet these objections .... There are others who say they can insure themselves against sickness, accident or death in any Friendly Society similar to an insurance company; but they can't in such societies insure themselves against want of employment. This can be done by a Trades' Union which is the only institution which can insure tradesmen a given sum per week when out of employment; and if this is adopted by our Trade those parties say they will join .... And to those who wish to uphold all the privileges of our Trade and all the benefits of our Association, we have all the Sections, which embrace all the benefits generally provided by such Associations for similar contributions'.

The contributions to the first section were a halfpenny a day (old money) or threepence a week to provide allowances against strikes or lock-outs, compensation for the loss of tools by fire or shipwreck, and generally to provide financial assistance for what was called trade protection. Entry money for this section was five shillings with current members exempted.

The second section covered all aspects of the first section but added to them unemployment benefits of eight shillings (40 new pence) a week for eight weeks and four shillings (20 new pence) a week for another nine weeks in any period of twelve months.

At this time the average wage for a shipwright was about £1.70-£2.00 a week. The contributions were a penny a day or sixpence a week for both sections with entry money of ten shillings for new members and five shillings for current members.

With regard to the third section covering 'friendly benefits' for sickness, accident or death, local societies were to be allowed to run them independently as in the past and to decide on the level of contributions and benefits. But there was a move towards uniformity here too. For example, the Tyne shipwrights reduced the level of contributions from fourpence to threepence a week to bring them into line with Scottish practice and added benefits of £4 on the death of a member's wife and £1 10s (old money) on the death of a child.

The proponents of a national organization recognized that the unemployment benefit was their main attraction in securing converts. They took great pains to explain its advantages and even indulged in sentimentality. 'Look for a moment at the picture so often presented in many homes during dull times; see the husband, the head of the family, coming home weary and footsore day after day, or it may be week after week and month after month and to the oft-repeated question, have you got a job? again and again; answer with a desponding look the cheerless reply of no success yet. Meanwhile the small savings have been exhausted, the household goods disappearing one by one, to stifle the cry of children for bread; with penury and want staring him in the face, his credit stopped, his independence gone, he either sinks into a nameless grave or he and his family become a burden on others or may be worse.

'There are some who take up the selfish argument and say I have always been constantly employed; I do not need to provide for idle times; I do not care whether my fellow-workmen live or starve. To all such we would say, you know not the day or the hour when your previous good fortune may desert you; and the fact that you have all along been constantly employed only increases your responsibility to make such a provision.'

While the benefits were designed as an incentive to membership and obviously provided a service, they were also vital to the organization of the Society or indeed to any trade union for two reasons. Firstly, by helping to tide members over bad times, such as sickness or unemployment, they discouraged individuals from undermining customary wage rates or working conditions which they might otherwise have been tempted to do. For a desperate need for money would put a strain, perhaps an intolerable strain, upon loyalty to the union. Secondly, benefits could be used as a disciplinary measure. Anyone breaking the union rules would not only be expelled, he would also lose any claim on the contributions he had made. This was another powerful factor in instilling a sense of unity and cohesion.

The meetings in the eleven centres were relatively well attended and secured decisions to call a Delegates' meeting in February to establish the Associated Society of Shipwrights.

The meeting was held at Neilson's Temperance Hotel in Ingham Street, Glasgow over three days from 2nd February with fifteen delegates representing the eleven branches. David Forrest, one of the two Govan representatives, was elected chairman and Joseph Heslop, representing Walker, was elected vice-chairman. Although historic, the meeting was remarkably low-key with an emphasis on business rather than rhetoric. The first day brought a general agreement to institute a new Association which would not be a rival to the United Kingdom Amalgamation of Shipwrights but rather an extension to it. The general proposition to form an Associated Society with a view to creating a national, closely-knit organization was approved unanimously.

On the second and third days delegates considered such details as the remuneration for officers and auditors, the printing of rule books and the initial operation of the sections covering benefits.

They decided that the Society should be called 'The Associated Shipwrights'. Its objects were to be to act as an 'auxiliary' to local societies in each port, to join the members of the trade 'in a stronger bond of unity' and to raise funds for the operation of various benefit schemes. There were to be branches in all ports with elected committees, presidents, secretaries and treasurers, all of whom had their duties precisely laid down.

The Association as a whole was to be governed by an Executive Committee consisting of seven members and the General Secretary. They were to be elected from those branches situated within a radius of six miles from the 'seat of government'. Any branch with one hundred members could apply for election as the seat of government and would hold that position for three years. The Executive Committee were to meet at least once a fortnight to transact the Association's business. They were to decide all cases of appeal and to interpret the rules or the spirit of the Association where the 'rules are silent'. They were to decide on the opening or closing of a branch, could call meetings in any branch or were to institute all legal proceedings in the Association's name. Committee members would receive 6d (2½p) a meeting, together with travel expenses if they lived more than a mile from the meeting place.

The principal official was to be a General Secretary. He would hold office for three years but would be eligible for re-election. A candidate must have held office in a branch, must have been a member of the Association for at least two years and must not be in arrears in his contributions. The General Secretary was to attend all meetings of the Executive Committee, conduct all correspondence and keep all documents, papers and accounts of the Association. He was to keep a clear account of the income and expenditure of the whole society and generally carry out the Association's business. Finally, it was laid down that 'The General Secretary shall devote as much of his time as the Society may deem necessary for the due performance of the business of the Association and shall be remunerated for his services as the Society may determine'.

The delegates adopted two slogans: 'United We Stand—Divided We Fall' and 'We Are As One'. And they used them as the basic themes in the preamble to the Rule Book. It began: 'According to the experience and testimony of high authorities in commercial circles, there has been and always will be, periods of prosperity and periods of depression in trade. That this is so, many shipwrights as well as other tradesmen can verify by bitter experience. During these dull times it has often been regretted by many shipwrights that no provision was made in our present societies for assistance during such days of adversity. Therefore to meet this much-felt want and also to bind the members of our trade into a closer bond of unity and to endeavour to dispose of many of the incongruities of our present system The Associated Shipwrights' Society was instituted.'

The delegates agreed that Glasgow should be the provisional 'seat of government' and that the offices should be at 8 Rosevale Street, Partick, Glasgow. They also agreed that Alexander Wilkie, the leading activist in the creation of the new union, should be the first General Secretary at a salary of £52 a year.

ALEXANDER WILKIE

Wilkie was a thick-set man with a powerful chest and well-set head. His hair was close-cropped, his ears large and protuberant and the lower part of his face completely covered by a large moustache and a full, if not luxuriant beard. Yet although a striking and somewhat awesome figure, his eyes gave him a much friendlier appearance. They almost twinkled.

Born in Fifeshire in 1850 and orphaned from the age of four, he had become involved in trade union affairs early in life. In the 1870's as a young man he had held various offices in the Glasgow Shipwrights' Society from auditor and collector to branch secretary. He then became General Secretary for the Clyde Shipwrights and the Associated Shipwrights of Scotland. In 1877, before he was 30 years of age he was made Secretary of the United Kingdom Amalgamated Society of Shipwrights. In that year a prolonged conflict between the Clyde shipwrights and their employers occurred which was eventually referred to an Arbitration Court. As Secretary, Wilkie was authorized to present the shipwrights' case. The manner in which he did so, the ability he showed in dealing with the intricate details at issue, the tact and judgement he displayed won him the respect not only of his colleagues but also of the Court president, Lord Moncrieff.

More generally, he demonstrated his ability in the part he played in dealing with demarcation difficulties, especially on the Clyde and the Tyne. He did a great deal of the work in drawing up lists representing the jobs to be undertaken by shipwrights and in presenting these lists to joint committees, arbitrators and umpires.

By 1881-82 he was still only thirty-one years of age but the experience he had gained at both local and national level, the ability he had demonstrated so often and his personal qualities of tact and moderation made him the obvious choice for General Secretary. He retained that position until his death in 1928.

The first fortnight's contributions were to be due on 7th March 1882 and all arrears of contributions were to be calculated from that date. To all intents and purposes, therefore, that date represents the effective inauguration of the new trade union. About 1,750 members enrolled immediately from branches at Govan, Partick, Renfrew and Clydebank, Greenock, Dundee, Aberdeen, Dumbarton, Leith, Walker, Hebburn and Jarrow. This compared with a total of about 20,000 shipwrights in the country as a whole.

In the first few weeks of the new union's life progress was relatively rapid. By April, when he presented his first report, Alex Wilkie was able to write: 'We can congratulate ourselves on the satisfactory progress we have already achieved, which proves most strongly the necessity of this "Association" and we urge all members and officers to further extend its circle for the mutual benefit of all.' In those few weeks from the Delegates' meeting in February to the submission of his first report in April, over 450 new members had enrolled, bringing the total to 2,200. Income for the two months under Sections 1 and 2 for Trade Protection and Unemployment had been £212 17s 7d and with expenditure of £7 3s 4½d, there was a balance of £205 14s 2½d.

Following the strict accountancy procedures that had been laid down, the Executive Committee had deposited £100 in the bank as 'working fund', had opened an account with the Post Office Savings Bank and had ensured that all branches had appointed auditors to examine the financial transactions for the quarter that would end in May 1882. Thus was instituted the simple and strict scrutiny of all monies for the security of members. Indeed the Committee even went so far as to instruct that no collector or officer should be recompensed for any expenses until the first quarter's audits had been completed.

The numbers in each branch belonging to the Associated Shipwrights' Society by April were:

Govan	449
Partick	424
Renfrew & Clydebank	192
Walker	216
Hebburn	51
Jarrow	77
Greenock	314
Leith	196
Dundee	181
Aberdeen	103
Dumbarton	No figures given

During May new branches were instituted at Preston, Port Glasgow, Kinghorn and Grangemouth and the total number of members went up to 2,577. Income increased to £427 15s 4d and expenditure to £53 2s 9½d, leaving a balance of £374 12s 6½d as the satisfactory outcome of the first quarter's operation. Mr Wilkie, however, urged greater effort. 'If the members would only put their shoulders to the wheel that sum could easily be doubled. Permit me to urge on all officers and collectors the necessity of pushing forward the second section (unemployment benefit) a little more. This is one of the special provisions a trade union only can supply and therefore we ought to give it a fair measure of support. It is as great a necessity or even more so for a working man to provide for an idle day as a sick day.'

That prophecy was soon to come true and there were to be many members who wished they had used a little foresight.

EARLY WORRIES

While the Society grew continuously, if not quite so quickly as the Executive Committee had hoped, there were two particular worries. One was that in these early months while the funds of the union were still being built up, there should be no serious dispute with employers. For although the reserves rose to £1,200 after nine months they were still perilously small. As the General Secretary wrote to members: ... 'This sum ... would be quite inadequate to meet any heavy strain. We would therefore most strongly urge on all our branches and members to endeavour so to act that, by a little tact, patience and conciliation, combined with firmness, we may avoid any differences either internal or external, and in all cases every means should be adopted before resorting to extreme measures and thus avoid the calamitous results of hasty and unconsidered action.'

So well was this advice followed and so moderate was the Society's approach to all aspects of industrial relations that in its first eighteen years only £7,500 was paid out in disputes pay compared with over £100,000 expended on other benefit payments to members. In some years indeed hardly a penny was spent through strikes or lock-outs.

The second worry concerned the lack of interest in the unemployment benefit. In the first year only £49 was paid into this fund compared with over £1,900 paid into the Trade Protection fund. Of the 3,700 members of the Society at the end of the first year only fifty-nine had paid into the unemployment fund. This was a remarkably low figure considering the widespread comments during the discussions over the inauguration of the union. Then it was claimed that an unemployment fund was the main distinguishing characteristic of a trade union and many prospective members declared that they would not join the Society unless it provided such a fund.

There could be a number of explanations for the failure. Partly, it must have been due to the boom conditions. Order books were high, unemployment low and indeed employers were anxious to take on all the extra labour they could find. In these circumstances it was difficult for shipwrights to imagine that depressions would ever return, even though the older members knew clearly from experience that shipbuilding was a cyclical industry, with good and bad times succeeding each other at five-yearly intervals.

Secondly, there was the undoubted fact that although unemployment benefit was not a novelty in the trade union movement, it was certainly a radical departure for shipwrights. They regarded almost with equanimity the cyclical nature of their industry and expected that every decade would contain a couple of bad years and a couple of highly prosperous ones. In these circumstances, unemployment when it came was regarded as an occupational hazard. They expected employers to cut wages and to lay at least some of them off during depressions as a means of cutting costs to encourage buyers to come forward to place orders for new ships. Thus the trade cycle would be reactivated. Conversely, at the height of the boom which followed, they would expect the employers to agree to their wage claims. These increases offset and to some extent compensated for the reduction of wages and the temporary unemployment which followed when the boom broke. Wage rates thus closely followed the switch-back nature of the production cycle. The men might not like the system but they regarded it as an inevitable part of the iron law of supply and demand.

Against this background, the Society's attempts to introduce an unemployment fund were regarded not so much with suspicion as with disbelief. Could a fund of this kind really provide worthwhile compensation? The benefits of eight shillings a week for eight weeks and four shillings a week for another nine weeks would not go far for a family used to an income of £2 a week or more. Furthermore the benefits were payable over a period of only four months in any one year. What would happen then? They would be in the same boat as everyone else, whether they had contributed to the unemployment fund or not.

The third argument used by members for not joining this fund, and the least justified, was that they simply could not afford the contributions of 6d a week. The recent wage increases, if nothing else, had clearly made this argument untenable. At the beginning of 1883 shipwrights in Aberdeen had secured a wage increase of a shilling a week and other concessions. By March shipwrights in Glasgow and along the Clyde had gained a similar increase with more to come in June. However, all the efforts and exhortations of the Executive Committee were of little avail, at least in the short run for twelve months later in March 1884, when the union had been in existence for two years, only sixty of the 4,500 members had subscribed to this fund, an increase of one over the previous year!

The value of the unemployment benefit was to be demonstrated within a few months for, by the autumn of 1883, the boom began to break and industrial output started to decline. The year as a whole saw the highest ship output ever recorded up to that date, with 897 vessels of an aggregate tonnage of 1·2m tons produced by 120 firms. Profits were correspondingly high. But that did not deter employers from reacting immediately to a reduction in ordering by calling for wage cuts. In Barrow firms notified the men of a reduction of 2s 6d (12½p) a week (about seven per cent). In Whitehaven and on the Clyde employers began by asking for reductions of 4s 6d an hour (about fifteen per cent). This figure was eventually reduced to 2s 3d an hour after very strong representations by the men. But still the unemployment section failed to attract the support of members and the Executive Committee had to consider further action, perhaps even making it a compulsory part of membership. The Annual Report for 1883/84 said: 'We contend that to "press" such men to make this provision would be a humane action indeed and a benefit to themselves, their wives, families, their fellow-workmen and the community at large. This we will not press further at present but the matter must be seriously faced in the future and some means adopted to secure the object in view.'

THE BREAK WITH THE 'AMALGAMATION'

But while these particular questions exercised the minds of the officials, the union was continuing to grow in numbers, in power and in usefulness. Its work was expanding all the time and it was able to play a more and more effective part in helping its members. Its action in securing a smaller reduction in wages than the employers at first proposed has been mentioned above.

Now in carrying out this work it was not only fulfilling the role that had been envisaged for it but it was also demonstrating in a practical way the weakness and ineffectiveness of the United Kingdom Amalgamation of Shipwrights. Whereas the latter was essentially a loose-knit federation of local autonomous societies, each with its own rules and regulations, the Society aimed to be much more powerful and purposeful. It was to represent the strength of conformity and centralization. With a strong executive it could assist each branch with its moral power, influence and information service, and it could fight harder to secure the best terms possible in any dispute.

It was also likely to be more efficient. And this proved to be the case, although any new organization was likely to be more efficient than the Amalgamation. It was a regular thing for minutes of the Amalgamation's meetings to be delivered only months afterwards.

The branches of the Society had come into existence as a result of frustration felt by some members in failing to persuade the Amalgamation to adopt a more dynamic attitude. With the blessing of the Amalgamation, the Society had been empowered to come into existence to prove whether there was a need for a more powerful union. After only a year, the Society believed that its existence was justified and that its impatience with the older body was confirmed. Members felt the need to consider once more the relationship with the Amalgamation. Accordingly a second Delegate conference was called in Neilson's Hotel, Glasgow in March 1883. Not surprisingly, the conference was highly critical of the Amalgamation and contrasted its ineffectiveness with the progress the Society had made in just over a year. After a day-long discussion, it was unanimously agreed by the twenty-three representatives that a further attempt should be made to secure changes in the Amalgamation's functions and that, if this proposal was not agreed, then the Society should break with the Amalgamation and refuse to pay subscriptions in the future.

The meeting itself was largely fruitless and indeterminate. Six months afterwards, the minutes had still not been received, which was a measure of the poor organization, a factor which rankled particularly with Wilkie. Society members also felt aggrieved that they should be allowed only seven representatives out of thirty, when seventy-five per cent of the shipping produced in the country came from ports where the Society was well represented, namely Scotland and the Tyne.

Feelings were exacerbated still further after the two London delegates stormed out of the meeting when one of their resolutions was lost. They declared that the rest of the meeting was thereby illegal. The chairman tried to calm matters, and assured everyone that everything would be all right. The Society representatives were not prepared to accept the assurance, however, and declared that their financial contributions would not be handed over until the minutes were sent out showing that the action by the London delegates had been cancelled or withdrawn. This was not done and the effective breach between the Amalgamation and the Society became wider.

It was formalized later that year at the Amalgamation's annual conference in Cardiff. For after a long discussion, the proposition that the Amalgamation should be reconstituted along the lines of the Society was lost by eighteen votes to ten. Society members intimated that they would have to suspend financial relations with the Amalgamation but they should still try to help each other in cases of disputes or lock-outs.

The Delegates conference in March 1883 dealt with two other important questions. One was the threatened resignation of the General Secretary, Alex Wilkie, for business reasons. Without going into details, he simply stated that the work had been extremely arduous and had occupied too much of his time. The delegates were shocked at the news. They knew how much the burgeoning Society owed to the driving force, vision and practical administrative ability of their General Secretary. A unanimous vote of confidence was expressed in his work and he was urged to stay on. To help him, it was agreed his salary should be raised from £1 a week to £3. He agreed to think the matter over and a few days later confirmed his acceptance. This compared with about £2 a week for a working shipwright.

The delegates also considered the question of the third section of benefits. These covered death and disability payments and had been left to the discretion of the individual local societies. Now, however, it was felt that they should be put on a uniform basis with regard to subscriptions and benefits. Branches were to be left to decide for themselves whether to adopt the standard regulations but by laying down guidelines it was expected, rightly, that most branches would accept them.

Later that year, three new branches of the Society were formed at Fleetwood, Barrow and Whitehaven, thus spreading the Society's influence beyond Scotland and Tyneside. It was also decided that the Society should be represented for the first time at the annual meeting of the Trades Union Congress, with Alex Wilkie, elected as the Society's delegate.

He was impressed by the efficient organization of the meeting and particularly taken by the final resolution. 'A strong union, with large funds, is absolutely necessary for successful competition with capital in labour diplomacy. The measure of value of a strong union lies not so much in the conduct of successful strikes as it does in the number of disputes its moral strength prevents. These are the great victories because they are bloodless .... Cheapness in contributions is often very dangerous and generally proves a broken reed in the day of necessity.'

The whole conference, Wilkie thought, had an 'elevating tendency'.

CHAPTER THREE

A TESTING TIME

The Society now entered a truly testing time and that it was able to survive indicated that it was based on sound principles. For the boom conditions which had coincided with the Society's inauguration were followed by a depression which was severe and long-lasting. In 1883 the country had produced over 1.2m. tons of shipping. The following year the figure slumped by forty per cent. As we have shown above, a natural consequence was a call by employers for a reduction in wages. At the very beginning of the year wage reductions of about 2s 6d a week had been enforced. In April a further reduction of 2s 3d was imposed along the Clyde. In Barrow and on the Tyne the reductions amounted to a shilling a week. The employers had originally proposed greater reductions but following the intervention of the Society's officers the smaller amounts mentioned here were agreed.

Similar success did not ensue in Whitehaven, however, where a very heavy reduction was notified. When the employer 'refused to listen to any reasons on behalf of the men why the reductions should be mitigated or withdrawn', the men went on strike. After five weeks, the reduction was withdrawn and the men resumed work at the old rate. But the dispute cost the Society £94. And in Dundee an employer posted notices of reductions of a halfpenny an hour, or six shillings and ninepence a week. 'Every effort, by letter or deputation, having failed to get the notice withdrawn, and no other resource being left to the members, they were reluctantly compelled to withdraw their labour.' At the end of three weeks, the reductions were withdrawn and the men resumed work at the old rate. In December 1884 the Clyde Employers' Association called for further reductions of a halfpenny an hour. After negotiations this was reduced to a cut of a farthing an hour.

In these circumstances, it was a remarkable achievement for the Society to continue its growth and to increase its funds, even if at a slower rate. For financially it was affected not only by heavier expenditure but also through a smaller income since contributions were waived at that time for unemployed members. The total income for first and second section benefit funds was £1,746 compared with £2,438 the previous year, while the number of members fell from 4,606 to 4,011. Yet the Society was able to make a net gain in the year of £615 to bring its balance to £3,542. 'Considering the small amount of contributions our members pay, and that only when working, and remembering the very depressed state of trade in the past year, this must be considered very satisfactory indeed', Alex Wilkie wrote in the third annual report. 'But we must impress this fact upon members—that while all things considered we are making very satisfactory financial progress, still the capital amount is nothing like what it will require to be to secure the deferred benefits of the Association, nor to meet any sudden and heavy calls that are made upon it.' The unemployment fund was in a particularly perilous state and for the first time more was paid out than put in for income was only £51 compared with expenditure of over £100. The result was that the credit balance at the beginning of the year of £90 was reduced to £41 by the year's end. 'This, considering the burden it has had to bear, is truly wonderful; and it has proved an immense blessing to those who, by their prudence and forethought, have made this provision'. It also provided yet more evidence to the Society's officials that a strong Association was more effective than 'a fossiled system of Federation'. For while no union could raise wages in a falling market, it could modify heavy reductions, as the Society's officials had been able to do in numerous negotiations. The Amalgamation meanwhile merely looked on passively and impotently.

The trade depression, the need to take firmer action to persuade more members to insure themselves against unemployment, the growing confidence of the young union—all these factors led to an impetus for greater cohesion and consolidation, for increasing the contributions and benefits and above all for making the unemployment section compulsory and for merging all the sections into one fund. The third Delegates Meeting held in the Alexandra Hotel, Clayton Street, Newcastle in April 1885, heard many calls for strengthening the Society and dealt with many amendments to rules to implement these calls. It is significant that unlike previous meetings which lasted three days, this one stretched over six.

On general principles there was a large measure of agreement; over details there was sometimes a marked difference of view. This was particularly true over the level of contributions. Mr George Innes, the Jarrow delegate, claimed that his members were 'pretty animated' over the higher contributions. The fact was that a shilling a week was more than his members wanted to pay, although his own view was that they must be persuaded to pay higher contributions. Mr David Chambers of Hebburn, however, said that his branch was strongly in favour of increasing contributions to a shilling a week, all of which should go into one consolidated fund. His members thought this was necessary and urgent and that no more time should be lost.

In fact the discussion went into a second day but the motion for a consolidation of funds, when put, was accepted overwhelmingly by twenty-two votes to four, with five abstentions. The delegates then went on to make adjustments to the rules to provide the following:

NEW MEMBERS

Applicants for full benefits under 35 years of age to pay £1 entry money; if they were over 35 years of age and under 40, they would pay £1 5s (£1.25). If they were over 40 years of age, new members could be admitted only to trade benefits. New members under 40 would then pay 1s (5p) or 9d a week, those over 40 3d a week.

For 1s 0d a week contribution they would be entitled to:

1st: Tool compensation—up to 50 per cent of cost to a maximum of £5.

2nd: Trade or Dispute benefit of 10s 0d (50p) a week.

3rd: Unemployed benefit—9s 0d a week for ten weeks, then 5s 0d for another ten weeks during any period of twelve months; then 5s 0d a week for twenty weeks during the second twelve months.

4th: Sickness or Accident Benefit—12s 0d a week for 13 weeks, 8s 0d a week for the next 13 weeks and 6s 0d for another 26 weeks.

5th: Superannuation—4s 0d, 4s 6d, 5s 0d a week according to length of membership.

6th: Funeral benefit—for member £10; for wife, if predeceased, £5.

For 9d a week contributions, members would be entitled to:

1st: Tool compensation—up to 50 per cent of cost to a maximum of £5.

2nd: Trade or Dispute benefit—10s 0d a week.

3rd: Unemployed benefit—9s 0d a week and as per scale.

4th: Sickness or Accident Benefit—6s 0d a week for 13 weeks, 4s 0d for another 13 weeks and 3s 0d a week for another 26 weeks.

5th: Superannuation—according to length of membership.

6th: Funeral benefit—for members £5, for wife, if predeceased, £2 10s.

New members who were over 40 years of age would pay 10s 0d entry money and 3d a week contribution when they were working for which they would receive:

1st Tool compensation—up to 50 per cent of cost to a maximum of £5.

2nd: Trade or Dispute benefit—10s 0d a week.

3rd: Funeral benefit—£3.

For full-benefit members, contributions were still to be paid even when they were unemployed. However, at the end of 20 weeks' unemployment in any one year, when the benefit payments would come to an end, the contributions would be halved to sixpence a week.

CURRENT MEMBERS

Current members of the Society were to be allowed to join the sections covering unemployment and friendly benefits for 10s 0d entry fee. Those who were already contributing to the friendly benefits section could join the unemployment fund for an entry fee of 5s.

The effect of the changes was immediate. In Walker branch a hundred members decided to pay full benefit. The total figures were: paying a shilling a week 363; ninepence 353; sixpence 299; threepence 2,786.

A SEVERE DEPRESSION

The mid-1880's were hard years for the shipbuilding industry, for the men who worked in it (many of whom were now unemployed) and for the burgeoning union. The boom had broken late in 1883. Through 1884 and 1885 the depression deepened and reached its low point in 1886. output in that year was only 483,000 gross tons compared with 1.2m. tons in 1883. Branch after branch reported on the depressing and depressed state of trade. In Govan it was 'very dull'; in Renfrew and Clydebank 'very bad'. In Grangemouth there was 'no work at all' and Port Glasgow 'never was worse'.

These general conditions were reflected in the men's wages. In March 1883 shipwrights on the Tyne received 40s a week for old work and 37s for new work. By March 1886 their wages were down to 37s for old work and 34s for new work. In Scotland the average wage had fallen from 37s a week for old work in 1883 to 32s in 1886. Aberdeen was always bottom of the league. Wages there fell from 30s a week to 25s. The depression also affected the numbers employed. If we take the first sixteen branches of the Shipwrights' Society, all of which were in existence by October 1883, we can see that the number of shipwrights in employment in those branches then was 3,348 compared with 1,430 in March 1886, a reduction of almost two-thirds. The number of members had also dropped to 3,732 compared with 4,600 two years earlier. In these circumstances income declined while expenditure increased, particularly on unemployment benefit. But even in the depths of the depression, the Society still managed a surplus although sometimes it was desperately small. In the spring quarter of 1886 income exceeded expenditure by only £44.

A NORTH-EAST DELEGATE

Despite the bad times the Society continued to move ahead. And indeed at the low point of the depression it even decided to take a bold step forward by appointing a full-time official for the North of England. Some members thought this was financial madness because of the extra costs at a time when the union's income was declining. But supporters of the appointment felt that a full-time official could help to increase membership and reduce expenditure by tackling union affairs in a more expeditious way. In particular, the right person if appointed would be able to sort out most local disputes as they arose and thus save the expense of Executive Committee members being involved.

Because the decision to appoint gives a good insight into the early workings of the union and shows that the Executive Committee feared to act without explicit instructions, we shall deal with the question in detail. The original proposition came from the Walker branch on 25th January 1886. In a circular, Joseph Heslop, the secretary of the Walker branch, wrote that it was in times of depression that a delegate was most wanted for it was in such times that most disputes occurred. There were over a thousand shipwrights working in the twelve yards on the river, only about half of whom were members of the Society. In the North-East as a whole it was estimated that 2,800 shipwrights belonged to the United Kingdom Amalgamation which employed a full-time official on the Wear at Sunderland. Now since these men were not well disposed to Society members, it was difficult for the latter to find work in the region except on the Tyne. It was further felt that an official would prevent so many members from falling into arrears and then lapsing from membership.

Of course there would be higher costs in the payment of a wage but this would be offset both by the reduction in committee members' expenses and in dispute payments.

The Executive Committee examined the proposal, found nothing in it contrary to the spirit of the constitution and circulated it to all members for their views. The Committee did make the comment that the proposition should be tried for a limited period to prove whether it would pay financially. 'The principal obstacle is the financial one in these depressed times and it is for the members calmly to consider the matter and forward their opinion thereon.' In other words the Committee was leaving the matter entirely in the hands of members, neither blocking nor encouraging its adoption.

Even this cautious approach led to some criticism. For some members felt that a decision should be taken only after the fullest discussion at branch level since it would involve more expenditure at a time of depression. The Executive Committee recognized the force of these criticisms and asked all branches to call special meetings of members on or before 29th May to discuss the question and record members' votes. It also printed the initial comments of branches.

The Govan branch was against the proposal for the time being. Jarrow was in favour of the Walker proposal but Hebburn was against by 29 votes to 5. Greenock, on the other hand, voted 48 in favour and 9 against. These and other votes clearly did not represent the full membership nor had members had the benefit of discussions to consider all the arguments on one side and the other. This the special meetings would now provide. When the votes were taken again there was a majority in favour by 611 votes to 390 but some of the individual branch returns reversed the earlier opinions. For example, the Aberdeen branch had voted in favour by 48 votes to 4 after a meeting held in St Katherine's Hall on 16th February. When a special meeting was held to discuss this question again in May, only one member voted in favour.

The Committee must also have been disappointed at the numbers who attended the meetings. While over 200 members attended the Walker branch meeting, only 30 attended in Jarrow or Hebburn. However, with a vote in favour, the Executive Committee now went on to find out feelings on the length of the appointment, for six, twelve or twenty-four months. It was overwhelmingly agreed that the original period should be for a year. But the Committee felt that before they could take things any further they should offer the opportunity of a similar appointment to all districts where there were three branches or more. They therefore suggested an extra set of rules should be adopted. Appointments should be for a year, applicants must have at least three years' membership and must have served at least twelve months in some office in the branch. The main task was to conduct the Association's business in any particular district. 'And in order that the Association may maintain its cohesion and unity—without which its influence for good and power to benefit the members cannot be secured—they shall not write against or take part in any meeting to oppose the actions of the Executive Committee.'

Although understandable, this was a remarkable statement as if to suggest the delegates were to be agents of the Committee rather than of the Association as a whole. With regard to disputes the delegates—as they were to be called—should do everything they could to reach an amicable solution.

Members were now asked to vote for these new rules and for the level of expenses and wages. They accepted the rules overwhelmingly and voted for 2s 0d a day expenses when delegates had to travel away from home. Surprisingly, they also voted for a wage of 40s a week rather than for any of the smaller amounts that were suggested.

Having laid down a framework for the appointment of district delegates, the Executive Committee now had to consider how to appoint the Tyneside delegate. They decided that again there should be special meetings convened at branch level to record members' votes. Three names were put forward: Joseph Heslop, the secretary of the Walker branch since the inception of the union; Alexander Clark, who had taken an active part in the formation of a branch at Port Glasgow; and Joseph Harris, the secretary of the Newcastle branch. By September, the votes had been collated, showing 400 for Heslop, 221 for Clark and 240 for Harris. Since none of the candidates had an overall majority, a second vote was taken between Heslop and Harris. As a result Heslop received 672 votes and Harris 353. Joseph Heslop therefore became the first North of England delegate, after a process of discussion, and election, that had taken nine months and roused a great deal of controversy. Indeed the Executive Committee felt it had to make a special call for feelings to subside and to urge that in future circulars should not be sent round the branches intending to sway votes one way or another.

Heslop seemed a good choice. Besides being secretary of the Walker branch, he had served in most of the other positions—as president, vice president and committee member. He had been in one office or another for over ten years. He had attended over 40 quarterly meetings of the local Societies in the United Kingdom Amalgamation of Shipwrights, knew the area thoroughly and got on well with fellow unionists and employers. He was generally regarded as being energetic and tactful and with an unwearying attention for detail.

These apparent qualities soon impressed the entire membership. When the time came to decide whether to continue the appointment of a North-East delegate or not, 538 voted in favour and only 22 against. The Tyne District Committee were particularly pleased with his work on a number of counts. They felt he had helped to secure work for over 100 members at a time of great depression by his intimate knowledge of the changing labour requirements of Tyneside firms. New members had joined the Society thanks to Heslop's 'energy and tact' while the amount of arrears had been substantially reduced by his 'persistent action'.

He had acted promptly to settle potential disputes at the yards of Armstrong, Mitchell and Company and Messrs Richardson. He had also been instrumental in the opening of new branches at Howdon, North Shields and Middlesbrough. Later, however, criticism of his work began to emerge and indeed became so widespread that he felt it necessary to resign.

FINANCIAL SCRUTINY

In these early years the Associated Shipwrights' Society seemed above all to be a kind of insurance company operating various funds for the benefit of members. Its other main role, in solving disputes, seemed of secondary importance. The quarterly and annual reports were taken up largely with financial matters carefully recording all items of income and expenditure branch by branch. They even listed the names of all members who had received benefit and how much.

Alex Wilkie, the General Secretary, who wrote the introductions to the reports often devoted more than half his space to financial affairs. In the annual report for 1885 he used the phrase '... in strength and power of union as contained in industrial insurance ...' suggesting that this was the only kind of strength he could envisage. Equally, almost the only time any emotion crept into his writing was in relation to finance. He would write that the Society had done 'wonderfully well' in increasing its funds at a difficult time. Or that a particular quarter's outcome was 'most satisfactory'.

Above all, he kept a close watch on all forms of expenditure and saw a close connection between industrial relations and the Society's finances.

As has been shown above, he was constantly urging members to settle disputes amicably, partly because he believed that conciliation and compromise were of the essence of industrial relations but equally because such an approach would not drain the union's resources which were still small. He scrutinized all payments most carefully. In his quarterly report for January—March 1886 he wrote: '... there appears to be a spirit abroad amongst some of the branches to spend as much as they can on any matter that crops up. This should not be. All branches should rather, especially in these times, curtail all unnecessary and not pressing expenditure.'

In the same report, he drew attention to a 'disagreeable' question, a charge by Greenock branch of £1 1s 6d for looking for another hall in which to hold their meetings. The Executive Committee felt that this charge was both excessive, being a third of the amount paid for hall rent for the whole of the previous year, and illegal since such expenditure was not allowed for in the Rule Book.

The Greenock report, given by the secretary, D. Sinclair, shocked the

Committee. He wrote: 'We know perfectly well it is not in the Rule Book but there is a great many items we pay that are not there as well as these, that we must pay in this branch, otherwise we cannot work it. If you can get your members to work for nothing, we cannot do it here. You state this must be rectified. All I can say in answer to that is, that I am instructed to say that the best plan would be for the Executive Committee or any of the other branches who complain, to send down or appoint from this branch who will work it themselves if not satisfied with the manner we are doing.'

The Executive Committee reacted sharply to this letter. Since Greenock recognized that the payment was illegal, it would have to refund the amount. 'If a branch can vote one pound from the General Funds illegally, it can vote a thousand,' Wilkie wrote, 'and if one branch had the right so should others.' What would be the result? confusion and extinction. No Association could be conducted on such a basis ... Other officers have worked the branch under the General Rules which guide all branches yet the present officers say they can't.... It has been the object of the Executive in conducting the business of this Association to place it upon a sound financial and commercial basis and to secure equal justice and equity to all Members.' To ensure that the rules were strictly adhered to the Committee called on members to support the following resolution: 'That the Executive be instructed to take what steps they may deem necessary to secure that this and all illegally voted money be refunded.'

Hardly surprisingly, the members voted by 422 votes to 114 to support the Executive. Only Greenock showed any opposition, with no members voting in favour and 91 against. But lest it be thought that Greenock was turning militant and divisive, it should be pointed out that these votes represented less than a fifth of the branch membership. Faced with such a clear expression of the members' feelings, Greenock backed down and refunded the money. Wilkie underlined the position by stating that the Executive Committee as empowered by Rule and now instructed by resolution would continue to take action—through the courts if necessary—to stop other illegal expenditure in the future. The Rules were quite clear as to what was permissible and what was not. Anything else could be paid out only on the authority of the membership or of the Executive Committee.

On another occasion, Wilkie wrote: 'While we are making considerable financial progress, still we must impress the fact on all members that the capital amount, satisfactory as it is considering the times and age of our Association, is yet not sufficient to meet the deferred benefits or the liabilities undertaken by the consolidation of the Sections; and in order to secure a stronger financial position, we will require much larger sums opposite each member; therefore we strongly urge on all members and branches to husband their resources and secure a fund equal to any emergency and wherever possible in these times to avoid disputes which, while frittering away the funds in hopeless contests, weakens our position to deal effectively with the difficulty when more suitable times arrive;

rather let us stoop to conquer. Keep united and bide our time which is sure to come sooner or later.'

It was true that at this time the Society's reserves represented only £1 12s per member. But even in 1900 when the membership had risen to over 18,000 and the reserves per member to over £6 3s, he was still urging the same caution in expenditure and the same diplomatic and conciliatory approach to labour relations.

No doubt this was part of the personality of the man. He had, after all, first sprung to prominence by his presentation of the shipwrights' case at the Arbitration Court in 1877. The judge had commended him for his tact and judgement. And throughout his career he constantly sought to settle disputes amicably and through negotiation rather than force. He sincerely believed this was the best way and that industrial action should be used only as a last resort and against an employer who refused all appeals to reason. Of these there were very few.

But more generally he felt that financial prudence was essential in the development of the Society and was indeed the bedrock on which its progress rested. Without constant efforts in raising income and reducing arrears and without eternal vigil over expenditure, the funds of the organization which had been built up so steadily would soon be dissipated. That would lead to collapse and disintegration. For Wilkie was aware that the benefit schemes it operated were the Society's main activity and reason for existence. Negotiations over wages or working conditions were carried out locally with help occasionally from headquarters and against the background of the Society's national strength. That strength was demonstrated most clearly in the balance sheet. It may seem a narrow view by today's standards. And one may wonder why it was felt unnecessary or inappropriate to motivate members by an appeal to higher idealism. But it must be recognized that in those early years an image of solidity, of responsibility and even of dullness was no bad thing in the search for new members and in the initial efforts to develop constructive relationships with employers.

SHIPWRIGHTS AND THE NAVY

The widespread unemployment of the mid-1880's forced many shipwrights to seek work elsewhere. Some emigrated, others left the trade altogether, while a third group joined the Navy. They were encouraged to do so by seductive advertising campaigns. But once they had signed on, individuals often found conditions far from what they had anticipated.

A number of them wrote to the Society complaining bitterly of the treatment they received in the Navy and urging potential recruits to consider the regulations carefully before agreeing to enlist. The complaints fell into two categories. The first concerned status. Unlike other tradesmen, shipwrights were regarded as ordinary seamen and were expected to take their share of menial tasks such as scrubbing the decks. They were also expected to mess with the crew. By comparison engineers, or engine room artificers, were given the rank of chief petty officers, were free of general duties, had a special mess and even had ordinary seamen to wait on them. The shipwrights felt aggrieved that they were not afforded similar privileges. The second grievance concerned pay. At a time when a shipwright could earn between 5s and 7s a day in civilian employment, his counterpart in the service received between 2s 3d and 2s 6d a day.

The Associated Shipwrights' Society was concerned at the harshness of these conditions, particularly since in the depressed state of the shipbuilding industry, a considerable number of shipwrights had felt they had little alternative but to accept them. The Society acted to try to alter the regulations but it faced a major difficulty. As long as members were continuing to sign on—however unwillingly—the Services were under little compunction to improve things. All the Society could do was to point out clearly and forcefully the conditions members would be exposed to and to await an upturn in trade which would reduce the pressure on members to enlist.

THE FIRST FIVE YEARS

The Society celebrated its fifth anniversary in March 1887. It had cause for quiet satisfaction rather than for great jubilation. Its greatest triumph in fact was that it was still in existence, having come through a severe depression relatively unscathed. True, the membership had declined from about 4,500 at the peak to 3,500 but the funds had continued to grow. They now stood at £5,400. Thirty branches had been formed and several thousands of pounds had been paid out in benefit to members. An effective administrative organization had been created thanks largely to the careful scrutiny of the Executive Committee in general and of Alex Wilkie in particular. Certain initiatives had been taken to negotiate on behalf of members involved in local disputes and in one or two cases, such as conditions in the Royal Navy, there had been attempts to act as a national pressure group on behalf of all shipwrights.

Against this impressive, if rather limited, list of achievements one has to present the other side of the picture. Firstly, the Society had been unable to convince the majority of the 20,000 shipwrights in the country to become members. It had even failed to secure a higher membership than the U.K. Amalgamation of Shipwrights which it denounced so frequently as an ineffective body. What is more, although it could boast of having opened 30 branches in five years, some of them were in a parlous state. Workington had only 8 members and Kinghorn and Paisley 12 each. Altogether 19 branches had less than 100 members. Their income was consequently small and in eight cases was exceeded by their expenditure (at least in the first quarter of 1887).

Part of the trouble no doubt lay in the failure to display a more vigorous attitude. While it was more effective than the U.K. Amalgamation of Shipwrights, the difference was one only of degree and was clearly minimal as far as outsiders were concerned. More generally, there was a failure to espouse a higher sense of idealism than represented by joint benefit between men and masters. In short, there was no political commitment as we would recognize it today.

Nor, despite the frequent votes on all sorts of resolutions (some of which were mundane and even trivial), was there a true sense of democracy. There were no annual conferences, no general discussions, no opportunities for the individual members to meet together except at branch level. And even on matters where votes were called, no great efforts were made to present all sides of the arguments to members. Perhaps most important of all, the Executive Committee still consisted exclusively of Scottish members or more particularly of members from three branches on the Clyde: Govan, Partick and Renfrew and Clydebank. Yet these three branches accounted for only a quarter of the membership. The inspiration for the Society had of course come largely from the Clyde, with important assistance from the Tyne, but if it hoped to become a truly national organization then there was surely an overwhelming need to widen the representation. Such a move would have had immediate benefits in improving the appearance of democracy, even if there was little change in fact. It would also have recognized that major progress could only be made through securing more members in England and would have helped that process by securing the active involvement of a larger number of individuals.

The fact was, of course, that power was largely concentrated in the hands of the General Secretary, Alex Wilkie. This was perhaps inevitable. He was after all an outstanding personality, a man of great ability, of undoubted dedication and of powerful presence. But added to these personal gifts, he had the authority of his position. He was the senior full-time official and he remained in office while the Committee members changed every six months. No wonder he gained a dominating position. No wonder he could steer the affairs of the Society and set its style of moderation and financial prudence. Because he personally wrote the quarterly reports, he in effect was able to choose the subjects for discussion and the areas for action.

As we have seen he put the emphasis on good housekeeping, on the settlement of arrears, the search for new members and the careful control of expenditure. In industrial matters he continually urged caution and diplomacy and when he introduced wider topics they were of the kind where he could expect the support of all members. Legislation to cover the loss of life at sea or improvements to the Service regulations for shipwrights were totally uncontroversial, certainly among his members. He could raise them therefore without the fear of internal friction.

Such a moderate approach was typical of the man but to be fair it must be said that this was probably the best way to encourage the growth of a young union. A more dynamic, more controversial, less practical approach may have won some converts but it would probably have deterred many more. In these early years a quiet period of development was needed. The fireworks could come later, if at all.

One must also recognize that in theory, if not always in practice, there was an element of autonomy in the individual branches. The Society certainly had a greater concentration of power in the centre than the U.K. Amalgamation but even so the branches had—and insisted upon—a substantial measure of independence. They had to be consulted on all important changes to the organization or operation of the union and only when their views were in a minority did they have to submit to other opinion. But that other opinion was not so much the view of the Executive Committee as of the majority of branches. Of course the Committee was in a powerful position to influence decisions but that is a different matter from making decisions itself.

Perhaps the most obvious symbol of the lack of central control was represented by the wage rates which varied from district to district and sometimes from town to town. The rates reflected an agreement between branch and employer and were determined above all by the state of the local economy. Tyneside was invariably at the top of the league with Scotland a little way behind followed by the West and South coasts. Aberdeen or Whitehaven nearly always seemed to be at the bottom. These variations were never queried, certainly in the first five years, and even in 1886 when the whole North-East coast was brought up to the same level as Tyneside, there was no attempt to carry the uniformity further to cover the whole country. Regional differences were seen almost as an act of God and no one queried the extraordinary fact that they all rose or fell together. Indeed, the branches would use the precedent of a wage rise elsewhere to press their claims while the employers would use the examples of wage reductions in other districts to call for the same from their workers.

There was therefore, after the first five years, a centralizing tendency, represented above all through the work of the General Secretary, but no true cohesion. That was to come much later.

CHAPTER FOUR

LOSS OF LIFE AT SEA

The Employers' Liability Act passed in 1880 was an important step forward in the recognition of the rights of workers. For the first time employers were to be made responsible for insuring their employees against risks or injuries which could occur at their place of employment. But although the new legislation was significant, it had a number of deficiencies. For example, employers were still empowered to persuade their workers to opt out of the provisions of the Act. More particularly, the Act did not cover seamen.

Now this was of considerable concern to the Society for an analysis of its records had shown that 12 per cent of the members who had died, had done so at sea while acting as ship's carpenters. 'Drowned at sea' was a fairly common description in the Society's obituary columns published in the quarterly reports.

Partly through the Society's pressure, the Government set up a Royal Commission to examine the question of the loss of life at sea and to make recommendations. The Society sought action on three main points: firstly the extension of the Employers' Liability Act to seamen; secondly, that all ships should be adequately and competently manned; and thirdly, that all seamen be compelled to pass a practical examination in their particular skills or trades. The last two points were necessary because the union found that deaths were occurring through the under-manning of vessels or the incompetence of the crew. The Board of Trade itself claimed that it had 'reason to believe that many ships are dangerously under-manned and that collisions and other casualties are the result'.

On the question of competence, the shipowners of the U.K. were in large measure in agreement with the Society. Indeed, at their annual conference in London in 1885 they proposed 'That masters and officers should be more thoroughly trained and subjected to an improved and more practical examination.' The ordinary seaman too should be 'able to read simple English composition, know the points of the compass, and be able to distinguish colours.' The standard of the crews must indeed have been poor!

But it was on the extension of the Employers' Liability Act that the Society placed most stress. Alex Wilkie raised the question at the T.U.C.'s annual conference at Hull in September 1886. And he persuaded Congress to agree to the following resolution: 'That, in view of the early issuing of the report and recommendations of the Royal Commission on the Loss of Life at Sea and the consequent legislation likely to follow thereon, it be a special instruction to the Parliamentary Committee (of the T.U.C.) to use its utmost efforts with the object of obtaining greater safety of life and limb at sea, to endeavour to secure in any Bill that may be introduced the insertion of a clause extending the Employers' Liability Act to seamen; and that all vessels shall be required by law to carry for their navigation sufficient and competent crews; that all seamen, firemen and tradesmen be required to produce a certificate of efficiency in their respective occupations before being allowed to proceed to sea; and that on all marine boards that are or may be formed, the workmen (seamen) shall have a just and adequate representation.'

The Executive Committee also sent a deputation to meet members of the Commission who included Thomas Burt, the M.P. for Morpeth, to press their case. Despite these efforts, the Society did not meet with any quick success. Another year elapsed before the Commission presented its report to Parliament and then there was a further delay before it was issued to the public. At the T.U.C.'s annual conference in Swansea in September 1887, the Society put forward the following resolution: That this Congress regrets the delay in the issuing of the report of the Royal Commission on the Loss of Life at Sea.

But the report, when it did come out a few weeks later, gave the Society's demands clear backing. The Commission recommended among many other matters that the Employers' Liability Act of 1880 should be extended to seamen and that a simple professional examination should be introduced for boatswains and carpenters. It summed up its report in these words: 'The measures which we have proposed in the interest of saving life at sea will also, we believe, tend greatly to the advantage of seamen. Any means adopted, within reasonable bounds, to increase the responsibility of shipowners for the safety of their ships, must also ensure to the benefit of all on board. It will become more important for shipowners to be careful in the selection of the officers and men they employ and there will be better and more continuous demand for the best men in the service and a gradual weeding out of it of those who by the want of qualifications or bad conduct give rise to complaints and of invidious comparisons with the seamen of other countries to which our attention has been called.

'Finally, we think it right to say that, although we have been unable to resist the conclusion that the loss of life and property at sea is excessive and is due to a considerable extent to preventible causes, yet we believe that never at any time in the history of the British mercantile marine has there been so great an improvement as in recent years in the construction of vessels of the first quality or a greater degree of safety to life and property in the vessels of the better class sent to sea.'

The Society itself was pleased with the recommendations. In the Sixth annual report Alex Wilkie wrote: 'What our trade has been contending for during these many years past is now recommended by the Royal Commission. We trust therefore every means will be adopted, every effort put forth to secure this recommendation becoming the law of the land.'

That was not to be. For although a bill was presented to the House of Commons early in 1888, it did not meet the Society's case or conform to the recommendations of the Royal Commission. The Home Secretary introduced the Employers' Liability for Injuries to Workmen's Bill, which extended the previous act to seamen. But there was a very important snag, for the Bill declared: 'The employer of the seaman shall not be liable to pay compensation for the injury unless it is caused by a defect in the condition of the ship.... or equipment of the ship existing at the time when the ship last proceeded to sea from a port in the United Kingdom....'

As Wilkie said, the Bill was carrying out the recommendations of the Royal Commission to the word but breaking it in the deed. It would be almost impossible for a workman to prove that the defect existed before the ship left the last port in the U.K. And what about defects that occurred at sea? If they gave rise to accidents, no compensation could be claimed. Such accidents were more than likely for gear and machinery were often put under great stress by captains endeavouring to earn high commissions through completing their voyage ahead of schedule. The Society had now to redouble its efforts to have the legislation changed.

One line of action was to try to raise the matter at the T.U.C. conference which in 1888 was held in Bradford. Wilkie was instructed to put forward a tough resolution: 'That this Congress is of opinion that the clauses of the Employers' Liability Bill, introduced by the Home Secretary, insofar as they profess to extend the benefits of that act to seamen, are entirely inadequate and do not meet the fair and just claims of the seamen.... And that all the representatives here present at this Congress pledge themselves to approach their respective members of Parliament and otherwise assist the seamen to obtain this long-delayed act of justice.'

The resolution was given unanimous backing by the conference. It was also agreed that a petition should be presented to Parliament protesting at the unsatisfactory provisions of the Bill and putting forward amendments.

On the question of introducing professional examinations, action was no quicker. In November 1888 Sir Hicks Beach, the president of the Board of Trade, put forward the draft clauses of a Merchant Shipping Bill which, among other matters, would call for an examination system for boatswains and carpenters. The shipowners, however, were opposed to certain clauses in the proposed Bill and asked for further discussions with the Board of Trade and with the unions.

This and the other issues on which the Society had campaigned were to drag on for a long time yet.

DRIVE FOR NEW MEMBERS

During the depths of the depression in the mid-1880's, membership of the Society slumped to 3,500. To counter the decline the Portsmouth branch suggested that the Executive Committee should embark on a drive for new members. In putting forward the proposal, the branch was no doubt aware that it stood in splendid isolation on the South coast, that its own membership was declining and that there were many shipwrights in various towns in the South who belonged to no union. The Portsmouth proposition stated: 'As many of those places have never been visited, or had an opportunity of being associated, then it becomes our duty to advance the right hand of fellowship towards them, bearing in mind that if not with us, they may be against us. As our Association has steadily made progress, let us forward on the good work in hand, by impressing on all around us the necessity of combination as to raise us to our proper position as a first-class trade.'

The Executive Committee, whilst sympathetic to the suggestion, were concerned at the possible expense involved and felt they should have a direct mandate from the members on this matter. The branches were divided in their views. Govan and Partick voted in favour of a membership drive unanimously. Walker was against for although 'this is a consummation devoutly to be wished, the times are too bad at the present. Our experience in this district is that to be able to gain members to our Association, times must be better ... We would recommend Portsmouth to get into communication with some member belonging to those ports who will take an interest and try to get some others to join and by that means form small branches. It can be done with very little expense which is the great desideratum at the present with us. We were successful in Bridgewater and Middlesbrough by the same course and we have no doubt Portsmouth will be the same.'

The Executive Committee accepted the objections but felt that something should be done and done quickly for otherwise it could be too late. 'Members must not forget that it was only by considerable outlay in missions that our Association was at first instituted and extended and if we mean to progress in this matter, we must be prepared to lay out a little in the hope of having a greater return.'

The members agreed and voted overwhelmingly in favour of a campaign particularly since it could coincide with the visit by Wilkie, the General Secretary, and Heslop, the Tyne district delegate, to the T.U.C. Conference at Swansea. A local delegate, David Tait of Portsmouth, was appointed to visit places beforehand, book halls, arrange for publicity and generally attract good attendances. But while they were still in Wales, Wilkie and Heslop held a number of meetings there.

On Friday, 9th September, they addressed a large number of shipwrights at Pembroke. After outlining the value of trade unionism and the benefits of the Society, Wilkie and Heslop faced numerous questions. The outcome was a unanimous decision to form a branch.

They also had meetings at Swansea and Bridgewater before going off on a tour of the South coast as arranged by David Tait. The first call was at Falmouth. Wilkie recalled afterwards: 'We had a pretty fair meeting of the men at night, one of the small employers attending to express his sympathy with the object in view as he held with the competition against the employers.' At the end of the evening a resolution was carried to form a branch and nineteen men said they would join. Then on to Plymouth. 'They all appeared favourable,' Wilkie wrote, 'but their difficulty was the want of work and thereby the want of means.'

There was a more positive attitude at Devonport. A large turnout of men agreed to form a branch and twenty-three signed on there and then. A long journey up to Portsmouth and although they left early it was late afternoon before Wilkie and Heslop arrived. The weather was bad with heavy, lashing rain but the meeting was well-attended. It was resolved to do everything possible to increase membership of the branch.

On Friday, 15th September 1887, the two officials were in Southampton for another well attended meeting. Another branch was formed.

Wilkie and Heslop left by the midnight train for London and then home. They had had an exhausting time with the T.U.C. Conference, visits in Wales and numerous meetings along the South coast. 'The distances in some cases were so great, in order to accomplish it in time for the respective meetings as arranged, we on several occasions had to travel all night.'

The grand tour had cost £29 10s 0d. Was it worth it? Wilkie said: 'We must state that our experience at this time has been that if we had waited as some suggested until we could get correspondence with these places, we would have had to wait for ever as it is only by a personal representative visit that we can arouse the members of the trade in some places even to attend a meeting.' Even the personal visit failed to do the trick however. For despite the good intentions expressed at the various meetings, Southampton alone translated the early euphoria into action and went ahead to form a new branch with 17 members.

Why there should have been such a disappointing outcome is not clear. And why the Executive Committee did not take firmer action to follow up the initial initiative is even more difficult to understand. In four or five places, potential members had come forward. Embryonic committees had been formed with chairmen and secretaries. But the impetus aroused at the meetings was allowed to dissipate. And only 17 members were gained from the ten-day tour and the expenditure of almost £30.

EIGHT HOURS A DAY

Following the successful trade union campaign initiated in the North-East in 1871 for a nine-hour day, the next target was obviously the establishment of the eight-hour day. In 1887, with the upturn in trade in many industries, the Parliamentary Committee of the Trades Union Congress felt the time had come to pursue the new goal. With the backing of Congress, the Committee circulated all unions to discover the feelings of members. Basically they needed to know if trade unionists wanted to push for an eight-hour day. Alternatively did members want to have a free day on a Saturday so that the 48 hours week (against the 54 hours norm then in operation) should be concentrated into five days. The danger with this option, of course, was that it would take the number of hours a day back to more than nine. In the Nine Hours Campaign, the unions had argued that this was the maximum number of hours a day that workers could be expected to work.

In putting this question forward, the Parliamentary Committee spelt out the implications: that it would almost certainly lead to a reduction in wages and that all overtime would of necessity cease. Otherwise such a change would be tantamount to a demand for higher wages because more hours would be worked at overtime rates. Or at the least such a reduction in hours was unjustified for there was more work available than could be completed in normal time. It is also worth pointing out that the working week on the Continent was greater than in this country and that with trade only just starting to turn upward after a long depression, this could have been considered the worst time to put foreign industry at an advantage. The Executive Committee of the Shipwrights' Society certainly felt unhappy on this point. They sought to gather statistics on the number of hours worked in various occupations in this country and in the shipwrights' trade in the colonies, Europe and the U.S.A.

But the Executive Committee were very firm in its view that such a concession, if it were to be aimed for, should be won by union agitation rather than Parliamentary legislation, an alternative course of action floated by the T.U.C. For the Committee felt that workmen would have no guarantee that their claims would be conceded. Furthermore, if Parliament were asked to deal with the hours of work, it might also claim to deal with wages (as it once had), to the detriment of workmen.

The Committee then made a very apt comment in the light of future events. They argued.... 'before we are able to move Parliament to our wishes in such a matter, we will require a Political Trades Union which will require to be supported same as the present Trades Unions.' It was not to be many years hence before the Independent Labour Party was formed to represent the working man in Parliament.

Despite the rather cautious attitude of the E.C., the members were wholeheartedly in favour of an eight-hours day, voting 854 in favour and 134 against. In some branches, the voting was virtually unanimous. In Govan, for example, 101 were in favour and none against, in Dundee 119 were in favour and just one against. Barrow, Newcastle, Howdon, Bridgewater and Southampton were the only branches to vote against, but only by small numbers.

The E.C. remained unconvinced. They linked the question with the widespread practice of overtime. Alex Wilkie expressed their views in this way: 'While overtime is so general it is mere hypocrisy to talk of establishing an eight hours' scheme. We have the power, if we like to use it, to kill this vicious system of overtime. Let us therefore set about it as an earnest statement of our genuine desire to really shorten the working week. Until we do so it is futile to plead that we are sincere in asking for an eight hours' day.' In fact more than thirty years were to elapse before the eight-hour day became normal. The 54-hour week remained the general rule in private industry until January 1919 when the 47-hour week was conceded. Government dockyards introduced the 48-hour week in 1894.

A NEW HEADQUARTERS

For the first six years of its existence, the Society had its headquarters in Glasgow. Equally important, the seven members of the Executive Committee were all drawn from the Glasgow area. They met every other Tuesday evening in the Society's offices at 27 Hope Street, Glasgow. Despite the various efforts to achieve an open and democratic system of government for the union's affairs, particularly with the frequent recourse to the ballot, it still appeared to some members that there was an undue concentration of power in Scotland and in the Executive Committee. Alex Wilkie was stung by these allegations and finally attempted to rebuke them in a vigorous manner. Writing in the seventh annual report, he declared: 'We are well aware it has not always been the fortune of the Executive to see eye to eye with all the branches or districts on every question that has arisen but as on the E.C. rests the responsibility according to our registered constitution, so with them rest the decisions.

'And in any case, any member or branch can, in the manner and method as provided by rule, appeal to the votes of the members of the Association whose decision is final and binding.' While this was true it is also fair to point out that the Executive had great influence which it could bring to bear before a ballot was held.

Wilkie went on: 'And as we have many men we will have many minds and if it is impossible for all to agree in every question yet at least all can agree to differ. When differences do arise, it would be much better if branches, instead of allowing feeling to engender, would request a representative, as provided by rule and resolution, from the E.C. to personally consider the matter with them. It would save both expense and needless irritation in working the Association because on many matters that crop up, it is impossible in a letter—no matter however cautiously worded or carefully framed—to avoid it seeming hard and formal and which in many cases is misconstrued; whereas that would be obviated and the objections urged or the resolution to be enforced, would lose its more pungent flavour when presented in friendly speech in the course of a friendly discussion with the opportunity of an immediate reply and explanation.'

Wilkie was clearly speaking—or writing—from the heart. There had been frequent examples of misrepresentation or misunderstanding. There had also been numerous cases of differences being resolved by personal intervention.

In October 1886 the Newcastle branch had resigned from the Tyne District Committee because of a number of internal differences. Further differences then arose between the Walker branch, the Tyne District Committee and the Executive Committee. At first it was hoped the issues could be resolved by correspondence. But as the files grew bulkier and bulkier, with no sign of a solution, the Executive Committee decided it must send a deputation to meet all the Tyne members. This was done and meetings took place over two days, 20th and 21st June 1887. The first meeting was with the Walker branch. After an 'animated discussion' it was clearly shown that considerable misconceptions had existed. These were dispelled. The deputation then met the Tyne District committee on the following day and those differences were settled. Another discussion took place on the differences between the Newcastle branch and the Tyne District committee. This too ended in agreement. Further, it was decided that the Tyne District committee should be reconstituted to allow representation from all branches on the Tyne. It had been part of the Newcastle branch's list of complaints that they had been excluded. All of these outline agreements were put to a general meeting of members in the evening. According to the official record: 'This was agreed to when the hope was expressed that all feeling and prejudice would now be cast aside and everyone act harmoniously for the interest and benefit of the Association and the trade in the district.'

Despite the obvious success of personal visits, they were too rare and only undertaken in extreme circumstances. Indeed, the Leith branch tried to make visits a formal matter, by proposing that the General Secretary or some one appointed by the Executive Committee should visit each branch at least once every twelve or eighteen months. This was carried by 376 votes to 141. It surely would have been better still for the Executive Committee to have been more widely representative of all members and branches. This would have given the Committee a better 'feel' of members' attitudes and, in return, would have helped the Committee to explain its views more thoroughly to a wider cross-section of the membership. The expense of travelling to meetings—which could perhaps have been reduced from once a fortnight to once a month—would have increased but this should have been seen as part of the price of administering the Association effectively.

In the autumn of 1887, the Executive Committee according to the constitution, called for nominations for the location of the Executive Committee and of the Society's offices for the next three years. Four places were put forward: Aberdeen, Port Glasgow, Glasgow and Newcastle. Each alternative satisfied two important criteria. They were situated in shipbuilding areas and they contained a number of branches within a given radius so that members of the Executive Committee could be drawn from a wide area. All the Tyneside branches were in favour of Newcastle while the Scottish branches were divided on the question. Govan, Partick, Dundee and Dumbarton favoured Newcastle, while Renfrew, Clydebank, Port Glasgow, Leith, Glasgow and Ardrossan all thought the headquarters should remain in Glasgow. Leith's attitude would seem to be odd in view of their proposition that there should be more personal visits by the General Secretary. It would be easier and cheaper for him to undertake regular visits from a more central location such as Newcastle.

When the votes were counted, Newcastle came out as the easy winner. It received 681 votes compared with 169 for Glasgow, 3 for Port Glasgow and only one for Aberdeen. The vote was not only interesting in itself but also for two other reasons. Firstly, even on an important matter like this, less than a quarter of the members bothered to vote. Secondly, the vote was entirely out of accord with the views of the branches. As we have seen, the branches were more or less evenly divided between Newcastle and Glasgow, yet the members voted overwhelmingly for Newcastle. It was clear, then, that in this matter at least, branch opinion in no way reflected the views of the members as a whole. It is interesting to speculate why. No doubt a principal cause was that then as now branch meetings were thinly attended. The views of the vocal and active minority were not representative of the majority.

Furthermore, on a technical level of voting procedure, branches voting in favour of Glasgow may have done so by a tiny majority, whereas those favouring Newcastle may have been almost unanimous. When all the votes were counted on both sides a different picture would emerge—as, of course, occurred.

Whatever the explanation, by the end of 1887 the members had voted emphatically for the Executive Committee and the head office to be located in Newcastle. Now occurred one of those incidents which could be said to demonstrate the democratic nature of the union but which in reality only demonstrated its lack of unity. The Executive Committee had decided that the move to Newcastle should take place in May 1888. This would obviate expenditure in paying double rents, rates and taxes since they had their Glasgow premises on an annual basis from May to May. They intimated their decision to the Tyne District committee, who took a different view. They wanted the move to take place three months after the vote was taken, i.e. in March. Although there was a difference of only two months (after the Committee had been located in Glasgow for six years), feelings became so heated that a ballot was called for as to when the move should take place. A ballot was duly held with 754 backing the Executive Committee's decision and 172 voting against. Such a difference of opinion, leading to this ballot, was silly. It also led to a rather sour atmosphere in which the move would actually take place.

While this incident rather clouded the future for Alex Wilkie, who as the General Secretary would be obliged to move to Tyneside, he must have been enormously touched by the compliments he received from his Glasgow colleagues before he left. At least two special gatherings were called in his honour. The Glasgow District held a social gathering on 7th May and presented him with an illuminated address 'in token of their confidence and respect, also recording their appreciation of the ability, energy and tact with which he had discharged the onerous duties of General Secretary.' The Glasgow United Trades Council also arranged a social evening at which he was presented with a splendid black ebony stick, mounted with silver, together with a morocco pocket book.

A few days later Wilkie had moved to Newcastle, the Society had taken offices at 3 St Nicholas Buildings, and a new Executive Committee had been formed with members from Walker, Jarrow, Hebburn, Newcastle, Howdon and North Shields.

Whether as a consequence or a coincidence, membership rose dramatically. By the end of 1888 over 800 new members had joined the Society, bringing the total to 4,389 in 38 branches, of which seven had been opened during the year. It is true that trade was beginning to pick up again but the move probably helped to stimulate the increase in numbers.

Having lost the Executive Committee, Clydeside now gained a District Delegate. Members voted overwhelmingly for the creation of this new position and subsequently for William Craig to fill it. He had joined the Society at its inception in March 1882 and indeed was the first president of the Executive Committee, holding office from 1st March 1882 to July 1884. Subsequently he worked in Merseyside for a year, returned to the Clyde for two years, moved to Belfast for a year and now returned to the Clyde once more. He was chairman of the Delegates meeting held in Glasgow in February 1883 and one of the delegates to that historic conference of the United Kingdom Amalgamation of Shipwrights held in Cardiff in June 1883 at which all the branches in the Associated Shipwrights' Society seceded. Yet despite all this experience William Craig was still only 31.

CHAPTER FIVE

RETURN OF PROSPERITY

By the end of 1888 the depression which had begun in the autumn of 1883 was over. Output in the shipbuilding industry rose to 903,000 gross tons compared with 573,000 in 1887 and only 483,000 in 1886. But it was not until 1889 that output exceeded the figure for 1883. Yards that had had to close were reopened. Berths that had been idle were busy once more.

More important, the number out of work dropped dramatically. And wage increases were agreed. In August 1888 shipwrights on the Tyne received an increase of one shilling and sixpence per week to 34s 6d for new work at a conference with employers. It was also agreed at this conference that a month's notice should be given by either side of general increases or reductions in wages. At the end of September shipwrights in Aberdeen received the same increase. In quick succession shipwrights in other areas were granted rises of about the same amount although in Scotland the increase was generally a farthing an hour or a shilling and three halfpence a week. Nearly all of these increases were achieved with the willing co-operation of the employers. Wilkie said there was a 'commendable spirit' on the part of these employers and he hoped other employers would follow their 'laudable example'.

The Society itself shared in the widening prosperity. It opened seven new branches during the year. In two cases they were existing branches splitting into two for the convenience of members. Renfrew and Clydebank split into separate branches and so did Walker and Wallsend. The other five new branches were at Londonderry, Stockton, Blyth, Glasson Dock in N. W. England, and Alloa. Membership also jumped by about 22 per cent from 3,578 in December 1887 to 4,389 at the end of 1888. It was particularly gratifying to see the members paying full benefit had virtually doubled in the year. The categories now comprised:

CONTRIBUTION	TOTAL MEMBERS
1s od per week	1,266
9d " "	409
6d " "	220
3d " "	2,429
N.F. " "	55
	4,389

The income for the year came to £4,420 which was an increase of 25 per cent on the previous year, itself a record. The increase was notably in entry money which had doubled. Expenditure was also at a record level but by only £126, a small increase compared with the increase in income. With actual expenditure of £2,652, there was a favourable balance of £1,765 bringing the Society's reserves up to £7,518. Wilkie's comment: 'Considering that the improved trade may only be said to have been felt by us in the latter part of the year ... this increase of funds and membership must be considered very satisfactory.'

MOVING AHEAD

While 1888 was satisfactory, 1889 was good. The key factor, of course, was the state of trade. As the year opened nearly all branches could report increased activity. Govan reported that the state of trade was 'very fair', Partick that it was 'good' and Renfrew that it was 'busy'. They were typical comments. The Tyneside yards seemed to be even better placed. Walker branch reported that trade was 'very good, all hands employed' and similar sentiments were expressed by Wallsend and Jarrow. Of the Society's 39 branches, only Ardrossan and Preston did not seem to share in the general business improvement.

Against this background, the union was able to negotiate wage increases for many of its members. In the Tyne and Blyth area members gave employers a month's notice, as agreed, of a request for an increase of three shillings a week to commence on 14th February. The employers replied by offering an extra one shilling and sixpence a week from 14th February, with a further shilling a week from July. The members accepted this offer, bringing their wages to £1 17s 0d for new work and £2 0s 0d a week for old work.

This success led to calls from other shipwrights in the North East for equal treatment. A conference was called at Sunderland on 11th February attended by members from other branches and also by members of other societies of shipwrights. Although the meeting was severely practical in its purpose and intention, it was historic in its importance. For this was the first occasion when shipwrights belonging to different unions had come together to secure a common objective. What is more, the conference represented a growing sense of stature on the part of the Associated Shipwrights' Society. As the more active union, it had deplored the laissez-faire approach of the United Kingdom Amalgamation of Shipwrights, had broken with it and had gone its separate way declaring: 'Those who are not for us may be against us.'

Now almost in a gesture of magnanimity, the Society was willing to call a conference of all shipwrights to agree a common approach to all employers on the North East coast. The aim was to bring all wages on to a par with Tyne and Wear. Only the twelve local shipwrights' societies in Stockton and Middlesbrough refused to accept the joint approach. To that extent the conference was not uniformly successful.

A few months later local Societies in Stockton, Middlesbrough and

Hartlepool did agree to united action which raised their wages by a shilling a week for new work from 14th May. Shipwrights in these towns also received an extra shilling a week from 15th July. All shipwrights in yards along the North-East coast now received identical wages.

Elsewhere Dundee branch secured an increase of a farthing an hour, or 1s 1½d a week, from 22nd February. Aberdeen secured a shilling a week on 14th March and another shilling on 2nd May. Barrow members gained an extra 1s 6d on 14th March and another shilling on 5th July. Leith seemed to secure the biggest increase with an extra 2s 3d a week.

Only on the Clyde was there any real difficulty. The members requested an extra halfpenny an hour (or 2s 3d a week) from 8th February. Employers refused but agreed to a meeting on 20th February. Some confusion arose at this meeting, for the men's representatives left with the belief that the employers had offered the extra halfpenny an hour from 8th April.

The members accepted the offer but when William Craig, the Clyde district delegate, told the employers of the acceptance he was informed that the offer had been made for a six months' period only. Both Craig and the men themselves reacted sharply to this extra condition which they felt had been sprung upon them. They therefore reversed their original decision and turned the proposal down. It looked as if the union could be face to face with a serious dispute. The Clyde district committee meeting on 20th March decided to make one final approach.

The employers agreed to meet them and another meeting was quickly convened. Alex Wilkie himself attended, together with representatives from both upper and lower Clyde branches. The outcome was an increase of one halfpenny an hour from 6th April to 6th September, when the level of wages would be reconsidered.

Because of the misunderstandings that had arisen, the Clyde employers decided to form a new association. One of its principal tasks would be to meet the union leaders every six months to discuss and arrange wages and working conditions. The Shipwrights' Society welcomed this initiative but hoped that negotiations could be conducted in a calm and sensible way and preferably as a result of written proposals by the management. This procedure would allow the men to consider matters 'quietly and calmly'. The union also hoped that the proposed method of conciliation would be more successful than previous attempts, and would allow all workmen to gain fair terms rather than only those who resorted to tougher tactics.

The increase in wages was not the only consequence of better business. There was also the drop in unemployment. This led the Executive Committee to suggest that all branch vacant books should be closed. No member need be idle and therefore no unemployment benefits should be paid. The immediate effect was to reduce expenditure by £100 in the quarter.

THE GLASGOW COMMITTEE

A further reduction of expenditure resulted from the decision to dissolve the Glasgow District Committee. It was felt that with a Clyde delegate and a Clyde district committee, a Glasgow committee was unnecessary. There would continue to be, as there had been in the past, continuous friction between the two and there was unnecessary expenditure. The Executive Committee in accepting the proposal to dissolve the Glasgow district committee, also suggested that no district committee should consist of more than nine members. The Executive Committee itself had never had more than nine members whereas the Clyde district committee consisted of sixteen. Such a large membership caused excessive expenditure on expenses. So did daytime meetings with payments in lieu of wages.

In 1888 committee expenses had come to £48, or almost £5 a meeting. If the committee met once a month at night with one member from each of the Clyde branches, the costs would fall to about £1 a meeting or £12—£15 a year. The members accepted the proposition by 954 votes to 34.

NAVAL PROGRAMME

The general upturn in trade was given further impetus by a large programme of warship building ordered by the Admiralty. It placed orders for 70 ships at an estimated cost of £21m. The total included eight first class battleships, two second class battleships, nine first class cruisers and 29 smaller cruisers. The programme was to be carried out in almost equal measure by Government and private yards. What a pity these orders were not placed three years previously when they would have gone a long way to offset the depression.

UNEXPECTED SUPPORT

It is worth noting that trade unions now received support from a most unusual quarter. Sir Charles Mark Palmer, one of the most important Tyneside shipbuilders in the second half of the nineteenth century, epitomized the virtues of the free enterprise system. He had created a huge shipbuilding, ship-owning and iron and steel making organization from nothing. As an archetypal Victorian entrepreneur he had been an early opponent of trade unions. He had wanted to deal directly with the men.

But now his views were mellowing and changing. Presiding at the annual meeting of the Newcastle Chamber of Commerce in March 1889, he even went so far as to congratulate working men for taking 'a wise and proper' course in joining unions. For as the unions continued to grow in strength, they were also growing in maturity. They now employed intelligent representatives or delegates and as the employers were doing the same, there was a mutual advantage. Serious strikes or lockouts were now infrequent and the system of conciliation must augur well for the future.

Such sentiments were clearly grist to the mill for the burgeoning

Shipwrights' Society. Alex Wilkie commented: 'This statement shows most conclusively the benefit of our organizations, not only to their members and the trade at large, but also to the community as a whole ...'

It certainly did seem that the Society was coming into its own.

THE WORK OF THE DISTRICT DELEGATES

Joseph Heslop, the North of England district delegate, and William Craig, the Clyde district delegate, were continuously developing and expanding their work. In so doing, they lifted a considerable burden from the General Secretary, Alex Wilkie, who besides the general administration of the union, was spending more time visiting branches.

The two delegates performed a great many functions. They administered the union's affairs at local level. They negotiated with employers. They wrote reports, led delegations, attended conferences. A look at their activities during the quarter January-March 1889 will provide an illustration of their range of duties. Joseph Heslop had to deal with several demarcation disputes where other tradesmen were encroaching on the work which shipwrights felt should be theirs. In particular there was a narrow dividing line between the work of joiners and shipwrights. The latter said they were willing to draw up a comprehensive list of jobs which could be assigned to one trade or another by arbitration but the joiners were not ready to accept such a proposal. A difference of opinion about the rails on top of iron stanchions led the shipwrights at Dobson and Company's yard at Low Walker on the Tyne to go on strike for seventeen days. Heslop was finally able to secure a satisfactory settlement after numerous meetings and negotiations.

He was also able to report progress on the question of overtime rates paid by Hawthorn, Leslie and Company of Hebburn. For over 20 years this firm had been paying for overtime at the rate of time and a quarter. But after six meetings Heslop persuaded the company to pay at the rate of time and a half.

He also spent considerable time negotiating wage claims with a number of firms on the Tyne and Blyth area who did not belong to the Employers' Association. In all cases, he was successful in securing an increase of a shilling an hour. He negotiated with other firms on the question of the requisite notice to be given when men were to be paid off. Some firms had not been providing the legal length of notice. Here too he was largely successful.

On the wider question of employment, he continued to act as a kind of one-man Ministry of Employment, putting men and jobs together. At this time with rising employment, it was not a question of finding jobs but rather of finding the men to fill them. Demand for labour was exceeding supply. With none of his own members out of work, he wrote to other branches but the general reply was that no members were idle.

He also helped to open a new branch at South Shields which would be more convenient for men living in that town than the branches at

Membership Certificate of the Associated Shipwrights Society.
By Courtesy of Tyne & Wear County Council, Sunderland Museum Collection.

Alexander Wilkie, First General Secretary, 1882-1928.

Jarrow or Wallsend. But even this was not the full extent of his work load. Other matters were 'too numerous' for report.

William Craig was equally busy on the Clyde. His main task was in the negotiation of the wage increase with the Clyde employers which led to some misunderstanding. We have already noted that two conferences were necessary before this question was made clear, but that eventually the employers agreed to 7½ per cent increase to run from 5th April to 6th September. Another conference was to be called then to consider the question again.

On the problem of demarcation, Craig was able to report more progress than Heslop. A joint committee of joiners and shipwrights had agreed to lines of demarcation and it was hoped to sign an agreement in the near future. Craig commented: 'We must express our feeling of satisfaction at the spirit in which the representatives of the joiners met us, all had come with the earnest desire to have this vexed question definitely settled and we trust that the good feeling created at those joint meetings may be the beginning of a closer relationship between the two trades.'

But elsewhere there was no progress. Craig had to spend a lot of time trying to settle disputes that arose from dock rules and byelaws. He felt it was time a new set of rules was drawn up by the shipbuilders' association and the unions.

Besides looking after the Clyde, Craig had been asked by the Executive Committee to visit Leith, Alloa and Grangemouth for although they were not in the Clyde district they were so closely allied that what affected the Clyde affected them. He reported that he found all of them 'getting on pretty well.'

Both Craig and Heslop were also involved in carrying out special audits at this time into the financial affairs of two branches, Greenock and Portsmouth. In itself this was a considerable undertaking but there was more to come. For the audits discovered that the rules of the Society were not being strictly obeyed. In particular there were three 'reprehensible practices'. The first was that the secretaries of the two branches, Donald Sinclair at Greenock and David Tait at Portsmouth, were both in arrears with their own contributions and had been at the time of their election to office. The Executive Committee took the strongest possible objection to this news, declaring that the future usefulness, power and prosperity of the union depended upon every member having confidence in the absolute truthfulness and honesty of all officers. The second malpractice was that all ledgers of income received in these two branches did not tally. Thirdly, some members had been paid higher amounts in benefit than was their due.

All of this led the Executive Committee to call for a special audit of all branch books. Furthermore, the two district delegates were instructed to visit all the branches in their districts quarterly, to audit and examine each quarter's transactions. Although understandable from the Executive Committee's point of view, the scale of this undertaking would be substantial, coming on top of the work the delegates already undertook. The Committee had been given a fright by what they had discovered. The Society's rules specifically covered the points at issue yet they had been ignored. And in the case of the two branch secretaries they were ignored deliberately. Only a more effective way of policing accounts on a regular basis would provide a degree of reassurance—and the two delegates were the obvious 'policemen' to use, at least in their own districts. Heslop and Craig agreed to undertake the new duties, but how willingly we do not know.

PIECE WORK

During the depression of the 1880's a number of employers experimented with piece-work arrangements. Under this system, men were paid not by the hour (time rates) but by the output or piece (piece work rates). The intention was to increase productivity and hopefully reduce costs by employing fewer men. The practice never became widespread and the majority of firms who did flirt with it soon dropped it. But one or two persisted, particularly on the Clyde.

The Associated Shipwrights' Society was very much opposed to piecework. They felt it was a 'selfish system' which led to bad and defective work, gave the dishonest worker an advantage and generally favoured quantity at the expense of quality. The union also refuted the claims of some employers that piecework was necessary because the men did not work as hard or as fast as they used to. Ships, they said, were being built in a shorter time than ever before.

And a well-known Tyneside shipbuilder, Wigham Richardson, supported the men in this. Speaking at a meeting in Newcastle in November 1887, he said: 'My sincere conviction is that there is more honest work and better work and harder work and less skulking today than there was thirty years ago.' In coming to this conclusion Wigham Richardson gave an interesting insight into working conditions. 'I have known quite well what it was to start in the dark on a cold morning with a cutty pipe in lieu of breakfast. I remember perfectly well the feeling of a cold chisel on a frosty day and the awkward apprentice hand which brought the chipping hammer down on the hapless knuckles instead of on the chisel head till your whole body tingled with sympathetic pain. And I know, too, that in those days when the cat was away, the mice would play.'

Several meetings were held in Glasgow to denounce the piece-work practice but still it lingered on with some employers. The union felt it would have to take stronger action. A meeting was called in the Glasgow Upper District on 23rd December 1887 and passed the following resolution: 'That on and after this date it shall be a standing order of this district that no shipwright shall take piece or contract for shipwright work. Any shipwright taking a contract for shipwright work in this district shall be expelled, if a member, from this Association.... Any shipwright working with a contractor after being notified to desist, shall be fined the sum of five pounds for the first offence and if persisted in shall be expelled from the Association.'

A special committee was also formed to try to persuade as many shipwrights as possible to abide by the resolution and sign a form to that effect. Over seven hundred did so. But some were still tempted. At R. Napier and Sons in Govan, three men—James Hutchison, William Hamilton and Donald McKenzie—broke their promises and undertook piece work. They were fined £5 each.

Another firm, A. J. Inglis, also refused to drop the practice. Alex Wilkie, the General Secretary, led powerful delegations to both yards to urge the employers to drop piece work but without success. Their efforts were undermined by a handful of mavericks who continued to accept the employers' offers. Wilkie had only scorn for them. 'They have betrayed their fellow workmen, broken their promises as tradesmen and dishonoured their signatures as men.'

The union was more successful on the Tyne. On 31st July 1888 four union officials including Wilkie, the general secretary, and Heslop the Tyne District delegate, attended a meeting with eight employers. Joseph Heslop opened by explaining the unfairness of the system and suggesting that piecework was as harmful to the employers as it was to the men for it led to poor workmanship.

The employers were not convinced. Mr White of Armstrong, Mitchell and Company of Walker, the warship builders, claimed that piecework allowed good workmen to benefit from their superior skills.

The union officials pointed out however that since the men worked in squads, no single man could receive the benefit of his alleged greater skill. Mr Black, also of Armstrong Mitchell, argued that he had heard no complaints from the men and indeed that they seemed to want piece work. To this the union men retorted that they were being offered no alternative. At the end of a lively discussion, the workmen's representatives were asked to retire. On being called back, they were told that the employers did not feel piecework should be abolished at least until further enquiries had been made. The employers also suggested that since it seemed the men were divided in their views, a ballot should be taken in the yards.

If that was meant to be a divisive tactic, it failed lamentably for the men showed they were virtually unanimous in their opposition to piecework. Armed with this verdict, the officials now sought further discussions with the employers. After two meetings, it was agreed that all work was to be done on a time-rate basis for the next twelve months and the position would then be reviewed. It was a victory for the men and the union in all but name.

On the Clyde, things were much more difficult. The firms of Inglis and Napier refused to soften their attitude, arguing that they had the backing of a considerable number of the men. At the beginning of 1850 the differences took a more serious turn when a long-serving employee of the firm of D. and F. Henderson of Partick was paid off, apparently because of the union's attitude to piecework.

A general meeting of employers' and union representatives was called for 4th February 1890 when a 'long and sometimes animated' discussion took place for three hours. The employers argued in favour of a flexible system under which they could operate either time rates or piece rates whichever seemed the more advantageous at any particular time or in any particular district. The union leaders reiterated the objection to the piecework system and drew attention to the 1887 resolution. The two sides were clearly still far apart and it was decided to adjourn for a week. When they reconvened the employers made two substantial points. Firstly, that other trades in shipbuilding were working the piecework system and unless the Society relented in its views, the amount of work going to shipwrights would be reduced; and secondly the employers said that the union was clearly not speaking on behalf of all its members since a good number of them were willing to work piece rates and were in fact doing so.

The union representative replied that certainly some men were breaking the union rules but they numbered only eighty and they could not be allowed to flaunt the wishes of the majority of members. To call the employers' bluff, Wilkie and the other trade union representatives agreed to put the whole question to their members again.

Meetings were held of all Clydeside branches, followed by a ballot. This produced thirty-three votes for piecework and 1,693 against. The employers refused to accept this result as 'conclusive and final ... inasmuch as in putting the terms of the Employers' proposals before the men to vote upon, the writer of the "Summons Circular" so prejudiced the whole case, that the members of your Association were not left free to decide the question upon its merits'. This reply naturally incensed the Executive Committee. But they were made even angrier because this reply was addressed not to them or to the General Secretary but directly to all the Society's members. The implication was that it was only the Executive Committee who were against piecework while the members would accept it if given a free choice. The Committee knew this was not the case. In this as in all other matters they felt they went to great pains to seek and then follow the instructions of members. But the employers' view was given credence by the Clyde District Committee who invited the owners to a meeting in Partick to address the men directly.

The issue had now reached a crisis. Who was speaking for the Society as a whole—the Executive Committee, or the recalcitrant members? And should the views of the majority prevail? The Executive Committee were in no doubt and acted decisively. They instructed members not to work at the yards involved in the dispute. They called upon them to pay an extra shilling a month for the next twelve months as a contingency and they asked the Clyde District Committee to defer its proposal for a meeting with employers.

The action met with qualified success. For while the members narrowly turned down the proposal for a 'fighting fund', the employers reacted positively by calling for another meeting. This was held on 19th May 1890. It proved an inconclusive and unsatisfactory affair. At the end of it, the employers suggested that the only option that was now open was to refer the matter to arbitration. The union delegation agreed to put this proposal to the ballot but there it was heavily defeated. The deadlock remained. And both sides were losers: the employers because they could not make progress on their full order books, and the union because its expenditure for dispute benefits shot up from £160 the previous year to £860 in 1890.

Having failed to gain backing for its request that the employers should meet the men, the Clyde District Committee now suggested that the issue should be referred to the Executive of the Federation of the Engineering and Shipbuilding Trades. This was done and a deputation of three were asked to discuss the question with members working piecework and those against the practice. Partly through these discussions and partly through the desire by Napiers to get on with their full order book, an agreement was reached. Under it, Napiers discontinued piecework and the Association withdrew all restrictions on men working at the yard. The move represented a victory for the union against one of the two firms who had fought hardest for the principle of piecework.

CHAPTER SIX

STRENGTH IN UNITY

At the end of the 1880's, as the British economy came out of the depression it had experienced for five years, there was a growing interest in trade unions. New unions were formed. Older unions found their membership increasing. And there was pressure for unions to combine. Writing in the eighth annual report of the Associated Shipwrights' Society, Alex Wilkie made an impassioned plea for all shipwrights to join together. He wrote: 'We for many years urged that the shipwrights of the different ports should become better organized and closer united together in a strong, consolidated Association which could provide all the benefits and enable members to insure themselves against all the disabilities that overtake workmen in disposing of their labour and in maintaining its value.' He thought that the small local societies were now completely out of date. For they could not offer members the benefits and the strength of larger unions. And individuals found it inconvenient to have to join a new society every time they moved from one port to another in search of work.

Wilkie wrote: 'It is generally admitted on all hands that local societies, like single individuals, are almost powerless to meet or combat the powers and influence of the large capitalists and great companies of the present day ... The urgent necessity of our trade being thoroughly organized was never more apparent than at present. And in their own interest, as well as that of the whole trade, we trust all shipwrights will terminate this isolated procedure, cast aside their mere prejudices and petty jealousies and embrace this opportunity of assimilating with the Associated Shipwrights' Society.'

Wilkie's call was given added significance by the decision of the employers in 1889 to come together in a National Federation of Shipbuilding and Engineering Employers. There were five objects:

1. To examine all Parliamentary Bills for their likely effect on shipbuilding and engineering and to make representations where appropriate.
2. To 'resist interference by workmen's associations with free contract work, number of apprentices engaged, etc.'

3. To support firms engaged in disputes.
4. To settle wage claims on a district basis for stated periods of time.
5. To prevent men from leaving their work and obtaining other employment under assumed names.

These objects were hardly neutral in their intention. Apart from the examination of Parliamentary Bills, they were clearly designed to strengthen the employers against the unions or to limit the unions' freedom of action. They were certainly interpreted by the unions in that way. Alarmed by this initiative, a number of unions called a conference in Manchester on 13th February 1890 'to draw ourselves a little closer together'. The conference was attended by representatives of the Amalgamated Carpenters, the General Union of Joiners, the Steam Engine Makers, the Associated Blacksmiths, the Co-operative Smiths, the Ironfounders and the Shipwrights. Alex Wilkie, the General Secretary, and Alex Elliott, the President, represented the Shipwrights. Robert Knight, the General Secretary of the Boilermakers' Society, was voted chairman of the conference.

The meeting decided on four main points. Firstly, other unions would not interfere in a dispute between a member union and an employer, unless requested to do so. Secondly, when a dispute occurred between a member union and an employer, other member unions would not do the work of the union in dispute. Thirdly, any dispute between unions in the Federation would be referred to arbitration. Fourthly, the Federation was to be of 'a neutral character', that is each union would remain autonomous.

Robert Knight thought these proposals were essential if the unions were to match the increased power of the employers. 'The very fact of a Federation being formed of all the shipbuilding and engineering trades will give us power and an influence we could not possibly exert as single societies and enable us to settle differences with our employers without having recourse to disputes. The object of the Federation is not of an aggressive nature but for defensive purposes and the protection of rights already acquired.'

Alex Wilkie commented: 'We can only hope that this Federation will be the means of more peaceful solutions of future great differences than has been the isolated actions of the past.'

The shipwright branches endorsed this view. One indeed urged an even closer association. Another branch called for a special contribution from all members to build up funds for the Federation. But this would have been to give the Federation an independent power and a financial strength it did not want and would have impaired the autonomy of the individual unions, a cardinal tenet of the Federation. The Shipwrights' Executive Committee felt that the proposals 'cannot but be of great benefit'. The members backed this view by 1,692 votes to 100. But the high hopes did not materialize in practice, at least not immediately. Three years later Alex Wilkie was to report to the Royal Commission on Labour that the machinery of the Federation was not always successful. 'We found a difficulty in getting it to work,' he said. The main defect was the refusal of the Amalgamated Society of Engineers to join. This was the biggest union in engineering and was consequently most affected by the constant flow of technical innovations. These innovations tended to stimulate the formation of specialist, sectional societies opposed to the general aims of the Amalgamated Society.

In these circumstances, it was unwilling to join a Federation where each of its smaller rivals had an equal voice. It would join only if it was given sufficient voting power to outweigh the smaller engineering unions. The latter would not agree to such a proposal; it did seem to strike at the very philosophy of partnership. To that extent, the Federation was not a success. Inter-union conflicts, particularly over demarcation disputes, continued. Often unions were more at logger-heads with one another than with the employers. And these internecine disputes further weakened the Federation as a powerful, multi-union organization in its dealings with individual firms or the Employers' Federation. But as time went by, the calls for more effective co-operation grew louder and the benefits of joint action became more and more obvious.

DEMARCATION DISPUTES

Disputes between unions, particularly over 'who did what?' were a constant source of irritation. They occurred almost as frequently as disputes with employers and were frequently laced with a greater degree of bitterness. A union official said in the 1880's: 'Here in Sunderland there is sure to be a dispute of some kind on every vessel before they start and half a dozen more before she is finished.' And Beatrice and Sidney Webb noted in their study *Industrial Democracy* published in 1897 that between 1890 and 1893 on the Tyne 'within the space of thirty-five months, there were no fewer than thirty-five weeks in which one or other of the four most important sections of workmen in the staple industry of the district (shipbuilding) absolutely refused to work.

'This meant the stoppage of huge establishments, the compulsory idleness of tens of thousands of other artisans and labourers, and the semi-starvation of thousands of families totally unconcerned with the disputes. Nor was the effect confined, as far as the trade unionists were concerned, to these sensational but temporary results. The men were, in fact, playing into the hands of those employers who wished to see trade unionism destroyed. The internecine warfare on the Tyne had left all unions concerned in a state of local weakness from which they have by no means yet recovered and under which they will probably suffer for many years. Their loss of members and of money is the least part of the evil. When one society is fighting another, the whole efficacy of trade unionism, as a means of improving the conditions of employment, is, for the moment, paralysed.'

The main difficulties lay with the shipwrights and for a good reason. The rise of iron shipbuilding strengthened the influence of the metal trades, particularly boilermakers, riveters and platers. The shipwrights, the masters in the old wooden days, saw their livelihood being increasingly squeezed while the ship joiners represented a danger of encroachment from another direction. A sixth of all the disputes involved shipwrights and joiners. The dilemma was well summed up in the following words: '.... the industry had the misfortune to be the meeting ground of many well-organized crafts during a revolution in its technique and to offer an expanding range of new jobs which lent themselves to much hair-splitting debate.'[1]

Many of the disputes led to serious aggravation between the unions concerned and even to strikes, for reasons that were well understood by one of the most enlightened Tyneside shipbuilders in the late nineteenth century, John Wigham Richardson. 'Imagine what your feelings would be if you believed (as if it were the Gospel) that you had a prescriptive right to certain work of which you were being unjustly deprived ... Unless you first realize that the men during a strike grow to look upon themselves as martyrs and to feel a martyr's exultation, you will never be able to understand how strikes last as long as they do, after the struggle is evidently hopeless.'[2]

And another Tyneside shipbuilder, John Price of Palmers, Jarrow, was quoted by the Webbs as saying: 'The principal difficulty in composing the disputes has arisen from the variety of practice in the different works and districts ... Each society proposes to itself to have the largest possible number of its members employed at the same time ... and to this end tries to secure the whole of the work it considers belongs to its members in accordance with usage and custom.'[3]

The shipwrights themselves put forward the view: 'While we do not object to any firms dividing their works into departments or sub-letting portions of the vessels they are building, still we do most respectfully and emphatically contend that no employers should, in suiting their convenience, give away another man's means of living, any more than that no workman would be allowed or justified to go into an employer's office and take his money from the safe and give it to another.'[4]

These comments help to throw some light on the increasing frequency of demarcation disputes during these years.

To overcome or at least to reduce these problems, there were many attempts to set up conciliation boards of one sort or another. One of the most successful attempts was on the Wear in 1885 when one of the regular disputes arose between joiners and shipwrights. They were regularly at logger-heads because their work was so similar. But these feelings came to a head in 1885 when the shipwrights went so far as to compile a list of 300 examples of pieces of work they should have been doing rather than the joiners. This list was presented to the conciliation board which after many meetings reduced the points of difference to eleven and then to three—which were submitted to employers for a decision. This was the beginning of better times.

A Sunderland shipbuilder, James Laing, was to tell the Royal Commission on Labour in 1891: 'Since then ... we have had no strikes on the Wear.'

The inauguration of the Federation of Engineering and Shipbuilding

Trades was a further step in this direction. For although it was formed in response to the employers' attempts to get together, an equally important aim was to reduce inter-union disputes through an arbitration system. It came not a moment too soon for these disputes were growing more and more serious. Indeed its arrival coincided with one of the worst disputes between the joiners and shipwrights, worse than the 1885 dispute. This dispute on the Tyne had been simmering for some months but by the autumn of 1889 both sides agreed to put the issue forward for arbitration. Alex Wilkie was to be the arbitrator for the shipwrights, William Patterson for the Carpenters and Joiners Society, with Thomas Burt, M.P., the general secretary of the Northumberland Miners' Association, to act as umpire. The Court met on twenty-four days over a period of five months and since the two parties could not agree, the umpire had to make a final adjudication.

Each side submitted a list of the work it felt entitled to by custom and practice. In many cases the lists overlapped. Each side then claimed that the other was encroaching upon its preserve. Wilkie argued that in the days of wooden shipbuilding the difference between the two trades had been quite clear. The shipwrights had done the heavy work and the joiners had 'fitted up the cabins'. With iron shipbuilding the distinction was not so clear and the joiners had used this change to extend their work. The question was further confused by the differing practices in different districts. Wilkie also argued that because joiners' wages were lower than shipwrights', there was a natural tendency for employers to favour joiners. He put forward the following definition as a basis for settlement: 'That whatever work is for the utility, strength and safety of the vessel to be shipwright work and that whatever may contribute to the elegance and luxury of passenger accommodation as in the cabins and saloons to be joiner work.'

William Patterson for the powerful Carpenters and Joiners Society, which had 25,000 members, argued that the Tyne was not typical of the whole country for in other areas joiners were doing work which the shipwrights would not accept. In any case the joiners had had wider duties than making cabins in the days of wooden shipbuilding. They were now simply maintaining the customary practices. It was the shipwrights who were encroaching on their work.

In giving his award in April 1890, Thomas Burt wrote that the questions at issue were 'numerous and complicated'. He felt that under any circumstances it would have been difficult to arrive at a just decision but that the difficulties were increased enormously by the parties being in direct conflict and by a frequent contradiction over matters of fact. The latter arose not from a desire to hide the truth but simply because in many classes of work there really was no uniformity. In such circumstances he felt it was no surprise that disputes occurred.

In coming to a decision he emphasized the need for give and take and for continuing current practices whenever possible. But where this was not possible he had decided to apportion the items of disputed work between the two unions. He gave lists of ninety-six jobs to be tackled by joiners and seventy-two by shipwrights.

The shipwrights accepted the findings as they had pledged to do when they agreed to go to arbitration. The joiners, however, were so incensed by the award that they refused to accept it, 'thereby breaking their pledges, repudiating their signatures and ignoring their public statements' (Wilkie). Despite continuous meetings an agreement could not be reached before 1st August when, according to the original Memorandum of Agreement signed by shipwrights and joiners, the award was to be put into effect. When the employers did so, 1,000 joiners from thirteen Tyne yards came out on strike. They received a uniformly bad press. The *Newcastle Daily Leader* of 1st August commented: '... It is not likely that any effective justification can be given for an act which needs a great deal more than an ordinary resort to forcible measures.'

The *Newcastle Daily Journal* of 4th October declared: '... the joiners do not possess the sympathy of other working men and their obstinacy in resisting every reasonable proposition seems to arise from an instinctive belief that no decision likely to be given by any impartial tribunal would be agreeable to them. But who is it they are trying to coerce? As we have said before, it is evident the employers are helpless even if they were willing to side with the joiners. The situation would not be improved so far as they are concerned by their provoking a justifiable strike of the ship-carpenters in place of an unjustifiable strike of the joiners ... What do the joiners want to be at? They are like spoiled children crying for the moon and refusing to eat their supper till they get it.'

After three months of deadlock, the Mayor of Newcastle, Thomas Bell, intervened and suggested that he should set up a Conciliation Board consisting of representatives of various independent unions to consider the dispute and make a final settlement. Both sides agreed to attend and to accept the Board's findings as final. The Board met continuously for ten days from 28th October to 10th November and made a number of amendments to Mr Burt's award. This in no way reflected on his work, however, and the Conciliation Board even went so far as to congratulate him on the way he had carried out 'a difficult and extremely delicate duty'.

The joiners ended their strike but the feelings between the two unions did not subside easily or quickly. The positions that had been adopted and the arguments that had been used were too strong for that. But the value of independent Conciliation Boards had been further vindicated and the gravity of demarcation disputes further underlined.

GOOD YEARS

All the omens for 1889 proved correct. It was a good year, the best that British shipbuilding had yet known. The industry was now producing four out of every five ships launched in the whole world. In this year it launched 790 vessels of 1,295,000 gross tons, thus just pipping the previous record set in 1883.

Wages too returned to the level of that year with the North-East coast again setting the pace. Shipwrights there were now paid £2 a week for old work and £1 17s for new work. Clydeside workers were a shilling or so behind these rates and Aberdeen again set the lower limit with £1 9s a week for new work.

The Society opened five new branches in the year—at Alloa, South Shields, Campbeltown, Devonport and Dundalk. It also incorporated the local society at Stockton so that membership there rose from twenty-two in December 1888 to 109 in December 1889 and at Middlesbrough where membership rose from 20 to 106. Total membership increased during the year by 1,061 to 5,450 in 43 branches.

Most pleasing of all was the financial side. Income almost doubled to £7,500 while expenditure went up by less than a tenth to £2,980. There was a gain of £4,700 on the year's transactions leaving the Society a balance of over £12,000.

The magical five-figure sum had been reached at last. Alex Wilkie was naturally jubilant. He commented in the eighth annual report that the increase both in funds and members 'must be considered very satisfactory indeed.'

The figures would have been even better but for the considerable amount of arrears in the payment of subscriptions. In fact only a quarter of the members were fully paid up. The majority were a little behind in their subscriptions but almost a fifth were more than five weeks behind. About 5 per cent were over twenty weeks in arrears. Alex Wilkie was distressed by these figures and scornful of the men involved. 'We have no patience with such men, they are the drags on the wheels of progress.' He urged all members to help to show up such men and to coerce them into paying up. 'It is really too bad, after the enhanced remuneration the Association has secured for the members that a number should lag behind in such a manner. In many cases the greatest kindness you can do to these men is to be firm and severe with them.' As a stimulus to action he compiled the financial position of all 5,400 members. This was a tremendous undertaking but if it helped to wipe out some if not all of the arrears 'it will in some measure repay us for the extra labour entailed on all by its compilation'.

The general development of the Associated Shipwrights' Society brought it favourable comment from the newspapers. The *Newcastle Daily Leader* described the union as 'young but vigorous' and said of the eighth report: 'The business of the Society is so fully detailed that its whole working is revealed and proves the management worthy of every confidence.' The Govan Press article commented: 'It is very gratifying to see such a large addition to the membership of the Association during the past year as it points to the fact that the shipwrights are at last becoming alive to their own interests and realizing that without union and organization they are at the mercy of all and sundry.'

The high tide of booming trade and full employment rolled through into 1890. Output was virtually as high as in 1889, wages continued to rise and more shipwrights joined the Society. In fact it registered its highest annual intake to date: 1,939 new members, bringing the total to 7,389, of whom 2,868 were paying full benefit of 1s 0d a week. Income for the year exceeded £10,000 and the balance at the year's end came to £16,688.

The Society opened no less than thirteen new branches in the year, of which ten were in England and assimilated local societies at Portsmouth, Hartlepool, Whitby, Ipswich and London. A large measure of this success was due to the effort of Alex Wilkie who made a fourteen-day tour of South coast ports from London and Sheerness through Southampton and Portsmouth to Milford Haven and Pembroke. It was an arduous undertaking, coming so soon after his work on the Tyne Arbitration Court and the compilation of the financial figures of all members. He was rewarded for all these efforts however. He was voted an increase of salary—from £3 to £4 a week.

TEN YEARS OLD

The Society completed its tenth year in December 1891 in high spirits. Shipbuilding output had remained at a high level, only fractionally down on the record year of 1889, and there was full employment. Wages had remained unchanged. Membership had gone up by 2,731 to over 10,000. And there had been no general disputes during the year, although there were one or two local demarcation difficulties.

It was all very satisfactory. The new union, launched just before the arrival of a severe depression, had proved itself. It did serve a need and did provide a powerful organization for the benefit and protection of shipwrights. These were the very things which the United Kingdom Amalgamation of Shipwrights had failed to do and which the Associated Society had been inaugurated to demonstrate needed doing. That demonstration had proved effective and totally convincing. The days of the Amalgamation were over.

In June 1891 a conference was held in Liverpool to determine the future of the Amalgamation. The conference came without difficulty to the conclusion that it had no future and resolved: 'That, considering the present position of the United Kingdom Amalgamated Society of Shipwrights, the manner in which strikes during the last few years have not been supported, also the unsatisfactory way in which the branches have contributed to the Central Fund, that the said Fund be divided, and each branch that has subscribed to the existing Central Fund receive their proportionate share, less an equitable proportion of expenses up to date of division.'

Alex Wilkie commented: 'This virtually means the demise of the Amalgamation after an existence of nearly half a century. In recent years the Amalgamation was only one in name, as its constitution did not meet the necessities of the times or the progress of the age. There can be no doubt if, at its institution in the second quarter of this century, it had like the other cognate trades' societies, instead of an amalgamation of atoms without cohesion, become a consolidated organization, we as a trade would now have been in a much better position.'

Despite its inherent weaknesses which were thrown into such strong relief by the growing industrialization and the formation of employers' associations, it is only fair to say that in its early years, during the 1840's and 1850's, it did provide an opportunity to come together to discuss common matters. It was a kind of meeting place, a forum and never set out to be much more. The fact was that a great deal more was required by the end of the nineteenth century, as the Associated Society had shown clearly.

The field was now clear for the Society to move ahead to recruit all shipwrights. 'That it has succeeded cannot be questioned,' the Society's tenth annual report stated, 'and we do trust that, with the difficulties ahead of our trade, that the shipwrights in all ports will sink all petty jealousies and local prejudices and unite in one consolidated and compact organization under one common flag and all maintaining our common cause.' This certainly continued to happen during the year with 16 new or assimilated branches, including Liverpool with 512 members and Hull with 716.

The Society also took the important step of admitting apprentices as half-members during the year. They would pay half the amount of adult members and receive half the amount in benefits. As a further inducement, the Society suggested it might offer to institute prizes of books, tools or cash to apprentices who secured certificates in Naval Architecture or at Technical Classes to supplement their practical training. As might be expected, the Executive Committee foresaw a problem with regard to numbers. The General Secretary wrote in the tenth annual report: 'This being a social as well as an economic question, is a most difficult one to deal with and will require to be fully considered from every point of view before any decisive action is taken, at the same time, while we have as yet fixed no limit, we may be forced to do so in sheer self-protection, if some firms persist in continuing to increase the number of their apprentices overmuch.'

There was one other important area where the Society made important progress during the year, in the appointment of more permanent officials. Besides the North-East of England and Clydeside, district delegates were now appointed for the Mersey and the Humber. It was another sign of the growth of the Society. Unhappily, the first Clyde district delegate, William Craig, died in June 1891 at the age of 36. He had done a good job for the union and had been one of its strongest supporters since its inception. He was replaced as Clyde district delegate by Robert Ramage.

The strong and steady growth of the Society was due, above all, to the General Secretary, Alex Wilkie. His energy and efficiency, his tact and moderation had played an invaluable part in bringing the Society through its early years. In recognition of his work he was presented with an illuminated address, a gold Albert and a purse of gold at a social evening in the Old Assembly Rooms, Newcastle, on 30th March 1891. In making the presentation, Joseph Heslop, the North of England District Delegate, said that Mr Wilkie had been actuated by one desire and that was to do right, no matter whom he pleased or offended. He felt sure that they would all agree that he had achieved this aim and that their progress as a Society was due in a large measure to his exertions.

In reply, Wilkie returned to one of his favourite themes, the need for moderation. He deprecated strikes because they were industrial warfare. As far as the Society was concerned, they had always tried 'by conciliation and conference to secure amicable arrangements'. Some had argued that the growth of a union in itself was a provocative thing. This was not his view. For they did not seek a war with the capitalists but simply the strength to secure a fair wage for their labour and a fair method of selling their labour.

It might be thought that this was something of a semantic argument, for who was to decide what was 'fair' and could not the pursuit of a 'fair wage' in itself lead to industrial warfare? Well, it could but in fact had not done so. The history of the first ten years shows plainly that the Society under Wilkie was a force for moderation. Time and again he urged his members to use every means of securing peaceful settlements in disputes with management. Even in the tenth annual report, which noted that the Society's funds stood at over £23,000, or more than £2 a member, he was arguing moderation.

'While we certainly contend,' he wrote, 'that it is one of the main fundamental objects of our Association to maintain and defend our trade, still we must earnestly point out to our members that this can far oftener be more efficiently done by care and watchfulness than by extreme measures. And we would urge wherever such differences do arise that every method be applied and no means be left untried to secure a just and amicable settlement.'

Wilkie's attitude derived partly from a desire to protect and nurture the Society's funds which even then could be quickly depleted by a major strike and partly from his own personality. He was a man of moderation himself. He probably also saw that the possession of power, the potential of power, is often enough in itself to achieve one's aims. It is not necessary to express that power through industrial action. The recognition by employers of union strength was frequently sufficient.

But as we have seen, industrial relations were now entering a new phase. For whereas the individual working man felt naked before the arrival of unions in his dealings with employers, now the latter felt unprotected against the power of the unions. As a consequence, they were forming employers' associations and the unions were replying by coming together in federations. The power game was escalating. It was all the more essential therefore to endorse the principle of moderation through conciliation. Wilkie wrote: 'Through the Federation of the Capitalists and Employers it would seem as if differences were to be fought out on a much larger scale than formerly. Therefore it is all the more necessary that the various classes of workers should have suitable machinery to arrange the differences between each other; and then by real and consolidated Federation be able to meet the Federated Employers on an equal footing. And thus by more perfect organization on both sides, instead of the barbarous methods of strikes and lockouts, the differences between Capital and Labour could be amicably and reasonably arranged around a conference table.'

In this escalating power game, the unions were often at a disadvantage. For it was far easier for employers to combine to deal with specific issues, such as wage rates or working conditions, than it was for the unions. For in shipbuilding in particular they were often wracked by demarcation disputes between each other with the employer standing by as a helpless spectator. Having clashed bitterly, it was then difficult if not impossible for them to come together to negotiate with employers. To continue to grow as autonomous individual unions remained their prime aim with a loose federation as an additional bonus where it could be achieved.

There was another difficulty, the growth of the 'new unionism', more militant, more political and more exciting than the sober unions led by moderate men. Towards the end of the 1880's a number of new unions had come into existence which seemed to differ strikingly from the older unions, or even from the Shipwrights' Society which, although a relatively new union, was modelled on the conventional form. The new unions tended to cater for the general labourer, rather than the craftsman, for the poorer workers rather than the richer. They did not prize efficiency and careful financing, did not see their role as providers of benefits and tended to be involved in political matters. Part of the impetus for these new unions and their attitudes came from the growing recognition of the widespread poverty and suffering in Society at that time. Part came from the growth of socialism represented by such organizations as the Fabian Society and the Social Democratic Federation. And part from the emergence of new leaders such as James Keir Hardie, the Scottish miners' leader, Ben Tillett, of the London dockers, James Havelock Wilson, the seamen's leader, Will Thorne of the gas workers, and John Burns and Tom Mann of the engineers. By and large these leaders were young, militant and believed in securing their aims not only by industrial power but also by political means, through securing representation in Parliament. In a pamphlet written in 1886, Tom Mann declared: 'To trade unionists, I desire to make a special appeal. How long, how long will you be content with the present half-hearted policy of your unions? None of the important societies have any policy other than of endeavouring to keep wages from falling. The true unionist policy of aggression seems entirely lost sight of, in fact the average unionist of today is a man with a fossilized intellect, either hopelessly apathetic or supporting a policy that plays directly into the hands of the capitalist exploiter.'

These sentiments found expression in various strikes, of which the best known was the London dock strike of 1889, in the formation of the new unions, and in the increasingly militant tone of the discussions in the T.U.C. The 1890 Conference saw the new men appearing in strength and one of them, John Burns, who was later to become a minister in the 1906 Liberal administration, has left this description of the contrast between the two types: 'Physically, the "old" unionists were much bigger than the new ... A great number of them looked like respectable city gentlemen; wore very good coats, large watch chains and high hats and in many cases were of such splendid build and proportions that they presented an aldermanic, not to say a magisterial form and dignity. Amongst the new delegates not a single one wore a tall hat. They looked workmen; they were workmen. They were not such sticklers for formality or court procedure but were guided more by common sense.'

This criticism reflected their view that the 'old' unions were concerned only with craftsmen, not labourers, maintained financial prudence, concentrated on their friendly benefits, abhorred militancy and accepted the general philosophy of the Liberal Party. For their part, they wanted to be open to all, militant, socialist and totally unconcerned about friendly benefits.

Although the impetus for the new unionism came largely from London, some of the first signs of its emergence appeared in the North-East. In 1886 a National Labour Federation was started on Tyneside by some Newcastle members of the Amalgamated Society of Engineers. Its intention was to recruit hitherto unorganized labour of all trades. But it was also open to trade unions, which could thereby take advantage of its supplementary strike benefit payments. Three years later in 1889 the Tyneside and National Labour Union was formed, subsequently called the National Amalgamated Union of Labour. Among the original leaders were Thomas Burt, the Liberal M.P. and Northumberland miners' secretary, James Havelock Wilson of South Shields, the driving force behind the new Seamen's Union, and Dr Robert Spence Watson, a well-known Newcastle philanthropist. Although this organization had originally been established to protect the platers' helpers and other assistants of the craftsmen boilermakers, it soon broadened its appeal and started to compete with the National Labour Federation for the less skilled production workers in shipbuilding, iron and steel, engineering and chemicals.

By and large this upsurge of a new kind of trade unionism hardly caused a ripple on the surface of the Shipwright Society's affairs although it agreed with the call for an eight-hour day which was the symbolic theme of the new unionism. But Wilkie did not stop preaching moderation or financial caution—indeed if anything they became even more important to him. Nor was there any intention of opening up membership or loosening the bonds of apprenticeship. Indeed as we have seen, apprentices were now taken very firmly into the structure of the union with their own scale of contributions and benefits.

Perhaps none of this is surprising for the Society felt, with justification, that it had made an excellent start in its first ten years. It had 10,120 members—half the shipwrights in the country—paying the following contributions:

1s 0d a week	4,054
9d a week	1,573
6d a week	1,185
3d a week	3,308

This total was spread over 72 branches, a far cry from the original 11. Income in a year had now reached £14,500 with expenditure around £7,500. And the funds stood at £23,000. All of this had been achieved by carefulness and moderation. For Wilkie and for the members as a whole there could be no question of throwing this away on militancy and financial madness.

CHAPTER SEVEN

SHIPWRIGHTS AND THE NAVY

While the Associated Shipwrights' Society could claim to have made considerable progress for the benefit of members, there was one important section for whom they had not been able to act. They were the shipwrights employed in Government dockyards on naval work. Although unions were allowed to organize in the dockyards, they were not given any formal recognition. Indeed, because of the nature of the work involved, there was a distinct feeling that unions represented 'interference' with vital matters of national security.

As a consequence the rates of pay and the general working conditions of shipwrights in the dockyards were not kept in line with similar conditions in private yards. The Admiralty saw no direct relationship between them. What is more, when comparisons were drawn, they could point out that Admiralty employees tended to have greater security of employment, being less vulnerable to trade cycles. They also received a pension, or at least those who were 'established' did. The others who were 'hired' did not, nor did they benefit from the security of the established man. The five main dockyards of Sheerness, Chatham, Portsmouth, Devonport and Pembroke employed together about 2,200 'established' men and the same number who were 'hired'. The benefits which the Admiralty mentioned so proudly were thus enjoyed by only half of their employees.

The wages were £1 10s 0d a week and had stayed at that level for ten years while the working week was 53 hours in the summer and 45 in the winter.

By comparison, wages in private yards had fluctuated but on the Tyne they had never fallen below £1 15s 6d in the depths of the depression and now in 1890 they were £2 1s 6d for old work and £1 18s 6d for new work. The working week was 54 hours in summer and 48 in winter.

The dockyard shipwrights had complained about the wide discrepancy for some time. Finally in February 1891 it was decided to press for action through a deputation to Labour members of Parliament.

A deputation of representatives from the five dockyards led by

Alexander Wilkie duly met a group of Labour M.P.'s including Thomas Burt and Charles Fenwick, secretary of the T.U.C.'s Parliamentary Committee, at the House of Commons on 19th February. They urged an increase in wages to bring them level with the average rate for the principal ports of the U.K. The M.P.'s were sympathetic and it was felt that the Government was too. There were frequent references to recent speeches by Government Ministers. One had said that the 'Government desired the men employed in the dockyards should be well paid and contented'. Well, then let the Government translate those ideals into practice!

Mr Fenwick promised that he and his colleagues would do what they could. Their demands were certainly 'equitable'. But meanwhile their case would be strengthened and the pressure on the Government would be greater if they encouraged all shipwrights to join the union. The stronger the Society, the more power it could bring to bear.

The union delegation fully accepted this point. It was grist to their mill for only 644 of the 4,500 shipwrights in the dockyards were in the union. They also accepted Fenwick's offer of help. After all, he had seconded a motion in the House of Commons only the previous week which at least partly seemed to cover their case. It was: 'That in the opinion of this House, it is the duty of the Government in all Government contracts to make provision against the evils recently disclosed before the Sweating Committee (of the bidding down of wage rates by unorganized labour), to insert such conditions as may prevent the abuse arising from sub-letting and to make every effort to secure the payment of such wages as are generally accepted as current in each trade for competent workmen.'

The motion, which received Government blessing, was designed with the building trade in mind. But the last sentence seemed to be of general application and the shipwrights seized on it eagerly.

However, this optimism soon evaporated. The Admiralty did concede a very small increase. But it still left the men well behind the general level of wages paid in private yards, particularly those building vessels for the Navy. Wilkie commented in the tenth annual report: 'There has been much dissatisfaction at the method of allocating the small increase given. ... But it will be apparent to any thinking man that the members of our trade in the dockyards must become thoroughly united with their fellow shipwrights throughout the country and all be firmly combined together before they can by their united efforts effectively use all and every legitimate means to have their just grievances redressed and their reasonable requests conceded. ... if they refuse or fail to join in with their fellow shipwrights and retain their present isolated and, in some respects, selfish position then they will have none but themselves to blame. ...'

His words and those of others had some effect. Membership at the five yards went up from 644 to over 1,000 in a few months. But the main grievance over wages was not resolved for some years yet. The Admiralty did concede the forty-eight hour week, however, in 1894, well ahead of normal industrial practice.

ANOTHER LOOK AT THE RULES

As the Society expanded both in membership and in range of interests, the need to re-examine the rule book and revise it where necessary became more pressing. Accordingly, a delegate conference was called for 1892. This was the fourth delegate conference in the union's history; the others were held in 1882, 1883 and 1885. There had thus been a considerable interval since the previous conference and the Society had added 54 branches and nearly 8,000 members.

The conference, held from Monday, 30th May 1892 to Saturday, 4th June in the Irish Literary Institute, Clayton Street, Newcastle, was attended by 51 representatives from 78 branches with a membership of nearly 12,000. It was the biggest representative gathering of shipwrights ever held up to that time. And according to Wilkie: 'The programme of business was both important, extensive and varied.' Over 550 proposals for rule revision were put forward, so great a number that the conference had to be extended into a sixth day. And on that final day, proceedings did not end until 11.15 at night after a nine o'clock start in the morning!

While some of the revisions called for re-wording or slight amendments, others were far-reaching in their implications, particularly where they referred to an increase in benefits. The Executive Committee were alarmed at the sweeping nature of some of the proposals and felt it necessary to warn members that they should be subjected to 'the most exhaustive and careful deliberations with full information on the respective points and principles involved'. The call for increased benefits could be satisfied only by an increase in levies which would not be popular. 'Therefore on sound business principles and safe financing, we would advise adequate contributions be paid for every benefit promised.'[1]

To emphasize this point, even further, the Executive Committee moved at the conference itself that there should be no increase in benefits unless accompanied by an increase in contributions. After a careful discussion, this motion was carried by a large majority.

Among general proposals, perhaps the most important referred to demarcation disputes. There was unanimous agreement to establish joint boards of shipwrights and joiners to decide on disputed work. Each trade would appoint three members to the joint board and the employers would appoint two members. The boards would try to agree on a demarcation of disputed work; if they were unable to do so, they would appoint a disinterested referee from a previously-agreed list of names, whose decision would be final and binding.

The next most important general question referred to certificates of competence for sea-going shipwrights. The Society had been pressing for Government action ever since the Royal Commission on the loss of life at sea. But despite their exertions and despite the backing of the T.U.C. and others, nothing had been achieved. The Conference called on all branches to raise the question with their respective members of Parliament. There were also calls for the raising of a Parliamentary fund to allow the union to put up its own candidate for Parliament specially to negotiate for this reform and for the Executive Committee to draft a bill which they could press on the Board of Trade. Neither of these suggestions found sufficient backing so the question was left with the branches and their local M.P.'s. But the Executive Committee was asked to consider the possibility of union-sponsorship of a Parliamentary candidate.

The Conference now turned to the detailed revision of the rules. One of the first items considered was the consolidation of various classes of membership. A sub-committee was set up to consider the question in detail and their report was considered on Thursday morning. This recommended that present trade benefit members under fifty years of age, paying only 3d a week, must at least join the Low Friendly benefits section covering sickness, at 6d a week. This was felt to be a step towards the ideal situation of only one class of membership with everyone paying the same contributions and receiving the same benefits.

Among the minutiae of rule revisions were some amusing examples, at least to our eye. The members themselves, however, seemed to treat them seriously. For example, they considered an alteration to rule 42 about members' conduct to the effect that: 'if a member is seen going into a public house the second time to be fined the sum of 2s 6d first offence and if he is found the third time his aliment to be stopped.' They also considered another amendment to another clause in rule 42. 'No undue advantage shall be taken of a sick member of this Society at any time; nevertheless if a member receive an accident by fighting, running, leaping, wrestling or any dangerous practice or act of bravado or for the venereal disease, he shall receive no sick pay, but should the disease occasion his death the funeral money shall be paid as at other deaths.' It may be said that neither suggestion was carried.

But above all, the Conference provided a substantial move towards the centralizing tendencies that had been working in the Society for some time. It agreed to recommend a general council of fifteen members from fifteen branches. It firmly laid down that all contributions paid by members belonged to the Society as a whole and not to individual branches. It authorized the appointment of the General Secretary to all committees, district or otherwise, without the need of election and it empowered the Executive Committee to look into the possibility of employing an assistant secretary to take some of the load off Wilkie's shoulders. All of these measures in effect reduced the power of the branches in favour of the centre. Coming at this time, they showed that the members as a whole were solidly behind the leadership they had had for ten years and were not tempted by the firebrands of the 'new unionism'.

Indeed Wilkie interpreted the Conference as calling for greater discipline and control. He wrote in the subsequent quarterly report: 'The delegates .... enforced the duty on the Executive that they should see that the rules were more strictly adhered to and carried out in the future and that those rules which after calm and careful consideration from all points of view, had been deliberately adopted as their safeguard by the whole

Association, should not be allowed to be overturned or set aside because they did not seem to suit the prevailing but fleeting feeling of the moment .... No community or organization could exist without rules and regulations and these having been deliberately adopted, all should loyally abide by, maintain and enforce the same.'

A number of matters were left for the Executive Committee to formulate specific proposals. This was the case with the proposed creation of three special funds: accident bonus benefits; a legal expenses fund to contest a case in the courts under the Employers' Liability Act; and a fund to enable the Society to sponsor a Parliamentary candidate. After giving these items due thought, the Executive Committee recommended firstly that if any member 'in benefit and in full compliance with rule' should be disabled through injury or accident he should receive a special bonus of £100 to be raised by a levy on all members. On the question of legal expenses to contest a court case under the Employers' Liability Act, the E.C. suggested that a new fund should be started into which members would pay a penny a quarter. Thirdly, they proposed that members should contribute another penny a quarter into a Parliamentary fund.

On being put to the vote, the first two were carried but, not surprisingly in view of the a-political attitude of the membership, the Parliamentary fund proposal was heavily defeated. Members were not interested in securing their aims through running their own candidate even when, on such matters as dockyard pay and conditions or examinations for sea-going shipwrights, they had had almost no success by negotiations.

The membership also turned down by 870 votes to 966, a proposal which sprang from the Delegate Meeting of establishing a General Council of fifteen members to consider and propose changes in the rules and any other matters that were referred to it by the Executive Committee. The motives for turning down this resolution were no doubt mixed. But the effect was to retain power in the hands of the Executive Committee and more particularly the General Secretary, Alex Wilkie.

THE EIGHT-HOUR DAY AGAIN

As we have seen, the Society first considered the possibility of an eight-hour day in 1887 and although the members were overwhelmingly in favour of pressing for its introduction, Alex Wilkie and the Executive Committee remained sceptical. The campaign, led by the 'new unionists' such as Tom Mann and the Social Democratic Federation, did not fizzle out. Rather it grew in intensity and became the symbol of the new approach to union affairs.

The T.U.C. annual conferences of 1888 and 1889 had considered the question but had not come to any clear decision. By 1890 the new unionists had arrived at Congress in force. They pushed through a clear-cut resolution that 'the time had arrived when steps should be taken to reduce the working hours in all trades to eight per day'. While the pressure came from the new men, they could succeed only because some of the traditional craft society representatives swung to their side. One of them was Alex Wilkie who, in contrast to his attitude in 1887, now felt that: 'The adoption of the eight hours in the shipbuilding trade would be a benefit to all outside workers as well as to the firms as the men would thereby be nearly able to see to work the full hours all the year round. The adoption of the nine hours did not make much appreciable difference to the shipbuilding trade as more and more tonnage has been produced since its adoption than ever there was before. And we do not believe the adoption of the eight hours would have any such disastrous effect as its opponents predict, any more than was the case in that of the nine hours.'

This statement represented virtually a complete revolution in Wilkie's attitude. It can be explained either by the successful advocacy on the part of proponents or by the difference in the economic climate. In 1887 the industry was only just emerging from a long depression. The introduction of an eight-hour day then would have helped foreign competitors as well as reducing take-home pay. Now in 1890-91, trade was buoyant, members were fully employed and they had had wage increases over the past three years. A change in working hours could therefore be contemplated with equanimity.

In fact, Wilkie's conversion was too late. Trade was about to turn down, wages were about to be reduced and the steam was about to go out of the Eight-Hour campaign. Congress remained faithful to the idea and every year up to 1910 renewed its call for its adoption but there was never any serious prospect of its being introduced nationally. In shipbuilding the firm of Short Brothers of Sunderland introduced the forty-eight-hour week in 1892 as a basic weekday of 7.30 to 5.0 and 7.30 to noon on a Saturday. This represented an eight per cent reduction in the working day and in return the men were asked to accept a five per cent cut in wages. The latter figure represented a smaller loss than it appeared however. For the relatively high level of absenteeism or late starting meant that on average the men lost three per cent wages throughout the year. The employers hoped that the shorter hours would reduce absenteeism or lateness, the firm would thereby benefit through better production, and the men through a substantially shorter working day.

The men accepted the proposition but very few of their colleagues in other yards were given the same opportunity for many years yet.

TRADE TURNS DOWN AGAIN

Towards the end of 1892 the turn-down in trade which had been threatening gained momentum. By the end of the year there were over 400 shipwrights idle on the Tyne and 520 in the North-East as a whole. Eight yards had no vessels on the stocks at all. The same was true all over the country with the Humber district reporting that: 'our building yards are almost bare' and the Clyde that: 'large numbers of our members are still going idle and no doubt some of them feel it very keenly as there are some who have been idle for several months.'

In the circumstances, the employers took the usual and, to them, inevitable course of seeking a reduction in wages. Barrow employers were the first to act calling for a ten per cent reduction which they modified, after discussion with the union, to a shilling a week from November 1892. In the North-East, the employers' original request for a five per cent reduction was modified after lengthy, and sometimes agitated, negotiations to a shilling a week from November and a further sixpence in January. And so it went on throughout the country with one district following another in having to accept reductions. Sometimes, as in Hull, Glasson Dock and Maryport, the men came out on strike when the employers refused to modify their original demands for large reductions, but on the whole the negotiations proved successful, if not exactly friendly.

Joseph Heslop, the North-East district delegate, commented: 'We are extremely sorry to announce any reduction but we are convinced by the smallness of our concessions, and the manner we got them put back, is due to having a well-organized society.' And Robert Ramage, the Clyde district delegate, reporting that the employers had accepted the union suggestion of a farthing reduction per hour, rather than a halfpenny as originally demanded felt that this result had been obtained by 'consolidation and moderation'.

CHAPTER EIGHT

SWITCH-BACK PRODUCTION

The middle 1890's produced an extraordinary pattern of switch-back production. Shipbuilding as an industry was accustomed to a cyclical pattern of output with a short series of good years succeeded by a short series of bad years, the cycle taking about a decade to complete its course. But now a foreshortened cycle set in, as the following figures indicate:

LAUNCHING OF SHIPS OVER 100 GROSS TONS
EXCLUDING WARSHIPS

Source: Lloyd's Register of Shipping

Year	U.K. Nos.	Tons	WORLD Nos.	Tons	U.K. % of World	NORTH-EAST Nos.	Tons	% of World
1892	681	1,109,950	1,051	1,358,045	81.7	251	570,296	41.9
1893	536	836,383	846	1,026,741	81.4	192	431,405	41.9
1894	614	1,046,508	932	1,323,538	79.0	252	544,768	41.1
1895	579	950,967	880	1,218,160	78.0	222	497,564	40.8
1896	696	1,159,751	1,113	1,567,882	74.0	280	611,727	39.0
1897	591	952,486	990	1,331,924	71.4	236	498,594	37.4
1898	761	1,367,570	1,290	1,893,343	72.3	299	763,825	40.0

After 1898, the normal cycle reappeared. The years 1892-1898 were so unusual that they created great problems for firms in determining demand and planning production and this had a consequent effect upon the unions through unemployment and frequent variations in wage rates. In 1893, the Associated Shipwrights Society found that much of its time was taken up with wage negotiations. Almost invariably, these negotiations proved successful in mitigating the reductions called for by managements and in some cases having them withdrawn altogether. In itself, of course, this reflected the uncertain attitude of employers who found it difficult to forecast future developments with any degree of confidence.

The depressed conditions were mirrored in the large increase in unemployment benefits, up from £3,637 in 1892 to £6,822 in 1893. But other benefits also showed a large increase. Trade benefit was up by £433 to £1,233, the largest amount paid in any year up to that time and was primarily caused by three demarcation disputes. The Sickness and Accident Benefits were £5,600, an increase of about 50 per cent. Tool compensation, Funeral Benefits and other outlays also went up. In fact, total expenditure rose to almost £21,000, which was £6,788 more than in 1892. This high level was partly due to the economic conditions. To be fair, it was also due to the rapidly-rising number of members. Sixteen new or assimilated branches were added, bringing the total to just over 14,000. In the circumstances, one would expect expenditure to rise. It was the widespread unemployment which caused the particular strain.

Even so, the Society still managed to pay its way for it had an income for the year of £22,600, which was £4,467 more than in 1892. It could transfer £1,800 to the balance of funds making a new total of £29,700 at 30th December 1893. In looking at the Society's income, it is interesting to see that although benefit contributions were by far the biggest source, there were in fact seven main categories of income, as under:

INCOME 1893

Fines	£121
Entrance and Assimilation Fees	£2,779
Levies	£608
Contributions to benefits	£17,795
Emblems, Rules, Cards	£317
Interest on Money Invested	£670
Refunded Monies	£331

These other categories were clearly of importance. Interest on investments, for example, was bringing in a substantial income, almost half of what the Society had received by way of benefit contributions in its first year. There were two main investments, with Greenock Harbour Trust and in preference shares with Sir W. G. Armstrong, Mitchell and Co. Ltd., the most successful shipbuilding concern on the Tyne, a firm in which many members of the Society found employment. Later the Society extended its investments.

Once again the Associated Shipwrights had shown that it could continue to make progress even during difficult times. If anything, more new members seemed likely to join in depressions than in prosperous times for they recognized even more fully then the urgent need for security and the advantages the union could bestow. In addition, the Society was now reaching the stage where a powerful snowballing effect on new members was taking place. Almost three out of every four shipwrights in the country were now members. In themselves they acted as unofficial canvassers. But added to the continuing work of officials there was very considerable impetus behind the membership drive. Even now, after twelve years, Alex Wilkie continued to lead the campaign and he scarcely ever missed the opportunity in any public speech or report to stress the need for higher membership. In the twelfth annual report, he wrote: 'Considering the splendid record of self-help, as shown by the transactions and disbursements of our Association since its institution, which must have been a great benefit to the recipients, and consequently of considerable advantage to the community, this should be a strong inducement to every member to greater exertions in the future so that we may ere long have every eligible shipwright in these islands within our organization.'

When these sentiments were supported, as they so clearly were, by a practical demonstration of the union's effectiveness in offering a wide range of benefits and in conducting negotiations almost continuously with employers, then it was little wonder that membership continued to surge forward as it did. The advantages were undeniable. And as membership increased, so did the number of full-time officials. A Bristol Channel district delegate was added to the payroll in 1893, the first incumbent being J. Jenkins. There were now delegates for North-East England, Clydeside and the Humber while Merseyside had two.

In 1894 trade picked up substantially again, offering fuller employment. The Society's pay-out for unemployment benefit dropped by about a sixth to £5,559 and strike pay dropped dramatically to only £175 compared with £1,233 in 1893. The latter showed there was not the same sort of pressure from employers to reduce wages, a popular source of friction. Six new or assimilated branches were added, bringing the total to 106 and the membership to 14,698. But three branches, at Glasson Dock, Campbeltown and Leeds, were closed temporarily for there were no members working there while Kinghorn with only eight members was in a dormant state.

The year saw the first results of the work of the Tyne Shipwrights', Joiners' and Employers' Standing Committee on demarcation problems which had been set up in 1893. Alex Wilkie wrote: 'While we consider some of their decisions are not what they should have been, still we cannot expect all in our favour—we must take the good and the bad.'

The committee's role was to act as a court of appeal if the representatives of the joiners and shipwrights could not agree on a particular point of conflict. The committee consisted of three members from each side and their decisions were to be respected for a year or of course longer if they were not called into question. They were not to open up the work done by Burt's award or the subsequent Conciliation Board but to add to and extend it where new disputes arose. If the committee itself could not propose a satisfactory solution, then it could have recourse to disinterested referees, a list of whom was drawn up. There was plenty of work for the committee to do and it considered a dozen cases in the first year. For demarcation disputes remained one of the most irksome aspects of union activities, so irksome indeed that Wilkie found it necessary in the annual report for 1894 to lay down a general definition of a shipwright's work. They were: '... constructors of floating structures, no matter whether composed of wood, iron, steel or other material, and erectors of structures temporary or otherwise required during their construction ... despite the alterations that have taken place in the construction of vessels, shipwrights' work, as in the past, is still so in the present, in so far that they commence with the initiatory work and continue right on during the various stages of her construction until she is launched, finished and ready for sea.'

A CHANGE OF DISTRICT DELEGATE

A curious incident in the history of the Association took place in 1894 with the resignation of Joseph Heslop, the North of England district delegate since October 1886. In the spring of 1894 the Executive Committee received a number of complaints about Heslop's work, particularly concerning his dereliction of duty, but before they could carry out an investigation, Heslop submitted his resignation.

Writing to Alex Wilkie on 18th April, Heslop set out his long record of service and added: 'When some of the men can show a record like this that they have been declaiming so loudly, judging so hardly and without charity, then they would have more room for condemnation.

'Let me at once say I have made mistakes but where is the man that has not made them and I can assure you it has not been no easy task (sic) on this river this last few years. You have to be the buffer between all parties. In fact, life has not been worth living this year. The strikes we have had and the men coming out against our rules and without consulting anyone and then when out some of them kindly turn round and try to put the blame on someone else's shoulders but not their own. Again I feel for some time that I have not been getting fair play in some branches on this river, and that some members have been pulling strings, some of them I know and their record is not of the best. This being so I think it is better to part as I am not prepared to be knocked about by some men in branches that take wild notions in their heads.'

It was all very emotional and lacked a constructive approach. It also seemed to indicate a man at the end of his tether, worn out by his exertions for the union, as he said, or overfond of drink, as his critics alleged. It was noticeable that neither Wilkie nor the Executive Committee made any comment, not even thanking Heslop for the work he had put in over seven and a half years, even if towards the end his standards had dropped.

Instead they went straight on to appeal for nominations for a replacement. Eleven candidates were nominated—including Joseph Heslop. This was an extraordinary turn of events, particularly since he had the backing of eleven branches. This placed the Executive Committee in 'an unprecedented and peculiar position' according to Wilkie, for by standing again he was virtually withdrawing his resignation. There must also have been a great deal of embarrassment all round. Indeed, it could be that he decided to stand again simply to spite Wilkie and to create the maximum amount of embarrassment. Alternatively, he might have thought that by resigning and standing again he would test the strength of his support and hopefully quieten his critics. But since, like all district delegates, he had to stand for annual election anyway, this hardly seems a rational explanation. The fact was that his resignation had caused an election in which he was now a candidate. The Executive Committee felt that in the circumstances they should carry out the investigation into the various complaints which they had previously felt was unnecessary because of his departure from office.

There were five main complaints, three of them concerning his lack of attention to duty and the other two referring to his drinking habits. One of the complaints declared quite specifically that 'he was incapable of doing business through drink'. In one case, the Executive Committee felt they had not got sufficient information to come to a decision but in the other four they found against Heslop. No action was taken against him but the whole matter was described at length in a quarterly report.

The investigation committee, which according to the Society's rules examined the credentials of all candidates for election to official positions, agreed with the findings of the Executive Committee but felt that, of themselves, they were not sufficient to debar Heslop. They did say, however, that they thought all candidates should be 'sober, steady men, of good moral character, of some ability and experience and be able with tact and discretion to allay instead of increasing friction in the many difficult questions which arise in connection with this position.'

To make their opinion of Heslop even more pointed, they went on to say that they were concerned at the expense and trouble to which the Association had been put and they suggested that resignations should be valid only if an individual agreed not to stand at the subsequent election.

These views had no immediate impact on members however for they gave Heslop the highest number of votes: 597 compared with 516 for John Ward, who had the next highest number. But since Heslop did not have a clear majority another election had to take place between him and Ward. This time Ward won by 1,731 votes to 1,260.

John Ward, a keen gardener in his spare time, had been on the Executive Committee for some time and represented them at the delegate conference of 1892. He was a representative on the standing committee of shipwrights, joiners and employers for the demarcation of work.

Even now this extraordinary incident was not quite over. For the Executive Committee discovered that there was an irregularity in the return of votes from the Southampton branch. This showed that 249 members had voted for Heslop and none for Ward. The Executive Committee subsequently discovered that only 63 members had been present at the meeting when the voting took place. They naturally deplored Southampton's behaviour, emphasized the need for impartial elections and fined the chairman and secretary £2 each.

As it happened this false return did not affect the outcome of the election. It did, however, affect the choice of Society delegates to the T.U.C. Conference in Norwich at the beginning of September. For Heslop was one of the three delegates elected out of a dozen nominations to attend the conference with Wilkie. And a very embarrassing session it must have been. It was only afterwards that the irregularity was discovered, putting Heslop into fourth place. By then it was too late. It would be fascinating to know Wilkie's feelings having had to tolerate Heslop's company for a whole week, unnecessarily.

SHIPBUILDING APPRENTICES

The various problems posed by apprentices were of continuing concern to the shipbuilding unions. In 1893 the Boilermakers' Society concluded an agreement with the employers under which there would be a five-year period of apprenticeship, apprentices would be indentured and there would be no more than two apprentices for every seven journeymen. This agreement put even greater pressure on the Shipwrights to try to regulate conditions in their own trade. For they felt that, with restrictions on entering other trades, there would be an even larger number of apprentice shipwrights coming forward since this was the only occupation where there was still an open door.

Govan branch drew attention to the 'deplorable' state of affairs in their area where there were 210 apprentices and 280 journeymen. Meanwhile 470 members were unemployed. This was totally unacceptable. If the ratio of 2:7 had been in existence, only 80 apprentices would have been allowed thus providing more openings for adult members. In other words, in times of depression such as occurred in the spring of 1894, unrestricted access for apprentices helped to increase unemployment.

The Govan branch put forward the following proposals:

1. That only two apprentices be allowed for every seven journeymen.
2. That no person be engaged as an apprentice over the age of 17.
3. That a uniform rate of pay be paid throughout the trade, namely 6s a week for the first year; 7s for the second year; 8s for the third year; 10s for the fourth year; and 12s for the fifth year.
4. That a committee be formed in each branch to give apprentices practical and theoretical training to enable them to become efficient tradesmen.
5. That any apprentice who acted 'disrespectfully' towards any journeyman who was responsible for teaching him a knowledge of the trade and who was responsible for all his actions while on duty 'shall be expelled from the instruction course or for a second offence should be expelled from the trade.'

It seems inconceivable to us today that training should be the responsibility of fellow-workmen rather than employers and that it should be left to workmen to lay down general conditions for the employment of youngsters. Employers seemed to be concerned only when there were such direct financial questions as members who were to be allowed to enter. In times of depression, particularly, employers saw apprentices as cheap labour and wanted the maximum entry, irrespective of the quality of work that was performed.

Other branches, while agreeing on restriction, had their own formula. Clydebank suggested one apprentice for every four men, Walker one in five and Wallsend two in eleven. Humber district took the matter very seriously and prepared a detailed report. It showed that on average there was one apprentice for every four men but this average covered marked variations. Some firms had no apprentices, others only one or two while some had an excessive number.

The Humber investigation discovered that some firms were trying to evade the usual custom of indenturing apprentices for a given number of years. Such an evasion gave an employer a 'whip hand' for he could dismiss apprentices summarily, particularly near the end of their term, on a trumped-up charge and replace them with cheaper labour. The lads themselves did not necessarily object to this system for sometimes they saw the advantage of hiring themselves to another employer at a higher rate of pay. But the Society members were extremely concerned for it led to the 'incompetent men we at times find sheltering under the ancient name and trade of a shipwright'. It also generated a system of special payments to certain individuals which was entirely against union policy.

The Humber district report produced proposals which were similar to Govan although there was a greater emphasis on the role of the indenture system or something equally binding.

The Port Glasgow branch felt strongly about this question and also produced a special report. It argued: 'Our trade is our capital, but when employers use that capital, in the form of apprentices, to the injury of the trade and the enriching of themselves, it is time to be up and doing something for ourselves.' Their suggestions, however, were hardly far-reaching. They wanted changes in the initiation ceremony and more courses of instruction.

Although the apprentice question clearly agitated many branches and although the Delegates Conference of 1892 had called for action, the Executive Committee seemed curiously dilatory. In fact, in the quarterly report of July-September 1894, it even went so far as to say: 'Although some branches have delivered themselves (of their opinions) they must not think because they have done so, action has to be taken at once on their proposals, many of which are neither possible nor practicable.' This was a particularly discouraging and unconstructive comment and would hardly lead other branches to put forward their views. Meanwhile the Executive Committee, while admitting that the question was 'more or less continuously before them', offered no lead. Despite protestations to the contrary, they seemed ready to let this matter drift.

DEVELOPMENTS IN THE T.U.C.

Alexander Wilkie was co-opted on to the ten-man Parliamentary Committee of the T.U.C. in 1890, the same year as the new unionists, such as John Burns and James Havelock Wilson were making such impressive gains with their election to the committee and their imposing calls for more 'socialist' revolutions. In himself, Wilkie represented a brake on the new unionists. They were clearly not getting things their own way. More important, the T.U.C. passed a resolution in that year that voting should

A Family Group—the Birkenhead Branch Officers and Committee in 1913.

A Sporting Occasion—the Chatham Dockyard Shipwrights' Tug-of-War Team in 1911.

no longer be by a show of hands but in proportion to the number of members. This decisively swung the balance of power towards the bigger unions, few of which were sympathetic to the new unions, and away from the smaller unions and the trades councils where the socialists had particular influence.

In 1894 the Parliamentary Committee revised standing orders. Trades councils were to be excluded, votes were to be proportionate to affiliated membership, and delegates must be either full-time union officers or still working at their trade. This meant the exclusion of such people as Keir Hardie, the militant Scottish socialist, who in that very year had seen Congress overwhelmingly accept his motion calling for the nationalization of the means of production, distribution and exchange.

The Committee also became more businesslike in its approach, preparing agendas much more carefully, concentrating on specific industrial and trade union matters rather than general political and social questions, and improving the efficiency of its administration under a new Secretary, Sam Woods. But while the T.U.C. thus acted to counter a socialist revolution, it moved some way to adopting the ideas and attitudes of the critics. It saw the need to be more forceful, and appreciated that it had achieved very little. It developed a marked hostility to the new Conservative Government of 1895 which although led by Lord Salisbury, was largely under the influence of Joseph Chamberlain, who had defected from the Liberal Party. In the report to the 1896 Congress, the Parliamentary Committee criticized the lack of 'any one really tangible and beneficial measure passed in the interests of labour'. The change in attitude by the Committee reflected changes within the unions themselves. The Associated Shipwrights' Society, for example, now supported both the eight-hour day and a fund to assist Labour candidates to Parliament, policies which a few years before it had opposed.

The Parliamentary Committee saw the need for a closer association of unions to offset the growing power of employers, one of Wilkie's favourite themes. It was no coincidence that in 1897, the year in which he was chairman, the Committee took two important steps. Firstly, they agreed on their own initiative and without the full backing of Congress, to support the engineers in their dispute and raised £23,000 out of a total of £116,000 subscribed. In 1893 the Committee had refused to help the seamen and dockers on strike in Hull. Secondly, the Committee proposed that Congress should take the initiative in forming a federation 'to render mutual assistance in disputes, strikes and lock-outs affecting any trades unions affiliated to the Federation.' Out of this proposal sprang the new General Federation of Trade Unions which forty-four unions joined, when it was established in 1899.

The Parliamentary Committee of 1897 also informed Congress that there was an urgent need to return more Labour members to the House of Commons, a call that was to be reiterated every year with growing force. By 1899 Congress was instructing the Parliamentary Committee to call a conference 'of all the co-operative, socialistic, trades unions and other working organizations to devise ways and means for securing the return of an increased number of Labour members to the next Parliament.' At that time there were only eleven trade union M.P.'s, mostly from mining constituencies. The miners in fact had five seats, of which three were in the North-East. Charles Fenwick, the Secretary of the Parliamentary Committee, sat for Wansbeck, Thomas Burt for Morpeth, both in Northumberland, and John Wilson for Mid-Durham. This level of representation was hardly very satisfactory considering that trade union membership now exceeded two millions. And this low level was no doubt the cause of the poor performance in the House. Much greater pressure was needed if the trade unions were to secure some of their long-cherished reforms.

It was in the growing recognition of the part that politics could play that the T.U.C. was moving closer to the calls from the socialists and others which had once been regarded as so radical. The 'new' and 'old' unions were in fact merging into one another.

DEPUTATIONS TO GOVERNMENT MINISTERS

The Society was involved in two important deputations to Government Ministers in the early part of 1895. It was represented in a large deputation of trade unionists who saw the Home Secretary, Herbert Asquith, to press for progress on factory legislation, employers' liability and other matters of interest to the trades unions. More directly, it asked for a meeting with Lord Spencer and other senior members of the Admiralty to complain of the encroachment by fitters on shipwrights' work in the Naval dockyards.

Alexander Wilkie led the deputation and began by thanking the Admiralty representatives for granting the eight-hour day and for offering small increases in wages. But he felt these were a just reward for the men who, even when offered higher wages in shipyards, refused them and 'stood loyally to the Admiralty and the nation.'

What was a shipwright? He was a builder of ships, no matter what the material which was used. When new materials came in, particularly iron and steel, they had adapted themselves to them and for the past thirty or forty years had claimed that such work was their own. 'And it must be remembered,' said Wilkie, 'that the shipwrights in the dockyards are workers in metal as well as in wood and that one half of them are men who have served their apprenticeship in H.M. Dockyards, all of whom have been more or less constantly employed on metal, the working of which is therefore their legitimate trade.'

Wilkie asked that the dispute caused by the engineers' claims should be referred to the Director of Dockyards. He should have powers to call in experts if necessary to find a solution to the question at issue.

Lord Spencer replied that the Admiralty was aware that any change would affect shipwrights in private yards as well as those in dockyards. The comparatively large number of shipwrights and the importance of the work they did made the matter one of great interest to the country. He had previously received a deputation from the engineers and he would now give the question careful consideration. He thought that it was a very reasonable suggestion to refer the question to the Director of Dockyards.

The Shipwrights' deputation were pleased with the reception they had been given and awaited further developments. Meanwhile they did think it was necessary to press two lines of action to try to secure 100 per cent union membership in the dockyards; and to have direct representation in the House of Commons. On the former point, they suggested that committees should be formed in each dockyard to recruit more members. While on the latter they felt that the Executive Committee should be empowered to raise up to £1000 from a special levy to pay the election expenses of a suitable candidate for Parliament.

The particular problem of the demarcation dispute between the fitters' members of an engineering union and the shipwrights dragged on for a long time. By the autumn of 1895 the Admiralty still had not been able to find suitable assessors. When at last they produced four names, the engineers' union refused to accept two of them on the grounds that they were dockyard officials and therefore not 'independent'. The shipwrights had never suggested that the assessors should be independent but that they should be experts and fully conversant with all the points under discussion. What is more, they pointed out that the engineers had not insisted on 'independent' assessors originally. They felt they were deliberately trying to be obstructive.

CHAPTER NINE

TYNE STANDING COMMITTEE

By the end of 1896 the Tyne Standing Committee of Shipwrights, Joiners and Employers which dealt with demarcation problems had considered fifty-three cases. Of these, it had adjudicated twenty-three in favour of the shipwrights and twenty-two for the joiners, with the rest divided between the two sets of workers. This was such an equal division one might be forgiven for thinking that they worked from some kind of mathematical formula. But even so, the 'lost' cases provided grounds for complaints, some members going so far as to doubt the value of independent committees.

The Executive Committee of the Associated Shipwrights' Society did not share these doubts and continued to argue strongly for an independent 'court of appeal'. It put the matter in this way in a circular to members: 'If a man steal our tools, we can take him before the Law Courts and if we prove our case obtain indemnification for loss sustained. But if he steals our trade, which alone makes our tools valuable to us as mechanics, we can have no redress when we have no Court or Board to appeal to.'

But while the Executive Committee supported the principle, they felt that the method of dealing with disputes was not ideal. The Tyne Standing Committee at that time consisted of three shipwright representatives, three joiners' representatives and three employers' representatives. If the representatives of the men differed, as they were likely to do for otherwise they could have dealt with the question at issue between themselves, then the decision rested with the representatives of the employers and according to the shipwrights' circular, 'we regret their decisions in some cases have not been as impartial nor equitable as we think they might have been.' Nor did the reference to a panel of referees work very well for it was almost impossible to get any decision altered. Later reference procedures benefited from the experience on the Tyne. When Standing Committees and Reference Boards were set up on the Clyde, in Dundee, in Barrow, in Teesside and in Hartlepool, they consisted of four shipwrights, four joiners and one employer who acted as chairman. If the committees failed to come to a unanimous decision or to achieve a two-thirds majority (i.e. even some of the members of the 'losing' trade must agree) then the issue was automatically placed before a committee of previously appointed referees as if no vote had been taken. By this means it was hoped to achieve an appeal to impartial and disinterested referees who would not be swayed by a previous decision.

Although this seemed a sensible reform, the members did not accept it. By 165 votes to 110 they turned it down. The Executive Committee were disappointed. They pointed first of all to the small voting figures, only 275 members voting out of a potential 1,820 in the eleven branches on the Tyne. Secondly, they felt that while the members had turned down this suggested reform, no other proposals had been put forward. They felt that another ballot should be held and that greater efforts should be made to stir up interest. A committee member should attend each branch to explain the matter more fully. It was becoming more urgent for it was suggested that the new method should be used to deal with a dispute with the blacksmiths. This particular case could not be dealt with until agreement had been reached on procedure.

The second ballot secured over 100 more votes, not a big increase, but the outcome was different. By about three to one members now favoured the proposed changes and suggested they be put into effect for tackling the dispute with the blacksmiths. This was done and an agreement was reached. The new procedure, although not perfect—perfection could not be expected in this emotional subject—was felt to be an improvement on the previous practice. It remained in existence for a good number of years.

DIFFICULTIES IN IRELAND

The innate conservatism of some of the local societies and their strong sense of independence had been a continuing problem for the A.S.S. in its efforts to create a centralized organization. By 1896 most of these problems were over. Few local societies remained. The advantages of a national union had been recognized almost everywhere, except in Ireland. Perhaps because of the distance involved, perhaps because of the character of the people, Ireland was one of the last places to accept the arguments for centralization. Six of the port unions had clung on to their independence fiercely as late as 1895.

In particular three branches were proving difficult. The Executive Committee accordingly despatched Alex Wilkie and William Millington, the Humber District delegate, to try to sort things out. They called first at Wexford where there were only twenty members and only one shipyard. Despite the precarious and isolated nature of their employment, these members had gone on strike because the yard had recently taken on two more apprentices. There were also complaints about the foreman. The union officials received no joy from their discussions with the firm or the foreman. The employers stated quite simply that they were not prepared to allow the men to dictate the number of apprentices who were employed. And the foreman was even more adamant in rejecting a request to comply with certain local working rules. Wilkie and Millington left rather with their tails between their legs, uttering the rather weak comment that: 'Great discretion is needed in such isolated one-yard places as Wexford.'

They journeyed on to Cork to visit the Passage West branch where a demarcation dispute was in progress. When they arrived they found that the manager of the Passage West Docks was on holiday but that he was expected back any day. They decided to wait. But one day turned into two and then almost into a week and still there was no sign of the manager. It became increasingly clear that his holiday would not end until they had left. So the Cork visit also proved abortive. Millington commented: 'The manager of the Passage West Docks is a diplomatist and our members and the E.C. will have to bear this in mind in any future dealings they may have with him and remember the first essential in cooking a hare is to catch it.'

Their spring visit to Ireland had so far proved unfruitful. But there was worse to come when they visited the Dublin branch with its hundred members. Communications between this branch and Head Office had been unsatisfactory for some time. Equally there had been inadequate supervision of branch affairs. No proper records had been kept of meetings nor of the collection of subscriptions and the payment of benefits.

On closer examination, Wilkie and Millington found things even worse than they had expected. For sickness and unemployment benefits had been paid to members who were not entitled to them while the branch officials had paid themselves salaries for work they had failed to do or refused to do. Head Office had been told that unemployment benefit payments had increased because more men were out of work but when Wilkie asked to see the local officials to discuss the irregularities they told him they were too busy to spare time for a meeting. In the circumstances he felt he had no option but to close the branch, to take possession of the books and to transfer all monies to Head Office.

Millington described the process as 'disagreeable', an 'unpleasant task' and 'a painful duty'. He also saw the main problem as the difference between a local society and a national union. 'The great lack apparent among some of our Irish fellow members is that they have not yet grasped the difference between the administration of the affairs of a large national trade society with an executive and branches, and a purely local society; consequently they require closer supervision and for some time to come in the interests of all they should be often visited and have instructions upon how to conduct their branch and keep its books and affairs correctly and in accordance with general rules.'

If the Society had adopted this policy before events had reached such a turn, the closure of the Dublin branch might have been avoided. With a dozen branches in Ireland, three of them in Belfast, the possibility of appointing an Irish delegate should also have been considered.

The end of 1895 and the early months of 1896 saw the shipbuilding industry very busy. Over 370 ships were under construction with a particular emphasis on sophisticated vessels which obviously provided more work. In addition, the Admiralty was to place orders during 1896 worth over £7m. The effect was to reduce unemployment and thereby the amount paid out in unemployment benefit substantially. While all districts shared in this general prosperity, the North-East of England was particularly well placed. Indeed, John Ward, the district delegate, even went so far as to say that: '... never in the history of our trade have the members of the N. E. Coast been so well employed. Nearly every yard has been full of work.'

The only reservation was that because of the high level of employment and the good weather through the winter of 1895/96 work had advanced so quickly that there was bound to be a lull in production 'causing us to have some idle members for the next few weeks.'

The *Newcastle Leader* of 26th March 1896 commented: 'The shipwrights are now in the happy position of being one of the busiest trades in the country.'

The men naturally wanted to take advantage of the rising demand for their labour to press wage claims. In the North-East they put forward their biggest demand so far, an increase of four shillings a week. A conference with the Tyne, Tees and Hartlepool Employers' Associations was held on 17th February 1896. The employers were naturally stunned by the request and pointed out with considerable vehemence that they were already paying the highest wages in the shipbuilding industry. This huge demand would further widen the gap whereas what was required was to reduce the differentials between the various districts. The men could not entirely disagree with this point and Wilkie remarked: 'This is a fact which the members in the district in their own best interest should carefully consider.' The meeting ended with the employers offering to pay an extra shilling a week from the first pay day in April.

While this offer was substantially less than the claim, the members recognized the dilemma that the employers had pointed out. They decided by three to one to omit any reference to a particular figure but to empower the negotiating committee to secure the best terms possible. At a second conference on 4th March, the employers agreed to increase the offer to one shilling and sixpence a week with immediate effect and the union representatives accepted.

This did provide an opportunity for other districts to close the gap. Workington members who were badly paid in comparison received an increase of a shilling a week from 27th February and another shilling on 21st May. In Ipswich, there was an agreement to provide an increase of a halfpenny an hour (2s 3d a week) and an improvement in overtime rates. But of course the most important area, alongside the North-East, was Clydeside where after long and often heated negotiations the employers conceded an extra halfpenny an hour with a farthing increase to be paid from 19th March and another farthing from 16th July.

THE CLYDE AND BELFAST

This concession was remarkable partly because of the length of the negotiations. The claim had first been submitted in May 1895. But more important, it was the first claim dealt with on a joint basis by employers on the Clyde and in Belfast. The Belfast employers had already offered an extra halfpenny an hour in old or repair work to bring the men into line with Clyde rates but declined to consider the claim for three shillings more for new work except on a joint basis with Clydeside employers. Clyde members had asked for an extra halfpenny an hour (2s 3d a week).

Although somewhat taken aback by this concerted approach, the men agreed to accept this new procedure and the first conference of the Joint Committee of the Clyde and Belfast Employers' Associations took place on 20th February. The union was represented by three delegates from Belfast and three from Clydeside together with Robert Ramage, the Clyde district delegate, and Wilkie.

The result of the Conference was to offer increases as long as no further demands were made for six months. Members in Belfast and on the Clyde were almost totally opposed to this proposition, turning it down by over five to one. A further conference was held on 5th March and it was agreed that the question of a standstill was separate from the wage claim and should be resolved separately. The Employers' Joint Committee then offered, and the union representatives agreed to recommend, an increase of a farthing an hour in both districts in March and a further farthing an hour from July. This was accepted by the members.

The joint arrangement produced differing views among the men. Robert Ramage, the Clyde district delegate, remarked: 'We will not disagree with this method if the wages of our members in the two ports are the same, because the governing of the question would be as easy to employers' and employees' associations in the two ports as it would be in treating with one district or an individual firm. But the results or effects produced by federated action, be they for us or against us, covers a larger field of action by both sides and therefore causes a greater expenditure to those interested.... We hope that trade societies will combine or federate for the purpose of dealing with the federated employers on questions which may be common to all trades.'

Wilkie felt that the change of procedure by the employers must lead to changes in the union's approach 'whether it be liked or not.' Many members did not like it but he felt that the end result had been satisfactory for both Belfast and Clyde members. 'They have received a substantial advance through their Executive grasping the changed position and acting decisively which deserves commendation, not condemnation.'

One can well understand Wilkie's feelings. It seemed sometimes as if the men would never be satisfied with anything. William Millington, the Humber district delegate, seemed to express the same view but this time directed at employers when he wrote that there had been a very heavy demand for shipwrights in his area. 'We say may this state continue but with less irritation, disappointment and clamour from those who are pressing us to supply them with what we have not at our command, viz a reserve stock of unemployed hands.'

In good times, as in bad, an official's life was never quiet.

A PROSPEROUS YEAR

The year 1896 was certainly good. Wilkie described it as 'the most prosperous in the annals of our organization.' Employment was high and wages continued to rise as one district followed another in securing increases from the employers. The Society had an income of over £26,000 and with expenditure at just under £16,000 there was a balance of £10,000 to add to the funds, bringing them to over £50,000. This was the equivalent of £3 10s 7d a member. The magic figure had been reached. For one of the original aims had been to establish funds of £3 a member or more. Now, after fifteen years, the target had been achieved. Wilkie thought it was 'most satisfactory'. But rather than allow a sense of complacency to set in, he immediately pointed out that the amount was not enough. A full benefit member could draw £20 6s od for sickness or accident benefit and £7 for unemployment benefit in any one year 'and remembering the great drain on the funds during the last depression of trade which, with the larger number of members, will be greater in the next .... then it can be easily understood .... we will require much more than double the amount per member accumulated at present.'

One new indicator of the state of the shipbuilding economy was the amount paid by the Society to members for railway fares. It had decided in 1895 to make loans available to members to cover rail fares from their homes to places of potential employment. The scheme helped the men, the employers and the union without any particular drain on union funds. For nearly all the loans were repaid without trouble—only a few members hung back. In 1896 the Society advanced £728 under this scheme, £540 more than in the previous year. Part of the increase was no doubt due to the wider use of the scheme but above all the huge increase was due to unprecedented demand for men from the outlying ports to come into the main shipbuilding centres where there was such an abundance of work.

Output was almost at record levels, not only in the private yards but also in the dockyards. But whereas the men working in the former had enjoyed the benefits of fuller order books in terms of higher wages, shipwrights working for the Admiralty received no such tangible recognition. Negotiations got nowhere. By mid-summer it was decided to present a petition to the Lords Commissioners of the Admiralty. It covered three main points. The first was for the abolition of different rates of pay for skilled shipwrights. They should all be put on the maximum level of 34s a week, still well below the rate obtaining in private yards.

The second point was to allow time served before men became 'established' (and on average this was as long as fourteen years) to count towards a pension. Thirdly, the Society wanted to protect its work against encroachment from other trades.

The Lords of the Admiralty were not very sympathetic. Nor were they receptive to a later petition dealing with the status of members who joined the Royal Navy. Unlike other tradesmen, shipwrights ranked only as leading seamen rather than as chief petty officers. This meant that not only did they receive a lower rate of pay but also they had to mess with seamen, take their turns in preparing food, scrubbing decks and other menial work and for their pains received only the same leave as an ordinary seaman.

When a year later, the shipwrights got an M.P. to raise the question in the House of Commons the Secretary to the Admiralty, Mr McCartney, replied: 'These alleged grievances have been carefully examined but it is not considered necessary to treat shipwrights in any exceptional manner as compared with other skilled ratings on board H.M. ships.'

During 1896 the union's membership went up to 14,235 in the following categories:

FULL BENEFIT	1s od a week	6,407
TRADE? LOW FRIENDLY AND UNEMPLOYMENT BENEFIT	9d a week	392
TRADE & HIGH FRIENDLY BENEFIT	9d a week	2,235
TRADE & LOW FRIENDLY	6d a week	1,817
TRADE	3d a week	2,690
APPRENTICES	6d a week	77
"	3d a week	513
"	1½d a week	104
		14,235

The branches which had closed temporarily during the previous depression were opened again and four new branches were added. They were in areas where there were branches already, such as Portsmouth, Devonport, Chatham or Tyneside (Bill Quay) but the new branches provided a more convenient service for the members involved.

In describing 1896 as 'the most prosperous in the annals of our organization', Wilkie could point to the high level of employment, which naturally reduced the call on the Society's funds. He could also itemize the reduction in stoppages caused by various disputes. But above all, he was pleased with the wage increases which the Society had helped to negotiate.

He wrote in the fifteenth annual report: 'One of the main if not the principal, object to be derived from our reconstituted and consolidated Association is to secure the best possible remuneration for our labour at the least possible cost to the members, individually and collectively.' That this had been achieved could be seen not only from the pay packets of members but also from the small amount expended in dispute benefits. In fact, only 3½ per cent of the Society's funds had been used for this purpose since its inception, a much smaller figure than the individual societies would have spent. 'This, to a great extent, has been accomplished by improved organization and management and a better understanding with our employers and mutual concessions across the conference table,' he wrote.

But if the Society had already proved more effective than individual societies, then the advantage was likely to be even more in its favour in the future. For two main areas—the North-East of England and Clydeside and Belfast—saw the employers acting in unison in joint conferences. Secondly, of course, an advance conceded or a reduction enforced in one district led to similar action in other districts. For all the claims of independence, the various districts and branches were closely linked with each other.

We can see this very clearly in the opening quarter of 1897. Trade continued at a very high level and for the second time in less than twelve months, members pressed for wage increases. As so often, the initiative came from the branches in the North-East of England from Blyth to Whitby. After two conferences with employers, they secured an increase of 1s 6d a week from 24th February 1897 making the rate 39s a week for new work and 42s a week for old or repair work. The Clyde and Belfast members now put forward their demands. After several conferences between employers and men, they secured an extra farthing an hour (1s 1½d a week). Belfast members were also given an additional 3d a week to bring their rates exactly into line with Clyde members, viz 37s 1½d a week for new work and 39s 4d for new work.

For many years the wages paid in Leith yards had followed Clydeside rates. They now went up accordingly. But Barrow members had also agreed with their employers in 1896 that their rates would be linked to the Clyde in future. Their rates were increased by 1s 1½d to make them 37s 7½d for new work and 40s 7½d for old or repair work. Virtually all other districts followed suit.

The start of 1897 was a very good period for shipbuilding and all the districts shared in the prosperity. John Jenkins, the Bristol Channel district delegate, reported that 'trade has been better than in any previous quarter for many years past.' In Merseyside the comment was that 'it has been the best we have had for some time.' In the North-East trade 'has been of a very satisfactory nature ... all our members here have been enjoying full employment.' And on the Humber 'the state of employment has been exceptionally good.' The only small cloud appeared on the Clyde where some vessels were not sufficiently advanced in construction and a few members had had to be paid off in the meantime. 'But we trust all will soon be employed again,' wrote Robert Ramage, the district delegate.

INDUSTRIAL TROUBLES

The high level of demand not only for ships but for all the other goods that an industrial economy working at full pitch could produce led to serious troubles in the summer. For a number of unions decided that this was a suitable time to press certain demands. In South Wales, miners agitated for a 'stop week' as a means of controlling output and thus securing higher prices and wages. The dispute indirectly affected shipwrights at Cardiff, Barry, Swansea and Llanelly, a considerable number of whom were out of work for four to five weeks. More important, the Amalgamated Society of Engineers decided that this was an opportune moment to call for an eight-hour day in the engineering trades in London. The employers reacted to this demand by imposing a lockout on 25 per cent of all members of the A.S.E. throughout the country. This lockout of engineers naturally affected many other trades with whom they worked, including many shipwrights.

The action by the engineers coincided with growing agitation within the Federation of Engineering and Shipbuilding Trades, to which the A.S.E. did not belong, for an eight-hour day. At the seventh annual meeting of the Federation at Hull in May 1897 it had been agreed to canvas all individual members on this question. The shipwrights voted by a large majority for an eight-hour day as their first priority and so did many other trades. The executive committee of the Federation requested meetings with various employers' organizations such as the Engineers Employers' Federation which had been set up in June 1896, to put the case for an eight-hour day. They found that the action by the engineers had queered their pitch. For the employers replied that 'under ordinary circumstances they would have gladly met the Federation representatives in conference but they cannot disguise from themselves that such a meeting would be liable to be misconstrued at such a juncture.'

The eight-hour day and the action by the engineers was also discussed by the T.U.C. at its annual congress at Birmingham. It expressed its 'entire sympathy' with the engineers' action and asked all other trades to help them 'morally and financially'.

Many members did so only with misgivings. Robert Ramage the Clyde district delegate of the Associated Shipwrights' Society, expressed in his quarterly report for July-September the widely held view that the engineers should be members of the Federation and that the eight-hour day should have been sought as a national aim and not simply for the engineers in London. He felt that 'many trades are now suffering that had no say in bringing about this state of affairs.' And he added that he thought the engineers should have at least sought the co-operation of the Federation before going ahead with its action.

But while criticizing the engineers for the way they had acted, he certainly supported the principle of a shorter day. For faster machinery was 'causing a very heavy strain in the body of man and a great tear and wear to his whole system; and he naturally desires more time for rest to be recuperated for another day's work.'

That Ramage was typical of the membership can be seen from the overwhelming vote in favour of a levy of 3d a week from 4th October to create a trade privilege fund. This would finance benefits of 9s a week to all members made idle through the lockout of engineers. Secondly, the members agreed to make a donation of £1,000 to the engineers, again to be paid out of a special levy on members.

The Society paid out over £3,000 on unemployment benefit during 1897, £2,000 more than in the previous year, and £3,698 as a trade privilege benefit. Those very high figures indicate the serious impact of the engineers' dispute on the shipwrights. In fact over six million working days were lost throughout industry as a whole in 1897 and a further million in 1898. The feelings aroused can be judged from the excellent response to the Engineers' call for subscriptions to the strike fund. Over £116,000 was raised, of which, as we have seen, £1,000 came from the Shipwrights. But, in the end, it was the engineers rather than the employers who were most anxious to settle.

By January 1898, after a number of conferences, an agreement was reached that the engineers would withdraw their claim for an eight-hour day. The employers on the other hand won the right to employ non-unionists, particularly to work new machines, to lay down suitable wage rates, to introduce piecework and to use as many apprentices as they wished.

All of these conditions represented a triumph for the employers who had come closer together as a result of the dispute. In particular, the Engineering Employers' Federation set up in June 1896 had got off to an excellent start. Its aims were to 'protect and defend' the interests of employers against action by unions in pressing for unduly restrictive working conditions such as 'unreasonable demands for wages, minimum rates of wages, employment of apprentices, hours of labour, overtime, limitation of work, piecework, demarcation of work, machine work and the employment of men and boys on machines.'

A NEED FOR CLOSER CO-OPERATION

The engineers' dispute had been a good test of the employers' strength. And the unions were not slow to appreciate its lessons. Writing in his sixteenth annual report, Alex Wilkie commented: 'The great difficulty in forming any consolidated and effective Federation is the fact that it must necessarily encroach more or less on the autonomy of the individual societies. As notwithstanding anything that may be said to the contrary, wherever there is to be active assistance or financial aid, there must be a corresponding control; otherwise, as the history of Federations has shown, they simply fall to pieces.'

The Engineering and Shipbuilding Trades Federation, set up in 1890, had done 'some very useful, if quiet, work on behalf of the societies forming the same, at a very small financial outlay.' But clearly something more powerful was needed and the T.U.C. at Birmingham had set up a committee to investigate the question. Wilkie himself favoured not only greater co-operation between unions but also the creation of a 'Court of First Instance' where differences between employers and employed could be discussed and arranged. Other courts could deal with disputes over demarcation problems between various trades.

'To obtain the best and fullest productive results,' Wilkie wrote in his sixteenth annual report, 'labour and capital must work in harmony together and history has shown that the best results have not been attained where the one unduly dominate the other.

'What is required is some means whereby the trade of the country could be steadied and developed not by spurts and starts but by a progressive continuous method which would give fuller and, if possible, constant employment to the workers and security to the employers of being able to fulfil their contracts.

'Trade unions, like Parliaments and Governments, may have made mistakes but no one dare deny that they have been a benefit not only to their members but also to all fair and generous employers as well as to the nation at large. Even their bitterest opponents have to admit that they have somewhat increased wages, reduced excessive hours of labour and otherwise ameliorated the position and condition of the workers. The proof of this is shown that where there is no union or where it is weak, wages are low, hours are long and conditions of labour oppressive.

'By fixing and maintaining a fair wage for all in the trade, they enable the fair and just employers to compete with the less scrupulous for what work there is in the market.

'Through their friendly and other benefits disbursed to their members, they relieve the rates of the citizens. By their educating influence with that of the Friendly and co-operative societies, they inculcate a spirit of order and discipline, without which, as many authorities have pointed out, every severe depression of trade would engender disorder inimical to the best interest of the State and Revolution would take the place of the quiet but progressive evolution of the times.

'He would be a saviour indeed who could formulate some practical scheme whereby capital and labour would automatically and mathematically each receive their fair share of the proceeds of their joint production and thus render these industrial wars unnecessary.'

This remarkable credo, while emphasizing the advantages of unions, largely ignored other questions. Wilkie did not refer to the position of the individual. For although unions were established on his behalf and apparently operated for his benefit, they must have seemed as powerful to the recalcitrant individual as the employers themselves. Even the union supporter must have wondered whether their actions were always to his benefit and whether he had sufficient control over the Executive. Nominally power lay in his hands but when he was only one among thousands what real power or control had he? What is more, was he always furnished with enough information to take meaningful and relevant decisions?

Secondly, one must regard the frequent and serious demarcation disputes which marred certain sectors of industry, particularly shipbuilding, as a grave by-product of the growth of unions. Such disputes, which were often more bitter than disputes with employers, arose from the division of trades into highly-organized unions which sought to establish clear-cut boundaries for their operations. This boundary-seeking was in essence selfish and was certainly at variance with the more general concept which unions expressed of the brotherhood of man. In this sense it was often easier for widely disparate trades to work together than for those whose work overlapped.

The third main area where lines of responsibility were uncertain was of course with employers. In seeking increases in wages or improvements to working conditions, there were no guidelines as to what was legitimate or what was not. It was simply a case of what the union or the employer could get away with. The approach was strictly pragmatic. Disputes arose not only when demands from either side were too high but also when it was felt that they were going into the other's preserve. In the engineering lock-out, the employers felt that the unions were overstepping the mark in seeking to lay down who should man certain machines. Equally, the unions felt they should be free to press their claims through collective bargaining or whatever other method they chose. But such questions as hours of work or numbers of apprentices were so central to both sides that it was even more difficult to define a 'sphere of interest'. Too often, it came down to power as we have seen. It was for that reason that the unions were determined to reply to the employers by strengthening their joint approaches.

On a personal note, the Shipwrights' Society lost the services of John Ward as North-East district delegate during 1897. He resigned through ill-health. He was never robust and the duties of the job eventually wore him down. But we can receive an insight into the special difficulties of district delegates from the following official comment: 'It would appear some members seem to think that when a man is elected to a responsible position, that he immediately becomes a target to be shot at for all sorts of insinuations and abuse.' Ward himself seemed to feel no rancour, however, and wrote: 'If I have made any enemies during my term of office it has been unintentional, to them I hold out the flag of truce with an earnest request that they will allow me peace and quietness for the remainder of my time on this earth.' He was succeeded by Richard Johns, aged 43, the chairman of the Newcastle branch and a member of the Society since its inception.

Another founder member, Joseph Heslop, who had been the first North-East district delegate, died during the year. Despite the differences of opinion which ended his official position within the union he was remembered by Wilkie 'as a loyal comrade, of a kindly and generous disposition and ever ready to assist anyone in difficulties, especially the widows and children of deceased members.'

CHAPTER TEN

A FEDERATION OF UNIONS

Wilkie's call for a federation of trade unions to match the growing co-operation and combination of employers found an echo in the Trades Union Congress annual conference in 1897. It was resolved 'to form one federation to render mutual assistance in disputes, strikes and lock-outs affecting any trade unions affiliated to the Federation.' A special committee was set up to devise a scheme. Robert Knight, secretary of the Boilermakers' Society and architect of the Federation of Engineering and Shipbuilding Trades, was appointed chairman of the committee. Alex Wilkie was one of the thirteen members.

The committee proposed that the new body should be called the General Federation of Trades Unions. Its objects would be to uphold the rights of combination of Labour, to improve the 'general position and status of workers', and to consolidate and unify action among all the unions. The emphasis was put on the promotion of industrial peace and the prevention of strikes or lock-outs. There would be a General Council consisting of two delegates from each member union, a management committee and district committees.

With regard to contributions, there would be two scales, the 'higher' and 'lower'. The first would amount to sixpence per member per quarter and the latter to threepence. These contributions would entitle unions to benefits of 5s per week per member or 2s 6d for the 'lower' scale when they were involved in disputes. These benefits would normally be payable only for eight weeks.

The contributions and benefits were seen as being the weakest part of the committee's proposals, partly because of the small amounts involved and partly because they were felt to be 'unsound', i.e. the income would not generate sufficient funds to meet likely outgoings. Wilkie answered this particular criticism by compiling a table of income and expenditure for various unions. This showed that on average unions needed to raise considerably less than 2s a member per year to pay out 5s a week in strike benefits. In the case of the Shipwrights' Society for example it would be required to pay about £1,331 into the Federation's funds whereas over the previous 15 years the Society had needed only about £430 a year to pay out full trade benefit. And the bulk of this expenditure was on demarcation disputes which were specifically excluded from the Federation's terms of reference. In Wilkie's view, whatever the deficiencies of the proposals, financial weakness was not among them.

While the financial aspects were the most hotly debated, there were many other areas for niggling criticism. The upshot was that a great many variations were put forward by individuals or by unions. The eighth annual meeting of the Federation of Engineering and Shipbuilding Trades held at Belfast in May 1898 had a long discussion on the question when many different views were put forward. The most strongly supported and indeed the one that won the day was for the establishment of a federation of kindred trades rather than for a general federation, a proposal with which Robert Knight himself agreed.

The T.U.C. Conference in Bristol in 1898 felt that the whole subject was so complicated and raised such strong feelings, as witnessed by the large number of amendments to the official scheme, that a special Congress should be convened in Manchester in January 1899. This was done and lasted three days. The debate did not live up to its billing. For, on the whole, the discussions were quiet and practical rather than impassioned. Perhaps this was the inevitable result after the first morning's session when it was decided by a large majority not to consider all the rival schemes but rather to consider the official scheme only and amend it as necessary.

This decision immediately reduced or made irrelevant much of the anticipated criticism. Even the levels of contributions and benefits, which had been so widely criticized, were carried virtually without debate.

The Special Congress ended by empowering the Parliamentary Committee to form a Provisional Management Committee. It was to circularize all trade unions to ask them to affiliate to the Federation and to call a General Council not later than July 1899.

Before the Special Congress had met, Wilkie had expressed the hope that 'it will discuss federation from a common sense and practical standpoint, clear the air of the many ideals and fallacies floating about and yet find the time opportune and the need essential to establish such on a sound, workable, practical and financial basis'. While the Congress lived up to all these hopes, the membership did not. For forty-four unions joined, representing 344,000 members, compared with the 1,184,000 affiliated to Congress. Many of the major unions refused to join. Even the Boilermakers who through their general secretary, Robert Knight, had played such an important part in drafting the scheme, turned it down out of hand. For while he had helped to draw up the proposals both he and his Executive Committee were critical of many aspects of them. Knight's views were particularly coloured by the satisfactory progress, as he saw it, of the Federation of Engineering and Shipbuilding Trades. Another Federation was not necessary, particularly one that demanded a subscription of £3,780 a year from his union.

The year 1898 was a record year for British shipbuilding, far outstripping anything that had gone before. More important, it was the start of a decade of massive output. Not until 1908-9 did production slip below the million-ton mark and then only temporarily. For most of the years straddling the new century, the average was about 1.4m. tons. Britain's dominance can be gauged from the fact that the output from all other countries combined did not even reach 500,000 tons. A fifth of the British output was for foreign owners.

Not only was the output huge, it was more varied than ever before, with ships of all shapes and sizes taking to the water. Some of them incorporated new design or engineering features. These were the early years of the turbine-propelled ships and of turret-decked vessels.

The shipwrights were able to benefit from the full-employment position. Alexander Wilkie wrote in the seventeenth annual report for the year 1898: 'Wages never were higher, nor conditions, generally speaking, more favourable.' On the Tyne, wages went up from £2 2s a week to £2 2s 6d for repair or old work and nearly all other districts had similar increases.

A Workmen's Compensation Act had been introduced by the Government in July 1898. Some union leaders who had been pressing for Government action for years felt that it did not go far enough but it certainly removed the legal requirement of proving culpable negligence on the part of employers in order to win compensation. To that extent it eliminated the need to engage 'costly and speculative solicitors'. In the first six months of the operation of the Act, for example, six claims were lodged with Cardiff and Barry employers, all of which were admitted. The six shipwrights involved received £1 a week each until their recovery, approximately half of their average earnings.

On Clydeside the employers agreed to introduce the payment of weekly rather than fortnightly wages. A meeting was held in September 1898 between the Employers' Association and the Federation of Engineering and Shipbuilding Trades. The employers were at first somewhat sceptical of the requested change. They did not believe that the majority of men wanted it. They also believed it would lead to worse time-keeping. Wilkie, who represented the shipwrights at the conference, argued that on the contrary it would improve things. It would also end the system of 'subbing' whereby workers were paid a 'sub' in between pay days and would reduce their dependence on credit shops. Employers knew that if they could bargain on a cash basis they could do infinitely better than on a credit basis and the workmen were in exactly the same position, he argued.

A few weeks later, after due deliberation, the employers announced that they were willing to introduce weekly payments of wages on the Clyde from the beginning of May 1899 on an experimental basis for a year. But if they found that time-keeping did not improve, but rather deteriorated, then they would want to revert to the previous system. Robert Ramage, the Clyde district delegate, commented: '... this being a matter in the men's own hands, we trust they will not give the Employers' Association the expense of calling another conference for the purpose of proving to our representatives that the new system was the cause of the men keeping worse time than in the old way of paying wages.'

DEMARCATION DISPUTES

But perhaps the most interesting aspect of the year was something that did not happen rather than something that did, namely the happy reduction in demarcation disputes. In the year as a whole the Society paid out only £361 in dispute benefits, in itself an indication of the reduction for in the previous year it had paid out £918. This was the first year of the demarcation agreement with the boilermakers and the blacksmiths signed in November 1897. The agreement set up a machinery for dealing with disputes. First an attempt should be made to resolve the issue at local level. If this failed, it should be referred to a joint committee consisting of five representatives from each of the disputing unions. If that too proved unsuccessful then the question would be referred to a board of referees. The agreement covered all shipyards on the Tyne and Blyth and was one more in the elaborate pattern of demarcation boards being set up in the shipbuilding industry in the North-East. By 1900 there were to be eleven conciliation boards, well ahead of the rest of the country. In fact according to one authority, 'the North-East coast was the only region where conciliation and arbitration machinery was developed to any extent'.[1] One estimate has shown that of 558 cases considered by conciliation boards in the North-East between 1897 and 1906 only ten resulted in strike action.'[2]

As we have seen so often, demarcation disputes were endemic in the shipbuilding industry because of the rapid changes that were taking place. In his seventeenth annual report, Wilkie wrote: '... scarcely any trade has had the number of difficulties, especially demarcation differences, to deal with. This is no doubt mainly caused by the continued changes in the structure of vessels and of a misunderstanding by others of the work of our trade as ship constructors.'

These disputes were not indulged in for their own sake but because they struck at the heart of the union's interest. 'These conflicts were not blind, insensible struggles but were dictated by the logic of craft organisation ... Without privileges to defend there would be no craft unions and if privileges were to be preserved they must be defended against all comers, whether employers, unskilled workers or other crafts.'[3]

But in trying to minimize or eliminate these disputes the work of demarcation boards of the Federation of Engineering and Shipbuilding Trades and of the General Federation of Trades Unions were of the utmost importance.

WORK OF THE SOCIETY

The Society's income for 1898 was no less than £33,840 and with expenditure of £19,810 there was a balance of £14,030 to add to the accumulated reserves of £54,892. With just over 15,000 members, the reserves were equal to £4 11s 4½d per member. But again Wilkie urged caution in considering these figures, pointing out that a table prepared by the Board of Trade showed that the average payments per member were among the lowest of similar societies. The same table also showed that the administration costs were among the highest.

The main disappointment of the year was again the lack of progress in dealing with the pay and working conditions of dockyard and naval shipwrights. Despite further conferences and renewed petitions to the Admiralty, the Society was getting nowhere. Yet they felt they had an excellent case which was heavily underlined by the well-known shortage of naval shipwrights. The Admiralty was even considering new ways of improving recruiting. But when the Society sought to explain the reasons for the shortfall, they continued to meet with rebuffs. Indeed in a letter of July 1898 the Admiralty even refused to accept that the Shipwrights' Society could speak for the men. 'I am desired to state that it is very well known to the dockyard employees that questions affecting their employment and pay can only be discussed with them through the recognized official channels and that following this practice, their Lordships' decision upon the subject of the workmen's petitions will be communicated to the Superintendent of the Dockyards in due course.'

Wilkie reported in the sixty-fifth annual report (April-June 1898): 'It will be seen that this is an evasive reply because the petition forwarded was, besides the dockyard shipwrights, on behalf of the naval shipwrights of the United Kingdom who would be willing to join H.M. Navy, and thus remove the present dearth of these men if their position aboard the ships of H.M. Navy was improved.' The lack of success, however, was clearly leading to strains. It was also clear that the Executive Committee did not know quite what to do next. Wilkie commented: 'The Executive shall be glad to consider any practical suggestion ... and while making no complaint, trusts that some dockyard members will be a little more considerate in the future, as whether successful or not, the E.C. have worked hard on their behalf and if grievances are to be redressed it will require all to pull and to pull strongly together.'

While life for Wilkie, other officials and members had its ups and downs, it was not all serious. Over the years, as the Society became more established and a band of comradeship developed, a growing number of branches looked to the social side. For example, the Tyne district held a 'Grand Social and Dance' in the Assembly Rooms, Westgate Road, Newcastle on 26th December 1898. 'About 170 ladies and gentlemen sat down to a substantial repast. The General Secretary (Mr Alexander Wilkie) presided and in a neat speech referred to the pleasure he felt at being present that evening and meeting them .... A splendid miscellaneous programme was rendered by a number of artistes of exceptional talent, Miss Leggatt rendered two extremely sweet and musical solos on the violin and mandolin .... Mr Glen was very happy in the rendering of the old nursery story "Old Mother Hubbard" brought up to date .... At the conclusion of the programme, the numerous company indulged in a series of dances which went off right merrily to the tripping and tuneful music of the band, of which Mr W. H. Smith proved a most efficient conductor. On every hand there was ample evidence that a most enjoyable evening had been spent and oftentimes as we went amongst the assembled company we heard the wish expressed that such a gathering would prove to be an annual one.'

A TRIBUTE TO WILKIE

Alexander Wilkie was now at the zenith of his powers as a trade union leader. Still only 49 he had been the general secretary of one of the most important craft unions in the country for almost twenty years. He had served on the Parliamentary Committee of the T.U.C. from 1890-1 and continuously from 1895. He had been chairman of the Committee in 1897. In the years to come he was to widen his scope by entering politics. He was to be on the Executive Committee of the newly-formed Labour Party from 1900-4 and to be a Member of Parliament from 1906-22. But as a unionist, he was already at the top.

One of his colleagues, William Millington, the Humber district delegate, paid him this tribute in 1896 when he was re-elected to the Parliamentary Committee with the highest number of votes:

'It is a tribute to his ability and earnest and indefatigable labours in the cause of our trade and trade unionism generally.'

The *Glasgow Herald* of 9th March 1898 must have also pleased him, with this comment: 'Mr Wilkie has just issued the sixteenth annual report of the Associated Shipwrights' Society and the publication is, this year at any rate, the best in get-up and matter of all the labour reports.'

But the highest honour was in being chosen by the T.U.C. as one of its two representatives to the Annual Convention of the American Federation of Labour held in Detroit in December 1899. He found it an exciting experience, with much to learn and much to impart.

In his address to the Convention, Wilkie outlined the solid progress made by the labour movement in Great Britain. There were now 1,267 trade unions in Britain with over 1.6m. members. Through union pressure over a million workers had received increases in wages in 1898. This progress had been achieved he said by hard solid work and attention to detail and not by agitation. 'As there is no royal road to Heaven,' he told the Convention, 'so there is no short cut to the milennium. In the future, as in the past, it will only be by hard plodding of hand and brain that labour will be able to work out its own emancipation.'

Wilkie was interested to learn that unlike the British T.U.C. every resolution submitted to the Convention was examined by a committee, thereby ensuring more detailed scrutiny than a large congress could give. It also meant that the final resolution had a large body of support for it and was invariably confirmed. He liked this system but felt that the composition of the committees needed greater care.

The Americans were particularly keen to hear of the latest developments on the political front for as the *Commercial Advertiser* of New York said in its issue of 18th December 1899 'the British trade unionist differs radically from the American in that he does not shun collective political action in his own behalf'. Wilkie reported that even the conservatives in the labour ranks were becoming dissatisfied with the lack of concessions by the Liberal and Tory Parties and that the movement to unite the working people on a common labour platform was making rapid progress. Indeed the 1899 T.U.C. Conference had instructed the parliamentary committee to 'invite the co-operation of all the co-operative, socialistic, trade unions and other workingmen's organizations .... in convening a special congress .... to devise ways and means for securing the return of an increased number of labour members to the next Parliament.' It was expected that the programme would contain a call for an eight-hour day, extensions to the Compensation Act, old age pensions and provisions for better housing.

After the Convention, Wilkie visited some of the principal shipbuilding centres on the Atlantic coast, including New York, Philadelphia, Baltimore and Newport Mews. He was particularly impressed by his tour of a yard at Newport Mews. He found that the very latest plant and machinery was installed there and that a good number of those holding responsible positions had emigrated from England.

Altogether Wilkie was away for seven weeks, a period which he found to be of 'untold value'.

FIFTH DELEGATE CONFERENCE

With the continuing expansion of the Society and the changing conditions of work, the members decided it was time for another delegates' meeting to revise the rule book. Considering that the third conference had been held in 1885 and the fourth in 1892, there seemed to be a pattern emerging of holding those meetings once every seven years. Coming at such intervals, these meetings do provide interesting vantage points for marking the progress of the Society. If we look back only to the third conference in 1885 we see that the Society had then 24 branches, just over 4,000 members and an annual income of £2,000. Now, fourteen years later it had 115 branches with 15,400 members and an income of £33,840.

This fifth delegates' meeting held in Newcastle from 29th May to 3rd June 1899 was attended by 82 delegates. Thomas Conner, a member of the Executive Committee, was elected chairman for the week. The meeting spent most of its time going through the rules and amending them where necessary in the light of changing conditions. It also looked at the salaries it was paying officials or committee members at district or national level and agreed on increases. Branch secretaries received a 25 per cent increase while Branch chairmen, treasurers and book-keepers received a rise of 10 per cent. Committee members were to have 1s a night.

District delegates had their salaries increased to £2 15s a week. There was considerable discussion about increasing the number of delegates but by a small majority it was decided not to do so. It was, however, decided to re-arrange their areas. The Clyde district delegate was to be responsible for the whole of Scotland and Belfast. He would have 31 branches and 4,800 members. Merseyside would be responsible for the whole of the North-West coast and for Ireland, except Belfast. The Humber would take in the East and South-East coasts with 30 branches and 4,200 members while Bristol would be re-arranged to take in all the South-West and Wales. Only the North-East of England delegate had his duties unchanged. He was already responsible for the area from Blyth to Whitby although he naturally concentrated most of his efforts on the Tyne where the Society had most of its members in the region.

The Executive Committee also received salary increases, the General Secretary going up from about £3 17s a week (£200 a year) to £4 16s. Executive Committee members were to have 2s a night and third-class fares paid and the chairman 2s 6d a night.

Two of the more general matters which were discussed referred to relations with outside bodies. It was agreed that the Executive Committee should do all in its power to ensure 'that all closely allied workers who have mutual interests should consolidate together'. It was also agreed that new efforts should be made to assimilate traditional shipwright societies, particularly in London, Liverpool and Sunderland who had so far refused all entreaties. Earlier that year the Society had assimilated the 250 members of the River Thames Shipwrights' Protective and Benefit Society. A fresh appeal should now be made to the others, 'in a lucid manner'. Failing success the Executive Committee was empowered to take such action as would be in the best interest of the trade and the Association. Members were clearly becoming impatient.

While such motions or the alteration of rules provided the meat of the conference, they were not perhaps the most important part. For above all the conference provided an opportunity for members from different parts of the country who never normally met, to get together, to exchange ideas and experience and to try to create a sense of comradeship. As one of the delegates wrote: 'There is another side and that is representatives being brought from all districts and getting to know one another and thus to a great extent be able to gauge the local circumstances attending each district and by knowing this the small lumps of local prejudice which may have existed have been rubbed off. We feel all the better for it ...'

In view of these comments which were typical of most delegates, it seems strange that no move was made to convene annual conferences to discuss not only the rules but also more general questions.

CHAPTER ELEVEN

PARLIAMENTARY REPRESENTATION

As the nineteenth century came to a close, trade unions moved perceptibly towards a belief that they must have greater representation in Parliament. After all they had now almost two million members yet there were still only eleven M.P.'s with labour interests. The unions had been faced with two particular obstacles. One was the political differences between the new and the older unions and unionists. Many of the new unionists espoused the cause of socialism under the banner of the Social Democratic Federation, founded in 1880, or other bodies. Older or more traditionally-minded unionists, such as Wilkie, thought that their aims could be achieved through the Liberal Party. They thought that the formation of a new party was an extra burden and some certainly did not accept the philosophy of socialism. Secondly, some unions thought that there should be an independent rather than a joint approach. This was particularly true of the miners. They had been represented by six M.P.'s for fifteen years or more. It was up to other unions to organize themselves similarly in likely constituencies.

Nevertheless, despite these difficulties, the progress towards greater Parliamentary representation continued. In 1897 the Independent Labour Party which had been formed four years earlier by Keir Hardie proposed a 'labour representation conference' to consider what action to take. A formal invitation was issued to the Parliamentary Committee of the T.U.C. and to its opposite number in the newly-formed Scottish T.U.C. The Scottish T.U.C. accepted the proposal in April 1899. The T.U.C. agonized over the question for a whole day at its conference in September 1899 and finally agreed that individual unions should attend if they wanted to. Any decisions or action taken would not commit unions which did not attend.

Alexander Wilkie, representing the views of the shipwrights, thought that greater efforts to secure members of Parliament should be made but not necessarily through the formation of a new party. He said: 'What is required at present is an industrial programme of a few clauses in the interest of the workers upon which most if not all trade unionists could agree. This should be pressed upon the House by a compact body of labour members, pledged to the same, leaving them otherwise free on purely party questions. Perhaps the special Conference about to be held ... may evolve some practical scheme.'

His views were very similar to those of Sir Charles Dilke, the influential Liberal M.P. who had held junior ministerial appointments. Dilke was sympathetic to the unions and even entertained the Parliamentary Committee to lunch once a year to discuss proposals for legislation on labour matters.[1] In 1899 he suggested the formation of a 'non-political party to deal with all labour questions of importance'. However, other views were to prevail.

The labour representation conference was called for February 1900 and held in London. Altogether there were 129 delegates representing 568,000 organized workers. The vast majority of these workers were represented through unions. The Independent Labour Party with 13,000 members and the Social Democratic Federation with 9,000 members were the two main political bodies present. The Shipwrights were represented. And so were the Engineers and the Miners' Federation for Lancashire and Cheshire. Other mining unions, however, did not attend. Nor did the Boilermakers' Society.

The nub of the conference lay in the difference between those socialist sympathizers who wanted a new party and the traditionalists who wanted an intensification of existing policies. This is seen most clearly in the debate on the nature of Parliamentary representation. James Macdonald of the Social Democratic Federation moved the original motion that there should be a distinct party with its own organization and having as its ultimate object the socialization of the means of production, distribution and exchange. This seemed to be going too far for some unionists. Alexander Wilkie led the main attack on the motion and moved an amendment. It said that although a Labour Party was the ultimate aim, in the meantime a programme of four or five main policies should be adopted to which every candidate should pledge himself. But on more general matters they should be willing to support any party. In fact the representatives should be left free on all purely political questions. Wilkie argued that this was as much as could be hoped for initially. He felt it would be a mistake to bind Labour members on other than purely labour questions. His amendment was seconded by John Jenkins, also of the shipwrights. After discussion the amendment was carried by 59 votes to 35. But the socialists, who wanted something more positive, were not yet finished.

Keir Hardie, of the Independent Labour Party, now moved another amendment to strengthen Wilkie's motion. It was that a distinct Labour Group should be formed with their own whips and their own policy. But they should also 'embrace a readiness to co-operate with any party which for the time being may be engaged in promoting legislation in the direct interest of labour and be equally ready to associate themselves with any party in opposing measures having an opposite tendency'. This amendment, which strengthened without destroying Wilkie's, was carried unanimously.

The socialists were equally adroit in the discussions about the formation of an Executive Committee. The original proposition was that it should consist of eighteen members, twelve of whom would be trade unionists. They would therefore be in a very clear majority. The socialists managed to have this domination reduced by arguing on practical grounds that eighteen members were too many. It would be difficult to get them together regularly and the expenses involved would be rather high. It would be better to have an Executive Committee of twelve, of whom seven would be trade unionists. This arrangement still gave the unions the majority voice. It did, however, materially swing the balance in favour of the socialists, particularly since they could hope that one or more of the trade unionists would be socialist sympathizers. And this in the end proved to be the case for R. Bell of the Railway Servants and P. Curran of the Gas Workers who were elected to the Committee were members of the S.D.F. The socialists were also successful in having one of their supporters, Ramsay MacDonald, elected to the secretaryship. But while they were successful in these ways, the socialists, particularly the Independent Labour Party, were careful not to frighten off the traditionalists. Instead they set out to court the unions. Reassured, Alexander Wilkie allowed his name to go forward for election to the Executive Committee and he won a place. Later he was elected vice-chairman.

He also urged his union to take up membership and the shipwrights were among the first of the forty-one unions who affiliated immediately to the Labour Representation Committee. Altogether these unions represented 353,000 members, about 30 per cent of T.U.C. membership. A new organization had come into being which was to have a far-reaching effect on the political development of the country. But its first test was to come too soon. For a general election was called in the autumn of 1900 and the Committee decided to field a number of candidates, including Wilkie. The new party had not had enough time to organize itself and with an annual income of only ten shillings per thousand members, it hardly had any funds. In fact its total expenditure on the election was just £33. Its two successes, Keir Hardie at Merthyr Tydfil and Richard Bell at Derby, were largely flukes. And in any case, these successes were countered by the loss of four of the former eleven trade unionists in Parliament.

Alex Wilkie stood for one of the two Sunderland seats as a Liberal along with Mr G. B. Hunter, the chairman of one of the biggest shipbuilding concerns on the Tyne.

Wilkie's candidacy had the backing of no less an authority than Sidney Webb, who wrote: 'I am glad to hear you are standing for Sunderland. Your successful organization of your trade proves you to be a first-rate representative. We ought to have more of the experienced trade union officials in Parliament. There are quite enough orators and lawyers and landlords and capitalists going there; what is scarce is the practical man. The work that you have done is a splendid training for Parliament and I sincerely hope you will get the votes of every working man in Sunderland together with those of everyone else who believes that we ought to have some more "Labour Statesmen" in the House of Commons.'

It was interesting that the two Liberal candidates should have been connected with the Shipbuilding industry, one a leading trade unionist, the other a major employer. Both were very much last-minute choices. For both the prospective Liberal candidates refused to allow their names to go forward as official candidates when the General Election was actually called in the middle of September. Wilkie and Hunter agreed to fill the breach. Wilkie had been adopted on 22nd September as the candidate for the Labour and Trades Union Party. He agreed to allow his name to go forward as a Liberal candidate too. He fought the election therefore as a Lib-Lab.

Both Wilkie and Hunter were adopted, as official Liberal candidates at a packed party meeting. According to the *Newcastle Daily Leader* of 24th September, Wilkie had a 'splendid reception'. He told the meeting that since three-quarters of the Sunderland electors were working-class, he thought they had a right to be represented by one of their own kind.

The Conservative Party also put up two candidates, Sir William Doxford, another shipbuilder, who had previously held one of the two seats, and Mr N. J. Pemberton, a landowner. The campaign itself lasted just over a week—there was no statutory three weeks as there is today. In that short time Wilkie could do little more than visit a few engineering and shipbuilding works and a few housing areas. In his speeches he gave special prominence to domestic reforms: the introduction of old-age pensions, better housing and education and land law reform.

Voting took place in Sunderland on 5th October. Again according to the *Newcastle Daily Leader*: 'Yesterday afternoon and towards evening the streets of Sunderland became densely crowded with people and nothing else but the election was thought of. The excitement reached fever heat.' The excitement can be seen in the voting figures for altogether 35,000 votes were cast compared with 26,000 in the previous election in 1895. Hunter and Wilkie came bottom of the poll, hardly a surprising result considering that they had little over a week in which to campaign. But Wilkie's votes of 8,842 were higher than the successful Liberal candidate in the previous election. As Wilkie himself wrote in the Society's 74th Quarterly Report: 'It is not given to many to win at the first attempt and while unsuccessful we are certainly not discouraged. Considering the short time at our disposal, we feel proud of the large measure of confidence obtained.'

Nor was the Labour Representation Committee despondent. On the contrary it said it had secured a 'remarkable success'. In every case but one where comparison with the 1895 election was possible the candidates of the working class had increased their votes. For whereas before they stood as individuals, now they could stand on behalf of a movement. The official report on the election by the Labour Representation Committee concluded with these words: 'This favourable result is due, in no small measure, to the existence of the Committee and its manifesto to the electors in the constituencies where its candidates were running was signed by all sections of the Labour movement. This is a happy augury for the future.'

A NEW CENTURY

The first year of the new century was an excellent one for British shipbuilding. Output was at or near record levels. Wages were high—£2.17½p a week on the Tyne for old or repair work—and unemployment low. Disputes, even between trades, were virtually nil. In the whole year the Society paid out only £19 for trade or dispute benefit, the lowest sum in its history. By contrast, the income for the year, at £38,800, was by far the highest recorded up to that time and after all expenses were paid, the Society was left with a balance of £96,670, equivalent to £5 5s 7d per member. This was 'a cheering account' according to the *Eastern Morning News* while the *Morning Mail* commented that 'its prosperous condition must be a source of great satisfaction.'

Part of the reason for the boost in income was the increase in membership to over 18,000 following the assimilation of twenty-two branches of the National Society of Drillers and Hole Cutters. The assimilation allowed the drillers to have a seat on the Executive Committee and suitable representation in other committees. The members were to pay the same contributions and receive the same benefits as shipwrights.

The Society introduced an interesting scheme for its members in the year to help with the purchase of houses. Following the resolution of the 1899 Delegate Meeting it instituted a scheme whereby the Society would provide advances to members secured by mortgage on their property. Members could receive a loan of up to £165, repayable over twenty years at £1 a month. The interest charged was 4 per cent. In the first year, ten members made use of the scheme and a total of £1,322 was advanced to them.

Wilkie was also interested in the broader aspects of housing. He was the chairman of the Newcastle and Gateshead Housing Reform Council which agitated for improved conditions. In the summer of 1900 the Council organized a deputation to the local authorities to urge them 'to make thorough and searching enquiries into the actual condition of housing and the best line to follow to secure practical remedies.'

Despite the general air of success and prosperity, the year also contained two notable reverses. The first concerned the payment of wages on the Clyde. For at the end of the first year of weekly pays, the employers notified the unions that they were to revert to the former practice of fortnightly pays. The unions were taken aback by this decision for they had believed that, once introduced, weekly payments of wages would remain indefinitely. The employers pointed out, however, that the agreement of 1898, which had come into effect in May 1899, gave them the right to revert to the former practice at the end of a year if they wished to do so. They did want to exercise that right and they gave as their reason the deterioration in time-keeping. Their statistics showed that while 39 per cent of the men had improved their time-keeping, 61 per cent had a worse record.

The question was taken up urgently by the Federation of Engineering and Shipbuilding Trades. While one or two members agreed that there were grounds for believing that time-keeping had deteriorated, they pointed out that the employers had carried out their survey during the worst part of the winter. The figures were therefore suspect. They also pointed out that the original agreement called for a conference to be held before the former system was re-introduced at which proof of deteriorating time-keeping should be brought forward. The employers had taken it upon themselves to interpret the agreement rather than seeking the views of the Federation.

Against the wishes of the employers, the Federation decided to ballot its members to test their feeling. The result was an overwhelming declaration in favour of weekly payments but, unfortunately, as far as the Federation was concerned, only a quarter of the members involved had bothered to vote. The Executive Committee naturally doubted the degree of interest among the members and certainly felt that they had no mandate to pursue tough tactics. They contented themselves therefore with a resolution which regretted the employers' action, particularly the refusal to submit the matter to arbitration. Any further action would be deferred 'until greater unanimity can be secured upon the part of the Clyde workmen'.

The other setback in the year was more serious and more general and concerned the legal position of trade unions. It arose from a dispute involving the Taff Vale Railway Company of South Wales and its workers who had gone on strike. The company decided to try to break the strike by taking legal action for compensation against the union for inducing the workers to break their contracts of employment and for interfering with the company's business by picketing. Bringing a legal action of this kind was unusual for it was generally thought that a union's funds were inviolate since they belonged neither to an individual nor to a registered company. In this sense, unions were regarded as being outside the law for they had no legal entity.

The judgement of Mr Justice Farwell, however, went against the conventional opinion. He declared that 'the Legislature, in giving a trade union the capacity to own property and the capacity to act by agents has, without incorporating it, given it two of the essential qualities of a corporation; essential I mean in respect of liability for tort ... the dependent society is, in my opinion, liable.'

Although the Court of Appeal reversed Farwell's decision in November 1900, the House of Lords was to restore it a few months later. This decision allowed the Taff Vale Railway Company to go ahead with an action for damages. This it did, the case being heard in December 1902 when both sides agreed to settle for a payment by the union of £23,000 to the company. Altogether the case cost the union £42,000 through other expenses that were involved.

This case was naturally an important one in the history of trade unions. 'It did not take union leaders very long to realize the crippling effects of this decision on their own prospects of successful strike action in the future.'[2] There were seen to be some disadvantages in that unions were now regarded as legal corporations but the fetters placed upon them from the action that had started in 1900 were felt to outweigh the benefits. In addition, this was no isolated case. In a famous judgement Lyons v Wilkins, it was laid down that 'picketing, except for the limited purpose of obtaining or communicating information, is illegal'. And in Leatham v Craig, it was ruled that 'The interference of a trade union to procure or induce the breaking of contracts is a conspiracy'. Only in Allen v Flood was there felt to be a judgement beneficial to trade unions.

Flood was a shipwright working for the Glengall Company in London. He and another shipwright, Taylor, were very much in a minority, however, for the other employees were nearly all members of the Boilermakers' Society. There was considerable feeling against Flood and Taylor which eventually came to the notice of Mr Allen, the Boilermakers' London Delegate. Allen advised the managing director of the company that unless he got rid of Flood and Taylor, the other men would walk off the job. The managing director accepted the advice and dismissed Flood and Taylor. Flood promptly brought a claim against Allen and the Boilermakers' Society generally. Although the first court and the Court of Appeal found in favour of Flood, the decision was overruled by the House of Lords to which the Boilermakers' Society appealed. It was thus laid down that both employers and employed were free to decide the terms on which they could buy or sell labour. A worker had the right to decide with whom he would work.

Officials or members of trade unions could threaten non-unionists with loss of employment or employers with suspension of work unless they discharged men obnoxious to the trade union.

This welter of legal action was interesting for two reasons: firstly, it indicated that employers were searching for new grounds to curtail the power of unions; and secondly that the legal position of unions was so vague in so many areas of activity. Now, however, they had received two particular blows with regard to picketing and with regard to the sanctity of their funds. These setbacks, as we shall see, were to stimulate greater interest in Parliamentary representation to restore the former position. More unions joined the Parliamentary Representation Committee and more serious attention was given to the political solution for industrial grievances.

Wilkie declared in his 20th annual report for 1901 that Parliamentary representation had achieved 'a mighty impulse' by the House of Lords' Taff Vale decision. He thought that and other legal decisions had 'revolutionized the previous understood and accepted view of the Law'. In his view, there was a law for employers and another for workers. For the employers were permitted to persuade men to take the place of their fellows but the unions were not to be allowed to picket peacefully to persuade them not to do so. He wrote: 'What is required is that there should be perfect equality before the Law.'

While the situation remained at best unclear and at worst unsafe for unions, Wilkie urged all his members, and particularly officials, to exercise the greatest care. 'Should any matter arise which seems to require instant action, let those involved enter a respectful protest to the management, then let work proceed until the Executive can be fully consulted.' The rest of his advice was underlined to emphasize its importance: 'We have to give clear and distinct notice to all whom it may concern that the Association shall not be responsible, or liable, for any action, taken by any of its members or officers, unless the Executive has been consulted and its consent obtained before any such action has been entered upon.' He was obviously determined that no imprudent action should land his union in the same position as the Railway Servants who had lost £42,000 on the Taff Vale case.

Meanwhile the Parliamentary Committee of the T.U.C. was urgently examining the situation and was consulting some of the best—and most expensive—lawyers of the day to consider what remedies could be taken. To many unionists, including Wilkie, the best course seemed to be in new legislation to clarify what had previously seemed to be clear. But the necessary legislation would be achieved only through a greater representation of working-class people in the House of Commons. He wanted 'no more quibbling over this matter as indulged in by some'. Their efforts and money would be 'much better employed in endeavouring to secure just laws and equitable treatment for the workers.'

The legal reverses they had suffered only served to reinforce the determination of unions to look after their members' interests and confirmed, even for reluctant or late converts like Wilkie, that industrial action was not enough. Only a change in the laws could produce the necessary remedies.

NAVAL AND DOCKYARD SHIPWRIGHTS

For years the Society had drawn up an annual petition to the Admiralty requesting various reforms with regard to the employment of shipwrights. Broadly speaking, the petition usually fell into two sections: for land-based shipwrights they urged an increase in pay and an end to the system of classifying shipwrights by merit; for sea-going men, they wanted the employment of properly-trained shipwrights and their elevation to the rank of Chief Petty Officers, a rank held by similar skilled craftsmen.

The Society had not had much success with these petitions because the Admiralty argued that while dockyard employees could belong to unions, it could not recognize them for purposes of negotiation. Instead, all questions dealing with pay and conditions must be considered through the men's superiors.

In 1901, however, the Society gained a little success. For as part of its petition it drew up very detailed tables comparing the hours and wages of shipwrights in private yards and in H.M. Dockyards. These tables showed that in private yards the average number of hours worked per week was just over 51 and the average wage just over £2.00. In the Dockyards, the hours worked were 48 and the average pay £1.65.

So the Dockyard men worked fewer hours but received considerably smaller wages. On the equal basis of a 48-hour week, the average wage in private yards would be £1.90, or 25p more than in the Dockyards.

Wilkie heard from the Admiralty that these statistics were 'practically in agreement' with its own figures. This admission in itself was a step forward. But it was followed within a few days by something more important. For speaking in the House of Commons on the debate on the Navy Estimates in June 1901, the Secretary to the Admiralty, Mr Arnold Forster, announced two concessions on the rates of pay and on the system of classification. He said: 'The shipwrights are a most important body of men in the dockyards and there can be no doubt that in some respects they have not hitherto been on all fours, as regards wages, with other skilled labourers ...' He also admitted that the system of classification had given rise to 'a good deal of dissatisfaction.' Accordingly, the Admiralty proposed to abolish classification and to pay established shipwrights £1.65 a week, hired men £1.70 and probationers £1.62½. Mr Arnold Forster said: 'By granting these concessions we shall give a substantial increase to by far the larger number of shipwrights.' He also had to confess that 'a very small number' would get no increase because they were already receiving £1.65 a week. In fact they totalled 352 out of a strength of 4,970. All hired men received an increase of either 5p or 2½p a week.

So at last the lengthy campaign was beginning to have some effect. Wilkie commented in the 77th Quarterly Report: 'No doubt the Dockyard shipwrights will fully appreciate the advance given but notwithstanding it cannot be gainsaid that the rates paid in H.M. Dockyards are still considerably lower than those paid outside doing work of a similar character .... We regret however that nothing has been done, so far as we are aware, to meet the just requirements and real grievances of the Naval shipwrights ....'

NEW OFFICES

Since its move to Newcastle in 1887, the General Office of the Society had been at 3 St Nicholas Buildings. Those premises were adequate at a time when there was a relatively small membership and a small staff. But over the years there had been substantial development with the result that the staff felt 'cribbed and confined for space.' The assimilation of the drillers with their staff and papers was the last straw. New accommodation simply had to be found.

The search led the Society's officers to Eldon Square, then one of the most fashionable parts of Newcastle, only a minute's walk from the City centre and handy for trains and trams. A Dr Williamson had recently died and his property at 8 Eldon Square was up for sale at £6,000. 'The Executive considered the opportunity should not be lost and resolved to secure it as an investment,' the official report commented.

And a good investment it certainly seemed. For it was a double-fronted house in excellent condition, five storeys high with a ground area of 522 square yards. Considering that land in that area was then valued at £10 per square yard, it seemed a bargain. And the cost would come to no more than two years' interest on the reserve fund. The membership approved the transaction and the deal was completed.

But just as the actual removal was taking place at the beginning of September 1901, Alex Wilkie fell seriously ill. No doubt overwork, not only on the Society's affairs but also on many committees, both regional and national, was to blame.

By Christmas he was able to return to the office but only for light duties. His absence for that long period brought clearly to mind the debt the Society owed to him. The Executive Committee decided to make a tangible sign of their appreciation and resolved to call the new offices 'The Wilkie Chambers'. They wrote in the annual report for 1901: 'The Executive feel sure that in taking this means of showing their sympathy with the General Secretary in his indisposition they are but re-echoing and reciprocating the sincere and earnest wish of every member as well as doing something to perpetuate for future generations the work and worth which have been the characteristics of our present General Secretary and who has done so much to help to alleviate, remove, brighten and ennoble the conditions of labour.'

It was a nice gesture and Wilkie appreciated it.

ANNUAL REPORT FOR 1901

His illness did not deter him from producing the most comprehensive annual report in the Society's history, running to almost 270 pages, with many illustrations of various Committees, delegates and ships. No doubt he was helped by the staff in the preparation of the details but he would be an active supervisor and his own introduction was the longest ever and one of the most pungent. On recent legal decisions he declared: 'The only real and abiding remedy is a clear, just and equitable rendering of the Law, by legislation in the House of Commons, placing trades unions in the position they were supposed to occupy by the Acts of 1871-6 but this certainly cannot be expected from the composition of the present House of Commons .... It is idle to talk of no class representation when the House is full of it.' On education, he urged the need to establish educational authorities elected by the people to deal with primary, secondary and technical education. He stated: 'National efficiency can only be obtained and maintained by a generous educational system, giving equal opportunities to all, removing every artificial restraint, eliminating all class and exclusive privileges from the path of deserving children which prevents or retards them from climbing to the highest schools in our country.' And on the housing conditions of many people in the country he had this to say: 'The housing question is a vital one, far more vital than many appear to imagine, it strikes at the very foundation of the social superstructure, the existence in our many towns of such insanitary and insufficient accommodation for the workers is, without doubt, creating evils, producing both intellectual and moral deterioration, the ultimate effect of which will be felt nationally and in these days of keen competition the maintaining of which is of primary importance.'

In these and similar comments, there was little sign of the illness which had afflicted him. Indeed, his comments were sharper and delivered with a greater authority than ever before. He had now emerged fully as a political as well as an industrial leader. Whereas his early years as the Shipwrights' General Secretary had seen him concentrate entirely on trade union matters, now he saw them in the context of the general political situation in the country as a whole. This transformation in his vision and attitude no doubt had many causes: the influence of the new unions and the socialists over the past twenty years; the growing recognition that Parliament could remedy certain grievances; and, from a personal point of view, the widening horizons which membership of national bodies had given him. He was, after all, no longer the leader of a small breakaway group but of almost 20,000 of the most skilled craftsmen in one of the most important industries in the country. That position alone gave him great influence. He was now developing it over a broader canvas.

In himself he typified the changing attitude of the unions. For the 'new unionism' of the 1880's was the conventional unionism of the 1900's. The assimilation of more unions under the banner of the T.U.C., the central role that the Parliamentary Committee played within that organization, the formation of the Labour Representation Committee—all of these steps indicated a great change on the part of unions. The change might have been too slow for some people. The Webbs, for example, were particularly critical of the Parliamentary Committee of the T.U.C. They wrote: 'The work annually accomplished by the Committee ..... has in fact been limited to a few deputations to the Government, two or three circulars to the unions, a little consultation with friendly politicians and the drafting of an elaborate report to Congress.'[3]

But while the change was slow it was sure. In this gradual evolution, the unions were of course expressing a characteristic which has since been noted many times: the paradox of organizations which demand change but which are themselves essentially conservative and pragmatic.

These general observations can be seen to be summed up in the person of Alexander Wilkie. At first, he was almost totally a-political and resoundingly moderate. But through the years he moved towards a political stance, partly through the pressure of outside events and partly through a growing sense of frustration at the lack of progress by other means. But having recognized the need for political action he preferred the cause of Liberalism and, as we have seen, argued for the unions to support the Liberal Party. But by 1900 his conversion to a Labour Party was virtually complete. It is interesting that he was originally adopted as a Labour candidate at the Sunderland election and only later, at the specific request of the Liberals, did he agree to stand as a Lib-Lab candidate. The process of shaping the new politics and political candidates, which had been slowly evolving, however, was now to be speeded up under the stimulus of the adverse legal decisions handed down by the Courts. The way ahead was now clearer than it had ever been.

TWENTY YEARS OLD

At the end of 1901 the Associated Shipwrights' Society was twenty years old. This was not only a significant year in its history but also in the history of British shipbuilding. For in that year over 1.5m. gross registered tons were launched, the highest in the history of the world. And there would be more to come for neither the technology nor the human resources had yet been fully tapped. As Wilkie wrote: 'The limit of the capabilities of the British artisan, either in energy or skill, has by no means been reached ....'

Membership was now over 19,000 which represented well over 90 per cent of all the shipwrights in the country. Wages remained high: £2 for new work on the Tyne and £2.15 for old or repair work. These rates compared with £2.20 a week for angle-ironsmiths, £2.10 for platers, £1.60-£1.90 for riveters, all of whom were members of the Boilermakers' Society. The average industrial wage for all workers at this time was just under £1.50 a week.

Income for the year was almost £40,000 and with expenditure of £27,000 this left a balance of £109,000 or £5.65 per member. While contributions at £32,000 were naturally the most important component of income, it is interesting that the union earned over £3,300 from its investments which, as Wilkie said, 'amply demonstrate the business capacity and wisdom exercised by the Executive Committee'. They had placed funds in such diverse investments as Greenock Harbour, Armstrong and Co Ltd, Co-operative Printing Society, Vickers, Sons and Maxim Ltd, Doxford and Company and Leicester Corporation. Altogether there were eleven main investments.

But while income was rising, so was expenditure. Indeed the latter was going up faster than the former and Wilkie feared that the limits of benefits had now been reached on the contributions paid. Sickness and accident benefit at £10,700 was again the biggest item but trade and dispute benefit which had been only £19 in 1900 shot up to £1,860 owing to two major disputes. Nevertheless, the 20th Annual Report was another 'gratifying record .... of stable development .... and further steady increase of members of reserve funds.'

CHAPTER TWELVE

The long-expected downturn in trade occurred late in 1902, starting on the East and South coasts and spreading to other parts of the country by the end of the year. Conditions in many parts were described as 'very bad'. Yet output for the year exceeded 1.4m. gross registered tons, the third highest output on record. Much of this production had been achieved at the beginning of the year and certainly by Christmas over fifty building berths on the North-East coast were empty, a sight that had not been seen for many years. One in ten shipwrights were thrown out of work.

Following the usual custom, the North-East employers asked for a wage reduction as a means of cutting costs and thereby stimulating orders. The request was for a decrease of 7½p a week, bringing the rates down to £1.95 for new work and £2.10 for old or repair work. The other indicators also flashed red. Unemployment benefit paid out by the Society shot up to £2,500, virtually double the previous year's figure. Equally, the amount advanced in railway fares to members seeking work away from home rose to £300, about 40 per cent up on 1901.

POLITICAL QUESTIONS

Despite trade difficulties, the concern with political and legal questions continued. Indeed because of the Taff Vale and other judicial decisions it deepened. For example, the Shipwrights' Society was among many unions represented at the Conference called by the T.U.C. on Old Age Pensions, held over two days in London in January 1902. The Conference provided the most pungent declaration yet heard for the introduction of old age pensions. It called upon the Government as a matter of urgency to introduce a scheme 'which shall be universal in its application to all citizens, male and female, on attaining the age of 60, the pension to be at the rate of at least 5s od (25p) a week and that the entire cost of such scheme be met by means of Imperial taxation.'

Of more immediate and direct concern was the new interpretation of the law of picketing and the protection of Trade Union funds. The Parliamentary Committee of the T.U.C., of which Wilkie was a member, spent a great deal of time considering the new situation and taking advice from eminent legal counsel and from leading politicians, such as Asquith, Haldane, Dilke and McKenna. The Committee recognized that its work 'has naturally been slow, yet deliberate and thoughtful.' They were very anxious on such an important matter, so full of intricacies, not to make any mistakes. One line of approach was for each union to create a subsidiary company which could operate the various benefit schemes. The funds of the unions would be put into these subsidiary companies so that they themselves had virtually no funds against which claims could be made. On the law of picketing it was suggested that an amending Bill should be introduced in the House of Commons permitting peaceful persuasion of workers to join a strike.

Meanwhile, the legal reverses had given a great stimulus to the work of the Labour Representation Committee whose membership rose during the year by a third to almost half a million, thanks to the affiliation of more unions. The main unions in coal and cotton still refused to join, however, and the Social Democratic Federation decided to withdraw, because of the absence of an overt Socialistic programme. The two places reserved for the Federation on the Executive Committee were given to trade unions which now had nine representatives out of the total of thirteen. In the House of Commons itself, Mr Beaumont, the M.P. for Hexham, called for new legislation 'to prevent workmen being placed by Judge-made law in a position inferior to that intended by Parliament in 1875.' In the debate that followed this resolution, it was suggested that a Committee of Enquiry should be set up to look into all aspects of the legal standing of trade unions. The Government was against such a move and the motion proposing the Enquiry was defeated, but only by a small margin. The unions felt particularly aggrieved that this reasonable suggestion, as they saw it, had been turned down. Some of them, including the shipwrights, circulated the Division List to their members showing how M.P.'s had voted. They advised their members to 'remember it accordingly when the time arrives.' Presumably a reference to their voting intentions at the next General Election.

The 35th annual Trades Union Congress held in London in September 1902 kept up the pressure. The president, J. E. Gregory, of the London Trades Council, in his address pointed to their growing strength. 'Our influence was clearly felt,' he said, 'in Mr Beaumont's resolution when the Government's majority was only 29—even one of their own whips voting against them.' He did not believe in unions turning themselves into companies to get round the law. Rather the law had to be changed and to bring that about, there had to be a new party. He said: 'We must build up a great Labour Party in Parliament from the ranks of the Trade Unionists.' With that declaration, there was now virtually no dispute.

CONSULTING THE MEMBERS

The Society canvassed its members' views regularly on a wide range of topics. Almost every month votes were called for on some question or another: elections for various positions; alterations in pay or conditions; the change of offices. Even accident bonus claims or the purchase of new banners had to be put to the vote. It certainly gave the appearance of democracy and of the members running the Society. Unfortunately the numbers who attended the branch meetings to discuss and vote on the issues at hand tended to be disappointingly small. Returns from a sixth of the membership were regarded as good. Paradoxically, one could have taken the claims for democracy more seriously if less matters had been put to members (especially concerning relatively trivial items such as the purchase of banners) but that when put greater efforts had been taken to institute thorough discussions. Above all, annual conferences of delegates from all branches and a more representative Executive Committee would have helped to justify the claims of democratic control. The Committee was still chosen on a lay basis from the Tyneside area. The main reason given for this procedure was to save expenses but while this may have been relevant in the early days of the Society, it was not so now that the reserves stood at well over £100,000. Nor would an annual conference have been an undue financial burden.

The members therefore lacked an opportunity to provide real control and to look ahead at the general development of the Society. What they had instead was frequent consultation on a whole range of relatively minor matters. All of this had implications for the work of Wilkie and his colleagues. On the one hand they were free to guide the general progress of the organization in one direction rather than another. But on the other hand they felt the need to get specific authorization for every executive decision.

Perhaps the greatest anomaly arose in connection with the district delegates who had to submit themselves regularly for re-election. As it happened the incumbents were nearly always returned but quite often the elections were close. No doubt these regular elections were useful in keeping the delegates on their toes but on the other hand they must have suffered from the feeling of insecure employment—a strange situation considering that they spent much of their time trying to obtain secure employment for their members.

THE MOSELY INDUSTRIAL COMMISSION

Alex Wilkie was invited to visit the U.S. for a second time in the autumn of 1902 as a member of a team enquiring into the conditions of American industry. The visit was arranged and paid for by the wealthy industrialist Alfred Mosely and the subsequent highly detailed report had an introduction by him. Wilkie produced a section on the American shipbuilding industry, having visited yards in Cleveland, Chicago, Philadelphia, Camden and Newport Mews. He found a greater use of machinery than in this country but nevertheless he concluded that 'it will be years before they can even approach, far less surpass, the British nation in shipbuilding.' The main reason was the British apprenticeship system which provided practical training and a skill in craftsmanship which was recognized the world over. Wilkie was particularly critical of the poor finish in the American ships he inspected.

His general views conflicted with those of Mosely who had mounted the U.S. investigation to prove how advanced American industry was compared with British, thanks largely to a policy of tariff protection. Wilkie and others disputed both the facts and the theory. It was untrue, as Mosely suggested, that American workers were paid 50 per cent higher wages and worked fewer hours. It was untrue that the education system was better. And it was particularly untrue that any supposed advantages derived from a policy of trade protection. In any case, said Wilkie, these comparisons were odious. 'No fair comparison could be made between this country and the United States—a continent in itself as against our little island.'

LABOUR REPRESENTATION COMMITTEE

The third annual conference of the Labour Representation Committee was held in Newcastle in February 1903. It was at this conference that the decision was taken to form a Parliamentary party totally separate from all others. Previously members could support any party as long as they obeyed the Labour whips on industrial matters. Now, in the words of the resolution put forward by Peter Curran of the Gasworkers, members 'should strictly abstain from identifying themselves with or promoting the interests of any section of the Liberal or Conservative parties.... Labour representatives in and out of Parliament will have to shape their own policy and act upon it regardless of other sections in the political world.' After a long discussion the resolution was carried overwhelmingly.

Membership of the Labour Representation Committee had jumped spectacularly over the previous year, going up by 84 per cent. Almost 130 trade unions were now affiliated, compared with 41 in the first year, and their membership was well over 800,000. There were also 49 trades councils rather than seven in the first year. Total membership stood at 861,000.

On practical grounds, perhaps the major decision taken at the Newcastle conference was that all Labour M.P.'s would be paid £200 a year. This money would be raised from a levy of a penny a member a year from affiliated trade unions. Trades Councils were specifically exempted.

THE SOCIETY IN 1903

Shipbuilding output in 1903 was considerably less than in the previous year. The inevitable result was another reduction in wages. The North-

East Coast Shipbuilding Employers had secured reductions of 7½p a week for time workers and 5 per cent for piece workers at the end of 1902. Similar cuts were introduced by the employers on the Clyde, at Barrow and in the east of Scotland in February-March 1903 and by the Belfast employers in October 1903. On the Clyde wages were now £1.88 a week for new work and £1.95 for old work. In Barrow the figures were slightly higher, £1.88 and £2.03 respectively, and in Belfast they were £1.90 and £2.02½p.

The effect of the depression was also shown in the dramatic increase in unemployment benefit which went up to £7,000, an increase of £4,500 on the previous year. This outlay brought the total disbursed under this heading since the inauguration of the Society to £43,550.

The biggest item of expenditure was again sickness and accident benefit, which came to almost £12,000. The Society had now expended £97,433 in sickness and accident benefit since its inauguration while almost £17,000 had gone in funeral benefits. It was equally proud of another figure because of its smallness—the dispute benefit. Only 3½ per cent of the £300,000 spent by the Society since 1882 had been for dispute payments, 'a sufficient and conclusive answer' thought Wilkie to those who denounced trade unions as 'fomenters of disturbances and a hindrance of industry.'

Despite the depression the Society's scheme to advance loans to members for house purchase continued to flourish. By the end of 1903, over £12,500 had been advanced out of the notional figure of £20,000 which had been set aside.

During the year, local societies at Gloucester and Newport were assimilated, taking the Society one step nearer to complete coverage of all shipwrights. Membership now stood at 19,300 in 140 branches. Of these, 11,000 were paying the full contribution of a shilling (5p) a week.

The reduction of wages consequent upon the depression of 1902-3 was not severe. On Tyneside, shipwrights were now paid £2.10 for old work and £1.95 for new work. These rates were slightly higher than on the Clyde. With the exception of the boom conditions of 1897-1901 they also represented the highest wages ever paid to shipwrights.

However the reductions occurred at a time when there was a perceptible increase in the retail price index.[1] In the latter part of the nineteenth century, the index had actually gone down. For example, in 1890 it was 91 (1850=100). It dropped slowly over the subsequent years until by 1896 it was down to 83. It then started to climb slowly again and by 1902 it was back to 91.

Over the same period shipwrights' wages on the Tyne also moved. In 1890 they stood at the historically high level of £2.07½ for old work. Because of depressions they fell to £1.95 in 1893-5 but then climbed up again and were £2.10 in 1897 and £2.17½ from 1898 to 1901. In 1902 they fell to £2.10. The prices index and wages had thus tended to rise and fall together and both coincided with the state of trade. But over the decade the shipwrights could certainly feel that their rates had kept pace with the cost of living. Now, however, a small but significant divergence was occurring with wages falling slightly while prices continued to push slowly upwards.

STAGNATION CONTINUES

The depression which had become visible towards the end of 1902 continued through 1903 and 1904. Output in both these years was around 1.2m. gross registered tons which may have seemed high in comparison with figures only a few years before but now with the rapid rise in capacity represented a considerable measure of under-use, in both material as well as human resources. In 1904 over 4,500 members of the Shipwrights' Society or about a fifth were unemployed for varying periods and the Society paid out £10,590 in unemployment benefit, the highest amount ever expended under this heading, far exceeding the previous highest figure of £7,000 recorded in 1903.

So large was the amount and so strange the paradox of a highly developed industrial nation standing idle that the underlying cause gave rise to speculation and to cries for 'systematic' action. In the annual report for 1904, Alexander Wilkie wrote that: 'This question of what is to be done for the unemployed will require to be faced and dealt with.' Such declarations represented a considerable move away from the free enterprise economy, which with exceptions had been the characteristic feature of Britain in the second half of the nineteenth century. The 'law' of supply and demand had been given a position of such eminence that workers, particularly in shipyards, had been led to believe that it was both inevitable and in their interests that wages should fall in times of depression. It was equally inevitable that unemployment would occur until the fall in wages stimulated new demand.

Wilkie now declared clearly that he did not believe in this inevitable process. In any case people had to live and to be given the means to live. 'If as a result of long unemployment, large batches of men become mentally and physically exhausted through the lack of the proper necessities of life, then the nation will be all the poorer, their best asset will be depreciated and the future commercial and industrial pre-eminence of our country imperilled.'

This question was so pressing that although no quick solution could be found a start could be made. The Government, however, had other priorities, particularly in foreign affairs and little was done, apart from the setting up of a Royal Commission. Instead, the 'inevitable process' went on. Wage rates which had been cut in 1902 were now cut once more. On the Tyne, new work was now paid at £1.87½ a week and old or repair work at £2.02½. These rates were on a level with what had been paid in 1896. But whereas then the average retail price index stood at the low level of 83 (1850=100), it now stood at 93. Shipwrights were thus worse off than they had been for a long time. In 1889 their rates had been £2 a week on the Tyne for old or repair work and £1.85 for new work. The average retail price index had been 91 then so that even on this fifteen-year view it had moved two points against them. In contrast other workers had had an increase of wages of 10 per cent on average between 1889 and 1904.[2] They would therefore feel—and indeed would be—better off. Even if we take the two years of 1896 and 1904, the average wage had gone up by ten points exactly in line with the retail price index, whereas, as we have seen, the shipwrights' wages fluctuated back to the level of 1896 so that they were considerably worse off.

THE EMPLOYMENT DEBATE

A Special Conference on Unemployment was held in January 1905 which called upon the Government to create a Labour Ministry with a Minister of Labour at its head. It also called upon local authorities to institute a programme of public works and to implement an eight-hour day. The following month a deputation from the T.U.C. and from the General Federation of Trade Unions called upon the Prime Minister, Mr A. J. Balfour, to put the case directly for Government action to create work. They found him willing to listen but unwilling to act. The difficulty as he saw it was to create a 'social organism' which would help the unemployed over a temporary period without encouraging them to look for permanent State aid.

Later in the year the Government did put forward a bill which became the Unemployed Workmen Act.

This was a mild measure enabling local authorities to set up Distress Committees and to offer relief from the rates but any payment of wages could only come from voluntary contributions. But innocuous as it was, it nevertheless established the principle of the 'right to work'. As Lloyd George said in the Parliamentary debate on 7th August 1905, it contained the 'germs of a revolution' but would 'do very little good except that it recognized a very important principle.... the right of a man to call upon the State to provide him with work. The State replied by recognizing the right but would not provide the work.' But at least the principle was established and upon that principle the unions could now attempt to build.

The Government also announced that it was to set up a royal commision to investigate the poor law and the general problem of poverty. This was, of course, a device for easing union and socialist disappointment and indeed resentment at the weakness of the Government's action as represented by the Unemployed Workmen's Act.

What was wanted, according to Wilkie, was something to help the unemployed 'in the direction of providing productive work which, while giving work to the unemployed, will be remunerative to the community, and help as a nation to distinguish between those willing to work and those who are not.'

Before anything radical was done, the economy was about to cure itself. The depression was coming to an end. Unemployment was dropping and wage rates rising. In fact in 1905 shipwrights asked for and received a restoration of their wages to the level of 1902-3. This was not as high as they had been in 1898-1901 but at least it was a step in the right direction. The Society's unemployment expenditure came down to £7,500, still the second highest in its history.

THE DEATH OF WILLIAM MILLINGTON

William Millington, the East and South-East district delegate for fifteen years, died in December 1905. He was without doubt one of the finest officers the Society ever had. He had been born in Hull in 1850, the same year as Alexander Wilkie and the two men had a great deal in common. Millington started work at the age of 11 and became an apprentice shipwright at the age of 15.

Like Wilkie in Glasgow, he became interested in union affairs early in life and in 1881, at the age of 31, Millington became assistant secretary of the Hull Shipwrights' Provident Association. By 1888 he was elected general secretary of the United Kingdom Amalgamated Society of Shipwrights and held the position until the dissolution of the society in 1890. In 1891 when all the local Humber societies became branches of the Associated Shipwrights' Society, he was appointed Humber district delegate and kept that position until his death. He travelled thousands of miles every year and visited every port in the country. Like Wilkie he came to take a growing interest in public affairs. He was a Liberal who, like Wilkie, came to support the Lib-Labs and then the Labour Party. In local affairs he was elected councillor in 1889. Wilkie and Millington were alike in their industrial philosophy, abhorring strikes except as a last resort. Considering that they had been so close and that their careers had been so similar, it was no wonder that Wilkie wrote of Millington that he had left behind 'a splendid record of a hard and strenuous life.'

CHARLES NEIL

A few months earlier, in May 1905, another long-serving official, Charles Neil, the Mersey District Delegate for thirteen years, had decided to retire. He had reached the age of 70 and was now in indifferent health. He had been 'connected actively since 1865 with every movement that has had for its object the improvement and maintenance of the shipwrights' trade.' Considering that the trade union movement was now actively campaigning for old age pensions, the Executive Committee thought it right to propose to the members that Charles Neil should be paid a 'retiring allowance'. They hoped the members would view the matter 'in a broad and generous spirit'. In fact they threw it out by an overwhelming majority. Only Barrow and Liverpool branches showed any sympathy—the rest voting solidly against.

THE SOCIETY'S AFFAIRS

Despite the depression, which was now lifting, the Society had another good year. Its income at £42,400 was the highest ever while expenditure declined a little thanks to the drop in unemployment benefit. There was a net gain of £4,900 bringing the Society's reserves to almost £130,000 or £7 11s (£7.55) a member. Its major source of revenue remained the contributions from members. But every year the income from shrewd investments became more impressive. In 1905 no less than £5,298 came from these investments, an increase of a quarter over 1904. There were 23 separate investments including company shares, bank accounts and local authority mortgages. The two highest investments, each of £20,000 were in the C.W.S. Bank and in the Prudhoe Street mortgage account in Newcastle. Interest on the former brought in £133 in 1905 and on the latter £712.

Membership declined slightly because of a more rigid attitude by branch treasurers in taking names off the ledgers if arrears of contributions persisted. The total numbers in the Society were now 17,800 adults and 660 apprentices, altogether 18,460. But while the numbers declined, more members were now paying the full contribution rate which had stayed unchanged at a shilling a week since the inauguration of the Society.

The opening years of the 20th century had not been kind to the trade unions. Important legal decisions, such as Taff Vale, had gone against them. An economic depression, lasting from 1902 to 1905, had further fettered them. Membership had declined. Wages had gone down. Unemployment had gone up. A new carefulness was called for, the result of which was to produce a period of remarkable industrial peace, lasting from 1900 until 1907.

But now things were to change dramatically. A new era was about to burst open. The shipwrights in particular were about to experience a golden year.

CHAPTER THIRTEEN

Some years are more important than others. They stand out as landmarks. Perhaps far-reaching changes take place or certain events occur which alter the progress of society or industry. Such a year was 1906. For it saw a change of Government and the arrival in Parliament of the Labour Party. It also saw the greatest shipbuilding output up to that time and the launch of some of the finest ships of all time.

THE SHIPS THEY WERE BUILDING

Three ships in particular gave distinction to the output of 1906: H.M.S. *Dreadnought*, the *Mauretania* and the *Lusitania*. The *Dreadnought* was not only one of the world's greatest battleships, it set a fashion for 'all big-gun' ships which swept the world until the outbreak of the First World War. It was the logical development of a particular philosophy of naval warfare and could be described as the inevitable outcome of improved technology and of politics based on power. 'The genesis of *Dreadnought* lay in the idea of a warship which would combine a very high speed with very great hitting power; which would be able to hit enemy ships at long ranges with devastating effect and which would at the same time be able to protect itself from the attack of small torpedo craft.'[1] The concept was given great impetus by the success of the Japanese Navy against the Russian fleet in 1905.

This decisive victory based on large, swift, powerfully armed warships set off an immediate explosion for bigger ships from every navy of consequence in the world. The British committee on designs advocated the 'all-big-gun' ship, H.M.S. *Dreadnought*, and within weeks her keel-plate was being laid at Portsmouth. She was being launched within three months and ready for service in just over a year. Fitted with ten 12-inch guns and 27 12-pounder quick-firing anti-torpedo-boat guns together with five submerged torpedo tubes, she was nothing less than a floating fortress. Three more *Dreadnought* class battleships were immediately ordered, two from Government dockyards and the other, the *Superb*, from Armstrong-Whitworths on the Tyne. In subsequent years the fever intensified both in this country and abroad, summed up in the famous slogan: 'We want eight (battleships) and we won't wait.'

While the naval dockyard at Portsmouth was busy on *Dreadnought*, two other yards were building equally famous ships. Swan, Hunter and Wigham Richardson on the Tyne were responsible for the *Mauretania* and the Clyde yard of John Brown for the sister ship, the *Lusitania*. These two ships built for the Cunard Steamship Company were of unprecedented speed and size and represented one of the greatest achievements of British shipbuilding. A contemporary account reported with obvious pride that the construction of these two ships was 'the most stupendous task ever entrusted to shipbuilders' for they involved 'the scientific solution of the most difficult problems in naval architecture and marine engineering.'[2]

They were 790 feet long, 88 feet wide and 60 feet high with accommodation for 560 first-class passengers, 500 second-class, 1,400 third-class and 800 crew—a total of 3,260 and each passenger had 50 per cent more space than in other liners. The ships were fitted with Parson's turbine engines which were just coming into commercial use at the time. In fact the adoption of this new kind of propulsion, which offered higher speed, less vibration and cheaper maintenance, by the two Cunard liners was regarded as an important step forward in its general acceptance.

Big and fast as they were, the ships were also noted for the excellence of their craftsmanship, the ornate decoration and the luxury of their furniture and fittings, a characteristic which earned them the titles of 'floating palaces'.

Although they were identical, the *Mauretania* always had the edge on speed and for 22 years from 1907 to 1929 she dominated the Atlantic as the fastest liner in the world. But even in 1933, after she had lost the title and just two years before she was broken up, she was able to achieve her highest-ever speed of 32 knots which she maintained for 112 miles. The *Lusitania* was sunk by the German Navy in May 1915.

The construction of these fast and beautiful ships was a great achievement for all the men who worked on them. For besides their naval machinery and huge size they contained many unusual features which must have caused innumerable headaches for the men. Yet at the same time the standard of workmanship in every department had to be impeccable. They truly represented the shipbuilder's art at its finest. The shipwrights and other men who worked on them and followed their outstanding careers could legitimately feel a continuing sense of pride and pleasure.

THE YEAR'S OUTPUT

The output of British shipbuilding in 1906 reached the staggering total of 1.8m. gross registered tons. This output was 15 per cent more than had ever been achieved up to that year and in fact was to be exceeded in only two other years in the future. The figure represented 62 per cent of the shipping launched throughout the world, not as high a percentage as had been achieved in the 1880's and 1890's when it had exceeded 80 per cent but still a most impressive amount, particularly in view of the developments in Germany and the United States. These figures indeed seemed to offer support to the unions who had been attacked by *The Times* in 1902 in a famous series of articles, entitled 'The Crisis of British Industry'. The newspaper argued that trade unionism and the restrictive practices that it encouraged had held back British industry at a time when the United States and Germany were forging ahead. Among the examples it chose was the shipbuilding industry where demarcation disputes and restrictive practices had led to 'long delays ... in the execution of orders'. The output of 1906 seemed to answer that charge. True, world shipbuilding had never been higher but Britain had confirmed her pre-eminent place. Indeed the North-East coast or Clydeside alone produced almost as many ships as the rest of the world combined.

Wilkie commented with evident pleasure in the annual report for 1906 that 'Our position, so far as shipbuilding is concerned, is far ahead of other nations'. And the unions received added support from Sir William White, Director of Naval Construction at the Admiralty, who in a series of articles in *The Times* in 1906 stated:

'One great advantage possessed by this country, but often overlooked, is the much greater number of highly-trained artisans skilled in all the trades connected with shipbuilding and inheriting from generations of predecessors special aptitude and information. Such a possession can only be obtained by lapse of time and accumulated experience. No doubt it is accompanied by drawbacks and difficulties which detract somewhat from its value but, on the whole, it is a valuable asset of the United Kingdom.'

The massive output of 1906 following high output in 1905 gave rise to fears that freight rates would slump leading to a reduction in ordering. For orders for new shipping—and therefore employment in the shipbuilding industry—depended on the level of freight rates. When rates were rising owners placed orders for new ships; when they were falling they abstained. The freight rates themselves depended on an interplay of many factors: the state of world trade; the size of various harvests; the availability of finance; the amount of tonnage in existence to handle world demand. When a great amount of new tonnage was launched it would have the effect of forcing down freight rates unless there was an even greater rise in world trade or old ships were placed out of commission or other factors intervened. So even outstanding years like 1906 brought their fears for the future. As Wilkie said: 'What the net result will mean of this extraordinary production which the last few years have witnessed it is difficult to forecast; time alone will tell.'

One of the reasons for the increase in output was the increasing size of vessels. The *Mauretania* and the *Lusitania* were both 32,000 gross registered tons while the *Adriatic* was almost 24,000 tons. Altogether twelve vessels of over 10,000 were under construction in 1906 compared with an average tonnage for steamers of 3,000 tons. More ships were also being fitted with turbine machinery. Besides the *Mauretania* and the

Lusitania another ten were fitted with turbines in 1906.

UNEMPLOYMENT REMAINS HIGH

Despite the massive output, unemployment among shipwrights remained naggingly high. Throughout the year no less than 3,450 members of the Shipwrights' Society drew unemployment benefit for some period or other. They represented 18 per cent of the membership and they received £5,000. An additional £1,890 was also paid out as a special benefit to those members indirectly affected by a wages strike by other trades on the Clyde.

The Society was becoming extremely alarmed not only by the continuing high level of expenditure on unemployment benefit but even more by the underlying trend which it represented. For the startling fact was that between 1904 and 1906 inclusive when the industry had turned out a record amount of shipping, the Society had expended no less than £25,000 on unemployment relief. Wilkie commented: 'It is a somewhat startling commentary on our social and commercial life in this country when we are faced with the fact that in a year which is supposed to have been a record one for British trade there should have been so many workmen who have been unable to find any employment.' He felt that one of the major reasons was the increasing use of machinery and the improved methods of production which allowed more ships to be turned out with fewer men. But while he was particularly concerned with the shipbuilding industry, the problem was general and ought to receive the full consideration of the Government. The measures already taken in allowing local authorities to set up Distress Committees were merely palliatives. 'No responsible Government or party whose objects are the uplifting of the industrial and social conditions of the people can afford to lose sight of this problem', he wrote in the annual report for 1906. But what action should be taken was not clear.

The general calls for public works and the more equal distribution of Government work were not relevant. There was no shortage of demand, particularly in shipbuilding and both the private and Naval yards had full order books. The fact was, however, that the work could be accomplished by fewer men. This was the new situation to which no one had an answer.

THE SOCIETY'S YEAR

This was the Society's twenty-fifth year, a time for looking back as well as forward. Since its inception it had raised £546,000 mainly from members' contributions, and expended about half of that amount on benefits to members. The remainder had gone into reserves (about a quarter of the total) or into administration, donations of one sort or another, the Parliamentary fund, railway fares and other items. Of the benefits, sickness and accident was by far the most important. £158,000 had been spent under this heading. Unemployment benefit was the second biggest category with £68,000, of which £25,000 had been spent between 1904 and 1906. Trade and dispute benefit accounted for only about 3 per cent of expenditure at £11,000. Funeral benefits had taken £22,000, accident bonuses £13,000, pensions £6,000 and tool compensation £2,600. The union could rightly feel that this was a proud record and that it had taken this burden of expenditure off central or local government.

In 1906 income was almost £44,000 which was the highest on record but not as high as it should have been if all arrears had been paid off. It was estimated that members' contributions alone should have produced about £40,000 instead of the actual level of £35,000. Considering that the requested contributions were so low compared to the level of benefits, it was felt that there should be fewer arrears. In fact on average each member was paying only 32s a year, which was not even one week's wages. Members' contributions did not cover total expenditure. Interest on invested capital and other items of income covered—and indeed exceeded—the deficiency.

Expenditure for the year also reached a record figure—£39,000. Sickness and accident benefit alone cost almost £14,000 and unemployment and special benefits almost £7,000.

The number of members went up by 586 to over 19,000 of whom 12,000 were now paying for full benefit by contributions of a shilling a week. With the bulk of the membership in this category it was felt that the time had come to reconsider the different classes and to reduce them from four to two. Such a rearrangement would not only reduce administrative work but would encourage yet more members to opt for full benefits.

GENERAL ELECTION

Without doubt the main event of the year however for the Society, for the industry and for the country as a whole was the General Election which took place in January. It produced a Liberal Government for the first time in ten years and a substantial number of trade unionist M.P.'s. For the first time it was possible to talk of the Labour Party in the House of Commons.

The Conservative Government led by Arthur Balfour but dominated by Joseph Chamberlain had resigned towards the end of 1905 primarily because of a deep division of opinion over the issue of tariff reform. One section of the party led by Joseph Chamberlain had come out in favour of abandoning free trade and replacing it with a policy of tariff protection against foreign goods. Free trade was for both Liberals and Socialists part of the natural order of things. It had been the ruling philosophy during the years of Britain's industrial greatness in the second half of the nineteenth century. To abandon it, they felt, was to return to an economic dark age. These views had been shared equally by the Conservative Party, at least until the turn of the century. In 1903 Joseph Chamberlain and others formed a Tariff Reform League to campaign against free trade and to demand duties on imported food, with preference for the colonies, and an average ten per cent tariff on foreign manufactured goods. They felt that this was the answer to the industrial depression Britain had been passing through. Free Trade was appropriate when this country was the outstanding industrial nation. But as other countries became more industrialized and started to compete more effectively, then it was necessary to take measures in self-defence, they argued.

Not only did this new approach split the Conservative Party, it was anathema to the Liberal Party and to the trade unions. The T.U.C. Conference in September 1904 declared its outright opposition for the increase in costs, which the tariffs entailed, would hurt the working class more than any other. In addition they were against a policy which aimed apparently at retaliation against foreign workers and against the spirit of international brotherhood.

That issue in itself was sufficient grounds for an election. But there were many others too. The T.U.C. put forward the following:

1. Support for a new Trade Disputes Bill which would give trade unions a secure legal basis.
2. An amendment of the Compensation Act so as to give compensation to all workers in all trades from the date of an accident.
3. An amendment of the Truck Act to prevent stoppages from wages for services supplied by employers.
4. The abolition of enforced Chinese labour in South Africa.
5. The introduction of a State Pension for everyone.
6. An extension of the Working Class Act.
7. Adult Suffrage, particularly for women.
8. The introduction of an Eight-Hour working day.

All candidates standing with the support of the T.U.C. were asked to pledge themselves to these measures. Equally all trade unionists were asked to vote only for such candidates. Most of these candidates also ran under the auspices of the Labour Representation Committee which had done an excellent job in preparing for the election. The Committee in general and its secretary, Ramsay MacDonald, in particular, had accumulated a mass of information about electoral prospects and were able to help Labour Candidates to find suitable constituencies. In addition, MacDonald had worked out a secret arrangement with the Liberal Party. In return for close co-operation, the Liberals agreed to let L.R.C. candidates have a clear run in thirty seats. That is, there would be no official Liberal candidates so that there would be either a straight fight with the Conservatives or at worst a mixed fight with some miscellaneous candidates. But there would be no Liberal to split the anti-Conservative vote. The effect of this electoral pact was to improve the Labour Party's chances immeasurably.

And so it proved. The Liberals gained a sweeping victory with a majority of 220 over the Conservatives and of 84 over all other parties. But the L.R.C. also scored a resounding success for 30 members were returned, 23 of whom were also trade union members. In addition there were 17 other trade union members of whom 13 were miners. Altogether therefore 47 members of the new House of Commons had clear organizational links with the labour movement compared with 15 before the Election.

The new party had taken a great step forward. The trade unions had achieved one of their main aims in securing Parliamentary representation. It was a turning point not only in the progress of unionism but in the political development of this country. One can accept the rather cynical comment of John Burns, once one of the 'new unionists' and soon to become the first member of the working class to gain a seat in the Cabinet, that 'the new Labour Party were floated into Parliament on the river of free trade' and that many of the candidates 'were elected by Radical enthusiasm, Liberal votes and trade union funds'. This does not detract from the achievement. Nearly all parties are elected on a negative vote, because they are less unpopular than their opponents. Few elections are won out of positive preference.

The fact was that a new political party had emerged from the working class. The organization of that embryonic party so that within six years it could achieve this level of success was a major achievement in itself. And it changed the face of British politics.

THE ELECTION AND THE SHIPWRIGHTS

The Shipwrights' Society put forward two candidates at the Election—Alexander Wilkie and John Jenkins, the Bristol Channel delegate. Both of them had been nominated as prospective candidates two years before and had had plenty of time to get to know their respective constituencies of Dundee and Chatham. Jenkins, a rather gaunt figure with a walrus moustache but no beard, had been a Cardiff City Councillor for some years and in 1904 he was Mayor of the City. He had a straight fight with a Conservative candidate for the Chatham constituency which had been won by the Conservatives at the previous election with a substantial majority. Jenkins was able to turn that into a Labour majority, polling 6,692 votes against his opponent's 4,020.

Wilkie had a less easy task at Dundee where the constituency consisted of two seats. Both had been held by Liberal members. When one of them, Sir John Lang, announced his decision not to stand, it was felt that this seat would represent a good opportunity for a Labour member like Wilkie. Unfortunately after his nomination another Liberal decided to put himself forward, indicating that the pact between the Liberal and Labour parties did not always work smoothly. Thus the contest was between two Liberals, two Conservatives and Wilkie, the Labour candidate. In the event Wilkie came second, a considerable way behind one of the Liberals but 711 votes ahead of the other. The two Conservatives were bottom of the poll. It was a gratifying result for Wilkie. He declared: 'My sole object in entering Parliament is to do something, in common with all Progressives, to assist forward the national welfare, when unemployment will be lessened, when children will have larger and better opportunities of life, when our women shall have brighter and happier homes to look after and when old age will have something better to get than mere Poor Law Relief tainted with pauperism. National good —not merely sectional ends—is my aim.'

Now 56 years of age, Wilkie was a bulky figure. He had always been solid, now he had the definite signs of a 'corporation' which he emphasized with a watch chain. His beard which had once been full was now trimmer and was indeed rather in the Van Dyke style. His hair too was thinner and on top he was almost bald.

His election had cost the Labour Party £925 (or 2s 10d per vote) by far the highest expenditure for any of the candidates at Dundee. The successful Liberal candidate, the Right Hon. E. Robertson, had spent £339. At Chatham John Jenkins' election had cost the Labour Party £686. Both Wilkie and Jenkins received £200 a year maintenance allowance from the Party, (this was before the payment of M.P.'s) in addition to their union salaries of £250 and £143 respectively.

Wilkie made his maiden speech in the House on 26th February on the composition of the Poor Law Commission. He regretted the absence on the Commission of a representative of the Scottish workers. The matter affected the workers directly and was one in which they were vitally interested.

None of those appointed could be said to represent the industrial community of Scotland. The President of the Local Government Board, John Burns, the former trade unionist, turned down Wilkie's demand. The Commission was too big already. Any more members would make it unwieldy. Wilkie could rest assured that Scotland's interests would be taken into account, a reply that was 'entirely unsatisfactory' to the *Dundee Courier* and no doubt to many others.

Two days later John Jenkins made his maiden speech in a debate on the Navy Estimates, when he took up one of the shipwrights' long-standing complaints about the pay and working conditions in the Government dockyards. The pay for all classes of workmen was too low, he said, and out of line with rates paid in private yards for similar work. He also called upon the Government to recognize 'the right of negotiation through the accredited representatives of the workmen'.

Mr E. Robertson, Parliamentary Secretary to the Admiralty and Wilkie's fellow M.P. at Dundee, replied saying that both points were fair and reasonable and were unlikely to meet with opposition. But the Government needed to study all the implications before coming to a decision.

Wilkie's first impressions of the House of Commons were mixed. The hours were long, much longer than in a workshop and there was always a great deal of correspondence. But the rules of the House came easily and relationships with members of all parties were good-natured. His greatest complaint was against the verbosity of certain members who took an hour to relate what could effectively be told in five minutes. On the whole he felt that the Labour Party made a good start and were making their presence felt. He told a reporter from the *Glasgow Weekly News* (March 10th) that in his view the Labour members were equal to any in the House. 'This is only to be expected when it is remembered that the bulk of them have been life-long lecturers on the questions of labour organization.'

THE WORK OF THE NEW PARLIAMENT

The Liberal Government which had now been returned to power was to be one of the great reforming administrations. It introduced old age pensions, and National Insurance against sickness and unemployment. It laid down minimum wage rates and took other measures to improve the lot of the working class. As one historian wrote: 'Social security was already becoming the key to British politics and the Liberal and Labour Parties after 1906 combined to satisfy part at least of the new demand .... Taken in bulk the Liberal legislation of the period meant that the States had at least accepted it as a duty to promote the welfare of its citizens at the common expense."[3]

In the first year there were two measures of importance to trade unions. One was the Trade Disputes Bill which had a chequered career through Parliament before finally emerging very much in the form advocated by various conferences of the T.U.C. Its progress was delayed largely by the Report of the Royal Commission which the Conservative Government had set up in 1903. The Report declared that the Taff Vale judgement 'involved no new principle and was not inconsistent with the legislation of 1871'. The Labour Party and the trade unions could not accept that view. Indeed, as we have seen, the Taff Vale judgement had provided the impetus towards greater Parliamentary representation. Now that it had been achieved, the unions certainly wanted their legal position clarifying beyond doubt. They insisted that the Liberals carried out their electoral pledges despite the publication of the Royal Commission Report. Henry Campbell-Bannerman, the leader of the Liberals and the new Prime Minister, had promised the Parliamentary Committee of the T.U.C. before the election to introduce a measure on 'the general lines' of the Committee's own proposals. This the Labour Party now insisted upon.

After considerable to-ing and fro-ing an Act was passed in December 1906 which clearly conferred upon unions the right of voluntary association and legalized peaceful picketing and persuasion. The unions had achieved their major objective.

The other measure was the Workmen's Compensation Act which closed a number of loopholes in the 1897 Act, improved the scales of compensation and extended the coverage to all workers. Wilkie called it 'one of the best pieces of industrial legislation during the Session of 1906'.

The advent of the new Liberal Government with strong support from the Labour Party was thus having an immediate effect on improving the status and conditions of the trade unions and of the working class in general.

WEEKLY WAGES ON THE CLYDE

This question had been hanging fire ever since the Clyde employers had unilaterally and summarily decided after the trial period of a year in 1899-1900 to revert to the fortnightly system of payments. Some unions had wanted to challenge the employers at that time but others were more reluctant. The depression of 1902-5 was clearly an inopportune moment but towards the end of 1905 the issue was raised in earnest once more.

The unions and many of the workers did not like the system of fortnightly payments. It tended to make it difficult for them to control their personal expenditure. It was quite common in the second week for workers and their families to have to resort to pawnbrokers or credit shops to obtain money for the ordinary necessities of life. Thousands of workers were thus regularly in debt, had to pay for the luxury of borrowing and found that credit shops charged higher prices. It was a perverse system which the employers favoured because it instilled a sense of loyalty and discipline among the workers. In short it tied them to the employers.

In 1905-6 the General Federation of Trade Unions and the Federation of Engineering and Shipbulding Trades joined forces to bring back weekly wages. They held a conference in Glasgow on 22nd December 1905 when it was unanimously decided to ballot the members of affiliated societies as to whether they would agree to strike action. The members supported this approach overwhelmingly. The two federations now felt able to pursue the question vigorously and when a Central Conference with employers failed to make progress they called a strike for June. Before it could take place, however, the employers backed down and agreed to the re-introduction of weekly payments.

The seventh annual report of the General Federation of Trade Unions commented: 'The best traits of trade union policy—patience, persistency and organization—were brought into play ... The employers' attitude in so strenuously opposing the demand is difficult to understand and has been severely criticized.... An employer who gratuituously gives his workers fair conditions is a good thing but a much better thing is to have a body of men who will see to it that, irrespective of the desire of the employer, fair conditions must be given.'

From now on, Clyde workers like those in the rest of the country were paid their wages each week and the amount of debt subsided substantially.

And so ended a remarkable year: a year when both output and unemployment were high; a year when tariff protection became an important issue in British politics and led to the overthrow of the Government; a year when a new party entered the House of Commons and when the rights of trade unions were secured. It was both a high point and a turning point.

CHAPTER FOURTEEN

From the high point of 1906 both the shipbuilding industry and the country as a whole were to plunge into a serious depression which made many factories idle and threw thousands of men out of work. National unemployment was to rise to almost 8 per cent of all workers. The capitalist system had two sides to it and the 'unacceptable face' was now to be seen in all its ugliness. In addition, the Society was to enter into its first full-scale dispute which placed a severe strain upon its funds.

THE WAGES QUESTION

The first important sign of impending trouble arose from requests for higher wages. In the autumn of 1906 petitions from shipwrights in the Naval Dockyards received a positive response from the Admiralty, which agreed to pay an extra shilling a week. Established men were to receive 34s a week and hired men 35s 6d.

When the men in private yards on the Tyne, Tees and Clyde put in similar requests the following spring they found a completely different response. The tide of work had changed dramatically in a few months. The high output of 1906 was being followed, as Wilkie and others had feared, by a downturn in ordering.

The Shipwrights' and Joiners' Standing Consultative Committee for the North-East coast lodged a claim in May 1907 for an increase of 1s 6d a week or 5 per cent on piece rates to take effect from July. They asked for a meeting with the employers to discuss the question. The employers turned down both the claim and the request for a meeting 'in view of the unsatisfactory state of trade and prospects of the shipbuilding industry'. The state of trade had certainly declined and even the Society's own reports for the Tyne indicated that at best it was only 'fair' and in some yards it was 'slack'. The Consultative Committee realized that they had missed their opportunity in the previous year and their reaction to the employers' decision was unusually mild. They took the view that 'it would be very unwise at the present to force a Conference with the Employers' Association at which, in all likelihood, we would only receive another definite refusal.' In the circumstances they agreed simply to write to the Employers deploring the lack of a meeting but to take no further action.

On the Clyde, the Society did slightly better. They at least managed to have a meeting with the employers on 11th June. But the outcome was the same; trade was turning down and this was no time to be offering wage increases. Mr C. Scott, chairman of the Clyde Shipbuilders' Association, mentioned the depressed freight rates which were deterring owners from placing orders, the high cost of materials, the low profits and the 'most gloomy' prospects. Here, too, the men felt they had no alternative but to accept the decision and to hope they could put in a fresh claim in the spring of 1908 if trade warranted it.

In Aberdeen shipwrights were more successful. Employers there agreed to an increase of just over a shilling a week as from July. Aberdeen was always one of the lower-paid ports and the increase brought the rates to £1 14s 10½d for new work and £1 17s 1d for old or repair work. By comparison, Clyde yards were paying three shillings a week more.

The increase was short-lived, however, for in the autumn the employers at Aberdeen followed the example of their colleagues on the Clyde in calling for wage reductions which exactly cancelled out the increases paid in July. The reductions came into force in January 1908 on the Clyde and at Leith, Dundee and Barrow as well as at Aberdeen. Similar reductions were called for on the North-East coast but, as we shall see, they were not acceptable to the men and a serious dispute arose.

SIXTH DELEGATE MEETING

The sixth delegate meeting held in Newcastle in October 1907 was a quiet, business-like affair with few clashes and no fireworks. Yet some important changes were made. The name of the Society was altered. It now became 'The Ship Constructive and Shipwrights' Association'. This longer title emphasized its members' role in the construction of ships. It also recognized the fact that the Society could organize on behalf of ship constructors, shipwrights (including loftsmen, erectors and liners off), ship repairers, yacht builders, barge builders, boat builders, mast builders, blockmakers, drillers and hole cutters. Above all the new name recognized the absorption of the Ship Constructive Association which organized Admiralty shipwrights.

The meeting urged that a greater effort should be made to assimilate those few local societies which still remained independent. Over the next year these efforts were to pay dividends. By the end of 1908 the Wear Shipwrights' Society and the London United Drillers' Society were absorbed, boosting the membership to 21,000. Among important shipwright societies, only the Liverpool society and the London Provident Union now remained aloof.

The meeting agreed to alter the scale of contributions, eliminating the 3d scale. In future all members would pay either 6d, 9d or 1s a week. In addition all members, except trade members paying 6d a week, should pay 6d a quarter to create a special fund for the payment of superannuation benefit which was becoming an increasingly heavy burden as the Society, and its members, grew older.

The most important change agreed at the meeting concerned the composition of the Executive. Until 1907 the Committee had been elected from among those members who worked within 25 miles of the headquarters. This rule had been laid down at the inauguration of the Society in order to save expense. But it was a restrictive rule and hardly in accord with the dictates of democracy. Now with virtually no discussion and certainly no opposition it was agreed that in future the Executive Committee should consist of one representative from each of the following districts: North-East, Scotland, North-West, East and South-East, South-West and Ireland. The drillers would also have a representative and the General Secretary would be a member. Thus the Executive Committee would consist of eight people representing the whole country. They would meet once a quarter.

Finally, the meeting took a range of smaller but by no means unimportant decisions. The General Secretary was to be elected for a period of five years and the district delegates for three, the latter to be known in future as 'technical advisers'. All General Office staff were to become members of the Association automatically. And, surprisingly in view of the state of the industry, it was agreed that all salaries should be increased by 10 per cent and that all paid officials should receive 14 days' holiday a year.

With the assimilation of the Wear Shipwrights' Society it was agreed to open new branches at Monkwearmouth, Southwick, Deptford and Hylton while Sunderland itself was to have a second branch. There were now over 1,200 members on Wearside and it was agreed they should have their own delegate, or technical adviser. Timothy McDonic was elected to the position. On the Clyde, Robert Ramage was replaced by Thomas Hill because of his alleged refusal to carry out two important instructions from the Executive Committee. The other technical advisers were Richard Johns (North-East), James Bridges (North-West), William Ford (East and South-East), John Jenkins (Bristol Channel and South-West) and Joshua Butterworth (Drillers).

The change in the composition of the Executive Committee did not make a great difference in terms of cost. The expenses, including railway fares, rose from about £120 a year to about £170 in 1908 and to £260 by 1910. This was hardly an unreasonable burden in view of the wider representation.

The election of the new committee took the best part of a year. Consequently instead of taking up office in January 1908, as originally intended, they did not meet until January 1909. The former committee remained in existence in the interim. The new committee was:

North-East—John Willcocks
Scotland—Edward Doherty
North-West—George Wills
East and South-East—Michael Jenkins
South-West and Wales—John Thompson

Ireland—William George
Drillers—Richard Tweddle

Each of them was elected for a period of two years but in order to get a rota system started some would retire at the end of the first year. Retiring members were eligible for re-election.

WAGES DISPUTE AND NATIONAL LOCKOUT

The winter of 1907-8 saw the start of the most serious dispute so far in the history of the Association. As on the Clyde, employers in the North-East called for wage reductions to counter the down-turn in trade. But unlike the Clyde members, the men in the North-East refused to accept the request.

The dispute began with a letter from the Associated Shipbuilding Employers of the Tyne, Wear, Tees and Hartlepool districts on 7th December 1907 calling for all shipbuilding trades to accept a cut of 1s 6d a week or 5 per cent on piece rates. The unions reacted strongly and quickly. They called a meeting of the Shipbuilding Trades Federation, which represented all the various trades. They agreed to act together on this question and to seek a conference with the employers. In fact, over the next few weeks and months numerous conferences were held with the employers who generally adopted a hard line. Wage reductions were necessary they declared as they had been in the past to stimulate orders during a depression.

Wilkie took up this central point during one of the discussions and asked bluntly: 'Will you be able to guarantee that we will get more work if we consent to this reduction?'

Skinner (Chairman of the Employers' Association): 'No.'

Wilkie: 'No, the point is, you had more work in 1901 when wages were higher than you have at the present time. Now if wages were the predominant factor, your yards ought to be full of work with the lower wages you enjoy at present.'

Skinner: 'We will do all we can to get work. It is not our choice that we pay off men. It is simply that we are compelled to do so....'

Wilkie: 'Do you not think that the men suffer enough by being idle?'

Jones (another employer): 'Well, before we can secure more orders the cost of production must come down. We have already pointed out that we do not come to the men first; that profits are the first thing we cut when orders become scarce....'

Wilkie: 'The high rate of wages is not the only thing preventing you securing work. There is the very high price which steel, iron and coal have reached...'

After further discussions, the unions decided to put up the suggestion that they would recommend to their members reductions of half the amounts called for by the employers. The latter refused however. They also refused to agree to the unions' suggestion of arbitration. According to John Skinner, their Chairman: We know our own business best and there is no arbitrator who could take up the position as we see it today.'

In other words they wanted the full reduction and they wanted it from 22nd January 1908.

The employers' continued firmness split the unions. The majority of those unions working piece-rates, e.g. the boilermakers, reluctantly agreed to accept the reductions. The majority of the time trades, e.g. the shipwrights, were against. In fact the shipwrights voted by 1,435 to 226 to resist the reduction by going on strike if necessary. This was an overwhelming majority even though only a half of the members had voted. Even when the employers amended their request slightly by suggesting that a reduction of one shilling a week should take place in January and a further sixpence in March, they remained substantially opposed. Deadlock was now reached and on 22nd January 1908 shipwrights, drillers, joiners, mill sawyers and furnishing tradesmen in the North-East came out on strike.

The Shipwrights' Executive Committee immediately recognized the strike as official and agreed to pay dispute benefit to all those members whose contributions were paid up and who had stopped work on 21st January. Members who were unemployed or who were receiving sickness or accident benefit on that day would not receive the dispute benefit. Strike Committees were set up in every branch.

The strike was well supported and remained solid throughout. Almost 3,000 shipwrights were affected, over 1,700 joiners and with the various other trades the total came to 5,150. By the end of the first month, the Executive Committee appealed to the whole membership for a special levy of sixpence a week so that all those on strike could be paid 15s a week. This was agreed, for there were clear signs that the atmosphere between the two sides was deteriorating. The employers were beginning to talk of further reductions beyond their original demands in order to bring North-East wages down to the level paid on the Clyde. And they were also threatening to close the yards as the strike was beginning to disrupt production. So serious were things becoming that the President of the Board of Trade, Lloyd George, asked representatives of both sides to see him but without success.

By the middle of March the employers had brought in their national federation and they asked to meet the union representatives at a conference in Edinburgh on 25th March. This was duly arranged and turned out to be a very large gathering indeed. No doubt each side wished to impress the other with the size of the delegation. The trick—if such it was—failed however, perhaps indicating that in such circumstances small, informal gatherings can make better progress. The employers argued that they could not understand why the men refused the reductions considering that the piece-work trades had agreed and that shipwrights in other parts of the country had accepted reductions.

The union leaders made no reply to this point but they did suggest a compromise: 6d a week off time rates immediately with another 6d in three months' time and 2½ per cent off drillers' piece rates. The employers retorted that they wanted the full reductions of 1s 6d a week and 5 per cent off piece-work. They would be ready to take 'extreme steps' if necessary.

Like the employers, the unions too had combined for extra strength. They had formed a body called the North-East Coast Workers' Central Committee. In view of the threat of escalation, the Workers' Committee felt they should ballot their members again, firstly, to see if they wanted to accept the reduction (which they did not); and, secondly, to see if they wanted the question referring to arbitration (which they did). Armed with this latest expression of their members' views, the union leaders met the Shipbuilding Employers' Federation in Carlisle on 24th April. They put up various suggestions but without avail. According to the Shipwrights' Monthly Membership Return for April: 'The employers would listen to no method of conciliation or arbitration and refused in any way to modify their original demand and consequently the Conference was abortive.'

The employers now took dramatic action. They imposed a lockout in Scotland and the North of England from 2nd May. About 15,000 men were locked out making another 22,000 idle as a result. The shipbuilding industry came to a halt in these areas and local economies suffered a serious decline. To mitigate the effect on their own members, the Executive Committee of the Shipwrights agreed to pay all members 12s a week in dispute benefit (members in the North-East had been receiving 15s a week). Even those members who were in arrears and would not normally be paid benefit money were to be helped. If they would sign 'promissory notes' agreeing to clear off their arrears as soon as they returned to work, then they could receive 9s a week benefit.

Meanwhile Lloyd George was continuing his efforts to end the dispute. But it was a Joint Board of the Trade Union Congress, the General Federation of Trade Unions and the Labour Party which found the eventual solution. It suggested a two-point plan. First, the men should agree to the reduction of 1s 6d a week and return to work. Second, the employers should agree to set up a joint conference with the unions to create permanent machinery to deal with all future disputes. The conference should be held within two weeks of a resumption of work.

The plan was put to a national ballot and was accepted by 24,145 votes to 22,110, a narrow victory after such a long dispute. The yards were thrown open again and the men resumed work on 1st June. Life returned to normal, or as normal as it could be after such a bitter conflict.

The strike had lasted 18½ weeks and cost the industry 1,700,000 working days. Well over £200,000 was lost in wages while the Shipwrights' Society spent £53,863 in dispute benefit payments. Some of this expenditure was covered by special receipts. The Society received £9,960 from the General Federation of Trade Unions and raised £7,679 from the special levy on members. But nevertheless the expenditure was a severe burden and a sad blow. For the first time the Association's expenditure exceeded income and by a substantial margin. In its first 26 years it had spent well under £13,000 on dispute benefit, something which pleased Wilkie and most of the members enormously. Now, in a few months, it had spent almost £54,000. Such an outlay might provide ammunition for critics. According to Wilkie in the 1908 annual report: 'The amounts expended may doubtless be seized upon by the opponents of Trade Unionism to show the futility of such organizations, but alongside the other benefits we certainly do not consider that the amount spent by our Association during its existence for militant purposes has been extravagant.' In fact while £15 11s had been spent over the 27 years on friendly benefits per member, only £3 2s had been spent on dispute payments. The latter figure, however, had risen enormously because of the events of 1908.

The joint conference between unions and employers duly met within a fortnight of the resumption of work to establish permanent machinery for the settlement of differences. Each side agreed to draw up draft proposals as the basis for negotiation. Further meetings were then held to bring the two sets of proposals together. By November the work was completed. An agreement was reached and ratified by all parties. In the Shipwrights' case the majority in favour was only 400 out of a total vote of 5,500.

In essence it laid down machinery for the consideration of all differences between men and employers. No stoppage of work was to be allowed until all the machinery had been exhausted. With regard to wage questions, any side wanting an alteration should request a preliminary conference with the other; should ask for a change of a fixed amount of 5 per cent for piece-work and 1s a week for time rates; and would not be allowed to ask for a further change within a period of six months. Any changes were to apply to all firms and all crafts. They were to be national rather than regional.

For other questions, settlement would be sought first at yard level. Failing that, a joint committee of employers and unions would consider the issue. If they too failed to provide a solution then the matter could go up to a Local Conference and finally a national conference of the Shipbuilding Employers' Federation and the unions. There was even to be a court of final appeal called the Grand Conference, consisting of the Employers' Federation and all the unions who were party to the Agreement whether they were involved in the dispute or not. But the employers were adamant in refusing the principle of arbitration or outside conciliation.

Despite this, the Agreement which was to last for three years gave the unions most of what they wanted. Wilkie commented: 'The Agreement concedes the principle of official recognition generally and can be made a very powerful instrument to draw every society into closer connection with each other which cannot fail to benefit the individual members of the various unions.' He hoped it would be given a 'fair trial', a natural reaction for a General Secretary of a union which had just seen a net loss of £40,000 on its year's operation. There were two particular criticisms, the employers' absolute refusal to accept the principle of arbitration; and the national rather than local negotiation of changes in wage rates.

Why did the dispute occur? As the employers pointed out other trades and shipwrights in other parts of the country had accepted the reduction. There seem to have been two main causes. Firstly, the men themselves felt that they were already suffering sufficiently by the high level of unemployment with one in five out of work. Shop floor feeling was rising against further demands on the men. There was 'a strong unofficial movement basing itself on the principles of "the living wage" and local union autonomy.'[1] Secondly, there was growing disbelief in the mechanism of cutting wages to stimulate orders. Wilkie wrote in the 1908 annual report: 'It was emphatically stated by the representatives of the men that a reduction of wages would neither bring work nor induce ship-owners to build ships which they could not use at a profit; and this has been proved as, although wages have been reduced, orders have not come forward, ship-owners are still disinclined to place orders and men still continue to be unemployed.' The strength of feeling among the men in the North-East gave an opportunity to test this theory and as far as the unions were concerned the theory did not stand up in practice.

SHIPBUILDING OUTPUT

Output from British yards showed a dramatic decline in 1908. The unprecedented production of 1906 gave way to a drop of just over 10 per cent in 1907 to a total of 1.6m. gross registered tons. But in 1908 that figure was almost halved to 930,000 tons and the following year it rose only slightly to 991,000 tons. In 1910 the total rose again but it was not until 1911 that the full effects of the depression were over.

World output fell too but not quite so steeply. The result was that the British proportion of total world production dropped to 50 per cent, a lower figure than it had known for many years.

With the fall in output, unemployment rose sharply. By 1908 well over 20 per cent of shipwrights were unemployed. Over 5,000 were out of work for various periods, excluding those affected by the dispute in the North-East. Altogether the Association paid out £17,353 in unemployment benefit, by far the highest outlay under this category during its history. The next highest year was 1904 when £10,590 was paid out and the average in recent years had been about £6,000.

The unions were in no doubt that the depression had been caused by over-ordering in previous years. Writing in the 1908 annual report, Wilkie commented: 'Under the present commercial system cycles of prosperity and depression are bound to occur, the output of new tonnage in the shipbuilding trade for the last few years has been far in excess of the requirements necessary for a profitable return and the reaction was bound to come.'

This view was given support by the *Glasgow Herald*'s annual industrial review: 'For some years the floating tonnage of the world has been far in excess of requirements, even in prosperous times. Boats are plying for rates of freight that scarcely pay working expenses, yet, notwithstanding the adverse conditions under which this trade is labouring, new vessels are, or at least have been until a year ago, continually being added to the already too large tonnage. The result of this so-called enterprise is strikingly indicated by the bare stocks of the shipbuilding yards today. The time has come when the world finds itself overstocked with ships.'

The level of freight rates depended on other factors than the amount of tonnage in existence. In particular, it is necessary to take into account the national economic situation and the state of trade. In this sense, freight rates were governed by the national economic performance and could be determined by national economic policies. The lack of Government action meant that the depression had to cure itself by waiting for an upturn in world trade and particularly in world harvests.

That upturn did not occur in 1909 when even more of the Association's members were unemployed and when no less than £25,700 was spent on unemployment benefit. The total included over £8,000 of special relief grant paid out at the beginning of the year. The massive payout under this heading meant that for the second consecutive year the Association made a net loss on its year's working. A total income of £47,354, was outweighed by a total expenditure of £64,250, bringing the reserves down to £88,563, the lowest figure since 1898. If dispute payment had not fallen to £66, the outcome would have been much worse.

GOVERNMENT ACTION

Faced with the depressed state of the economy, union leaders looked to the Government for action. In 1906, John Burns, the former trade unionist who was now President of the Local Government Board and therefore responsible for dealing with unemployment, had arranged for a grant of £200,000 to the local Distress Committees. This was a start even if it did not go far enough. The Parliamentary Committee of the T.U.C. commented: 'We frankly admit that this sum is totally inadequate from the point of view of the magnitude of the problem but we must not forget that this is the first time a Government has realized its responsibility towards the unemployment problem, by a grant from national funds.' Burns was unwilling to commit the Government to any other action until the Report of the Royal Commission on the Poor Law was ready in 1909. This was an impossibly long period from the union's point of view. Burns' reputation deteriorated rapidly. In July 1907 Ramsay MacDonald introduced the Labour Party's answer to the problem, a 'right to work' Bill or The Unemployed Workmen Bill as it was properly called. This called upon local authorities to compile registers of the unemployed and 'to prepare schemes for providing work' to be paid for out of the rates. The bill did not reach a second reading. It was reintroduced, however, in March 1908 and was supported by 116 members, after what Wilkie called 'a spirited discussion'. Herbert Asquith, who had succeeded Campbell-Bannerman as Prime Minister, promised legislation in the following year and meanwhile increased the grant to the Distress Committees to £400,000. Keir Hardie declared that 'this would be quite inadequate to meet the pressing demands of the unemployed this winter.' Wilkie said: 'It is perfectly true that the causes are many and the remedy not to be found in a single Act of Parliament but at the same time if we are to do anything as a nation, the first step is to recognize our responsibility to the unemployed.'

The Royal Commission on the Poor Law reported early in 1909 and union leaders immediately began to press for the implementation of some of its many proposals. David Lloyd George who was now Chancellor of the Exchequer and Winston Churchill as President of the Board of Trade were more than willing to help. Their main measure was the establishment of labour exchanges.

In introducing this scheme, Churchill said it sprang from two defects noted by the Royal Commission—a lack of mobility and a lack of information. In setting up the scheme he wanted 'to co-operate in every way in the closest and frankest terms with the unions'. The proposed measure would also be linked with a system of compulsory unemployment insurance with contributions from the State, the workers and the employers. By the beginning of 1910 nearly 100 exchanges, controlled by the Board of Trade, had been set up. Critics pointed out that the exchanges could not produce work, only information. But as Wilkie wrote in the 1909 annual report: 'It is true they will not provide work but they create a common meeting ground for both employers and workmen who have mutual interests to serve in this respect and if thoroughly used by all sections of the industrial world will mitigate the hardships and needless tramping of men in search of employment from place to place and standing at yard gates day after day. With the advent of the advisory committees, composed of an equal number of employers and workmen, the Labour Exchanges should speedily prove their usefulness and utility in the industrial world.'

The T.U.C. Conference in September 1910 wanted more action. It called upon the Government to resurrect the 'right to work' bill. It also wanted legislation to govern minimum rates of pay and basic working conditions. 'Sweating', as it was called, existed in many industries other than tailoring, box-making and lace-finishing where the Government had set up Wages Boards in 1909. The unions wanted minimum rates fixed for all industries and in particular a 3s a week minimum for adult government workers in London. They were also critical of the national old-age pension scheme introduced in 1909. This provided for pensions of 5s a week for those over 70 with incomes of less than 10s a week at a cost to the nation of £7.5m., a far cry from the original demands.

In all of these measures, the Labour representatives in the House of Commons, including Wilkie and Jenkins of the Shipwrights' Association, felt that they had made some progress despite the disappointments. Certainly compared with the previous Conservative administration the period 1906-1910 had been one of progress. 'Thus it came about that while many of the rank and file became critical of the limited attainments of

The Men who launched the *Mauretania*, one of the world's greatest ships, on 20th September 1906.

The Executive Committee and General Staff of the Shipconstructors' and Shipwrights' Association in 1908.

their parliamentary representatives, the latter, though they wanted more and complained of the government's tardiness and parsimony, were conscious of much solid achievements.'[2]

In other words, union leaders were ready to take what they could rather than what was ideal. On old age pensions, for example, Wilkie had this mild comment: 'Later on, efforts will be made to further extend the Old Age Pensions by reducing the age and increasing the amount.' Hardly a sweeping criticism but he, like other trade union members of Parliament, was finding that the Liberal Government under Asquith was not as congenial as it had been under Campbell-Bannerman. His natural moderation and the financial losses of the past two years were other factors. It was better to wait until the economic and industrial climate improved. In fact, things were to get worse rather than better.

CHAPTER FIFTEEN

Although trade now began to improve noticeably and the pace of shipbuilding quickened, it did not lead to an equal reduction in unemployment. In fact the country faced a paradox of a booming economy unable to provide work for all who sought it. Partly as a result but also due to other factors, a period of considerable industrial unrest was about to begin. The legal position of unions was again put in jeopardy—this time over their right to spend money on political purposes and constitutional crises wracked the country. But overlying all the growing complexities of industrial life, there was a still greater threat; the unmistakable signs of impending warfare.

WARSHIP BUILDING

As the century progressed, the demand for warships became more rather than less intense. It was an appetite that fed on itself as countries vied with each other to have the latest 'machines of death'. Some countries, notably in South America, were spending a quarter of their national income on warships. Others doubled their expenditure on these mighty men of war within the space of ten years. In fact in the ten years from 1904 to 1914 the eight leading navies of the world spent an estimated £1,340 million, a half of which went on new warships. Nor was this country exempt. Britain had moved from a position of 'splendid isolation' in her foreign policy to one of alliances with various countries, particularly France, while Germany, Austria and Italy were bound together in another alliance. Europe was now divided into two rival armed camps which viewed each other with great suspicion. Every move made by one power was countered by a move from another.

In particular, Germany and Britain were watching one another with great alarm and apprehension. When Germany started a building programme which would give her thirteen extra battleships and armoured cruisers by 1912, there was instant reaction in London. But while reaction was instant, it was by no means unanimous. A split developed in the Cabinet between those who thought four new battleships would be sufficient and those who wanted six. The Conservative opposition was more united and more insistent. They wanted eight and campaigned under the slogan: 'We want eight and we won't wait'. The Government compromised by ordering four new battleships with a further four to be laid down if events in Germany warranted it. Warship fever had afflicted this country as much as any other. While the implications of this fever were ominous, there were at least some beneficial effects in terms of the extra work created. As Wilkie commented in the 1910 annual report: 'It is said that the money now spent on naval preparations could be spent more profitably in other channels of social reform; that may be but of that we have no proof as yet. But what we do know is that a wholesale reduction of armaments would create an army of unemployed workmen which there is no guarantee would be relieved.'

With regard to the central discussion of whether to rearm or not, Wilkie took the conventional view. 'We are no advocates for unnecessary expenditure on armaments, at the same time it is necessary for us to deal with the condition of things as they exist. If other nations are rapidly increasing their naval strength, then, in the interests of national security, whether we like it or not, we are bound to do the same.' It was the prevalance of this point of view which helped to stoke the fires of war for, pushed to its conclusion, warfare became inevitable.

The Labour Party was deeply concerned about the trend of events and called a special conference on disarmament and the international situation in January 1911. Ramsay MacDonald, who took the chair, made a highly impassioned speech in which he restated the traditional aims of the Party. 'We are going to feed the underfed child, we are going to take care of the underfed man, we are going to take the lost and abandoned woman by the hand and lead her into better ways and better paths ... We are going to stretch our hands to our French comrades, stretch our hands to our German comrades and all other comrades from the North Pole to the South and from the rising to the setting sun and we are going to proclaim that blessed day when the sword will be finally sheathed and when nations will pursue the ways of peace and follow the arts of war no more.'

The conference then passed a motion highly critical of Government policy protesting against 'the heavy and growing burden of armaments which arrests social reform and endangers international solidarity, goodwill and peace.'

Unfortunately such resolutions, no matter how impassioned, were of little use in stopping the inexorable movement towards war.

STATE OF TRADE

While naval building was going ahead very rapidly, private shipbuilding was also picking up. Output in 1910 was 1.1m. gross registered tons, 10 per cent up on the previous year, and Britain's share of world output returned to 58 per cent. Among the year's launchings was the White Star liner *Olympic*, the largest vessel afloat. Built by Harland and

Wolff in Belfast it was 45,000 tons and 882 ft. long. There was accommodation for 2,500 passengers and 860 crew.

At the beginning of the year many areas were reporting that trade was 'very bad', as at Walker or Barrow, or 'slack' as at Newcastle or Sunderland. By the end, typical reports were that trade was 'fair', 'improving' and in some places 'good' or 'very good'.

But notwithstanding the improvement in trade there were still many members out of work. In fact over a quarter were idle for varying periods and no less than £28,000 was spent by the Association on unemployment benefit. The sum included £20,000 paid out as a special grant to members affected by the 14-week dispute involving the Boilermakers. The dispute led eventually to a lock-out by the employers which affected shipwrights as much as other trades. The dispute cost the General Federation of Trade Unions over £53,000. The special grant was proposed by the Executive Committee and endorsed by a large majority. It was to be recouped by a levy of 3d a week from all members.

The dispute indicated that the Shipbuilding Agreement of 1909 needed further amplification. Meetings between unions and employers were held late in 1910 when it was eventually agreed to add some explanatory clauses. In particular, machinery was necessary to decide whether or not a stoppage had taken place in breach of the Agreement. It was decided that local committees should be called upon to adjudicate. Although this got over the special difficulty, it did not go far enough for the unions. Wilkie was still lamenting the absence of conciliation machinery. 'The lesson which experience of the Agreement in its working and the dispute enforces seems to be plain, that is the necessity for either a neutral chairman or the inclusion of a final clause providing in the end, for any matter under dispute to be submitted to a reference'. The employers were still absolutely opposed to this idea.

The large expenditure on unemployment benefit meant that for the third year running the Association made a loss on its operations. With income of £57,864 and outlay of £67,328 there was a net loss of £9,564 bringing the reserve fund at 31st December 1910 down to £79,098. In the three years 1908-10 the Association had made a total loss of £67,000 virtually halving its reserves. In the circumstances, Wilkie regarded it as essential that the funds should be built up again through the levy of 3d a week. In view of the rising level of trade he felt that this would be no hardship. Nor did he have much time for those who complained that they had never received anything from the Association. They ought to be thankful that they had never been unemployed or ill and therefore in need of benefit. 'By our rules and regulations', he wrote, in the annual report for 1910, 'the many have to assist the few, the fortunate to aid the unfortunate, the employed the unemployed, the healthy the sick, the young the aged'. As fine a declaration as one could hope to find of the brotherhood of man which underlaid the work of trade unions.

The Association now had 21,631 members with the assimilation of the Wear, Tees and Hartlepool Drillers' Society and there were 141 branches.

THE OSBORNE CASE

The Osborne case was one of those important legal disputes which seemed to put a new constraint upon the unions. Like the Taff Vale case in 1900 it appeared to impose restrictions which were not there before. The case which was heard in 1909 was a simple one. Mr W. V. Osborne was a branch secretary of the Amalgamated Society of Railway Servants. Although a strong unionist, he believed equally strongly in personal liberty. He thought it was wrong for funds to be raised by unions solely for the support of the Labour Party. He stated to the T.U.C. Conference in 1905: 'Let them have Parliamentary representation as much as they like but let it be by and under the control of their own people'. The 1906 conference, however, accepted a socialist motion binding future union parliamentary representatives to the Labour Party. Osborne was so upset by this decision that he sought an injunction against the decision in the law courts. It was granted in 1908 and upheld by the House of Lords in December 1909. The Railway Servants Union was to be prevented from spending its funds for political purposes, a decision which seemed to threaten all trade union political activity and to undermine support for the Labour Party.

This decision in fact went further than Osborne intended. For he was not opposed to political action as such but rather to the compulsory political levies which some unions, including the shipwrights, had introduced and to the inevitable association with the Labour Party. He was an old-fashioned Lib-Lab himself and would have preferred a wider choice of political bed-fellows than the unions allowed.

The unions were naturally quick to react. A special conference of the Labour Party, the T.U.C. and the General Federation of Trade Unions was held in February 1910. It agreed to uphold the right of trade unions to engage in political activities 'provided that a majority of members agreed' and sought immediate action to amend the law. Immediate action was not forthcoming, however, partly because the unions were not unanimous. Some members were undoubtedly opposed to compulsory levies on all as the result of majority votes and some were undoubtedly unhappy about the automatic support for the Labour Party. It was November 1910 before the Asquith Government announced its intentions. They were far-ranging. Members of Parliament were to be paid and so were their official election expenses. This would reduce the need for political levies. But Unions could still raise such levies if they wanted to and the raising of such funds was to be included among the purposes of trade unions. But 'there shall be no compulsion upon any member to contribute to the fund'.

The constitutional crisis of 1910 which led to two general elections within a year, the Irish crisis and the Home Rule Bill, delayed comprehensive action. The State payment of M.P.'s was introduced in 1911. Legislation to restore the unions' freedom to raise political levies had to wait until 1913. This legislation when it did come, safeguarded the right of an individual not to pay such a levy and without the threat of victimization if he refused. It stipulated that political levies were to be paid into a separate fund quite distinct from the general funds. These levies could be introduced only after a ballot showing a majority in favour. The Trade Union Act of 1913 thus virtually restored the position as it was before the Osborne case but in the meantime the Labour Party had suffered some reverses.

GENERAL ELECTIONS

Two general elections were held in 1910, an unusual event in itself. But more important, both elections were concerned with a question of fundamental importance to the political and social development of Britain: whether the House of Commons which was elected by the people (or at least a large part of them) was to be supreme or whether ultimate power lay with the House of Lords, representing hereditary power. The country had arrived at a constitutional crisis and two general elections were needed to break the deadlock.

The issue was the reforming legislation being put forward by the Liberal Government. For while the pace of social and industrial reform might have been too slow for the socialists and some trade unionists, it was certainly too fast for the Tories, especially as they were represented in their massed ranks in the House of Lords. They had not liked the Trade Union Act of 1906 which in effect placed unions outside the law. They did not like the proposals for old age pensions, particularly the call for a State contribution of £1.2m. Such a measure reflected the State's acceptance of the principle of promoting the welfare of all citizens at the common expense, a dangerous doctrine according to the Tories, all the more abhorrent because it implied the redistribution of income and shifting the balance of taxation. The budget of 1907 had started this process by taxing 'unearned income' more heavily than 'earned income'. The budget of 1909 went a great deal further by proposing a 'super tax' on incomes over £5,000, higher death duties and a tax on unearned rises in the value of land. All of this was too much for the Tory-dominated House of Lords. They took the unprecedented step of refusing to pass the Finance Bill which contained the Budget provisions. So clear an affront to the Commons had never been given before. Relatively small measures had sometimes been sent back to the Commons for further consideration. But not something as important as the budget.

The Liberal Government retaliated by calling an election in January 1910 on the theme of who was to govern—'the People or the Peers'. The outcome was never in doubt although the Liberals did lose some seats. But its alliance with the Labour Party, which was firmer than ever, and the support of the Irish Nationalists, who backed the Liberals' Home Rule proposals, ensured a decisive Government majority.

The Labour Party put up seventy-eight candidates, including miners' representatives who now agreed to fight under the party banner. Of these, forty were successful. The party lost eight seats and won three. The result, according to the Labour Party's official record indicates that it had 'a wonderfully strong grip upon the country'. Its total vote was 505,000, up by 183,000 since 1906 and representing 36 per cent of all constituencies where Labour Party members stood. Despite the increase, John Jenkins, the shipwrights' Bristol delegate, lost his seat at Chatham. He was defeated by 7,500 votes to 6,130. The total number of votes in his favour was slightly down on 1906 but the Conservatives had increased their votes substantially from 4,000 in 1906.

In Dundee, Wilkie held one of the two seats with a big increase in his vote. He polled 10,369. The other seat was won by Winston Churchill with 10,746 votes.

The Budget now went through the Houses of Commons and Lords. But when the Government put forward legislation to prevent this sort of constitutional crisis occurring again, the Lords demurred once more. They did not exactly turn it down but they did the next best thing. They put forward so many amendments that the Government felt it had no recourse but to go to the country again.

The issue of 'People versus the Peers' had been answered decisively although in the end it required a threat from George V that he would, if necessary, create 250 Liberal peers to ensure the Bill's passage through a reluctant and obstructive House of Lords. In the same year the Government pushed through a measure to pay members of Parliament.

Of more direct relevance to the general public and the trade unions in particular was the National Insurance Act. Wilkie called it 'the outstanding Act of the year' and said 'its supreme importance to the trade unions of the country cannot be over-estimated'. This far-reaching and complicated Act set up a vast contributory scheme to insure all the working classes against sickness and unemployment. Now such an insurance scheme was very much of the essence of trade unions' work. Indeed, it would not be too much to say that many members belonged to trade unions simply because of the benefit schemes of which sickness and unemployment benefits were the most important. The Act, therefore, could have undermined the union's work and purpose. Cleverly, Lloyd George got around this potential opposition by proposing that trade unions (and established friendly societies) should be classified as 'approved societies' for administering the monetary benefit to their members.

Wilkie wrote in the 1911 annual report: 'The essential point which concerns our Association and our members as trade unionists is how to adapt our machinery in order to obtain fullest advantage of the Act and at the same time retain our fullest freedom as a trade union to assist our members in improving their conditions and increasing their remuneration. The most effective way in which we can do this is for all our members as trade unionists to make their own Society the Approved Society under Part I of the Act. It is not a matter of competition with the great Friendly Societies of the country who under the Act will still have an enormous field hitherto untouched to work on but the question of our members and trade unionists generally making it their first duty to preserve their trade union intact.'

Combined with free medical inspection and treatment of children in schools the new Act did a great deal to improve the nation's standards of health. The unemployed provisions allowed for benefits of 6s a week for fifteen weeks. The worker was to contribute 2½d as was his employer, and the State 1d.

Because of Lloyd George's astute move in bringing unions into the scheme, there was not only no adverse effect but on the contrary a positive advantage. Union membership, particularly among the lower grades, increased markedly. The total number of union members represented at the 1911 T.U.C. was 1·6m; by 1913 the number was 2·6m, an increase of 60 per cent in two years.

BOOM TIME

The economic depression was now over. For the four years leading up to the war shipbuilding output excluding warships was always in excess of 1·6m gross registered tons. In 1911 the total was 1·8m tons which represented 68 per cent of total world output.

With the dramatic increase in production, unemployment fell and the Association paid out only £1,000 for unemployment benefit, mostly in January. Correspondingly, there were increases in wages. The Shipbuilding Agreement was used to secure general wage increases of a shilling a week (or 5 per cent for piece workers) in February and a similar increase in October. Shipwrights on the Tyne now received 39s 6d for new work and 42s 6d for old or repair work. In addition, the Association was able to settle a 'long vexed question' of securing parity between wage rates in the North-East and in Scotland at least for new work. Shipwrights on the Clyde and in Dundee, Aberdeen, Leith and Grangemouth were given an extra farthing an hour so that in all in 1911 they received increases of 3s 4½d a week to bring their rate to 39s 6d for new work. Other parts of the country were also successful in securing increases. In London, there was success of another kind. Employers conceded the 48-hour week in both winter and summer. Elsewhere, the working week remained at either 54 hours throughout the year or 54 hours in the summer and 48 in the winter, mainly because of the darker days and later starting.

The outstanding feature of the year in industrial relations was the plethora of strikes. Over 870 were recorded resulting in over 10m. working days lost. A particularly severe strike occurred in the Welsh mining industry. It lasted for ten months and was marked by rioting. Dockers and seamen were also very militant in demanding new wages. There was a short general strike in the London docks and a more prolonged affair in Liverpool. The railwaymen also called the first national railway strike which lasted for only two days but which gained the men the recognition by the employers that they wanted.

Wilkie commented: 'Never in our history has there been a year of such industrial unrest.' He ascribed the cause to the recent depression, the reduction in earning power and the disparity between the incomes of various classes. In addition compulsory education had led to an awakening of expectations. 'The unrest is the natural result of the awakening. It is the voice of the masses demanding more of the material things of life, better opportunities for themselves and their children, a greater recognition and a more adequate return for the social services they render. The unrest has not been the work of a few. It is the work of the people themselves, it is the revolt against low wages, long hours, bad housing and unfair conditions; it is a demand for equal opportunities to participate more in the world's treasure, its leisure and pleasure.'

Despite the general unrest, the Association's outlay on dispute benefits came to only £3,000. Unemployment benefits were also substantially down and even sickness and accident benefits cost only £15,400 which was £1,000 less than in 1910. The upshot was that total expenditure was £43,700 which was £24,000 less than in the previous year.

Income, on the other hand, was at a record level of £67,000 or £10,000 more than in 1910 thanks to full employment and the 3d levy. As a result the Association had a net surplus of £23,000, the first in three years, and the funds went up to £102,000. Membership rose to virtually 23,000.

CHAPTER SIXTEEN

Industrial troubles which had been so prevalent in 1911 reached a crescendo in 1912. Almost 41m. working days were lost, the third highest figure on record. But although the disputes affected many sectors of industry, the Shipwrights escaped. They had one of their best years.

INDUSTRIAL TROUBLE

The omens were bleak as the year opened. It was only too clear that the miners and the mine owners were on a collision course particularly after the men had seen the effective use of the national strike weapon by the railwaymen in August 1911. By February 1912 the Miners' Federation had called a national strike to secure mimimum wages of five shillings a shift for men and two shillings a shift for boys. The owners had claimed they could not afford such a concession at a time of falling output per man and the miners struck. Almost immediately large sections of British industry were affected and within a few weeks railways as well as factories were grinding to a halt. The Government decided it had to intervene and after consultations with both sides rushed through Parliament a bill setting up local boards with independent chairmen to lay down minimum wages, but not necessarily the five shillings that was demanded.

Wilkie felt strongly about the dispute. Writing in the Quarterly Report for January-March 1912 he said: 'Had a few trade unionists caused such an upheaval in our industries, the whole country and the press would have rung with their denunciations, but when a few coal-owners, quite indifferent to the interests of the community, by their attitude bring about such a condition of things, then little or nothing is said.'

The Government's initiative was just enough to satisfy the miners. After a ballot they agreed to return to work in April. Thousands of other workers could also return to normal.

Hardly had they gone back than there was another serious strike, this time in the London docks over the employment of non-unionists. The National Transport Workers' Federation called out all its members throughout the country because of the tough attitude adopted by the newly-constituted Port of London Authority, under its chairman, Lord Devonport. The call for a national strike, clearly imitating the action of the railwaymen and the miners, largely failed. The dockers did not have the same sense of national unity. Only the Bristol docks offered genuine support. The strike collapsed and by August many of those involved were desperately trying to get their jobs back.

These two strikes were largely responsible for the appallingly high number of working days lost but even in 1913 and 1914 without any national strikes, the figures remained near the 10m. mark.

The causes for this remarkable outburst of militancy have engaged the attention of commentators and historians ever since. It is probable that they were numerous and intertwined. The Trade Union Act of 1906 which restored the legal immunity of trade unions and their freedom to engage in peaceful picketing removed a restraint. The full employment conditions following the depression of 1908-10 provided an opportunity and the sharp rise in the cost of living offered a motive. Since the end of the nineteenth century the cost of living had been rising gently. In the six years 1902-1908 it went up by 4 to 5 per cent but between 1909 and 1913 it shot up by another 9 per cent. The pressure on unions and union leaders to counter its effects by securing wage rises was correspondingly increased. Not all industries had the machinery, as the shipbuilding industry had, to absorb this pressure in a peaceful way and to respond to it. Indeed, in some industries as we have seen, the employers hardly recognized the unions and this was a fundamental element in many of the disputes. Wage rises may have been the ostensible cause but union recognition was even more important as the basic aim.

Equally there was a growing conviction that there should be a more equitable distribution of the nation's wealth. Wilkie returned to this theme time and time again. Writing of the outcome of the miners' dispute he said: 'We wish it had been more favourable to the men who have made such a splendid stand for a decent wage and fair conditions of labour.' In the 32nd annual report for the year 1913 he widened his remarks to describe in general terms the 'fuller life' as he saw it. It would be: 'a life which will enable them to live decently, under proper housing conditions, to obtain a larger measure of the reward of labour, to develop his (sic) mind, to have greater opportunities for leisure so that himself, his wife and children may become real citizens. ... The problem of wealth production has been largely solved: improved machinery, invention, better organization of industry has increased our productivity as a nation enormously. What we must bring our minds to is to more equally distribute the product of that wealth so that all willing and able to work shall be assured a living wage based on a reasonable standard of comfort, decent conditions of employment and proper housing accommodation.'

Will Thorne, of the Gasworkers, who was President of the T.U.C. in 1912, made the same point in his address to conference. 'Labour unrest cannot cease,' he declared, 'nor can the tide of industrial revolt be stemmed until remedial measures are brought about and the present social inequalities removed. We want a better distribution of wealth.' He estimated that in 1869 when the first T.U.C. conference was called, gross national product had been £800m., of which the workers had received half. In 1911 the country's output was £2,000m., of which the workers received £800m., much less than half.

The 14th annual conference of the Labour Party held in January 1914 accepted unanimously a resolution which claimed that labour unrest could be ended only by the abolition of the capitalist system. There should be a legal minimum wage for each industry, a maximum working week of 48 hours, the abolition of unemployment and decent homes for all.

The trade union movement which on the whole had been concerned initially with the conditions within industry and with operating various benefit schemes for members, now almost without exception saw its role in a wider political and social context. It also saw that many of its grievances could be resolved only by political action. As Wilkie said, workers had to use 'all the means at their disposal either by trade union effort or by Parliamentary action, to obtain a fairer share of the wealth they help to create and a more equitable distribution of the results of industry.'

Other unionists wanted even stronger action. They were disillusioned not only with the state of society but also with the remedies proposed by their more conservative colleagues. Thus we see the growing call for industry unions (i.e. unions based on particular industries rather than on particular crafts) and for syndicalism or the control of industry by the workers. The employers were to be eliminated, not by the socialist process of nationalization, but by revolution. The workers would then be in full control deciding how much to produce and by what methods.

They were radical measures and they failed. There was only one important union amalgamation on an industry basis before the First World War. Three railway unions joined forces to form the National Union of Railwaymen but their success was incomplete. For the footplatemen and the clerks refused to join and their unions remained independent. Equally the syndicalist movement had some success among the miners of South Wales but overall had little impact. The respect for parliamentary methods, despite frequent denunciations of 'judge-made laws' as in the Osborne case, was widely and deeply held among nearly all sectors of trade union opinion. Revolution was not for Britain.

THE ASSOCIATION

The widespread labour unrest hardly affected the Shipwrights. In 1912 it expended only £1,450 on strike pay and in 1913 the figure was even better at £715. Such low outlays were 'in great measure due to the work and efforts of your District and General officials who have in many cases at all hours and in all weather, to travel many miles to reach the seat of dispute and deal with it before too much feeling is engendered.'

(Annual Report 1912, page 14.) Nor were the shipwrights affected indirectly by the other disputes. In 1912 unemployment benefit cost only £550, the lowest level since 1899 and in 1913 it was £1,174.

These low figures reflected the state of trade which was buoyant. In both years shipbuilding output was near or at historically record levels. District delegates or technical advisers as they were now called could all report surging demand. Timothy McDonic talked of an 'unprecedented boom in trade' on the Wear and Tees in the spring of 1912. By the winter he was still commenting: 'The boom in shipbuilding in our district still continues.' Thomas Hill on the Clyde was saying the same thing. In spring 1912 trade was in a 'prosperous condition'. By the year-end: 'It is very gratifying to state that our members in Scotland are fully employed and there is every indication that the same briskness will continue in 1913.' It did.

In the circumstances wages rose continuously. In 1912 shipwrights in the Clyde, Tyne, Tees, Wear, Barrow, Hull, Birkenhead, Leith, Dundee and Aberdeen areas known as the Federation area got an increase of a shilling a week or 5 per cent on piece work. Their colleagues in other parts of the country secured advances too, in some cases even greater. At Preston and Fleetwood, wages went up by two shillings a week and in Bristol drillers received an extra 2s 6d per week.

In 1913 similar advances were agreed, bringing the rate to 41s 6d per week for shipwrights in the Federated area, basically the North of England and Scotland. For old or repair work the rate was three shillings higher at 44s 6d.

Even in the Dockyards where annual petitions had to be submitted, often with little effect, there was considerable success. The Admiralty agreed to increase wages for shipwrights in the dockyards from 36s to 38s a week, an increase which cost the country £35,000 a year. All of these increases had been secured by negotiation, another example according to Wilkie, of the benefit of union organization and another reason for 100 per cent membership particularly in the dockyards. 'We consider we are justified in respectfully appealing to all Dockyard Shipwrights who are not members of our Association to join,' he wrote in the 1913 annual report.

This appeal was successful in the dockyards and elsewhere. By the end of 1913 there were 171 branches. One of the oldest and most independent of the local societies, the London Provident Shipwrights' Society, had agreed to assimilate, taking membership up to almost 27,000. Only the Liverpool Provident Shipwrights' Society now remained aloof.

The reduction in expenditure and the rise in membership income produced good financial figures. In 1912 there was a net surplus of £24,000 and in 1913 of £8,400, taking the reserves up to £135,000. This was still short of the figure of £147,000 reached in 1907 but the climb back from the three disastrous years of 1908-1910 had been dramatic. In the first thirty-two years of its existence it had raised almost £1m. and expended about £840,000. As Wilkie said in the report for 1912: 'When we inaugurated our reconstituted Association thirty-one years ago, few of any of the founders ever dreamed of the vast amount of work that would be accomplished in thirty-one short years.' It certainly was an achievement of which he in particular could be proud. It may have been unspectacular but it was solid, purposeful and very effective.

WILKIE AS AN M.P.

One marvels at the work that Wilkie and fellow trade union leaders got through. Running a big union like the Shipwrights was job enough with all the detailed work that it entailed. But to be an M.P. as well with prime responsibilities towards the constituents of Dundee and his colleagues in the Labour Party was surely herculean. Of course 'Sandy' Wilkie, as he was called by his friends, was well rewarded. He now received £275 a year from the union (about £5 10s a week, more than double a shipwright's wages) and he also received £400 a year from the State as an M.P.'s allowance. Equally, he had an assistant and more district representatives and committees on which to devolve some of the work. It was still a heavy burden, particularly for someone as conscientious as Wilkie.

The burden will become clearer if we examine his Parliamentary work. As one would expect, he nearly always took part in the debates on the Naval Estimates which considered the Government's spending on the Navy and the programme of construction. He was concerned with two major themes; the conditions of employment including the rates of pay; and the building programme with its implications for world peace. On the first theme, he was particularly concerned with naval shipwrights. In the debate on 21st March 1911 he pointed out that there had been no alteration in their ratings for the past thirty-four years. He could not understand why the Admiralty stuck to 'fossilized old notions'. If the country depended upon the Navy, as the Admiralty said it did, then the safety of ships themselves depended upon the skilled shipwrights and carpenters on board. 'That being so, what we do ask is that they should be put on an equality of rating with the new rating the Admiralty are establishing as on their work and their ability depends the safety of the ship.' In 1912 the situation was made even worse by the new pay and conditions offered to certain ratings but not to all. He asked on 31st March 1913 in that year's debate on Naval Estimates: 'Why should the Admiralty, to men with equal responsibility and of equal rank, mete out so much difference in the pay and also in position? I think this sort of thing should stop and, whatever is done, they should all have fair play from the Admiralty.' He pointed out that a skilled engineer, as chief petty officer, received 5s 6d a day while a skilled shipwright with equal training and skill received only 4s a day. 'You can see why there is unrest and discontent when these inequalities exist,' he declared.

He was also concerned about the fluctuations in trade. At certain periods unemployment among dockyard shipwrights reached 30 per cent; at other times there was over-demand for their services. On 4th July 1911 he said in the House of Commons: 'The workers are asserting that they are either starved to death or, as at present, worked to death.' He thought there was need for a better system of evening out the flow of work to mitigate the normal fluctuations in private shipbuilding.

His most bitter comments were directed at the Government's defence policy which he thought brought the chances of war nearer. He blamed the Government for the world-wide demand for Dreadnoughts and warships. In the debate on 31st March 1913 he declared: 'Who started the "Dreadnought" building and the "Dreadnought" scare? It was started by the hon. Gentlemen opposite (the Tories) when they were in power in 1904 and 1905 and they built the first "Dreadnought" in twelve months and they went swaggering all over the world declaring we could build ships quicker than others and that we had the ships and the men and the money too. That is one of the causes of the naval laws in other countries and it is more or less the cause of the naval unrest right throughout the world. That is the cause of all the smaller nations in the Western hemisphere building "Dreadnoughts".'

In a statement of faith which was to occur to many others then and since, he said: 'I do not say a word of disparagement against Germany because the workers of the world have no quarrels one with another. Quarrels are made by the rulers and as soon as we make this House thoroughly democratic, and it is becoming more democratic year by year, and as soon as we can get the views of the people properly and clearly expressed we will be able to get nearer and nearer to the real democratic sentiment of the world.'

Even the argument about providing employment, which he had used in previous years, no longer seemed to carry so much weight with him. There would, he said, be plenty of employment in maintaining and repairing warships.

When the same view was put during the Navy Estimates debate in 1911 it was defeated. Mr G. H. Roberts of the Typographical Association had moved that 'the increasing expenditure on the Navy is not justified by foreign events and is a menace to peace and national security' but it was defeated by 54 to 216. Surprisingly, similar motions were not put forward in the following years when they were even more urgently needed. The Labour Party at this time was concentrating on a number of measures including an amendment to the Trade Union Law (after the Osborne case), the right to work, an eight-hour day and minimum wages of 30s a week for adults in urban areas. It was also concerned with the provision of school meals and the nationalization of coal mines. It did not have any success with any of these measures with the exception of the amendment of trade union law.

Wilkie took part in national debates but also showed interest in more local matters. For example in 1911 he raised questions about the training of teachers in Scotland. In 1912 he probed the way that a smallpox epidemic in Scotland was dealt with. And he was concerned with the operation of the Shops Act in Newcastle.

With the retirement of Thomas Burt, Wilkie, now aged sixty-three, was the oldest trade union general secretary in the country and with the growth of the shipwrights' union, that job alone remained an onerous one. He was an active Member of Parliament. He was a Newcastle City Councillor. He was a trustee of the General Federation of Trade Unions and he sat on many committees. It was a demanding life and it is no wonder that his health began to fail a little. In 1913 the attacks of sciatica and lumbago which had plagued him for some years intensified. He was now in considerable pain. In the end he could stand it no longer and was ordered by his doctor to rest and to have remedial treatment. He went to Vichy in France for a few weeks, thus missing the annual general meeting of the General Federation of Trade Unions for the first time. It was held at the beginning of July. But by 14th July he was back at work and taking part in negotiations.

CLOSER UNITY

Numerous attempts were made at this time to achieve closer unity among trade unions. The 12th annual report of the General Federation of Trade Unions noted that the Federation had 'continually advised and sought to promote the amalgamation of unions entering for similar occupations'. But without much success. On a higher sphere there were proposals to amalgamate the Federation, the Labour Party and the Trades Union Congress.

The Labour Party was particularly anxious to pursue this proposal and urged its serious consideration. It also wanted a central building in Westminster for the labour movement. But the General Federation, despite its call for union amalgamation, was unwilling to agree to this scheme. It felt that the 'best results' could be achieved by maintaining a 'separate identity and autonomy' but co-operating with other bodies on all matters of national importance. The Federation took this view because it 'had quite enough work in the ordinary industrial side'. Indeed, the work had increased enormously in 1911-12 when it had been involved in 719 disputes. But, more important, the Federation was opposed to any scheme of amalgamation which had a 'distinctly political basis and aims'.

In vain, Arthur Henderson, M.P., general secretary of the Ironfounders, and others tried to describe the effects of separate bodies. At the Federation's 13th annual meeting in July 1912 he said: 'They had been speaking in the name of Labour with more than one voice. If, as a Federation, they were going to do any political work, they ought to do it in the closest co-operation with those who were in a better position to do it than they were. No middle course could be satisfactory.' His motion was defeated however by 46 votes to 21.

When the Trades Union Congress at its conference at Newport in 1912 turned down a proposal for unification put forward by the Boilermakers' Society, that was the end of the matter. The Labour Party was left as the only supporter of the scheme. The 13th annual report commented: 'We regret that the efforts of the past few years have ended so unfortunately particularly in view of the welcome tendency to closer organization that is evident in the trade union world generally. Nevertheless we trust that the movement as a whole will at no distant date come to share our continued conviction that the proposals for which we have been responsible are both essential and desirable, if the industrial and political interests of the organized workers are to be promoted in the most effective and efficient manner.'

SHIPWRIGHTS AND BOILERMAKERS

While there was little progress in general, the Shipwrights and Boilermakers did achieve considerable success in producing closer working arrangements. Representative committees of both unions had four meetings of which the first was held on 28th October 1912. At this meeting each union submitted proposals which were then taken away for consideration. A year then elapsed before the second meeting on 28th November 1913. That meeting unanimously accepted the principle of closer unity as a step towards amalgamation and set up a sub-committee of five from each side to draft detailed proposals for a further meeting on 14th-15th January 1914.

The proposals, when delivered, were far-reaching. They were that joint action should be taken on all matters affecting both unions, particularly concerning the alteration of working hours, changes in wage rates, organization including questions of non-members and members in arrears, and yard or shop conditions. There was to be a joint fund created from contributions of 3d per quarter per member. This fund would be used to pay out dispute benefits of 3s a week for eight weeks in addition to the amounts paid by each union to its members if there should be a dispute arising out of joint action against employers. Payments out of this fund could be authorized only by the Joint Central Board consisting of five representatives of each executive. The two general secretaries would be appointed as 'central administrative authority'. There were also to be joint district boards for each area of the country with district delegates or technical advisers acting as joint convenors.

Furthermore, there was to be a court of reference. In the first instance, this was to consist of three members from each union. If they failed to agree three 'disinterested' trade unionists from the district were to be selected as referees to decide the issue.

These proposals were accepted by the January meetings and recommended to members as the first step towards complete amalgamation. They 'would keep the object free from intricate and enormous difficulties of merging contributions and benefits of both organizations into one and would be of immediate and practical advantage to the members of the respective organizations and the initial step to the fuller consolidation of the two societies in the future.' They were also seen as an effective answer to the growing solidarity of employers' organizations.

When put to the shipwrights, the proposals received approval but by only a small majority, 2,427 voting in favour and 2,185 against. The Boilermakers' vote was even more confused. Their attitude seemed to be that only full amalgamation would produce the desired benefits. Before further action or a clarification of views could take place, war intervened. The proposals were shelved.

Three years elapsed before they were looked at again. Then, on 1st June 1917, the Executive Committees of the Shipwrights and Boilermakers, on the initiative of the latter, looked at the question once more. The previous division of opinion still persisted. The shipwrights wanted to resuscitate the agreement of January 1914 which they thought would provide an effective start to eventual amalgamation. The boilermakers wanted to go for complete integration straight away despite the difficulties. After further discussions, however, they accepted that the previous agreement was better than nothing at all and it was decided to send out a joint circular to members of both unions calling for approval or the original agreement. This time the vote by the shipwrights showed an overwhelming majority in favour, by 4,878 to 988 while the boilermakers too accepted the practical agreement as the best way forward.

The two executive committees met again in the Station Hotel, Newcastle, on 18th August 1917. John Hill, general secretary of the Boilermakers' Society, expressed the hope that eventually full amalgamation would be achieved but that meanwhile they had gone as far as they could. He wanted the Joint Fund to be set up as soon as possible to provide 'a full consummation of the scheme'. The meeting agreed that the first subscriptions to the Fund should be paid in the current financial quarter, i.e. before 30th September 1917. Over £700 was put into the Fund by the shipwrights in 1917 and over £1,660 in the first full year.

Strangely there was no official comment about the scheme in the annual report. Such an important measure, so close to Wilkie's heart, would surely have merited an entry, one would have thought, but not so. It was an odd omission.

In looking ahead to the eventual outcome of the agreement between the boilermakers and the shipwrights, we have slid over an event of vital importance to the union and to the world as a whole, namely the First World War. We must now turn to study its impact.

CHAPTER SEVENTEEN

The war which now paralysed Europe, slaughtered and maimed millions and adversely affected the social and political life of the country, was paradoxically a good period for the shipwrights. In the four years wages almost doubled, employment was constantly high and the hours of work came down from an average of 54 per week to 47. But, on the wider view, Britain's pre-eminent place among the world's shipbuilding countries slipped as other nations boosted their production. And this caused grave fears for the future because high production on the one hand and good wages and working conditions on the other went together.

THE APPROACH TO WAR

War overtook the shipwrights as it overtook British society, almost by stealth. There was an overwhelming tendency to ignore its approach, to dismiss the rival armament programmes and to continue with 'business as usual', in Churchill's phrase. This country had been at peace for a hundred years. It was difficult, indeed almost impossible, to imagine war. Such episodes as the Crimea or the Boer War had been regarded as rather romantic ventures, at least by those not involved in them and that included the vast majority of people. For them war was an unreal condition and its approach seemed equally unreal.

Industrial life went on as usual. No special preparations were made. No Government plans were announced. There was no need for panic. The employers and the unions could carry on as normal. And so the shipwrights' quarterly reports dealt strictly with union matters. Even the report for the first quarter of 1914 which was prepared in April-May started with the words: 'Trade continued good during the quarter and our members were fully employed in both new and repair work.' Equally, the technical advisers concentrated on their usual business. But by the end of the second quarter there could be no escape. And on 4th August 1914 war was declared against Germany.

At first, the attitude of the Labour Party and of the trade unions was in some doubt. As we have seen, they were opposed to war and said repeatedly that they had no quarrel with their brother workers in Germany. But only the Independent Labour Party maintained this attitude once war was declared. Ramsay MacDonald, who had been the leader of the Labour Party since 1911, and who was firmly opposed to the war, resigned from the parliamentary party. So did six of his colleagues. The majority of the party, however, and the overwhelming bulk of trade unions accepted the declaration of war and pledged themselves to the defence of the country. Wilkie wrote in the second quarterly report for 1914:

'....... the blame for the catastrophe lies not at the door of this country. We have laboured for peace and for the continuance of friendly international relations, but peace can only be maintained, with honour to ourselves, and with due regard to our national undertakings and the observance of our International Treaties and obligations (sic). Nations, like individuals, must honour and implement their signatures, must respect their guarantees and must recognize their pledged word. On this rests the whole basis of civilization and the proposals made to this country through the medium of diplomatic conversations were such that no self-respecting nation could have accepted without sacrificing their right to be regarded as a nation whose word was its bond.

'..... The magnificent unity which all sections of the community have shown in this present emergency proves conclusively that no matter how much we differ on internal questions when Our Island Home is threatened we are all one and we are facing this struggle a United Great Britain and Ireland, standing manfully by each other against the common foe.'

The decision by Ramsay MacDonald and the I.L.P. members to oppose the war was dismissed as irrelevant. Arthur Henderson, of the Ironfounders, M.P. for Bishop Auckland in County Durham and known universally and affectionately as 'Uncle Arthur', was elected chairman of the parliamentary party in MacDonald's place. The latter's action and that of other I.L.P. members was to stigmatize the Labour Party for years to come as 'pacifist cowards' even though they represented only the smallest element in party thinking. Arthur Henderson represented the typical view. He became a minister in 1915 and a member of the war cabinet from 1916 to 1917. Many labour leaders spoke on recruitment platforms and they constantly urged vigorous conduct of the war and the ending of sectional differences. Wilkie wrote in his third quarterly report for 1914: 'This war has brought home to all the advantage of the unity and consolidation of all classes ....'

But while they gave full support to the war effort, trade unions and members of the Labour Party were anxious to protect the workers' living standards. On 5th August, a special conference which had been arranged some time earlier of all sections of the labour movement, decided to establish a standing committee entitled The War Emergency Workers' National Committee. Meeting weekly it helped to formulate policy to safeguard the interests of the workers and their families. Or as Wilkie put it: 'As trade unionists and part of the great industrial movement we must be absolutely united together to assist our less fortunate brethren, to look after the women and children and to do everything possible to mitigate the hardships which this war will bring in its train. This is a time to show our great sympathy and comradeship one with each other and face the future with courage and assurance so that when the war is over and the battle flags are furled the Labour Movement may be bound closer together, more united in its requirements and common interests.'

Just over a fortnight later, on 24th August, a meeting of the Joint Board of the T.U.C., the General Federation and the Labour Party urged an industrial truce for the period of the war. All existing disputes should be brought to an immediate end and 'a serious attempt' should be made to avoid any future conflicts. The employers did their part too. For example, they agreed to release workers to help on military work. The Wearside Shipbuilding Employers posted notices informing the men that they were 'at liberty' to leave for the purpose of assisting Admiralty contractors in work on war vessels. Many men answered this call but some refused to do so. Wilkie complained: '... in certain places it would appear as if it was next to impossible to persuade certain of our members, even when unemployed, to recognize their duty to the State as well as the danger to their craft in refusing to go to other places where men are urgently required. This is not a time for people to quibble over paltry excuses when their craft is in danger and the need of the nation vital ...'

On the other hand, the unions were alarmed by the 'insidious movement' on the part of some employers to undermine, if not destroy, certain trade union safeguards which had been established over many years. One of the most important examples concerned the 'dilution of labour', that is, allowing unskilled or semi-skilled people to carry out certain tasks normally performed by skilled craftsmen. The problem arose partly through a shortage of manpower as military recruitment built up and partly through a rapidly rising demand for armaments and munitions. A Treasury Committee on Production looked into the problem and recommended the 'dilution of labour' as the best solution. Within a few days, employers and unions in the engineering industry had signed the 'Shells and Fuses Agreement' under which women were allowed to do jobs formerly carried out by skilled workmen on the solemn understanding that the original trade practices would be restored once the war was over.

Realizing the importance of this agreement, Lloyd George, who was still Chancellor of the Exchequer, summoned union leaders to the Treasury from 17th to 19th March to consider the application of a similar agreement to the whole of the industry. Lloyd George pressed two points: the relaxation of trade practices including 'dilution of labour' and compulsory arbitration of disputes. Union leaders were ready to accept these terms but only on three conditions. Firstly, they wanted firm assurances, as had been given in the engineering industry, that the former trade practices would be restored when the war ended. This promise was given and, more surprisingly, kept. Secondly, firms were to be so taxed that they did not receive higher profits as a result of the new working arrangements, but this did not happen. Thirdly, the unions were to be represented on the local joint committees which were supposedly to direct industry and labour. In fact, they never functioned properly and were basically concerned only with dilution. On the question of arbitration the Committee on Production presided over by Sir George Askwith was set up on a permanent basis to consider questions of arbitration.

This 'Treasury Agreement' as it was called, was a triumph for all concerned. Lloyd George called it the 'great charter for labour'. Wilkie said it was 'an arrangement which we venture to state safeguards the interests of the trades unions during the war and after the war is over. The Government have guaranteed that no individual will suffer nor the rights and interests of trade unions be imperilled.'

And so the nation geared itself for war. It had been unready for the cataclysmic event but once it arrived there was an immediate and virtually universal response to the national appeal. Industry and the unions accepted new working arrangements with little argument. And the public, who had thought the war might be over by Christmas, prepared for a long, drawn-out affair.

IN TIMES OF WAR

The British industrial war machine was being brought to maximum output, especially in shipbuilding and armament manufacture. The demand for shipping was enormous and it ran parallel to a big increase in repair work. 'In common with many other British industries, that of ship repairing had unprecedented demands made upon it as a result of the exigencies of war. It is now common knowledge that these demands increased and became more and more pressing as the war went on until the enemy submarine campaign brought this country to the most dangerous crisis it has ever had to face. The call for ships was insistent and imperative and the whole resources of the ship repairing industry were taxed to the utmost.'[1] Altogether 7,856 war vessels and merchant ships were dry-docked in the North-East alone during the war and in addition 20,245 ships were repaired afloat.

Other areas were equally hard-pressed. And so were the men. Overtime was being worked almost every night. Sunday work was a regular thing at the beginning of the war. The shift system was introduced widely. But still it was not enough. In particular there was a serious shortage of shells on the western front. In June 1915 a Ministry of Munitions was set up to rectify the shortage and Lloyd George was put in charge. He ran the whole department as 'a business operation' and soon there was no shortage any more. Over £2,000 million was spent by the new Ministry, 218 national factories were set up and 20,000 smaller ones built or converted.

Within a few months production of armaments of all kinds had gone up enormously and by the end of the war the country was actually producing more weapons and ammunition than the Services could use. The 'scandal' of the shell shortage upon which certain newspapers had campaigned was in fact due to nothing more than the rapid increase in the armed forces. It was easy to enlist thousands and thousands of servicemen; it took longer to arm and equip them.

Another criticism was harder to identify and tackle. It was claimed, even in a Government White Paper, that the shortage of supplies was due to slackness among the workers. Their time-keeping had deteriorated. Their workmanship had slipped. And, on the other hand, their drinking habits had increased. Given full employment and fatter wage packets, the men had relaxed their discipline.

Union leaders such as Wilkie were appalled at these suggestions. 'The steady men in all trades are justly indignant at the assertions made in the so-called White Paper,' he wrote in the Quarterly Report for January-March 1915. 'Its publication has done more harm than good and too strong a protest cannot be made against the way in which the workmen, as a whole, have been maligned in this White Paper .... some lists supplied by firms have been found to be most carelessly compiled and inaccurate in many details .... Now let it be most clearly understood that we are not defending the shirker or slacker or the minority who could do better but we must protest against the wholesale statements that the lost time is due to drink and high earnings as we are informed a considerable amount of time is lost by men who are total abstainers.'

As one suggestion, he put forward the idea of works canteens where men could obtain food and non-alcoholic drinks at reasonable cost. This suggestion was taken up and factory canteens became a common feature of British industry. In addition, restrictions were placed on the drink trade. Pub opening hours were cut and afternoon closure was introduced, beer was reduced in strength and its price increased.

These measures tackled the myths, rather than the problem itself which was a severe shortage of labour. As far back as November 1914 the shipyard trades representatives had pointed out to the employers at a conference in York that it was physically impossible to double or quadruple the number of skilled craftsmen, as had been requested, particularly when men were volunteering for the forces. The unions had suggested that the employers should release about 10-15 per cent of their labour force so that they could be drafted to war work, the first time unions had even condoned the direction of labour. The employers had announced that men were 'at liberty' to leave to do war work and although some men had moved voluntarily, they were not enough. The compulsory scheme suggested by the unions was taken up, however, neither by the employers nor by the Committee of Production. This was odd in view of the fact that the Government was taking sweeping powers in other directions. In July 1915 the Munitions of War Act gave the Government enormous powers over the munitions industry and its workers. There was to be compulsory arbitration of disputes, suspension of trade practices and the introduction of 'Leaving Certificates'. Unless he obtained such a certificate from his employer, a worker was not allowed to leave the munitions industry.

This Act formalized the Treasury Agreement of March. The unions were so put out by the operation of a formal Act rather than an informal agreement that the Government had to consider amendments. In January 1916 an Amending Act provided certain safeguards in the use of Leaving Certificates. It also allowed unskilled workers to receive the skilled men's rates of pay under the 'dilution of labour' scheme.

The shipyard trades benefited in at least one way from the edict that there should be no stoppage in Government work. At the beginning of 1915 the boilermakers, shipwrights and other shipbuilding trades asked for wage increases of 6s (30p) a week or 15 per cent to pieceworkers. This was the highest wage demand ever lodged in the industry's history at that time.

At a conference on 23rd February between the Shipbuilding Employers' Federation and the unions, the request was modified to 4s 6d (22½p) a week or 10 per cent to pieceworkers, still very high figures. The employers replied by offering 2s (10p) a week or 5 per cent to pieceworkers. At that, the conference broke down. On the following day, 24th February, the Committee on Production headed by Sir George Askwith was asked to look into the dispute. After giving the question 'full consideration' the Committee agreed that the men's claim should be met or nearly so: 4s (20p) a week extra for timeworkers and 10 per cent more for pieceworkers. The unions accepted the offer unanimously, as one might expect, and agreed to 'urge our members to continue to improve, where possible, on the timekeeping and the production of ships and munitions of war and everything necessary to our national welfare in this grave national emergency.'

The case was interesting in that although the Government was taking unprecedented powers it still preferred conciliation. Lloyd George liked to think of himself as a man of the people and as the politician who, above all others, secured widespread acceptance of the war effort. There were other cases where his intervention on behalf of the workers, despite the Government's legal powers, was even more dramatic but the shipyard case was one of the first to illustrate the new power of certain groups of key workers in a war situation.

The arbitrator's decision brought shipwrights' wages in Scotland and the North of England to 48s 6d (£2.42½) for old and repair work and 45s 6d (£2.27½) for new work, the highest they had ever been. The outcome, said Wilkie, was 'very satisfactory'. In fact the whole year had been a good one. Membership had risen to 29,500. Income had gone up substantially to £80,000 while expenditure rose to £64,000. The excess of income over expenditure took the reserves to £176,000. The increase in income was almost entirely due to the National Emergency levy under which members made a small contribution for the benefit of the families of those who had joined the forces. By the end of 1915 nearly 2,000 shipwrights had enlisted and over £16,000 had been paid out to their families. The scheme was greatly appreciated, as Wilkie commented in the 34th annual report. 'It has lightened the burden in many a home, it has brought cheer to the children left behind and it has been a source of great comfort to our members, facing dangers on land and sea, to know that the members of their organization have not forgotten them in this time of national stress and peril.'

THE WAR GOES ON

The early hopes that the war would last only a few months had now completely disappeared. It was going to be a long struggle. Faced with this prospect, Herbert Asquith, the Prime Minister, decided to form a coalition Government to emphasize the need for national unity. Bonar Law, the leader of the Conservative Party, became Colonial Secretary; Arthur Balfour, the Conservative Prime Minister in 1902-5, became First Lord of the Admiralty; Arthur Henderson, leader of the Labour Party, was made President of the Board of Education; and overshadowing them all was the brilliant Welshman at the newly-created Ministry of Munitions, David Lloyd-George.

He was at least partly responsible for a decision which, far from uniting the country, widened divisions of opinion. This was compulsory conscription to the forces. For the first eighteen months the war had been prosecuted on the basis of voluntary enlistment and about four million men had joined up. This was a magnificent expression of loyalty and, as we have seen, in the early months recruitment was higher and faster than the service departments could handle. But in the autumn of 1915 public opinion, encouraged by certain newspapers, hardened to the view that conscription was needed. Partly this was a reaction to the stories (or rumours) about slackers which had been given credence by the Government's White Paper. And partly it was a yearning for dramatic action in the light of the dawning realization that the war could drag on for years. Lloyd George, among others, was a principal supporter of conscription.

The unions were almost totally opposed. They felt that there had been a splendid response to voluntary recruitment as there had and that to introduce compulsory measures was an insult. The T.U.C. Conference held at Bristol in September 1915 unanimously approved a resolution condemning conscription. Moved by Mr J. A. Seddon, the President, the resolution declared that it would 'divide the nation at a time when absolute unanimity is essential.' No reliable evidence had been produced to show that the voluntary system had failed and the unions would continue to give 'every aid' to the Government to secure all the men necessary without conscription. Speaker after speaker supported the motion. Mr Shaw of the Textile Workers said: 'There is no genuine need for this demand for conscription and it will split the nation asunder.' Mr Bramley of the Furnishing Trades said: 'I shall vote for the resolution because I believe it to be the duty, the absolute duty, of this Congress of Labour to declare unanimously against the conscription campaign which has been foisted upon the country by the newspaper adventurers who are in utter ignorance of the true meaning of patriotism.' There was one lone voice speaking in opposition. Mr D. Carmichael of the Shop Assistants' union cleverly pointed out that 'we are coercing the workers into the Army today as ruthlessly as if we had conscription fully enforced.' His view was that there may as well be conscription. The conference did not agree, rejecting it unanimously 'amid loud and repeated cheering and the waving of handkerchiefs.'

Wilkie alluded to the question in the Quarterly Report for July-September 1915. He felt that the voluntary system was being given 'a full and fair opportunity' of providing the required manpower and that the efforts of the Joint Labour Recruitment Committee would produce the necessary numbers.

The Government took the opposite view for political rather than practical reasons. In January 1916 it passed the Military Service Act which imposed compulsory conscription on unmarried men between the ages of eighteen and forty-one. In the event the political storm which had been feared failed to blow up. Labour members protested against the bill but finally accepted it while about thirty Liberals voted against it.

Alexander Wilkie found himself in trouble over the matter. His constituency party executive in Dundee passed a resolution expressing 'its strong disapproval of those members of the Labour Party who have lent their support to the Military Service Bill, viewing such action as a gross and humiliating betrayal of their trust as guardians of working-class interests.' Wilkie sent a long reply to the 'carping criticism and unjust aspersions.' He said that 'it seems strange that those men who are against compulsion want to compel me to vote as they direct' and he wanted to know the justification for the assertion that he had betrayed working-class interests. The envisaged conscription was 'the mildest form of compulsion ever invented'. After eighteen months of war he still felt that the country was in great danger so that he would 'shrink from no sacrifice of wealth or men that will enable us to come out of this conflict in a satisfactory and successful manner.'

His reply did not satisfy his party executive but it did satisfy the shipwrights in Dundee who called a special meeting to discuss the matter. They expressed their 'unabated confidence in Mr Wilkie, endorsing his action in supporting the Government during the national crisis and approving his votes in favour of the Military Service Bill.' Since only 14 of the 300 shipwrights in the local branch attended the meeting it is not clear whether their views were typical of the whole or not. Nor is it clear whether they had been under some pressure to call the meeting.

In the event, conscription failed. In the first six months, the average recruitment figure was just over 40,000 a month compared with 85,000-90,000 previously. This reduction resulted from the large numbers, well over two million, who were exempted by the new law because of the essential nature of their work in the mines or on munitions. Previously, at least some of them had enlisted but now they were not given the chance. In despair, the Government passed a second Act covering married men as well so that military service became general up to the age of forty-one.

The Acts frequently caused friction between the unions and the War Office over individual cases and between the union leaders and their own members.

Wilkie maintained his attitude of backing conscription as a necessary evil. Writing in the Quarterly Report for January-March 1916, he said: 'No one wants compulsion for compulsion's sake but if Compulsory Service is the only way by which this war can be brought to a successful termination, then, if we really want to win the war, the Nation must rise above the mere academic considerations or abstract principles and organize its resources not only in manpower but in self power as well so as to bring both, if necessary and required, to the services of the State and not to the services of individuals.'

But while Wilkie supported the Government in this, he, like other trade unionists, was becoming increasingly concerned at the rapidly rising profits being made by shipbuilders and shipowners. The Treasury Agreement and the subsequent Munitions of War Act had received union support on the understanding that companies would not be allowed to make undue profits out of the new, more flexible, working arrangements. The fact was that by 1915-16 shipping companies' profits on average had risen by 77 per cent over the previous year. Equally, the need for more merchant tonnage was leading to speculation in ship ownership. In 1916 a small steamer built in 1878 which had been sold for £6,000 in 1906 changed hands for £41,000. In another case a ship sold for £22,300 in 1907 was sold for £56,500, while in a third case a steamer sold in July 1915 for £65,000 was sold in March 1916 for £178,000.

It was natural that such a situation should antagonize the unions and matters were made worse by the sharp rises in food prices and the consequent increases in the cost of living. In the annual report for 1916 Wilkie lashed out. 'Profiteering,' he wrote, 'must be put down with a strong and resolute hand .... There is no doubt that the War has resulted in the people, as a whole, being exploited for the benefit of the few and it is not sufficient to tell us that the nation has taken over a certain percentage of excess profits ... all excess profits should be the property of the nation as a whole and no one has any moral right during the continuance of this great struggle to expect to reap a monetary advantage out of the necessities of the country.'

The unions wanted firm Government action. They wanted to see national control of all essential foodstuffs, the commandeering of ships, the controlling of freights and freight rates, the supervision of industrial production to achieve maximum output and the taking over of the coal mines. These demands had been put forward with increasing pressure over the past few months and were to meet with a ready response. In December 1916 Lloyd George replaced Asquith as Prime Minister and immediately brought to bear greater energy and efficiency in the prosecution of the war effort.

A war cabinet of only five members took over supreme control. Besides himself there was Viscount Milner, Arthur Henderson for Labour, and two Conservatives—Bonar Law and Marquis Curzon. Under the cabinet, new departments were set up: shipping, labour, food, national service and food production. They introduced many of the measures the unions had demanded. In fact socialism came to Britain almost overnight and under the guise of the war effort. For example, all merchant ships were requisitioned, all food production was controlled by government, mines were nationalized and rationing was introduced. And above all prices were regulated on the basis of 'cost plus', so that the cost of living was stabilized until the war was over. These sweeping, radical measures, greater and more extensive than anything ever contemplated in Britain before, were introduced with a very large measure of co-operation from all concerned and not only the unions. Shipowners, for example, whose ships had been requisitioned, were made managers. Farmers still tended their own land even though they were told what to produce and at what price they could sell. It was all seen as part of the necessary sacrifice for the war effort.

With the demand 'for ships and yet more ships' by the new Prime Minister, shipyard employment remained very high. In fact the Association paid out only 18s 4d on benefit in the year, the lowest figure ever. Meanwhile wage advances were agreed of three shillings (15p) a week for shipwrights in both the dockyards and private establishments.

The radical measures taken by the new Government did not entirely succeed in removing ill-feeling and unrest. And the Government set up a number of Commissions of Enquiry which uncovered a wide range of grievances. Essentially, however, they sprang from one basic cause, a conviction that sacrifices had been borne unequally. While Wilkie had shared this view, he felt that the reconstruction of the Government and the introduction of new policies improved the situation immeasurably. He now lent his whole-hearted support to the new Government. In the annual report for 1917 he wrote: 'We must have industrial peace at home and if difficulties do arise we should endeavour to have them settled with the minimum of friction so that all can concentrate their energies in bringing about the defeat of Prussian militarism and Prussian autocracy.' He also lent his name to a circular put out by the Federation of Engineering and Shipbuilding Trades in February 1917 which called for still greater output from the shipbuilding yards and armament factories. 'We do not doubt,' said the circular, 'that all workmen connected with the twin industries of engineering and shipbuilding will strain every nerve to do their utmost in the national interests, by reducing lost time to a minimum, by abstaining from anything that tends to create industrial disturbance and by devoting themselves, body and soul, to the work of overthrowing the enemy's plans. You may be sure there is no lost time in the German shipyards.'

NEW PARTNERS

During 1917 there were two important changes in the Allied camp: the United States entered the war and Russia, wracked by the revolutions of February and October, virtually dropped out. The British cabinet was naturally disturbed by the Russian revolution and the emergence of the Kerensky regime. It sent Arthur Henderson to Moscow to discuss the implications for the war effort. While he was there he had long discussions and left persuaded that the Kerensky plan for a negotiated peace was the right solution. He put this view to a specially-summoned meeting of the Labour Party which agreed with him. The war cabinet was appalled at the suggestion. He was summoned to a meeting but was kept waiting 'on the doormat' while the other four members discussed his attitude. When allowed in, he was reprimanded by Lloyd George. In the circumstances he felt he had no alternative but to resign, which he did. Labour kept its place in the coalition, however, by the admission of George Barnes, former general secretary of the Amalgamated Society of Engineers, who had been Minister of Pensions.

Henderson's call for peace by negotiation and his resignation in support of his views served to endear him yet further to the labour movement. He was given a tremendous ovation at the 1917 T.U.C. while the following year his proposal received overwhelming support. There was now a clear division of opinion in the country as a whole between the Government's policy and the views of the labour movement and this division of opinion helped to heal the breach between trade unionists and their leaders which had been evident the year before.

Meanwhile the war was entering a crucial stage with the Germans stepping up their submarine action as a means of starving England out. As the loss of ships rose higher and higher, the demand for replacements became more and more insistent. In December 1917 the Prime Minister, David Lloyd George, declared: 'Victory is now a question of tonnage and tonnage is victory. Nothing else can now defeat us but a shortage of tonnage.' And the following March, the First Lord of the Admiralty, Sir Eric Geddes, set the target at three million tons annually and complained that only a third of this total was being achieved. In order to boost output his department authorized the building of 45 additional berths in private yards. It also decided to establish National Yards, much against the will of the industry and announced that between them they would have 34 berths. Such measures obscured the real problem which was a drastic shortage of materials, particularly steel, and to a lesser extent a shortage of labour. In the circumstances the authorization of new berths could not help. Nor could the renewed criticism of the efforts of the workforce. Geddes referred to this aspect time and time again. So did the employers. *The Shipbuilder* magazine, which echoed the thoughts of employers, declared in April 1918: 'The output of skilled labour at present employed in the shipyards will have to be increased. There is no doubt of that .... Nothing less than a full week's work, when the circumstances permit it, should be tolerated from a healthy man.'[12]

The increasing demand for ships led the unions to request an increase in wages. When the employers refused to agree, the question was referred to the Committee on Production under the chairmanship of Sir George Askwith. The Committee laid down an increase of five shillings (25p) a week for all trades from 1st April. The Association's members, perhaps flushed with this success, agreed that their own officials and officers should have increases. Branch officers were to receive an extra

25 per cent and full-time officials an extra 12½ per cent.

Conditions of limitless demand won the shipwrights further increases—an extra three shillings (15p) on 1st August, an extra five shillings (25p) on 1st December and then a war bonus of 12½ per cent on all earnings. In August 1918 there was another all-round increase of 17½p a week.

Membership of the union jumped during the year by almost 5,000 to 35,723 and twelve new branches were opened, bringing the total to 177. In 1918 there was an equally big increase in membership taking the total to 41,000 and the number of branches to 196.

Throughout 1918 the belligerent armies continued to hammer at one another with little impact as they had done over the past three years. It was a classic war of attrition and of few real successes. But in September 1918 the first signs appeared that the German power-bloc was about to totter. The Turkish army was defeated. Eastern Europe was beginning to crumble. The German army was now open to a new attack. In October the German government appealed for an immediate armistice and for the opening of peace negotiations. The terms were hard but no harder than might have been expected. The German army was to be withdrawn from all foreign soil in both West and East Europe and all arms, armaments and warships were to be confiscated. The Germans had little option but to accept and signed the armistice on 11th November. The war was over.

Its consequences lingered on for a generation or more. Three quarters of a million men from the United Kingdom had been killed—in France the figure was nearly twice as high—and one and a half million were permanently crippled. The economy had been massively disrupted and there was a great shortage of many items. The National Debt had leapt to fourteen times its pre-war figure. Paying the interest on it took up almost half the yield from taxation. In all, the war had cost the country £9,000m. Over 5m. tons of British shipping was lost. Of this three million tons was replaced while two million tons of naval shipping had been achieved.

The Shipconstructors' and Shipwrights' Association had done its part. About 3,500 members had been on active service and hundreds of them were killed. The Association had spent £30,000 in relief to their dependents. In addition, it had offered £90,000 to the nation in War Loans. Writing in the annual report for 1918, Wilkie had this to say: 'We can all rejoice that the struggle is over, that we and our allies have fought and won that great battle for freedom and democracy. In the midst of those feelings let us remember with gratitude those who have made the supreme sacrifice as well as those who, while fighting, have been maimed and disabled. Nothing we can do as a nation can ever repay our debt to them and it must be the duty of every citizen to see that adequate means are taken to make sure that those who have been left dependent and disabled will not suffer in consequence of the sacrifices which have been made.'

While the Association could aspire to this limited aim, it could not secure its members against the economic deprivations which followed the war or the alarming industrial unrest which reflected it.

CHAPTER EIGHTEEN

The immediate post-war period saw the Association continuing to make progress. It added to its membership by absorbing the last independent society and it opened negotiations for full integration with the boiler-makers' and blacksmiths' unions. In the shipbuilding industry, however, progress was less happy. Output went up for a couple of years and then shared in the general economic slump which affected the whole country. On a wider view still, there was persistent and widespread labour unrest, worse than the country had ever experienced before.

THE 'KHAKI' ELECTION

As soon as the war was over Lloyd George called an election to gain popular support for the coalition which had been formed during the exigencies of war. He received an immediate blow with the defection of the Labour Party. They refused to serve under a peace-time coalition. On the contrary, they wanted to be an independent and autonomous group, offering the policies of a real opposition and providing new solutions to Britain's problems. Henderson, who had been humiliated by the war cabinet because of his views on a negotiated peace, was an especial supporter of taking the Labour Party into opposition, thus repaying the old score to Lloyd George, but the party as a whole were firmly behind these tactics anyway. But Lloyd George was to have the last laugh for Henderson lost his seat, a victim to the general view that the Germans should be dealt with severely. Pacifists proper such as Snowden and MacDonald and members of the I.L.P. also lost their seats. But otherwise the Labour Party did well, increasing its membership from 39 to 59. The coalition group had an overwhelming victory, however, winning 474 seats. Liberals who did not support the coalition were decimated. But while Lloyd George had won a famous victory he had split the Liberal Party irrevocably and thereby opened the way for the Labour Party as the second party in the country.

The Shipwrights' Association had decided to field six candidates, including Wilkie. But because the Election was called in a hurry only one of them, apart from Wilkie, was able to find a constituency. He was

A. W. Tapp who fought the Gillingham constituency and came in second with 4,705 votes compared with 12,455 for the Conservative candidate. Wilkie again stood in Dundee and again he and Winston Churchill won the two seats with most convincing majorities. Indeed Wilkie's majority was the largest Labour vote in the country.

A couple of months after the Election, Alex Wilkie 'reluctantly' came to the decision that he would not contest the seat at the next Election. As we shall see, he had been appointed General President of the temporary executive committee formed to amalgamate the shipwrights with the boilermakers and blacksmiths. He felt that this new work was 'of the very highest importance' and that he 'should devote as much time as possible and practicable in the building up and the welding into one the three great respective organizations.'

The news was received by the *Dundee Advertiser* with 'regret'. The issue of 12th January 1920 commented: 'For all questions of politics apart, Mr Wilkie has proved himself a very careful and attentive representative of the city—always willing to identify himself with its larger interests and never forgetting that he was the Parliamentary mouthpiece of the whole constituency and not merely a section of it. Mr Wilkie's decision is a matter of regret on other grounds. At a time when Labour is setting before itself very large aims in the sphere of politics and when men of all shades of opinion, from Bolshevists to Constitutionalists, are claiming to speak in its name, the movement can ill afford to spare a representative in Parliament of his sturdy good sense and sane outlook.'

The Newcastle *North Mail* commented: 'Mr Wilkie is one of the fine veterans of the Labour movement and the passing from political activity of such men as he in a time of industrial ferment like the present is always a matter for sorrow.'

The Lord Provost of Dundee, Sir William Don, wrote Wilkie a personal letter in which he said: 'I regret that you are not again to contest Dundee, more especially as you were so agreeable and willing to undertake all that has been asked of you by the community.'

Despite the general compliments and the genuine reason for his standing down, there was still a feeling that the relationship between Wilkie and his local Labour Party never fully recovered from the war-time conscription issue. Certain passages in Wilkie's resignation letter give a hint of this feeling. In one paragraph, he wrote: 'While there have been differences during the war, the electors of Dundee have appreciated the services I have rendered ......' and elsewhere: '..... while feeling satisfied that I would retain to the full confidence of the Dundee electors ....' These passages indicate a person who seems in need to justify himself. Furthermore, the standard letter from the secretary of the Scottish Council of the Labour Party seemed a little formal and lacking in warmth. 'You will certainly have the satisfaction of recollecting not only that you have polled the largest majority for Labour throughout the country but that you were one of the pioneers in Labour representation in Scotland and a conscientious member of Parliament for the largest Scottish single constituency.' Fine, but Mr Shaw's letter does not read as if it was sent

William Westwood, Second General Secretary, 1929-1945.

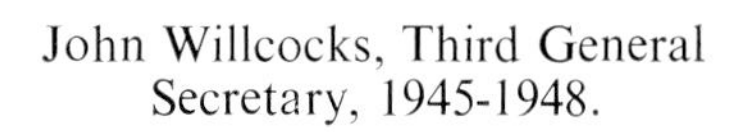

John Willcocks, Third General Secretary, 1945-1948.

Sidney Ombler, Fourth General Secretary, 1948-1957

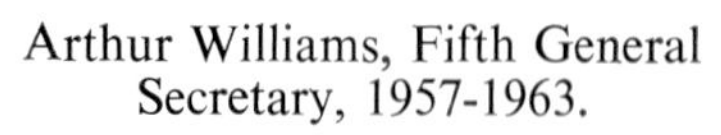

Arthur Williams, Fifth General Secretary, 1957-1963.

to a friend. It is easy to make too much of all this, and perhaps that is the case, but a suspicion of disaffection still remains.

RESTORING THE ECONOMY

With the election over and the return of a powerful Government dominated by Conservatives but headed by a Liberal, at least in name, Lloyd George, the immediate and urgent problems were to negotiate the terms of settlement of the Peace Treaty, to demobilize the troops and to restore a peace-time economy. The first problem is outside the concern of this book. The second problem, of the rapid release of hundreds of thousands of servicemen on to the economy, was thankfully eased by an economic boom. Large-scale unemployment did not occur, not until 1920 at least and then for a different reason. The third problem was to prove the most difficult although in advance it looked the easiest to solve.

The basic policy was to return to the practices of 1914 and to dismantle the tentacles of Government intervention. In Alan Taylor's phrase, 'Freedom burst out overnight. Price controls, control of raw materials and of foreign trade, direction of industry, were swept away.'[1] One of the first measures was to repeal the compulsory arbitration provisions of the Munitions Act. Another was a Restoration of Pre-War Practices Act which the Government had promised the unions when they signed the Treasury Agreement in March 1915. This forced employers to return within two months to previous practices and customs including the use of skilled men only for certain work. The 'dilution' of labour was over.

A departmental committee headed by Sir Alfred Booth was set up by the Board of Trade to consider the position of the shipping and shipbuilding industries. It recommended that the industries should be released from Government control and that everything possible should be done to increase their efficiency and to re-establish Britain's former position. The country should set itself a shipbuilding output target of 2m. gross tons a year—which in fact it achieved only once—and skilled shipyard men should be among the first to be demobilized. Shipbuilders should be free to buy steel without being handicapped by any system of priority certificates.

The committee made almost no comment on labour relations despite the criticisms that had been made during the war and despite the evident fears of employers. An editorial comment in *The Shipbuilder*, said: 'The attitude of the shipbuilding workmen, and more particularly of the "iron men", during the course of the war, has caused much anxiety to many as to the future of the industry. The earnings of the "iron men" have largely increased and at the same time their output has diminished. The time-keeping of a large section has been bad and their general readiness to strike or to threaten to strike on any pretext has been distressing to those desirous of getting on with the war.'[2]

The employers saw the solution as lying in payment by results for all the workers in the industry rather than for only those trades for whom this was traditional. But the unions would not have it, much to their long-term disadvantage. There seems no doubt that a golden opportunity was lost for creating a new Britain in many ways.

There was a particular problem with regard to apprentices whose training had been interrupted by war service. It was felt that they needed to be encouraged to continue their training for otherwise they would end up as semi-skilled and industry would be short of the highly-trained people it needed. The Shipbuilding Employers' Federation and the many unions involved in the industry drew up a scheme to come into effect on 1st January 1919. Under it, apprenticeship could be reduced by the length of war service if it was spent at a trade, or if it was not, by a maximum of 2½ years. The other key point was the level of wages. And here, in order to prevent former apprentices from drifting off to semi-skilled but higher paid work, it was agreed they should receive the prescribed rate for their class with only a small deduction. On the other hand, if training was carried out at a technical institute and not in an employer's workplace, then the State would pay a maintenance allowance of at least 33s a week.

The ending of the war saw a period of rapidly-worsening labour relations, despite everyone's hopes that things would get better. The number of working days lost by strikes jumped from 5m. in 1918 to 55m. in 1919 and 86m. in 1921. The main centres of trouble were the mines and the railways. As early as January 1919 the miners came out with demands for a six-hour day, a 30 per cent increase in wages and the nationalization of the industry. They got a seven-hour day without a reduction in wages while nationalization, although recommended by the Sankey Commission which the Government had set up, was deferred.

The resort to industrial action swept the country. Even police forces in certain areas went on strike. Perhaps it was no surprise, therefore, when some of the men in shipbuilding came out over the new working arrangements. At long last the union officials had persuaded employers to reduce the number of hours from 54 to 47, a big improvement. This had been achieved at a conference in November 1918 just two months after the T.U.C. annual conference had called for a 48-hour week without a reduction of wages. The various unions submitted the proposals to their members who endorsed them by a majority of 177,000, the voting being 337,000 to 160,000.

But militant groups of shop stewards wanted more. Some demanded a 44-hour week, others 40 hours. Boilermakers, shipwrights and blacksmiths on the North-East coast, with the exception of Wearside, did not return to work after the New Year holidays in 1919 when the new hours were to be introduced. Later their example was followed by workers in Belfast and on the Clyde. Their action was unofficial and led *The Shipbuilder* magazine to comment: 'The action of the men in not carrying out their agreement indicates a spirit full of menace for the future and creates working conditions under which no industry can flourish.'[3] Even the T.U.C. was obliged to condemn their action.

The annual report for 1919 declared: '.... in as much as the 47 hours agreement had been endorsed by the votes of the members, it became the bounden duty of the minority to loyally abide by the decision of the majority. Unless this course is taken a very serious blow will have been struck at the fundamental principle of trade unionism—namely collective bargaining.'[4] The men continued their protest for eight weeks before returning to work; the 47-hour week was accepted.

But so widespread was industrial action becoming that Wilkie had to counsel his members in the annual report for 1919: 'Everywhere in the industrial world there is unrest, culminating in many instances with disputes and dislocation of industry. It is not in one industry but in most. It may be said that this is the aftermath of war. So it is but if the reconstruction of this and other countries is to be resolved or work accelerated, the road is not by industrial unrest or the adoption of some of the methods we have seen taken in recent disputes, many of which have been organized not for trade union purposes but for other objects quite outside those for which the Trade Union Movement stands.'

The disputes over the introduction of the 47-hour week cost the Association £36,600 in benefits, the largest figure since 1908. This massive expenditure was the main cause of the tiny increase in the organization's reserves of only £424 in 1919 despite a record income of £122,000. That income came largely from members' contributions of £81,000 from levies and entrance fees of £27,000 and from dividends on investments of £9,000. The main items of expenditure, apart from disputes benefit of £36,000 were sick benefit of £22,000, pensions of £11,000 while management expenses including salaries had risen to £42,000.

Meanwhile employers and trade union officials continued to discuss the possibility of a further reduction in wages. On 28th August 1919 the Shipbuilding Employers' Federation and the Federation of Engineering and Shipbuilding Unions signed an important agreement which said:

1. That working conditions on a 47-hour week basis be adjusted with the least possible delay, and
2. That a joint committee of employers and unions be set up to 'investigate the economic relation of production to hours of work and, in this connection, the methods of manufacture in the shipbuilding and engineering trade in this and other countries.'

The second point was a most important one for the employers for they continually complained of the lack of sufficient output and of the strides that other countries were taking while Britain was locked in the conservative attitude and practices of the unions.

FULL SUPPORT—AT LAST

On 1st January 1919 Alexander Wilkie and the other founding fathers achieved a life-long ambition with the assimilation of the last independent local society. The Liverpool Shipwrights' Association agreed to become part of the Shipconstructors' and Shipwrights' Association. The union was now complete. It organized all shipwrights in the country. That is not to say that all shipwrights belonged to the Association, for that was not the case. In the 38th annual report for the year 1919 Wilkie reported that membership had risen by about 3,700 to 45,000 but he added: 'There is still room for a further increase in the membership in the various districts and we trust that no effort will be left untried to bring into the Association every eligible man working at the craft as it is only by strengthening our organization in every way that we can hope to achieve many of the objects for which we stand.' What the assimilation of the Liverpool Shipwrights' Association did mean was that there was no rival organization of any significance in any major port.

The assimilated members totalled 850 plus 270 apprentices, mainly working in Liverpool but with some in Birkenhead, Wigan, Portmadoc, Garston, Litherland and Salterforth.

Upon assimilation, they received the full benefits of the Association, i.e. a member paying a contribution of a shilling a week (5p) received trade or dispute benefit of 12s (60p) a week, unemployment benefit of 12s a week for fifteen weeks, sick benefit of 15s (75p) a week, reducing in steps to 4s (20p) a week after 26 weeks, superannuation ranging from 4s 6d (22½p) to 8s (40p) a week depending on length of service, funeral benefit of £10 and tool compensation up to £5. The same benefits applied to all members over 65 years of age paying 8d (3½p) a week. Members paying 2d (1p) a week continued to do so and received only funeral benefit amounting to £6. Apprentices paying 2d a week received sickness benefit of 4s a week for 16 weeks and then of 2s a week for a further 16 weeks, funeral benefit of £4 and tool compensation of £2.

Assimilated members were qualified to hold office in the Association while the two full-time officials at Liverpool were taken over for twelve months and the positions retained thereafter subject to election. The Association took over all assets of the Liverpool Society which amounted to £2,500.

Although the assimilation represented the culmination of a lifetime's work for Wilkie, he made no reference to the historic event in the annual report. He was generally so particular in recording each milestone in the Association's progress that the omission seems all the more remarkable.

MOVING TOWARDS AMALGAMATION

Perhaps he was absorbed by an even more important event, the proposed amalgamation of the Association as a whole with the Boilermakers' and Blacksmiths' unions. Amalgamation of course was not new. It had been considered just before the war but had not been achieved. Now all parties made a more vigorous approach. No doubt they were influenced by the T.U.C. resolution of 1918 which 'welcomed the growing tendency towards union by industry as an improvement upon sectional unionism or union by crafts alone'. It recognized the special nature of craft unions whose value was above purely industrial considerations by 'improving technique and cultivating pride and pleasure in the work itself.' But it urged that more amalgamations should take place where appropriate and set up a special committee to advise Congress on demarcation lines between unions and industries and to provide suggestions for 'the unification of the forces in each industry'. The shipbuilding unions therefore set to with a will to emulate the progress being made in other sectors of industry.

The shipwrights' executive decided that they must make every effort to get all members to vote on the question. Instead of relying on the usual method of branch meetings which were invariably thinly attended they arranged a postal ballot of all members. They also decided to hold a number of consultative conferences in different parts of the country which they and the General Secretary, Alex Wilkie, attended. They were held in Edinburgh on 8th July, Newcastle on 11th July, Bristol on 15th July and Belfast on 22nd July. These meetings generated considerable interest, certainly more than branch meetings would have done, but not quite as much as had been hoped. Equally, the postal ballot produced 22,500 votes compared with the normal total of about 5,000 through the branch meetings but the figure was still only half of the membership. However, Wilkie and the Executive Committee claimed 'very satisfactory results' and the vote in favour was very decisive. It was:

For amalgamation:	17,204
Against amalgamation:	5,270
Majority in favour:	11,934

This represented a majority of 3½ : 1. The majorities among the other two unions were even greater:

Boilermakers and Iron and Steel Shipbuilders

For amalgamation:	46,738
Against amalgamation:	4,488
Majority in favour:	42,250

Associated Blacksmiths and Iron Workers' Society

For amalgamation:	9,146
Against amalgamation:	1,512
Majority in favour:	7,634

The clear majorities encouraged further progress. It was decided that the temporary executive committee should start work on 5th January 1920, that the offices should be at 9 Eldon Square, Newcastle (next door to the Shipwrights' headquarters) and that all members of the three unions would be issued with cards giving the name of the new amalgamated union, namely: 'The Amalgamated Union of Shipbuilding, Engineering and Constructional Workers'. Alex Wilkie was to be the General President, John Hill, general secretary of the Boilermakers, was to be General Secretary and William Lorimer, general secretary of the Blacksmiths, was to be Finance Secretary.

Meanwhile the usual work of each organization continued although the respective district delegates were 'strongly urged to consult and work together in all matters which may arise.' Joint District Boards were created to deal with matters of interest. The temporary executive took over immediately responsibility for disputes. No stoppages of work were to occur without its approval while it would pay disputes benefits. But above all, true amalgamation depended on the attitude of the individual members. The executive of the three unions in a statement on 8th December 1919 impressed 'the necessity of the members co-operating in every yard or shop as closely as possible so that the greatest possible good may be derived from this great and far-reaching step which has now been taken by the three societies.' The statement also recognized that 'many difficulties' had yet to be overcome.

In the annual report for 1919 Wilkie said that the proposals were the 'most important event of the year' and that they 'ought to make for the more complete consolidation of the three organizations' and that 'if consummated on equitable lines' they would be 'of benefit to all concerned'.

Hopes were high at the beginning of 1920 that amalgamation would be achieved. Wilkie talked of it becoming an 'accomplished fact' within twelve months. Unfortunately the first signs of disunity now began to appear. The Boilermakers' Executive suggested that the Executive Council should consist of six members not twelve as originally agreed, with the other six sitting on sub-committees continuously. The suggestion gave rise to 'very protracted discussion' among the executive committee of the shipwrights who finally demanded that the original proposals should remain. They did understand that the workload would be very heavy and some of this could be shed to a sub-committee. In particular, it could draft the Constitution. But the full temporary executive committee should sit one day a week for administrative purposes.

As the work proceeded, more and more difficulties seemed to arise. How could the three executive committees be integrated; which of the district delegates would continue and which should be asked to stand down? The integration of rule books, of contributions and benefits was relatively simple compared with the personal problems. The Boilermakers' Executive Committee were particularly reluctant to give up office. The Shipwrights' Executive Committee agreed that all the members of the Boilermakers' Executive should become members of the first executive committee of the amalgamated union for two years whilst shipwrights and blacksmiths would have only a certain number of representatives. The chief officials —Wilkie, Hill and Lorimer—were to hold office for three years before being subject to election. With regard to district delegates, the continuity of their jobs was to be assured by appointing in each district, a resident delegate, a full-time district secretary and a full-time auditor. If new districts should be found necessary with full-time officials, then the retiring members of the shipwrights' and blacksmiths' executive committees should be appointed.

The difficulties were sometimes balanced by constructive approaches. The Federation of Foremen's Association signed articles of agreement under which each organization would recognize the other. More important, the Amalgamated Society of Carpenters and Joiners initiated discussions on closer working arrangements. But despite such steps, the high hopes began to evaporate as progress became slower and slower. An enormous amount of work was being done, innumerable meetings were being held but the central aim was being lost in a mass of detail, some of it petty, some of it obstructive. No agreement was reached by 1920. In fact the only notable advance during the year was the drafting of a bill for presentation to Parliament on the 44-hour week. Under pressure from their members and particularly from shop stewards, the leaders of the embryonic amalgamated union decided to draw up this measure which Wilkie and other Labour members would present. It called for a working week of no longer than 44 hours and a working day of no longer than eight hours. Such a measure caused alarm among employers who thought they had offered sufficient concessions in wages and hours already. The leading industry magazine, *The Shipbuilder*, commented: 'Shorter working hours and decreased production have had a disastrous effect on industry since the Armistice. The bill as drafted is wholly wrong in principle. It is an infringement of the liberty of the subject, some of its provisions are unworkable and it would set up a trade union bureaucracy which would be just as harmful to the individual workers as to the country generally.' This was nonsense but as it happened the employers had nothing to fear. The measure soon disappeared from view.

By the beginning of 1921 the chances of failure had to be faced. In a speech at a presentation ceremony in South Shields on February 1921, Alexander Wilkie seemed full of foreboding. He did not mention the great goal that lay ahead but only the obstacles. 'It is a difficult and arduous task,' he said, 'to arrange the administration of the three combined societies and legislative work entailed in order to put them on a proper working basis.' As progress slowed down, difficulties over the drafting of the Constitution loomed ever larger until finally the Shipwrights' Executive felt that it should call for a vote as to whether to continue or not. The answer was overwhelming:

Against proceeding:	20,364
For "	4,213
Majority	16,151

Amalgamation was dead. Or as Wilkie put it: 'That, so far as our Association was concerned, concluded the tentative arrangements'. Why did it fail? Wilkie put it down to the meddling, unconstitutional action of 'outside committees' which had 'entered into disputes of great magnitude which have dissipated the funds of the unions'.

It would be simpler and fairer, however, to say that the real will was not present. The ever-increasing emphasis on petty detail was indicative of fear, rather than of trust, of security rather than co-operation. The mass of minutiae could—and should—have been left to the consideration of the Executive Committee of the new union rather than constituting an inevitable part of the negotiating process. Lengthy discussion of detail is always likely to lead to failure and the longer the discussions go on covering one little point after another, the more likelihood there is of failure. If a general agreement to work together for the common good could have been signed within a few months of the opening of negotiations, then the amalgamation would have been an accomplished fact. It would then have been much more difficult for any one of the organizations to pull out and any disagreements would have been within a single unified union rather than between three unions which still basically considered themselves to be independent.

The failure contrasted with a number of successful amalgamations achieved among other unions around this time. The Amalgamated Engineering Union was created in 1921, the Transport and General Workers' Union in 1922 and the National Union of General and Municipal Workers in 1924. The movement towards amalgamation was mainly prompted by two factors, the increasing unity among employers and the desire to maintain a growth in membership, and was made easier by the Trade Union (Amalgamation) Act of 1917.

Over the two years of negotiation, discussion and meetings between the shipwrights, boilermakers and blacksmiths, the Shipconstructors' and Shipwrights' Association spent £5,300 on administrative work and expenses connected with the amalgamation. On the other hand, part of the salaries of the General Secretary and his assistant were paid by the temporary executive council. In 1919 the General Secretary's salary had been £518 while his assistant had been paid £305. In 1920 they received from the Association £295 and £152 respectively and in 1921 they received £326 and £180. The Shipwrights' Association thereby saved £693 on salary payments.

In addition, from 27th December 1919 to 25th June 1921 the Association had paid into the temporary executive council's funds total sums of £6,958, the equivalent of three shillings (15p) a member. The Blacksmiths had paid in £3,974 and the Boilermakers £18,000. Out of this income, the council paid salaries or part salaries, administrative costs and dispute benefits in 1920. The shipwrights received £2,045, the boilermakers £12,988 and the blacksmiths £142. Despite these outlays there was still over £9,000 in the funds on 25th June 1921 when the negotiations finally ended. It was decided to divide the amount among the three unions according to the size of their membership. The shipwrights were to receive £2,311 but because they had not paid the last subscription of 1s 3d (7p) a member, the actual amount handed over was £447. If one, finally, adds in the original contribution made in 1919, then the total costs to the Association of the abortive attempts at amalgamation were of the order of £12,000, or about 30p a member.

AN INCREASE IN WAGES

During the war, demands for increases in wages had been considered by the Committee of Production and on average they had agreed increases about every four months. The total increases agreed by the Committee came to £1.40 a week plus 12½ per cent on earnings in the case of time-workers and not less than £1.7½p a week plus 10 per cent on piece rates and 7½ per cent on earnings in the case of pieceworkers. The Committee last sat to hear a claim for the shipbuilding workers in October 1918 when an increase of 25p a week was agreed from 1st December.

The Committee had been dismantled by the Government and bargaining returned to the pre-war practice of negotiations between the Shipbuilding Employers' Federation and the Federation of Engineering and Shipbuilding Trades. During 1919 the unions submitted a claim for an extra 75p a week for men and 37½p for youths and apprentices. The employers rejected the claim on the grounds that the state of the industry did not justify such an increase. The men for their part claimed that with an increase of 120 per cent in the cost of living index between 1914 and 1918 they were worse off in real terms. This in fact was only true of the better-paid workers. The lower paid had had a dramatic increase. A worker earning £1 a week in 1914 had had increases of 172 per cent but for those on £2 a week the increases were 92 per cent, which was less than the rise in the cost of living, and so on.

The disputed claim was referred to an Interim Court of Arbitration under the Wages (Temporary Regulation) Act of 1918. The Court felt that rises in the cost of living had already been taken into account by the Committee of Production in October 1918 and that there had been no significant rise in the cost of living since then. But with winter approaching, the Court felt that further rises in prices may occur and it awarded an increase of 5s (25p) a week to be paid from 4th December 1919.

The unions were decidedly unhappy about the outcome. By this time, the Government had decided on a more permanent mechanism for settling industrial disputes, namely the establishment of a full-time Industrial Court. The shipbuilding unions decided to present their case to this new body and they received a hearing in February 1920.

The Court spent some time looking at the general arrangements for wages. For a time-worker received a basic rate, a flat advance and a percentage on total earnings. The arrangements for piece-workers was similarly complicated. The Court commented: 'The arrangements at present in force bear indeed all the appearance of having been devised to meet an emergency.... It cannot be claimed that they represent a satisfactory basis upon which the industry should continue.' The Court recognized however that such matters were outside its competence.

The Court argued that during the war when the determining factors of supply and demand were in abeyance, consideration of the cost of living was an important factor in deciding changes in wage rates. But now that the war was over supply and demand should assume their full importance and the cost of living was no longer relevant. This was orthodox capitalist philosophy relying on market forces to adjust wage rates, increasing them during boom periods and depressing them during slack times. That being the case, one would have expected that the Court had finished its work. But not so. For in the next breath, it adopted an interventionist attitude. It now argued that there was a great demand for more ships to make good the ravages of war and wages in the industry must be kept on a par with wages in other industries. Why the market forces which the Court extolled could not take account of this situation is unclear, hardly a surprise since its general philosophy was unclear. In any event it ordered an increase in two instalments of 6s (30p) a week for time-workers and of 16 per cent for piece-rate workers over and above the increases agreed by the Court of Arbitration. The decision meant that the unions had achieved an increase of 11s (55p) against their claim of 15s (75p) for time-rate workers. This brought the level of shipwrights' wages on Tyneside to £4.05 for new work compared with £1.90 pre-war, plus 12½ per cent bonus.

Three months later the unions went back for a further increase. This time they wanted another 6d an hour (2½p) or £1.17p a week for adult workers and half that amount for boys. *The Shipbuilder* magazine commented: 'It is quite evident that neither the shipowning nor the shipbuilding industries can stand such huge increases. If such concessions are made as the result of trade union pressure, it is believed that the result will in the end lead to unemployment and prove disastrous.' The employers were firmly against this later demand and this time the Industrial Court, which nearly always took a middle or compromise line, turned the application down completely.

In December the unions brought the question up again with the employers but without result. There was a growing feeling that the peak demand for ships and therefore for labour was easing. This was no time for further increases.

MEMBERS AT SEA

The work that the union had been able to do in improving the pay and conditions of most of its members was not matched by equal progress for ships' carpenters and joiners. Even as late as 1920, 38 years after the formation of the union, the annual report could state officially that 'the conditions of labour for ships' carpenters are so bad that economic circumstances only compel our members to accept the job at all.' And the report was equally frank in determining the cause. 'The reason for this is undoubtedly to be laid at our own door. It is a thousand pities that the efforts that are being made today to improve the position were not made many, many years ago. We have got to realize that we are endeavouring to break down conditions which have been growing from bad to worse for a generation.' The Union had not acted energetically but where it had acted was in relation to Admiralty employees. Its seafaring members in private employment had been virtually ignored. In 1920 at least the means whereby greater action could be initiated were clarified. The Association affiliated to the Seafarers' Joint Council which represented all seamen on all questions. Secondly, a National Maritime

Board was established for the industry to lay down fair wages and conditions. The union's grievances were similar to those in which it regularly petitioned the Admiralty. Firstly, wages were too low. Carpenters were entitled to receive between £17 and £21 a month depending on the size of ship which was little more than their land-based colleagues, despite the extra responsibilities and in any case many were not receiving these amounts. Secondly, status on board was inferior to that of other craftsmen. Thirdly, the hours of work were not governed by statute so that unscrupulous employers could demand long hours with no overtime payments. Finally, there were complaints about the manning requirements and the standard of accommodation.

Affiliating to the Seafarers' Joint Council was the first move in seeking to put things right. And this was given extra strength by the inauguration of local seafarers' councils in London, Liverpool, Glasgow, Hull, Southampton and South Shields. The Shipwrights' Association urged its members to seek representation on these councils as it had done nationally on the parent body. By joining, the Association had 'for the first time established our claim to speak on behalf of the men engaged at our craft at sea.'

On wages, the Seafarers' Council lodged an application for an extra £5 a month or its equivalent for all grades which was 'strenuously opposed' by the employers who threatened to lay their ships up rather than pay it. It was indeed a bad time to press a wage claim with the economy turning down. In the circumstances the Council felt it was 'desirable to withdraw the application for the time being.' In addition, the Shipwrights' Association faced a special difficulty in pressing a claim for it simply did not have the numbers on board vessels to demand action. On many ships there were no carpenters at all, on others there would be only one, while even on the biggest vessels there would be no more than four, hardly a powerful bargaining counter unless they acted together. It was for that reason that the union concentrated its efforts upon organization. 'We must concentrate our efforts upon building up seafaring branches in all the ports—having got our seafaring branches going we can then set about improving the conditions of labour', said the annual report for 1920. Only then could they rectify the 'degrading conditions of today'.

TROUBLED TIMES

The new decade heralded one of the most extraordinary periods in British economic history. For from the heights of a boom Britain slumped almost overnight into the depths of a severe depression. Within three months, from December 1920 to March 1921, unemployment doubled and by June 1921 the figure exceeded two million. In many towns in the North where there was a heavy dependence on coal, cotton, engineering or shipbuilding, more than half of the working population was made idle. *The Economist* magazine called 1921 'one of the worst years of depression since the industrial revolution'. The dramatic change had its origin in world factors, particularly the over-production of primary products but it was exacerbated by Government action, particularly in this country. For Government spending was slashed from £2,500m. in 1917-18 to little over £1,000m. in 1920-21. The budget showed a surplus of £230m. at a time when the Government should have been creating work by budgeting for a deficit.

In shipbuilding, the position was especially severe. In 1920, the industry produced an all-time record of two million tons of shipping. But now with a short-fall in the demand for primary products leading to a cut back on exports of all kinds, there was more shipping than products. Consequently shipowners cancelled orders for new ships with the result that by 1923 only 600,000 tons was produced. With the dreadful drop in output prices, wages, employment and profits all went tumbling down too. The same was true in world shipbuilding which fell from 5m. tons in 1920 to 1½m. tons in 1923.

By the spring of 1921 the situation was already alarming. The employers took the usual course of asking for reductions in wages. They called for a 6s (30p) a week reduction in time rates and for a 15 per cent reduction in piece rates to take effect from the end of April. Most of the unions agreed at a conference in Carlisle on 19th April as long as the reductions could take effect in two instalments on 7th May and 4th June. The shipyard joiners refused the request and went on strike. They stayed out until August but had to agree to the terms in the end.

The reductions did nothing to stimulate new orders. The employers now gave notice that they were going to abolish the Ministry of Munitions' war bonuses of 12½ per cent to time-workers and 7½ per cent to piece-workers in three instalments from November 1921 to January 1922. Harsh though these measures must have seemed, the men agreed to accept them in a ballot. The Shipconstructors' and Shipwrights' Association voted in favour by 4,900 to 3,270.

The men had to suffer more than reduction in wages. Up to 8,000 of them were unemployed too. So widespread was the unemployment that the Executive Committee decided to give a special grant of 75p per week for six weeks from 30th May. This was later extended to the 30th July. A further special grant of 37½p a week for four weeks was then agreed. Altogether these special grants cost the Association £72,387 in addition to the normal expenditure on unemployment benefits. In the year the total outlay was £117,000. Wilkie commented in the annual report: 'We do not know of any other society in the industry which has spent, in proportion to their numbers, a similar amount in special grants to relieve their members.' He added: 'We are satisfied that the amount spent was of great benefit not only to the individual members but to the members' wives and families and relieved the distress caused by unemployment to a considerable extent.'

That was true. But when branches made requests for an extension of the special grant, the Executive Committee 'could not see their way to make any further extension'. To meet the outlay already agreed, the Executive requested a special levy of 2p a week per member. Part of the reason for turning down the new appeals related to the extra help offered by the Government. Unemployment Insurance had first been introduced in 1911 and was limited to the three million workers in the building, engineering and shipbuilding trades whose work was expected to fluctuate regularly. In 1920 at the height of the boom the scheme was extended to cover twelve million workers, virtually the whole of the working population, mainly to provide insurance against casual, short-term unemployment. At the time, no one had envisaged that unemployment would reach such levels or last so long but having introduced the scheme there could be no turning back. In fact, Lloyd George and his Government never contemplated turning back. Instead they developed the scheme further. In March 1921, 'uncovenanted benefit' was allowed, that is a period of insurance which had not been paid for and in November 1921 the benefits were extended to provide allowances for wives and families. All of this provided a fundamental change in Britain's economic life. It took away some of the injustice and deprivation of unemployment. It prevented mass rioting for a 'better Britain'. Yet at the same time, by making unemployment bearable, it retarded the growth of industrial Britain and discouraged workers from moving from declining industries or areas to ones which offered brighter prospects for the future.

If recession, reductions in wages and widespread unemployment were not enough to make 1921 a highly memorable year, there was another outstanding feature—an enormous number of days lost in strikes. Almost 86m. working days were lost, by far the highest number ever, with the sole exception of 1926. This extraordinary total was largely due to a three-months' strike by the miners against a heavy cut in wages imposed by the coal owners. They had received their mines back from the Government on 31st March 1921 at the end of a period of temporary Government control during the war and could see no other way of restoring the industry's financial viability but by a substantial reduction in wages. The Railwaymen and the Transport Workers, who with the Miners, formed an informal Triple Alliance of industrial power, agreed to begin a sympathetic strike on Saturday, 16th April. To avert this escalating clash, the Government intervened and tried to start fresh negotiations. They were called off by the miners, however, and at that the leaders of the Railwaymen and the Transport Workers refused to sanction the sympathetic strike. The miners stayed out and still refused to negotiate. They felt betrayed by the other unions and dubbed Friday, 15th April 'Black Friday'. The Triple Alliance was dead, relationships between the three unions deteriorated sharply and indeed the unity of the whole trade union movement were badly shaken.

Alexander Wilkie referred to this parlous state of affairs when addressing the annual conference of the Federation of Engineering and Shipbuilding Trades in Portsmouth in May 1922. The object of the Federation was, he said, to do away with strikes. He was sorry that that had not matured and that they were in greater trouble than ever before. 'Strikes and lockouts are all barbarisms of a bygone age which should be done away with.' In a dispute a conference was always necessary so why not have it sooner rather than later and while negotiations were taking place work should go on.

The Shipconstructors' and Shipwrights' Association had little expenditure on dispute benefit in 1921 which was just as well considering the enormous outlay of £117,000 on unemployment. It paid out only £779 for disputes. But the income and expenditure account suffered its worst result so far. Income at £137,000 was approximately £7,600 up on 1920. But expenditure at £232,000 was £110,000 more than in the previous year, producing a loss of £95,000 and bringing the reserves down to £174,000. This was an alarming result and led Wilkie to call for higher contributions. Writing in the annual report for 1921, he said: 'If the Trade Union movement is to maintain its position and assist its members to the full, then the members must be prepared in good times when work is plentiful to pay into their unions a much higher contribution during such a period of prosperity so that when the days of adversity come they will be able to get a greater amount of benefit than during the present unfortunate period of unemployment.'

There was some joy to be found during the year despite all the gloom. One piece of good news was that the valuation of the funds of Approved Societies under the Insurances Act of 1911 showed that up to the period December 1918 the Association had had such a healthy surplus that it was now able to pay additional benefits to those members who had joined the Approved Section. From 4th July 1921 those members could receive an extra 5p a week under the State sickness benefit scheme, an extra 2½p for disablement benefit and an extra 10p for maternity benefit. The annual report said these were 'very satisfactory results'.

The Association itself saw the assimilation of more sailmakers. Another 120 joined mainly in London, Southampton and Lowestoft to add to the 250 who had joined in 1920, the first year of assimilation. It also continued to receive tangible benefit from its membership of the General Federation of Trade Unions. In 1921 it received £1,883 in dispute benefit accruing from disputes involving the Association's members in the previous year. On the other hand it sent contributions of £1,717. In the three years, 1919, 1920 and 1921, to go back no further, it received total dispute benefits from the General Federation of £5,594 compared with total contributions of £4,970. Of course in a quiet year, it would not expect any return from the General Federation but payments in such years were in effect building up the kitty for bad years. This was the essential practice which Wilkie and others preached for the Association itself.

CHAPTER NINETEEN

The first half of the 1920's was a highly volatile period in many ways. The economy moved from boom to recession to semi-boom, although unemployment remained above a million. The number of days lost in strikes fell from 86m. in 1921 to only 8m. in 1925. Trade union membership also fell away. The peak membership of over 8m. in 1920 dropped to 5.5m. in 1925 and was to go lower still. Shipbuilding output which had been 2m. tons in 1920 fell to 0.6m. tons in 1923 and then jumped up to 1.4m. in 1924. Politically, the Labour Party continued to gain strength while the Liberals continued to decline. The parties were in an equal state of flux internally, each adopting new leaders, and there were three general elections within a period of two years, leading to the first Labour Government in January 1924.

POLITICAL CHANGES

By 1922 the peace-time Coalition of Conservatives and certain sections of the Liberal party was suffering severe strains. In October the strains, especially over foreign policy, proved too much, the Conservatives decided to fight the next election as an independent party, and Lloyd George, perhaps the most creative and the most unscrupulous premier of the century, resigned and was never to hold office again. His time at the top had been a brilliant, even mercurial display of instinctive and intuitive political dexterity which left behind some great and solid achievements as well as many colourful anecdotes. Politics was to seem much duller although still highly absorbing because of the constant flux within and between the parties.

A general election was called for 15th November 1922. For the first time this century Alexander Wilkie was not to be a candidate. He had fought the Sunderland constituency unsuccessfully in 1901 before becoming one of the two M.P.'s for Dundee in 1906. He had held that position for almost seventeen years and had already announced that the 1918 election was to be his last although the reason he gave then, namely his work on the amalgamated union, no longer applied. But he was now 72 years of age and thought it right to confirm his previous decision. On 30th October 1922 he wrote a farewell letter to the electors of Dundee.

Recalling some of the measures which he had supported in Parliament, such as the introduction of old-age pensions and national health and unemployment insurance, he claimed that he had 'broken no pledge nor violated any principle' for which he stood. Although a Labour member he had sought to speak on behalf of the whole community. 'I have always conceived it to be my duty, although having a special knowledge of the industrial classes, to represent the whole of the electors, and to in no way narrow my interest to a section but to endeavour to benefit all.... A sound, sane trade union and Labour policy which aims to embrace the good of all, not at the expense of any one class, but the benefit of the whole, has always been my object, and to which, after long experience I still adhere.'

He went on to speak of the need for co-operation to solve the problems which cut deep into the social life of the country, such as unemployment and housing, and ended with the words: 'I have not sought any material advantage during those years nor any personal advancement in other directions, believing that service is man's highest ideal and that:

The reward is in the race we run
and not the prize.'

The Labour Party had over the years been building up its constituency strength and fielded 414 candidates in the election. They were opposed by the Conservatives, led by their new leader, Bonar Law, by the 56 National Liberals, led by Lloyd George, and by the independent Liberals, led by Asquith. The results were most encouraging for Labour which received 4.2m. votes and won 142 seats, twice the previous number. The Conservatives with 5.5m. votes and 345 seats were the majority party and formed a Government. The Liberals were torn asunder. For although they polled almost the same number of votes as Labour, they were divided between the two factions giving the party as a whole only 117 seats. Labour was now confirmed as the second party and as the official opposition. Even Winston Churchill lost his seat in Dundee while Wilkie's place was taken by E. D. Morel, secretary of the Union of Democratic Control.

Labour was not only a bigger Parliamentary party, it was also a radically different party. Whereas the Labour members in the previous Parliament had nearly all been union nominees and had all been from the working class, now there was a heavy infiltration of middle class representatives. Clement Attlee, who was to become leader of the party and prime minister, entered Parliament at this election. He was a lecturer in social science at the London School of Economics and had been educated at a public school and Oxford. Mr C. P. Trevelyan, later Sir Charles, was a large landowner in Northumberland. He was to become the first Labour Minister of Education. Arthur Ponsonby, son of Queen Victoria's private secretary, was, like Trevelyan, a fugitive from the Liberal party. Both were founder members of the Union of Democratic Control which had been set up in 1914. Supported by middle class intellectuals and closely allied to the Independent Labour Party, it urged negotiations to end the war and more open or democratic diplomacy in peacetime. The Labour Party was thus more national than ever before and more critical of the existing order, particularly in the fields of foreign policy and economic policy. The U.D.C. members provided the main criticism of the former while the working-class socialists from Scotland known as the Clydesiders, were particularly critical of capitalism. The basically conservative attitude of the former trade union M.P.'s such as Wilkie had thus been replaced by something wider and more bitter. This was recognized by the re-election to the leadership of Ramsay MacDonald, at that time the outstanding personality in the party and one of its most radical members.

FURTHER REDUCTIONS IN WAGES

The reductions which had taken place in 1921 had virtually no effect on stimulating new orders. In fact work in hand continued to decline. By mid-1922 tonnage under construction was only half what it had been a year earlier. The employers' reaction nevertheless was to call for yet further cuts, despite the clear failure of this policy. In response, the unions became more resistant. Wilkie wrote in the half-yearly report ending June 1922: 'It would be far better if all sections came together and thrashed out the whole position of the industry, both with respect to costs and wages, and endeavour to find out if there is not a better way of fostering the industry than merely by depressing wages to the lowest level and thus decreasing the purchasing power of the worker, consequent upon (sic) the lowering of his standards of life and comfort.'

The employers were determined, however. They wanted to withdraw the cost of living advance of £1.32½ which had been offered to time and piece-rate workers in 1917, 1918 and 1919. The men refused to accept these conditions, voting by 5,800 to 1,300 against the reduction. When the employers intimated that they would have to accept the cuts, the men went on strike from 29th March. From the employers' point of view the strike was almost welcome since they had so little work on hand. A strike would reduce their wages bill. On the other hand, the strike cost the union almost £22,000 in the six weeks it lasted. By then, the shipwrights and others realized that the employers were in no hurry to settle. Unwillingly they returned to work and in a second ballot agreed to the reduction of 16s 6d (82½p) by 5,500 votes to 4,200. Towards the end of the year, they agreed to empower their officials to negotiate with the employers in the abolition of the final 10s (50p). In negotiation, the best that could be achieved was to phase the abolition over four equal steps from November 1922 to January 1923.

All of this meant that wages fell to £2.60 on the N.E. coast for old or repair work, a massive drop from the heady peak of £4.20 in 1920. They were now only 37½p better off than they had been in 1914, despite a big increase in the cost of living.

Meanwhile the union officials also suffered a reduction. Following the general fall in wages and the burdens that members were shouldering, there was a call for branch, district and general officials to have their wages and expenses cut. This was agreed and reductions of about 20 per cent took place. Wilkie's salary came down from £524 in 1922 to £426 in 1923.

FORTIETH ANNIVERSARY

In March 1922 the Shipwrights' Association was forty years old. It was also virtually half-way through its existence for it was to be absorbed into the Amalgamated Society of Boilermakers, Shipwrights, Blacksmiths and Structural Workers in the mid-1960's. The forty years had been a great success in some ways, perhaps most importantly in establishing the union's dominance. When it started it had 1,750 members in 11 branches. A great number of local societies were in existence and proud of their independence. None now remained. The Association organized for the whole craft throughout the industry. There were 226 branches, 40,000 members and 14, full-time officials. Second, the financial basis of the union had been well and truly laid so that it could withstand the massive payments of the early 1920's without undue worry. In 1922 its expenditure exceeded income by £76,000, but at the end of the year it still had £100,000 in reserves. This of course was a big drop from the £240,000 held in reserves in 1920. But the fact was that the Association could afford these payments because of the careful husbanding of its resources in better times. And, of course, reserves were there to be used in bad times and it was hoped that the early 1920's represented as difficult a period as the Association was ever likely to face.

Its financial strength gave it the opportunity to carry on making benefits to members above the financial limits imposed by one year's income. But even in normal times the benefits that were paid out were a highly important part of its operation, some would say the most important of all. The amounts spent on benefits since its inception were:

Trade and dispute	£161,909
Tool Compensation	£5,958
Unemployed Benefit	£373,584
Sickness Benefit	£472,997
Superannuation Benefit	£147,579
Funeral Benefit	£79,174
Accident Bonus	£24,275
Medical Advisers	£5,383
TOTAL	£1,270,861

In recent years the expenditure increased. Just taking the four years leading up to 1922 gives these impressive figures:

Benefit	*1919*	*1920*	*1921*	*1922*
Trade & Dispute	36,000	22,000	2,500	25,000
Tool Compensation	100	200	300	400
Unemployment	2,600	3,300	116,000	64,000
Sickness	32,000	22,700	24,500	27,600
Superannuation	11,000	15,000	18,300	22,000
Funeral	4,500	4,300	4,400	4,200

All of these benefits represented a total expenditure of over £460,000 in four years which if nothing else represented a very considerable insurance policy for members against the hazards of a working life. In turn, these benefits were dependent upon a solid and reliable administration and this certainly had been achieved. There were from time to time the odd cases of fraudulent conversion of monies but this is likely to happen in any walk of life where individuals are made responsible for money. As a system the Shipwrights' Administration was effective and competent. All monies could be accounted for—and were accounted for—in the quarterly and annual reports while the level of contributions was kept extremely low for the benefits involved. There is no doubt that membership of the union represented good value for money.

When we turn to wages and working conditions, the union was much less successful. The state of trade still remained the main determinant of wages rather than the strength of the union. During the war wages had risen spectacularly due to the extraordinary demand for ships. Equally, in the early 1920's wages fell sharply as demand fell away. By 1923 they were only 37p above what they had been ten years earlier. It may be said that without union power wages would have fallen still further. But there is no evidence to confirm that one way or another. Certainly the employers were able to secure the reductions they called for and even a strike in the Spring of 1922 did not produce any concessions from them. With a thin market for ships they were able to sit back and wait for the unions to return to work. Indeed to some extent a strike suited their purpose for they did not have to pay wages for the duration. Of course it may be that the employers could secure the wages they felt the market could bear because they knew how to pitch their demands in such a way as to get union approval and in that sense the union could be said to play a part in determining wage rates. Without a union, rates might have fluctuated more sharply than they did. That is a clear possibility although unlikely. It must also be said that there was a paradox in the union's attitude. In general, like nearly all other unions, it was in favour of greater Government regulation, except over wages and working conditions. Then it believed in collective bargaining. But it was in wages that one could see most clearly the interplay of the market forces of supply and demand and the relative weakness of union power.

When we turn to working conditions, we see little impact by the union. It took many years to achieve a reduction on the 54-hour week and when the 47-hour week was introduced, it was received with a good deal of dismay by large sections of the membership who felt that a greater concession should have been achieved. Nor did union officials have much success in dealing with either the Admiralty or private employers over working conditions for sea-going members. By and large their working lives improved hardly at all in the first forty years of the union.

What the Association did in this period was to make it simpler to deal with the employers and brought about a greater degree of unity to match an increasingly united front on the part of employers. The whole of

Scotland and the North of England, the 'federated' area as it was known, now negotiated with the employers as a single unit and other parts of the country could equally be dealt with en bloc. Negotiations were to that extent less time-consuming. The union could speak on behalf of all shipwrights and shipconstructors rather than just a portion of them.

On the other hand, control of the union was still too much in the hands of the Executive Committee and particularly of Wilkie. There had not been a delegates conference for many years. No constructive approach had ever been made to the membership about the future development of the union. They were left simply to react to proposals put up to them in the regular ballots held at branch meetings. But such proposals generally dealt with nothing more momentous than the selection of candidates for the T.U.C. Conference and as a result few members, generally no more than one in ten, turned up at these meetings.

A particular aspect of this problem was represented by the succession to Wilkie as general secretary. He had held the position ever since the inauguration of the union. Now well over 70 there were no signs of his standing down or of a successor being sought and groomed. The annual reports which were largely written by him were meanwhile becoming less and less informative and more and more personal documents containing press notices of his activities and speeches. The regular reports from the districts written by the technical advisers were dropped during the war and never revived. The quarterly publication of reports was replaced by half-yearly publications. The amount of detail, for example, on wage rates, was reduced.

There can be no doubt that the members were growing restive under the interminable length of Wilkie's service. He began to receive anonymous critical letters which he dismissed as cowardly. But more important by the beginning of 1922 there were growing calls for the restoration of small, independent societies to achieve a greater sense of democratic control. Again Wilkie dismissed these calls—'we cannot too strongly condemn the attitude of these individuals as it is against all reason and against the tendency of present-day development of trade unions,'—but they were a sign that members wanted more control and a greater say in running the union and determining its, and their, future. Wilkie had done an excellent job in laying the solid foundations of the union. His reputation would have remained higher, and his value to the union would have been greater, had he retired in 1920 at the age of 70 rather than lingering on for another eight years.

A TERRIBLE YEAR

The depression which had started at the end of 1920 still hung over the country in 1923. It was the length as well as the severity of the slump in activity which was so remarkable. At one time two million men had been unemployed and even now well over a million were out of work. The cost to national and local government in relief was over £100m. a year. Even those who were employed were suffering because of the widespread reduction in wages which the T.U.C. estimated at £676m. over the whole of industry.

In shipbuilding the picture was gloomier than it had been for many years. The output of merchant ships at 600,000 gross tons was lower than at any time since the inauguration of the Lloyd's Register lists in 1892 with the sole exception of the war years. Unemployment was rife. Writing in the half-yearly report for January-June 1923 Wilkie said: '..... it will be found that never in the history of shipbuilding and shiprepairing in this country has there been such a vast number of men unemployed .....' In two and a half years the union had spent £200,000 on unemployment relief, a graphic illustration of the problem. Another way to judge it is to look at the number of shipwrights unemployed month by month. In January 1923 well over 8,000 were out of work, more than one in six. The number came down to 6,640 in March. But then started to rise again. Even the summer months made no difference and by August the figure was 8,878. It remained around this high level during the autumn but began to fall in November and December, ending the year at 5,800. This was a prelude to relatively happier times in 1924.

The causes of the depression and possible solutions were discussed and put forward the whole time, but with no clear agreement from all sides and certainly no great sense of conviction. One point did emerge clearly, that a reduction in wages did not provide the stimulus to new orders which employers suggested. On the contrary, by decreasing spending power employers and governments were accentuating the depression. This is not to say that wages should be increased at such times but that deficit budgeting, a policy only vaguely understood at the time, was needed. Such action was implicitly called for in the proposals that the government should institute public works programmes but this was nearly always turned down on the grounds of financial difficulty.

This point was discussed by the Prime Minister, Arthur Bonar Law, when he met a delegation from the General Council of the Trades Union Congress at No. 10 Downing Street on 16th January 1923. The delegation had called to protest at the 'indifference to the chronic suffering of thousands of men, women and children directly affected by the long-continued unemployment' and for the recall of Parliament to 'deal with this problem as a national emergency of vital importance.' After listening to the views expressed to him, the Prime Minister ranged over some of the solutions which were put forward at various times, including the stimulation of public works by borrowing money. He thought this was unsound and that 'the first essential to real prosperity was to pay our way and balance our Budget.' He appreciated that the effect was to make unemployment 'a great deal worse' but the Government thought that 'such a course as massive borrowing would have to be paid for by greater suffering afterwards.' He declared simply: 'I am certain that if, in order to meet your views, we were now to borrow money and employ it in any way you like so as to get the stream of wages going, we should be permanently destroying the chance of getting back to normal conditions.'[1] Like so many other deputations before and since, the T.U.C.

General Council left No. 10 empty-handed.

Conditions in the shipbuilding industry were made even more difficult by a paralysing strike of boilermakers. At the beginning of 1923 the Employers' Federation and the Confederation of Engineering and Shipbuilding Unions reached an agreement on overtime and night-shift working. The agreement was turned down, however, by a ballot of members of the Boilermakers' Society. They went on strike and this led to a lock-out being imposed from 30th April in the yards in the federated area. The effect was devastating. Many ship repair contracts were sent abroad. Such shipbuilding work as there was came to a stop. The Boilermakers' Society was expelled from the Confederation for refusing to accept the terms of the agreement. From now on the employers would have to negotiate separately with the Boilermakers' Society and the Confederation. Wilkie, like many others in the industry, was appalled at the situation. He said: 'Whether we like it or not there must come in the very near future a method by which these unfortunate disputes or lock-outs can be avoided and an appeal made to reason rather than the arbitrament of force.'[2]

Shipbuilding was an important industry in the economy of the country. 'No one trade or any body of employers has a right to destroy that industry, as both are simply partners in it.... and when differences arise they should jointly meet together and find a way out of their difficulties in a spirit of mutuality and conciliation ... The spirit of conciliation has certainly not been evidenced ..... We can only hope that when this unfortunate lock-out is ended both sides will sit down and endeavour by calm reason and cool judgement to evolve machinery that will be as far as possible equitable and fair to both sides.'

The lock-out had an effect on shipwrights and other workers not directly involved in the dispute. For not only were they prevented from working and receiving wages, they were also denied their State Unemployment Benefit because of the operation of Section 8 of the Insurance Act of 1911. Many representations had been made in Parliament to have the section altered so that a person not involved in a strike or lock-out but who was paid off as a result should receive unemployment benefit. The Labour Party had been given a promise that a suitable form of words would be inserted in the Act but nothing had been done so far, with the result that many shipwrights and other workers did not receive their state unemployment benefit.

By September 1923 not only shipyards but also engine works had to close. Even those yards struggling on with apprentices were working short time or had to dispense with many other tradesmen. The Shipbuilding Employers' Federation and the Confederation of Engineering and Shipbuilding Unions met in Carlisle in September to discuss a solution. The employers called for an enquiry or for arbitration. The unions refused saying that in their view neither was necessary. They felt that the Boilermakers' Society had been a party to the overtime agreement and that if they now refused to accept it then their expulsion in May was justified. This attitude did not help to resolve the matter however and on 26th September the General Council of the T.U.C. decided to set up a special committee to 'conduct an investigation into the circumstances of the dispute.'

On 1st October the Committee was successful in arranging a meeting between the Boilermakers' Society and the Federation of Engineering and Shipbuilding Trades despite the high feelings running between the two. As a result of this meeting it was decided that an approach should be made to the Employers' Federation who were asked to state the terms of a possible agreement. This the employers did. They wanted the boilermakers to return to work under the agreement and to put down their objections in writing. The employers for their part would give 'special consideration' to calling a conference to deal with these objections.

These proposals did not go far enough for the boilermakers who turned them down.

The T.U.C.'s special committee then decided to have another meeting between the boilermakers and the other trades. It was held on 1st November. The committee put forward a proposal which was to provide the breakthrough. They suggested that the boilermakers should be allowed to negotiate directly with the employers. The Federation was asked 'to place no obstacle in the way of free negotiations between the Boilermakers' Executive and the Employers' Federation.' The committee who had been having separate negotiations with the two other groups 'recognized in view of what had taken place that this was calling upon the Federation to take an important step'. The Federation agreed. Negotiations were opened between the boilermakers and the employers and on 19th November a settlement was reached. The shipyards could return to normal. The T.U.C. could feel it had rendered valuable service to secure a settlement which without its intervention would certainly have been postponed.

Despite the strike and lock-out and the continuing effects of unemployment the Shipconstructors' and Shipwrights' Association paid out only £3,900 in unemployment benefit in 1923 as against £117,000 in 1921 and £64,000 in 1922. On dispute benefit it paid out only £1,600 compared with £25,000 in 1922. The impact on the Association's finances was thus sharply reduced. However it still made a loss on its year's transactions, the third in a row, bringing the reserves down to £82,000, the lowest since 1910 and the second lowest of the century.

The main cause was a dramatic drop in income. At £62,000 it was £56,000 less than in the previous year and £75,000 less than in the peak year of 1921. The drop was accounted for by a number of factors. First and most important, membership had fallen to only 34,000 compared with 47,000 in 1920. This sad decline can be attributed to some leaving the industry, some going abroad to Canada, Australia and elsewhere, but mostly to those who simply allowed their membership to lapse. Many others, although still members, were becoming less regular in their payment of contributions. In 1921 income per member from all sources, but mainly contributions, was over £3. Now it was just £1.87½. If all members had paid their contributions regularly the Association would have received £70,000 in 1923 instead of the £50,000 it did receive from this source. Levies, interest on investments and other items brought the total income to £62,000. Expenditure also came down spectacularly to £79,000 from £194,000 in 1922 but was still greater than income. The main reason for the fall was the substantial reduction in dispute and unemployment benefits. The Association's bill for administration also showed a considerable reduction following the revision of salaries, being £31,000 instead of £48,000.

Despite these improvements, the financial situation was becoming more and more alarming. It led Wilkie to propose once more that contributions be increased or benefits reduced. Both courses of action were fraught with danger in the current circumstances. An increase in contributions would have been rejected out of hand by the members. They had recently forced the Executive Committee to withdraw the general levy of 2p a week introduced in 1921 as a means of recouping the £72,000 spent in special grant. They clearly would not accept an increase in contributions. Equally with the membership falling away so rapidly, dropping by a quarter in just three years (47,000 in 1920; 34,000 in 1923), this was no time to reduce benefits and thereby the value of belonging to the union. This would have produced an even greater fall. Yet one can understand the deep worry and concern of the Executive Committee as they watched helplessly while the reserves disappeared. At least in 1923 the extent of the fall had been moderated:

	LOSS
1921	£93,000
1922	£76,000
1923	£17,000

In the circumstances the union could but trim its administrative costs and live in hope that the economy would recover, bringing with it greater employment, higher wages and an increase in membership and wages. These hopes were sadly not to be realized for a number of years yet.

ANOTHER ELECTION AND A LABOUR GOVERNMENT

Towards the end of 1923, with world trade reviving only slowly and unemployment remaining obstinately at well over a million, Stanley Baldwin, who had taken over as Conservative Prime Minister on the death of Arthur Bonar Law, resurrected the policy of Protection. This involved raising tariffs against foreign goods as a means of stimulating home manufacture. So sudden was Baldwin's decision, so contrary to the policy stated so clearly by Bonar Law, and so devastating its effect on British politics that Baldwin had to call an election.

Substantial sections of the Conservative Party supported Free Trade, so did the Liberal faction under Asquith. The Labour Party was even more firmly committed to it. They felt that Protection would not work, that it would lead to other countries doing the same thing in 'beggar my neighbour' retaliation and it would destroy the international spirit of labour co-operation which the Party and above all the T.U.C. was doing so much to foster. Indeed the attitude of the unions, of the T.U.C. and of the Party deserves the highest praise for its wisdom and its selflessness on this question.

The election of December 1923 was fought on this one issue alone. The public had mixed feelings on the subject, just as the politicians had. They therefore voted more or less as they had done in the previous election but gave the Conservatives 100,000 fewer votes, the Liberals 200,000 fewer and the Labour Party, which had put up a spirited campaign on funds of £23,000, raised mainly from the unions, an increase of 100,000 votes. In percentage terms these were small changes. The Labour vote rose from 29·5 per cent to 30·5 per cent. But because of the somewhat freakish nature of the British electoral system, these small voting changes produced substantial effects in the House of Commons. The Conservatives lost 90 seats, the Liberals gained 40 and the Labour Party 50. No one party had an overall majority. The Conservatives were the biggest but having lost the election could hardly continue in office. The Liberals having opposed them on the policy of Protection during the election could hardly now join them in coalition. The Labour Party with 191 seats was clearly destined for office.

And so it proved. In January 1924 when the new Parliament met, the Conservative Government was defeated and George V asked Ramsay MacDonald to form a Government. In his diary that night the King wrote: 'Today, 23 years ago dear Grandmama died. I wonder what she would have thought of a Labour Government.' Whatever she might have thought, things were not to be very different. The new ministers were even willing to wear court dress despite a terrible fuss from left-wingers; they were willing to carry on the Parliamentary traditions and above all they were willing to be influenced very largely by their civil servants.

All of this created a sense of frustration, of disappointment and even of anger in more radical breasts. But in reality the new ministers had little choice. They were a minority government with little room for manoeuvre and even less power to force their policies through Parliament. With two exceptions, Arthur Henderson and Lord Haldane, none of them had had any previous ministerial experience. Even the Prime Minister had never held office before although certainly he was a man of wide executive experience. But above all they were demonstrating for the first time that a Labour Government although highly sympathetic towards, was nevertheless to be independent of, the trade unions and even of the Labour Party. It was and is answerable first and foremost to Parliament and the British public. It was a hard lesson for some to learn but it was a fundamental tenet of the British constitution. The same point can be made in a different way. Where the Labour Party was initially the political wing of the trade union movement, this was no longer the case. Of the 191 Labour members of Parliament only 98 were trade unionists. The shipwrights were not represented at all. Their only candidate, John

Moses, was unsuccessful in his campaign for the Drake Division of Plymouth. Of the twenty Cabinet ministers only seven were unionists. Thus the Party and the Government were clearly distinct from the unions and the Government was distinct from both.

There was another important reason for the lack of a charismatic Labour Government: the appalling nature of the problems facing the country, whether at home or abroad. The state of trade and industry, the education system, the chronic housing situation all weighed very heavily on the shoulders of the new Government, while abroad it had to try to grapple with the continuing problem of war reparations which six years after the end of the First World War had still not been solved. The problems were so great and so widespread, it was all the Government could do to keep its head above water. The unions were given an insight into the Government's difficulties when a delegation from the T.U.C. met the Prime Minister on 2nd May. They presented him with petitions on old age pensions, unhealthy offices and unemployment. On pensions, they wanted the abolition of the means test which was 'calculated to penalize the provident and the thrifty' and the payment of a full pension to all 'irrespective of any income received from any other source'. They petitioned for statutory regulations covering ventilation, sanitation and space to be introduced in offices. But naturally their main concern was unemployment. The Congress had expressed its 'deep dissatisfaction' with the Government's plans and called for 'adequate and effective measures' both to alleviate the grave physical and mental consequences to the unemployed population and to remedy the serious social distress to which multitudes of men, women and children are being condemned'.

The Prime Minister replied that the problem facing him and his Government was time. There were so many things they wanted to do and so many opportunities of compelling them to go slowly that he could see a very great accumulation of things that would have to be dealt with one after another. They would have to be a little bit patient.[3]

The T.U.C. would not—and could not—be patient. It continued to work on the unemployment problem, both on its own and in collaboration with the National Unemployed Workers' Committee Movement.

The two organizations drew up an Unemployed Workers' Charter which called for the immediate development of Government schemes to absorb the unemployed at their own trades, the reduction in the working week and the establishment of training centres to give proper training to unemployed workers. The General Council of the T.U.C. sought to highlight the situation and to increase the pressure for action by organizing a week's campaign in the main industrial centres during May 'to call public attention to the unemployed problem and to make representations to public bodies.'

At its annual conference in September 1924 the T.U.C. went further still in approving what it called an Industrial Workers' Charter. This brought together some of its main demands in numerous areas:

1. Public Ownership

   (a) nationalization of land, mines and minerals

(b) nationalization of railways
(c) the extension of State and municipal enterprise for the provision of social necessities and services
(d) to make proper provision for the adequate participation of the workers in control and management.

2. Wages and Hours of Labour
   (a) a legal maximum working week of 44 hours
   (b) a legal minimum wage for each industry or occupation.
3. Unemployment
   (a) suitable provisions in relation to unemployment with adequate maintenance of the unemployed
   (b) establishment of training centres for unemployed juveniles
   (c) extension of training facilities for adults during periods of industrial depression.
4. Housing
   Provision of proper and adequate housing accommodation.
5. Education
   Full educational facilities to be provided by the State from the elementary schools to the universities.
6. Industrial Accidents and Diseases
   Adequate maintenance and compensation in respect of all forms of industrial accidents and diseases.
7. Pensions
   (a) State pensions for all at the age of 60
   (b) State pensions for widowed mothers and dependent children.

The Charter with the instruction that a 'vigorous campaign' should be instituted all over the country to mobilize public opinion behind it, was a most important document, setting out clearly and forcefully the principles for which the Movement stood (some of which were of course not new) and calling for action upon them.

The Government acted where it could. It extended unemployment benefits and amended the Insurance Acts. Payments were increased from 75p a week to 90p for men, from 60p to 75p for women while the children's allowance was doubled to 10p. These were of course palliatives. They eased the distress; they did not tackle the roots of the problem. Perhaps the Government could not be expected to do so for there was no clear answer. Its members were deeply divided over the question of public works. More than one minister spoke out strongly against 'artificially creating work'. At the same time, the Chancellor of the Exchequer, Philip Snowden, a prominent member of the Independent Labour Party, was turning out to be a very orthodox Chancellor. Despite his calls in the past for social reforms of many kinds, he proved himself in office to be the most conservative of Chancellors, demanding a balanced budget and rigorous economy. The effect was to make the depression even deeper and the tension within the Party and between the Party and the unions even greater. The T.U.C. annual conference was to hear W. J. Brown, of the Civil Service Clerical Association, declare: 'There are certain things which have been done by the Labour Government that this Congress ought very emphatically to condemn.' His voice was not alone.

But the Government did have success in two fields. In housing the Minister, John Wheatley, one of the Clydesiders, quickly drew up a plan for building 2.5m. houses within fifteen years, increased the subsidy available, placed the responsibility on the local authorities and ushered in a period of co-operation between government and industry. The President of the T.U.C., Mr A. A. Purcell, M.P., called it an 'historical industrial document, a complete census of the industry with a practical workmanlike survey of the changes in organization, equipment and power needed to get the required results. I commend this process of enquiry and constructive criticism to all concerned with other industries.'[4]

The other success of the Labour Government was in education where Trevelyan, the minister, set up a committee of enquiry whose report largely fashioned the pattern of education up to the present time. It called for the raising of the school leaving age to fifteen and, more important, the division of education into two sectors: primary and secondary. At that time the State system provided only elementary schools which catered for all children from five to fourteen years of age.

These achievements, although important in themselves, were not enough. When after nine months of minority Government, MacDonald called for an election the Labour Party were defeated and the Conservatives, who had renounced Protection once more, were returned with 419 members, 161 more than in 1923. Labour lost 40 seats, giving them a new total of 151. But if any party really suffered it was the Liberals. Their numbers fell from 159 to 40. From now on they were to be the third party, wandering off increasingly into the wilderness. Labour, although out of office, was confirmed as the second force in British politics. It had served its apprenticeship. It was now ready to share with the Conservatives the alternating responsibilities of government and principal opposition. As Wilkie said in the annual report for 1924: 'They showed their capacity in administering the affairs of the nation and of the British Commonwealth and were quite equal to those older parties who have had the monopoly of governing for so many years. It lies with the working men and women of the country when the opportunity again occurs, not only to put a Labour Government into office, but to place them in power to make the reforms desired, not only in the interests of the industrial classes but of the nation as a whole and effective to the betterment of all.' The opportunity was not to occur for almost five years.

CHAPTER TWENTY

The first Labour Government had come and gone. Britain, still in recession, settled down under the torpor of the inactive government of Stanley Baldwin. Events would have to cure themselves, however long that took. And it was to take a long time. Not until the Second World War, fifteen years hence, did the British economy, or at least heavy engineering and shipbuilding, reach peak performance again. Under this torpor industrial relations became more peaceful with the devastating exception of the General Strike in 1926.

AN INDUSTRY STILL LANGUISHING

Despite an improvement in freight rates between 1923 and 1924—they went up by 22 per cent on average over the whole world—the increase in ordering was not dramatic. New work laid down in federated yards rose from 400,000 in 1922 to 950,000 in 1923 but then slipped back. In 1924 the average number of shipwrights unemployed at any one time was 3,500 but by 1925 the figure had gone back up to 4,500.

In this situation, it was particularly galling to see British owners placing contracts abroad. Furness Withy ordered five 10,000-ton motorships from a German firm because the contract price for each ship was £60,000 less than the lowest British tender—£170,000 against £230,000. Lawrence Holt, a member of the well-known Liverpool shipowning firm, gave his reasons for German success after a visit to that country:

1. Lower wages
2. Widespread piece-work operation
3. Longer hours of work
4. No restrictions on labour-saving machinery
5. No demarcation obstacles between trades
6. No redundant labour in the yards

Comments of this sort and the relative success of foreign firms were worrying. As a result the employers and trade unions in the industry decided to set up their own Joint Committee of Enquiry. Its purpose was to examine the state of the industry with special reference to foreign competition. The Joint Committee produced an interim report in the autumn of 1925, dealing with hours, wages and conditions on the Continent as compared with this country. The second part of the report published in June 1926 looked at costs arising outside the industry, for example the price of steel was £2 a ton cheaper on the Continent, thanks to cheaper coal. The report found that the prices for some articles were 100 per cent and sometimes 200 per cent more than pre-war. Occasionally this was caused by trade associations forcing them up. The report also complained that the burden of local taxes and rates was often three times as heavy as pre-war and that it fell especially on the depressed areas where the shipyards were situated and where unemployment was highest. These areas were having to pay for their depressed state twice over.

The first section dealing with costs and conditions over which the industry had control created greater divisions of opinion between union leaders and employers but was nevertheless enlightening. The investigations showed that wages were higher on the Continent but so were the working hours at least in Germany and Holland where 54 hours was the norm but no comparison was made of the relative productivity per £ of wages. But the report did deal with the comparative attitudes on the Continent and in this country towards greater inter-changeability or flexibility in working practices in order to speed up production. The employers felt that a more flexible approach was possible without infringing upon the broad principles of craftsmanship.

The report had a generally favourable reception from the employers. *The Shipbuilder* magazine which reflected management views, commented: 'The report is unique in British industry. It represents an attempt by all concerned—capital, management and labour—to investigate the causes of our loss of shipbuilding supremacy.'[1] In 1913 the U.K. had built 60 per cent of world output whereas in 1926 with a comparable total world output, British production accounted for just over 40 per cent.

While the report had a generally favourable reception from the bosses, union reaction was mixed.

The Executive Committee of the Shipwrights, together with the district technical advisers discussed it at length before giving their verdict, that it 'takes us very little further towards the elucidation of the problem of the revival of the industry, its increased prosperity and therefore greater continuity of employment to those engaged in the industry.'[2]

The shipwrights saw the proposals on interchangeability as an attempt 'to impose upon the shipyard workers a new set of working conditions, abrogating all previous agreements and customs.' As a result, they declared: 'We are of the opinion that all questions of interchangeability must be settled amongst the trades concerned as occasion arises and that the proposals of the employers are impracticable and will increase rather than minimize trouble.'

They did agree with the report that Government action was needed to create an international agreement on the length of the working week and that piece-work proposals should be studied closely by the unions.

If the report did little to improve matters, the same could be said of the continuing activities of the T.U.C., the General Federation of Trade Unions and the National Unemployment Workers' Committee Movement. But at least they kept up the pressure. They never allowed the apparent lack of progress to drive them into apathy. The T.U.C. selected 21st June 1925 as Unemployment Sunday when demonstrations were held in all the major towns. And it 'pressed these demonstrations to the fullest conclusion' by holding a special conference in the Central Hall, Westminster on 24th July. The conference, which turned out to be a mass demonstration on behalf of all unions, passed a number of resolutions deploring the 'appalling increase in the number of unemployed compared with the pre-war period' and declaring that 'such a state of affairs cannot be allowed to continue indefinitely.' The Conference was 'to exert the utmost possible pressure upon the Government to take such steps as are necessary for the remedying of the present critical situation'. What those steps should be, the Conference did not say except for the pursuance of a foreign policy calculated to develop amicable diplomatic relations which in turn should help exports.

The shipwrights did call for very specific action at the annual meeting of the General Federation of Trade Unions held in Blackpool on 9th and 10th July. They looked to barge-building for a revived canal trade as part of an overall solution. They put forward a resolution which viewed with alarm the depression in the shipping industry and called for 'an exhaustive enquiry into the ports and waterways of Great Britain with a view to improving freightage facilities, reducing costs, and affording employment to ship, boat and barge builders.'

In an interview with the President of the Board of Trade, Sir P. Cunliffe-Lister, in November, the shipwrights pointed out that other countries were developing their canals and spending considerable sums on barges while this country had spent virtually nothing on new works since 1830 and not enough on maintenance to keep most in a good state of repair. The union pressed for work on three projects: The Trent Scheme which would link Nottingham to the national network; the 'Cross' Scheme which would link the Mersey, the Thames, the Humber and the Severn; and the Mid-Scotland Ship Canal which would connect Glasgow and Edinburgh. These schemes, relatively cheap to carry out, would benefit the engineering, shipbuilding and barge-building industries and create considerable employment for both skilled and unskilled workers. The minister said he was impressed by the case and would make sure it was considered by the various Government departments involved. The delegation felt that 'a decided move forward had been made'. Nothing more was to be heard of it. Yet this was one of the most imaginative proposals put forward at the time. It would have been relatively cheap, quick to put into practice and would have been of inestimable long-term benefit to the country.

In September 1925 the Admiralty increased the sense of desperation hanging over the industry when it announced that it was to put on a 'care and maintenance' basis two of its dockyards, at Rosyth in Scotland and Pembroke Dock in Wales. In other words, no further orders were to be placed in these yards. Admiralty work was to be concentrated in the other Royal Dockyards. The effect would be very hard on these two towns which were largely dependent on the dockyards for their prosperity.

The T.U.C. was in conference at Scarborough when the news came through. Leaders of unions which were involved tabled an emergency resolution viewing the decision 'with alarm' and calling upon the Government to countermand it. Mr J. T. Brownlie, of the Amalgamated Engineering Union, moved the resolution seconded by Mr John Hill, of the Boilermakers. Hill said that the decision was a serious matter not only for the men but also for the many retail businesses in the two areas. The Pembroke dockyard was the only industrial facility in the whole county. In Rosyth there had been considerable expenditure not only on the dockyard but also on social amenities, such as housing and schools. All of this would be placed in jeopardy. He saw it all as part of the conspiracy between the Government and private enterprise. 'It is part of the policy to close down all Government work and throw the work more and more into the hands of private employers,' he declared.

Mr W. Jackson spoke on behalf of the shipwrights. He put in a plea for those transferred to Rosyth from other places who would now be cast adrift. 'An enormous amount of money has been spent on this dockyard and if it was to be closed it meant that all that money would be thrown away.'

In arguing for Rosyth and Pembroke to stay open, T.U.C. delegates made it clear that they were concerned with employment not with armaments. This was a difficult point which J. H. Thomas of the National Union of Railwaymen and Colonial Secretary in the first Labour Government, put most clearly when he said that Congress would be united in agreeing to a reduction on expenditure on armaments. But closing Rosyth and Pembroke would not cut down on such expenditure. The work was to be concentrated in other places. The delegates could oppose the closure of these two docks and urge a reduction in expenditure on armaments at the same time. That would be a consistent policy. Congress agreed and the emergency resolution was passed.

The T.U.C. was represented in a deputation which saw the Civil Lord, Lord Stanhope, on 17th September. So was the Federation of Engineering and Shipbuilding Trades. The deputation was led by Wilkie who spoke of the hardship which would be suffered by the men. The Admiralty could not divest itself of its responsibilities to the townships as easily as it imagined. In view of the serious consequences to the men and their families, the Admiralty was asked to think again.

Lord Stanhope was unyielding. The Admiralty had to carry out economy measures and it was more economical to carry out work in large yards than in small. 'The Admiralty deeply deplored the necessity which gave rise to the hardships.' But he could hold out no hope of the decision being reversed and he could give no more assurance for the future.

It was very depressing and another nail, or so it must have seemed, in the coffin of British shipbuilding. A month later another deputation met the Prime Minister and Lord Stanhope with the same outcome.

THE ASSOCIATION'S AFFAIRS

The Association reflected the conditions in the industry with membership, income and reserves all continuing to fall. Membership drifted down to 29,000 which was in effect setting the clock back ten years. Income was down to £65,000 by 1925 having been £68,000 in 1924. Expenditure also came down from £79,000 in 1924 to £72,000 in 1925. The reserves fell once more, for the fifth consecutive year and, by December 1925 stood at only £63,000, the lowest level since 1897.

Wilkie ended his annual report for 1925 with these words: 'In concluding the review of the work of the Association for 1925 we regret that it is not of a more cheering character but in common with other shipyard unions, we have had to pass through years of depression unparalleled in the history of the Society and industry.'

Despite the heavy depression, there was one bright note, a small increase in wages. In February 1924 the Confederation of Engineering and Shipbuilding Unions asked for an advance of 50p a week. The timing of the claim might have seemed extraordinarily inappropriate but the unions argued that wages were now below a civilized standard and that engineers, their colleagues in the Federation, had not given up the last 50p of the £1.32½ war bonus as all other trades had. The employers showed sympathy but nothing else. At a time when contracts were being taken at small or even no profit, they said that they had no room for manoeuvre.

The unions refused to accept this argument and in June a Board of Arbitration was set up to discuss the matter. In their evidence to the Board, the employers threw some interesting light on the effect of competition during the previous two years. On forty-nine contracts for new work taken between June 1922 and June 1924 an aggregate of £233,000 had been lost. And on a further eighty-three contracts for new work not then completed, they estimated that a total loss of £785,000 would be made even with wages at the existing level.

The Board, however, took into account other factors: the noticeable rise in freight rates, the extra work being ordered and the extra berths being occupied. It was for these reasons that the Board granted 35p of the claim, to be paid partly in June and partly in September. The increase brought the basic wage for shipwrights in the federated area of Scotland and the North of England to £3.20 for new work and £3.35 for old work. A similar request in January 1925 was turned down. In fact there was to be no further increase until the summer of 1928.

The improvement in labour relations—or at least the dramatic reduction in working days lost through strikes—was shattered by nine days in May 1926. Large sections of British workers, two and a half million in all, came out on strike in support of the miners, producing the nearest thing this country has ever known to a General Strike. In fact the episode is generally referred to in such terms although it was not really general. Besides the miners, transport workers, printers, some building workers and those in the power and iron and steel industries were called out. But textile workers—after miners the most important industrial group in the country—remained at work. So did post office and distributive workers while the shipyard workers and those in engineering were only called out after a week had elapsed.

The General Strike had its origin in 1925 when the coal-owners put forward wage proposals which the Miners' Federation rejected. This was hardly surprising since the proposals involved a reduction of 10p a shift in the Scottish and northern coalfields to about 40p a shift. They also provided no national minimum which the miners had been seeking for some time. The Executive of the Miners' Federation asked to meet the General Council of the T.U.C. which decided to support them in their opposition, or as the T.U.C. put it, 'to co-operate wholeheartedly with them in their resistance to the degredation of the standard of life of their members.' In July 1925 another meeting took place between the Miners' Executive and the Special Committee which the T.U.C. had set up. The T.U.C.'s understanding of this meeting was that the miners 'made it plain that they were placing their case unreservedly in the hands of the General Council.' The miners were later to dispute this interpretation.

But for the moment there was general agreement. Other unions pledged their support. The railwaymen and transport workers agreed to place an embargo upon the movement of coal. This sign of solidarity made matters much more serious and almost constant meetings were being held between all the parties. The Prime Minister, Stanley Baldwin, took over personal responsibility on the Government side. At first his attitude, as expressed at meetings or in his statement on 30th July, was 'that the Government are not prepared to give a subsidy to the industry' but that they would establish 'an authoritative enquiry to try to get to the bottom of the economic difficulties of the industry .... with a view to putting the industry as quickly as possible into a more healthy condition in which it can afford a better level of wages.'

The following day, after he had met the owners and miners once more and seen how entrenched their positions were, he learned that they were willing to take part in an enquiry. He therefore announced that the Government 'was prepared to render assistance to the industry until the Spring, by which time the enquiry would be completed.'

The assistance was intended to maintain the previous rate of wages and to amount to £10 million. In fact it cost £23m. and helped profits as much as wages. A royal commission was set up under Sir Herbert

Samuel, a former Liberal Minister, and spent the winter hearing evidence and preparing a 300-page report. When it came out, it offered little immediate hope or help to the men. It put forward numerous proposals for the development of the industry such as the amalgamation of smaller pits and the improvement of working conditions. But on the immediate, pressing question of wages, it agreed with the owners, there would have to be a reduction. The men refused to accept such a finding while the owners rejected reorganization. The two were now on a collision course. The current wages agreement, extended by the Government's offer of subsidy, expired at the end of April 1926. On 1st May the men were locked out. The same day a special conference placed authority in the hands of the general council of the T.U.C. which decided that a national strike in support of the miners should begin on 3rd May in certain industries.

Their call was obeyed almost to a man. Only 1 per cent of railwaymen turned up for work. Buses and trams virtually disappeared from the streets. No newspapers were published. Docks, furnaces, power stations closed down. Following a carefully drawn-up plan the Government drafted in troops and police to maintain essential supplies while volunteers were asked to come forward to drive buses, unload cargoes and undertake other jobs. Large numbers of people, particularly students, volunteered and thoroughly enjoyed themselves.

In fact, of all the puzzling features of the General Strike, the most extraordinary was the camaraderie of it all and the lack of tension. One reads of police and strikers playing football together while in Newcastle the local strike committee actually helped the district commissioner to unload and deliver food. If any single piece of evidence demonstrated that this was not a political strike and that there was no attempt to overthrow the Government, then it was surely provided by the atmosphere of those nine days.

After a week Sir Herbert Samuel took the centre of the stage once more. Working in a personal capacity, he drafted a memorandum to settle the dispute, principally on the basis that wage reductions should take place but only after the reorganization and modernization of the industry had been accepted in principle by the owners. This was the concession which the negotiating committee of the T.U.C. had been looking for. Despite the dissension of the miners, they called off the national strike unconditionally on 12th May. The miners who found that the T.U.C. had taken the initiative from their hands continued the struggle alone for six months but in the end they were forced back to work by starvation and had to accept longer hours and lower wages while the owners refused to do anything to reorganize or improve the industry.

Shipbuilding workers had been called out by the general council only for the last two days of the strike and, if Wilkie's comments were any guide, came out rather begrudgingly. He talked of the 'disastrous general strike and the coal dispute' which dislocated every industry and prevented 'the necessary material being to hand for the production of new shipbuilding and repairs.'[3] The effects had been 'calamitous'. Tonnage under construction in September 1926 was only 774,000 tons compared with a million tons a year earlier.

It is easy to understand his feelings of exasperation. Shipbuilding, with cotton and engineering, had borne the brunt of the depression. Unemployment had been higher in these industries than elsewhere. His own union had suffered falling membership and reserves. Each time it looked as if things might at least start to improve some new obstacles came in their way. It was understandable, yet his attitude contrasted with the solidarity of the movement as a whole.

In fact the shipbuilding trades did not have a good record with regard to the call to support the national strike. 'Instead of an all-round and unanimous response to the appeal there was only chaos and disorganization.'[4] While recognizing the prejudiced source of this comment, there was more than an element of truth in it. The shipwrights certainly were reluctant to stop work, as were the boilermakers, while a mass meeting of all shipyard trades at Middlesbrough decided that they would not come out with their respective unions. It was estimated that 95 per cent of the men employed on the North-East coast shipyards remained at work while on the Clyde 75 per cent did so. Since the shipyard workers were called upon by the T.U.C. special committee only after the first week, their true attitude did not have any chance to show itself before the strike was called off. But certainly there was no unanimous and immediate response to the strike call as there was in other industries.

Wilkie took the opportunity to state once more the case for moderation and effective machinery of arbitration. '..... It appears to us that the time has come when a closer survey of the methods by which these disputes can be avoided should be considered and, wherever possible, with the spirit of reasonableness on both sides, measures should be adopted to prevent a recurrence of these calamitous disputes which in the end have to be settled by the arbitrament of reason rather than force,' he wrote in the autumn of 1926.[5] Pious platitudes alone would solve no problems. No one had gone into the strike willingly but unless they had abandoned their principles they had no alternative but to go on.

At least the T.U.C. and the Labour Party had tried to put forward constructive proposals in calling for public ownership and control. As Mr Pugh, President of the T.U.C. in 1926, said in his address to the annual conference in Bournemouth: 'Change of ownership will not solve the problem. But if, with public ownership there is invoked a spirit of new endeavour, of co-operation between the workers of hand and brain in place of the present antagonism and strife, coupled with a genuine effort to modernize the industry, to enlarge its scope, improve its methods and bring it back into line with the tendencies of economic evolution and scientific discovery, we have then these conditions necessary for the development of the industry as a great public service in which real justice can be done to the workers by a progressive improvement in their standard of life..... The strike reflected the growing discontent of the workers with the whole structure and policy of the industrial system and their determination to resist the traditional idea, that bad trade can be made good and industry placed in a healthy condition by the mere expedient of degrading the standard of life of the working people.' There was in this an element of compassion and positive thought that Wilkie's comments lacked.

SHIPYARD AGREEMENTS

The massively disruptive effect of the General Strike—the *Economist* estimated that it cost the country between £400m. and £500m.—the debilitating effect it had on union funds, the serious punishment inflicted on the miners, who had to accept the owners' terms after losing £60m. in wages, all these factors led to a new peace in industry. Disputes fell away completely and for the next two years there were fewer days lost in disputes than at any time since records were kept.

It was in this new atmosphere, of calm after a storm, that the shipbuilding employers and most of the unions signed the formal agreement dealing with disputes procedure that still stands today. Apart from questions relating to piecework and piecework prices, the following procedure was agreed:

1. A dispute was first to be discussed at yard level between the employer and a deputation of the men concerned.
2. Further meetings at the yard attended by local officials of the employers' association and of the union directly concerned.
3. A formal local conference between the local employers' association and the union or unions involved.
4. A central conference attended by national officers of the employers' federation and the union.
5. If the central conference also failed to find a solution, then the dispute could be referred to arbitration by mutual consent.

Where general questions that were raised locally were common to two or more unions, the Confederation of Engineering and Shipbuilding Unions could represent the workers at local or national level but the unions concerned and not the Confederation had to accept the responsibility for any settlement. The Agreement made a special reference to piecework and piecework prices. If there was no agreement at yard level, the question would go to a joint committee consisting of three employers and three representatives of the union or unions concerned, none of whom were to have any connection with the yard where the dispute had arisen. If they failed to agree, a local or national conference could be called.

This important Agreement, so close to the heart of the Shipwrights' Executive, went unobserved and un-noted. Yet at the very moment the Agreement was being worked out the Quarterly Report was making the general comment that there ought to be a spirit of co-operation between the two sides in order to steady and develop the industry but the spirit of co-operation in the industry should not be on a one-sided nature but a genuine desire on both sides to arrange as far as possible to avoid disputes and settle them without resorting either to lock-outs or strikes.'

Well here was the practical means of putting that general desire into practice. Why did not the union give it open backing and support? It is hard to escape the conclusion that the union was lacking effective leadership. One feels sympathy for Wilkie in the ill-health that dogged him—he had not been able to attend the T.U.C. conference in September 1926—but why did he not stand down? Why did he not appreciate that his most valuable contribution now would have been to give way to a younger man?

CHANGES IN THE PENSION FUND

During 1926 membership continued to fall reaching 26,000 by the year's end. This was a drop of 3,000 or about 10 per cent. Reserves also continued to tumble, falling by £21,000 to only £42,000. At this rate they would have been exhausted and the Association would have been bankrupt within two years. The Executive Committee decided that drastic surgery was needed. Looking at expenditure they recognized that the superannuation benefit was the heaviest outlay. It was costing the union over £20,000 a year and was rising. With more and more members reaching retirement age, the financial burden could become intolerable particularly when income was falling or at best was only stable. The Committee decided to recommend a bold but harsh course of action. Superannuation benefit should be paid for only five years. Any members who had received the benefit for that period would have the payments stopped. The recommendation was likely to cause a good deal of antagonism or at least soul-searching. But this was a measure of the perilous financial situation facing the union. The tremendous drain must be stopped. The period of five years was chosen because in that time a member of as long as forty years' standing would have received his contribution back, even if he had never been a beneficiary of any of the other schemes.

To set the recommendation in context, the Executive Committee suggested that there could be two alternatives. Firstly, the payment of superannuation benefit in proportion to the amount received from members each quarter. Secondly the total suspension of all superannuation payments. The Executive Committee also proposed that the union should pull out of its membership to the Labour Party, the Trades Union Congress and the General Federation of Trade Unions. It also proposed the setting up of a special committee to have another look at the Association rules.

The members agreed by 2:1 that the union should pull out of the various bodies but they were opposed to alterations to the superannuation scheme. The Executive Committee were left in a difficulty by this decision. After considerable discussion they decided to put the question to the members again but this time as a simple resolution: either the stopping of payments after five years with the levy remaining as it was or the total suspension of the benefit until the Rules Committee had had time to examine the scheme afresh. This time the members agreed. So superannuation benefits were to be paid for only five years. Any members who had already been in receipt of payments for such a period would have their benefits stopped.

Although the new rule did not come into effect until 31st July, it had a dramatic impact on the union's expenditure for payments under this heading; they dropped from £20,462 in 1926 to £14,498 in 1927 and to £13,045 in 1928. Equally, there were considerable savings from pulling out of the various bodies mentioned above. Affiliation fees to the T.U.C. had cost £400 a year, to the General Federation £1,200 and to the local and national Labour Party £700. All of these sums were saved. There were naturally squeals of disapproval from certain quarters. Some members thought the moves were harsh. The T.U.C. sent a delegation to try to convince the Executive Committee to change its mind. But they remained resolute. As a result they managed to stabilize the accounts —but only just. In 1927, after six successive years of heavy losses, there was a small surplus of just £308. It might have been small but the surplus was a notable event, all the more remarkable since membership was continuing to fall. By December 1927 it was down to 24,379. Nevertheless income remained at £57,800 thanks to a really determined attempt to collect all members' contributions. With expenditure down to £57,500 there was at last a sign that the worst was over. Stringent economy was paying dividends. But there was to be a fierce struggle yet over many years before finance ceased to be a pressing concern.

CHANGES IN THE RULES

The changes in the superannuation fund which had been agreed by the members were also considered by the Rules Revision Committee which met in the first half of 1928. The Committee endorsed the new policy of limiting payment to five years, pointing out 'that every member who draws this benefit for the period mentioned will receive more than it was possible for him to have paid in to this organization during his membership.' Assuming that he joined the Association as a full member as soon as he ended his apprenticeship, a member would pay just over £100 in contributions. At 8s a week pension, he would receive £100 in five years as a union pensioner. The Rules Revision Committee described the Pension Scheme as 'the most important one in our Association'. Following the changes, this no longer remained true. The sickness benefit scheme became marginally the most important, at least in terms of outlay.

The rules of the organization had not been subject to revision for a good number of years and were in urgent need of re-examination particularly in view of the sharply-altered financial position. Partly because of that position it was decided not to convene a delegates' conference as had been done in the early years of the union but instead to entrust the work to seventeen members elected by their colleagues. Besides financial considerations, it was also hoped that this procedure might produce better results more quickly. This seemed to be the case and the Committee expedited matters still further by setting up a small sub-committee to tackle particular problems as they arose, for example the question of drafting.

The Committee made a number of important proposals for altering the rules. On contributions, it proposed that they should be all-inclusive in the hope of dispensing with levies. The quarterly superannuation levy, the legal levy and the payment for reports would be assimilated into the weekly contributions without any extra cost to the individual member. It was hoped that the saving in administrative time and labour would balance the loss of revenue. The local contingency levy was retained, however, in case a branch needed special funds for an emergency or special situation.

On benefits, the Committee proposed that all payments should be in full without a deduction for contributions. This system would then show clearly the actual cash paid to the individual member. The Committee wanted a change in the law so that state unemployment benefit could again be paid through the Association rather than through the Ministry of Labour. It also suggested that friendly benefits for such things as funeral payments should be optional 'in the desire to have a complete organization of all eligible workers.' At the same time the Committee 'strongly recommend all members to continue paying for friendly benefits whenever they can do so.'

The Committee made a number of interesting recommendations on the organization of the union. It suggested that the Executive Committee should be reduced from seven members to five but that they should be full-time, giving 'the whole of their time and interest to the Organization'. The number of district delegates should be reduced from thirteen to nine which would produce a considerable saving in administrative expenses. So too would the election of district committee and secretaries on a local rather than a national basis. Full-time officials, however, should continue to be elected nationally. The elections of officials was to be statutory and was to be on the basis of:

General Secretary—every five years
Assistant General Secretary—every three years
Executive Representatives—every two years
District Delegates—every two years

They also decided that all full-time officials should retire at the age of 65.

The proposals were lucid, coherent and relevant to the union in its new situation. By June 1928 they were ready to be put to members. In order to make sure that they were properly understood it was decided to hold a series of area conferences at which members either of the Rules Revision Committee or of the Executive Committee would explain the proposals to members. Through the second half of June and the first half of July sixteen area conferences were held and in all were attended by about 5,000 shipwrights. These special conferences were not always successful in convincing members of the soundness of the proposals.

When the vote was taken in October, the Govan, Partick and Port Glasgow branches voted solidly against. So did North Shields, Southampton, Hull, Grimsby, Goole and a number of other branches. But in other areas, the recommendations were well received and in total the members voted: For 2,783; Against 1,857. The changes came into force on 1st January 1929. The union started a new era.

CHAPTER TWENTY-ONE

The union entered a new era in 1929, partly due to the introduction of the new rules and partly due to the death of Alex Wilkie and the election of a new General Secretary and other officials. Britain, too, entered a new era. A second Labour Government was elected, more experienced and confident than the first. Soon it had to face the impact of the Great Crash and the Great Depression which, within eighteen months, made one in every five working men unemployed. The twenties had been a difficult decade for shipbuilding; the thirties were to be devastating.

DEATH OF WILKIE

The death of Alexander Wilkie on 2nd September 1928 marked the end of the first phase of the union's life and, as it happened, the first half of its existence as an independent union. He had almost been its progenitor, certainly he was its greatest servant, a shrewd, capable and energetic man who had won great respect for himself and his union. Under his guidance and leadership, it had grown from 1,750 members to well over 45,000 representing almost all shipwrights in every part of the country with a reserve fund of over a quarter of a million pounds. But since that high-point, it must also be admitted that there had been a terrible reversal with membership slipping back to only 22,000 at the time of his death and the reserves down to £42,000. The main cause lay in the appalling state of the industry. But on the other hand, he did little to prompt the kind of financial tourniquet which eventually had to be applied.

For all that, his services to the union were enormous and undeniable. The *Newcastle Daily Journal* said of him: 'No man worked harder for the Labour movement and for the interests of shipwrights in particular than Mr Wilkie.... Displaying fine organizing ability, Mr Wilkie steadily increased the strength and influence of the Society.'[1]

He was seventy-eight when he died and had held official positions for over fifty years, first as secretary of the Glasgow Shipwrights' Society in the early seventies, then from 1877 as secretary of the Federated Societies and of course from 1882 as General Secretary of the Associated

Shipwrights' Society. The period of office in itself was remarkable. But, even more remarkable, was the fact that for most of that time the work was arduous and pioneering, culminating in the unsuccessful but whole-hearted attempts to create one union for the shipwrights, boilermakers, blacksmiths and other workers in the shipbuilding industry.

His union work, although the first priority, was only one side. He was also a political figure. He sat in Parliament for fourteen years and as a Newcastle Councillor and Alderman for twenty-four. He was a leading member of the T.U.C. and of the Labour Party. As such, he sat on many committees and took part in many high-level meetings and deputations. He was also a director of the Percy Building Society and of the Co-operative Printing Society. All in all, it would be impossible to disagree with the tribute of the *Newcastle Daily Journal* that he was 'a worthy Scot who served his fellow well', were it not for the fact that he was created a Companion of Honour. That distinction really was most unusual for a trade union leader, no matter how diligent. It indicated that there was something of a higher quality in him too and that the *Journal*'s assessment was not really sufficient. Certainly his own colleagues were in no doubt about his contribution. The President of the Executive Committee, James McWhirter, wrote: 'We feel certain that his work and his achievements will remain with us, and will act as an incentive to those who are toiling on, in whatever capacity, to do their best in helping on the work of the Society and the Movement as a whole.'[2]

He was buried in Heaton cemetery, Newcastle, not far from his home at Leven House in the prosperous residential area of Lesbury Road.

ELECTION OF A NEW GENERAL SECRETARY

Wilkie's death occurred at a time when the union was in the process of consulting the members about the proposed revision of the rules. Rather than interrupt and possibly complicate that process, it was decided to go ahead with the ballot and empower the Executive Committee to take any action that was necessary to continue the union's affairs.

Meanwhile Frank Purdy, the Assistant General Secretary, who had been made Acting General Secretary, at the time of Wilkie's illness, was to continue in that capacity. The ballot on the rules was held in October and the new constitution came into effect on 1st January 1929. It was therefore the new year before nominations for the position of General Secretary could be requested. Four candidates were put forward.

The Acting General Secretary, Frank Purdy, was an obvious nomination and he was put forward by forty-six branches. Aged fifty-six, he had been a member of the general office for thirty years and had worked closely with Wilkie as his assistant. He knew the administration of the union intimately. If the members wanted continuity and a smooth transition from one chief officer to another he was their man.

The technical adviser for the Cardiff area, E. P. Harries, was another candidate. Although he had only been the adviser for four years he had 'pulled the area together'. His main claim, however, was that he was the union's representative on the Admiralty Industrial Council which meant that a great deal of business affecting members in Government employment went through his hands. His main disadvantage was that he was not widely known. Only sixteen branches nominated him, all of them on the south coast or in Wales.

The same could be said of Sam Mason of London. Apprenticed in Liverpool where he became a union officer, he was asked to move to the London area where there was a great deal of work to be done. In 1923 he was made the district technical adviser. He was particularly noted for his tactfulness.

The fourth candidate was also a technical adviser. He was William Westwood of Glasgow, who was nominated by fifty-eight branches. A driller by training, he was a dynamic, outward-going personality, who had become widely known not only for his industrial work but also as a shrewd political figure. In fact he was the Labour Party agent in Dundee where he had worked on behalf of Wilkie and helped him to secure his highest majority. Later he fought Perth as a candidate himself but without success, although he was said to have put up a very good fight. His proposers said of him in putting forward his claims for the position: 'He is an able debater, a fluent speaker, active, tactful, diplomatic, and possesses good initiative while he has a strong personality, is a fearless fighter, just, firm and combines patience with good temper.'

After such a glowing reference, it is perhaps surprising that the members did not elect him immediately. But they did not. The first ballot taken in April 1929 gave him the lead but not by such a margin as to invalidate a second election. The figures were:

Westwood	2,948
Purdy	2,118
Harries	1,041
Mason	737

The two bottom candidates were eliminated and a second election was held in June between Westwood and Purdy. The result was:

Westwood	4,825
Purdy	2,275

In other words, Westwood picked up not only the vast majority of votes which had gone to Harries and Mason, but he also attracted the votes of those members who had not voted the first time. His victory was now decisive but even so only a third of the members had taken part in the ballot.

So William Westwood, who had been born in 1880 in humble circumstances in Dundee became the second General Secretary of one of the most important unions in the industry.

He had actually started work at the age of eight, knocking up the jute workers for their early-morning shift beginning at six o'clock. This meant that young William had to be up at 4.30. He also sold papers and delivered for the local grocers in between finishing his short education. When he left school he had a number of jobs before starting an apprenticeship as a driller at the age of sixteen.

Even from this early age he was politically motivated and he saw his future as a union official. At the age of nineteen, while still an apprentice, he became the branch secretary and the following year he became the youngest delegate to the Trade Union Congress. At about this time another strand in his personality asserted itself. For he took his first step into the world of commerce. On the spur of the moment at an auction he bought a riverside cottage where he had once sheltered, for £90. Within a fortnight he sold it for £180. This was the first sign of an acumen that was many years later to turn him into a highly successful businessman. But for the moment the union was his career. In 1909 his reputation increased considerably when he played a major part in the settlement of a dispute in the jute industry. Meanwhile his spare time study of industrial insurance secured him by competitive examination the position of National Supervisor with the Association in 1913. He held this appointment in Glasgow until he was elected General Secretary.

He was to remain in the position until 1945 by which time he was to be a tremendous figure in union and political circles and be created a Baron. That lay in the future. His first task, as he told members in a special address to them, was to appeal for loyalty and co-operation for without these he would not be able to bring about the changes which would restore the union's lost prestige.[3] He wanted to see the membership increased and in particular to encourage apprentices to join the union. He recognized that differences of opinion would occur but he urged members to bear in mind that the officials were only human. 'If criticism is offered let it be of a constructive and not destructive character.' He went on: 'We are anxious that the rules should be administered in a common sense manner by all officers, so let us forget any mistakes of the past, in order that a real awakening can take place, and if we all pull together we can inspire the much-needed enthusiasm which will bring about an increased membership, combined with a strong financial position.'

He reiterated this view in his first newspaper interview after his election, when he said: 'My main ambition is to gain for our Association the standing with the trade union movement which it should have. We are hoping that this will come about as a result of the improvement in the industry and the improvement which will take place in our organization at an early date.'[4]

There was no doubt that the Executive Committee were prepared to give Westwood their backing. They offered him their 'fullest loyalty and support' and hoped he would be able to 'inspire greater confidence within the society and as a result once more raise it to its proper place among the trade unions'.[5]

His election and the start he had made were well received in wider circles. A trade paper, *The Syren and Shipping*, commented: 'When Mr

William Westwood succeeded the late Mr Alexander Wilkie as General Secretary of the Shipconstructors and Shipwrights' Association, it was generally admitted that one able trade unionist and sane administrative had followed another. Mr Westwood, like Mr Wilkie, had made for himself in general labour politics a reputation for breadth of outlook and statesmanlike grasp of the things that really mattered and everyone knew that if the old union was in difficulties, he was the best possible man for straightening things out.'[6]

Meanwhile the Acting General Secretary, Frank Purdy, who had been unsuccessful in the ballot, felt he had no option but to resign. He had been so closely involved with the Wilkie regime that to have stayed would have been embarrassing. More important, there was no job for him to return to, for his previous position as Assistant General Secretary had been the subject of a ballot at the same time as the General Secretaryship. He had lost the latter and the former position was closed to him. He had no alternative but to resign, which he did on 30th June.

OTHER ELECTIONS

The contest for the Assistant General Secretary attracted seven candidates and required two ballots. Ultimately John Willcocks, the Tyne and Blyth technical adviser for thirteen years, emerged successful. Slightly younger than Westwood, he had been elected secretary of the Jarrow branch when he was only 22. In 1908 at the age of 25 he was elected to the National Executive of the union and the following year he was elected the first President. As a recognized authority on demarcation problems, Unemployment Insurance and the Workmen's Compensation Acts, he had done a great deal of work of great worth to the union. It was calculated that he had been instrumental in securing over £20,000 for members in compensation claims during his years as a technical adviser. He and Westwood were to form a very effective team.

Once Westwood and Willcocks had been elected, members could turn to the elections of a full-time executive committee of five, according to the new rules, and of seven district delegates plus two drillers' organizers. In these elections also two ballots were necessary but by September the process was complete and the new officials had taken up their duties. They were:

EXECUTIVE COMMITTEE

President:	John Stewart (Glasgow)
Vice President:	Joseph Harrison (Tyneside)
	George Burke (Bristol)
	A. C. Allen (Plymouth)
	P. F. Smith (Sunderland drillers)

DISTRICT DELEGATES

G. W. Cable (Tyne and Blyth)
M. Mackenzie (Clyde)
T. McDonic (Wear, Tees and Humber)
S. Mason (London and Southampton)
W. Dunham (North-West)
E. P. Harries (Bristol Channel)
W. W. Robertson (Ireland)

DRILLERS' ORGANIZERS

T. Butterworth (England and Wales)
J. McMillan (Scotland and Ireland)

Within a few weeks E. P. Harries resigned as Bristol Channel delegate to take a job with the T.U.C. and was succeeded by W. H. Ford. Otherwise this was the team which now set to work to revive the union and put it on a new and more dynamic course. The first task was to look at the general administration of the office. New methods were introduced, creating greater efficiency. For example, a new duplicating machine increased output with less labour. Stationery supplies were rationalized producing a saving in costs. All printing work was automatically put out for tender which meant keener prices. The Monthly Returns which were costly to print and of little interest to members were discontinued although the branches still sent the forms to head office for information.

There was also a physical rearrangement of the office under which all departments were concentrated into No. 8 Eldon Square, thus vacating No. 9 and making it available for letting. Furthermore, as a result of discussions with the local authority, it was agreed that no rates should be paid on No. 9 as long as it was untenanted. This meant a saving of £90 a year in rates alone. There would of course be other savings on heating, lighting and other services. The cost of heating No. 8 was also examined because of the high bills. It was decided to put in a new central heating system which reduced the costs substantially.

Two members of the National Health Insurance Department who had left were not replaced. The Audit Department was instructed to examine all quarterly reports from branches as soon as they arrived so that any irregularities could be put right without delay. New methods of payments of money to the branches were introduced which were less cumbersome and less costly. A new system of registration of members was introduced so that the exact numbers could be ascertained. The old system had got completely out of hand for the actual registration number now was 103,800, whereas the membership was just over 20,000. No proper account had been taken of dead or lapsed members. This would be put right.

It was not all a question of retrenchment and economy. Westwood suggested that there should be a Quarterly Report or Journal for members. This would be not only a record of work carried out. It could also become a means of arousing greater interest by members in their organization. The Annual Report could also be made more attractive and at the same time less expensive by omitting some of the statistics and re-introducing reports from the various districts. Of wider significance, the Executive Committee felt that the union should rejoin the Federation of Engineering and Shipbuilding Trades, the Labour Party and the T.U.C. It had pulled out of them all in 1927 as a means of saving money by not having to pay the subscription fees. Nothing was done immediately, however, in relation to the Labour Party and the T.U.C. because a levy would have been needed and the time was not appropriate. There was one other point of particular concern, the administration of National Insurance by the union as an Approved Society. The cost of this administration, in particular the payment of branch officers' salaries, was now greater than the income justified and the account showed a deficit. It was agreed that the union should take steps to stop being a reimbursing society by the end of the year.

All of these decisions implied a new energy, a new determination and a new spirit. New men had taken over. Armed with new powers, such as full-time responsibility, and faced with a perilous financial situation, they acted with resolution and flair. The Committee in effect became a Management Committee meeting at frequent intervals. For example they met on 1st, 2nd, 3rd and 4th October as they grappled with the immediate problems of administrative reorganization. Later they could meet at four- or five-weekly intervals but the meetings themselves generally lasted for two or even three days. In this way they were able to keep in close touch with what was happening both at head office and in the country. Regular contact with the members was indeed one of the main elements of the new policy. As Westwood said at the first meeting of the new Executive, the Committee members must get round their districts as early and as often as possible to start the drive for new members and explain the new methods of administration. They also kept a close check on branch records. A whole series of area conferences, district and branch meetings were in fact held in the autumn of 1929 up and down the country to outline the union's parlous position, to detail the steps being taken and to solicit the support of members, particularly new members. The cumulative effect of all these actions was dramatic. The union gained a sense of confidence and of purposeful progress. Within a few months Westwood could say: '..... many of the difficulties which confronted us when we took up our duties have now been overcome and we are now on the right road to success.'[7] As a single piece of evidence he could have pointed to the fact that between 20th July and 26th November, 919 new members were enrolled.

As a final example of the thrusting work that was done in the first few months of the new leadership, it must be said that all existing agreements were reviewed. As a result a new understanding was reached with the National Union of Seamen about the contributions to be paid by sea-going joiners and shipwrights. In addition, outlets for employment in new industries were sought. An agreement was signed with civil engineering contractors giving greater opportunities for employment. Similarly an agreement was reached with the Aircraft Constructions Works at Brough under which the union was to be allowed to organize certain sections of the men. It was decided to form a suitable section in the union for this particular class of men who would be admitted as trade members only.

THE HEALTH OF THE UNION

While the steps that the new officials had taken would put the union on the right road, the journey was to prove a very bumpy one. Membership continued to decline despite the new members and so did the reserves. The small surplus achieved in 1927 after six years of loss proved only a temporary respite. In 1928, 1929 and 1930 the expenditure exceeded income, even if only narrowly. The membership figures which were down to 21,000 were more encouraging than they might have seemed. For this was a true figure. The previous totals contained many members who had fallen seriously behind with their contributions. Such members, in Westwood's word, were 'purged'. The 'purged' members exceeded the new recruits in the first few months. This made the drive for new members even more important. Westwood put it this way:

'Our Association, like every other trade union, is a business concern and its chief business is to protect and improve the general conditions of employment of its members—and those who ought to be members. We do our best to help any individual in matters that affect him alone; try to please dissatisfied members; help members who have met with misfortune; and are constantly working for the realization of the ideals and aspirations of those who are discontented with things as they are and desire something better for themselves and their fellow workers. The work of the Association cannot be carried on without money—without the subscriptions of its members and the task of collecting it (sic) is not always easy or agreeable. It is essential that members pay their contributions regularly in order that branches can remit properly, otherwise efficiency is impaired ..... Our desire is to be one of the finest and best-managed trade unions in the country; but it cannot be this without you.'[8]

His words and the better administration produced results and would have done so on a more spectacular scale but for the depression which set in during 1930 and made 30 per cent of the membership unemployed by the year end. In the first quarter of 1930 membership increased by 137 and a surplus of £1,465 was produced. Unfortunately, this was wiped out in the ensuing months so that the year ended with a loss of £1,824.

STATE OF THE INDUSTRY

Westwood's first nine months as General Secretary from June 1929 to March 1930 saw the industry in a relatively prosperous state. Output at 1.5m. gross registered tons was slightly up on the previous year and in his introduction to the annual report he could say: 'We have every reason to be optimistic of the future', an unfortunate prophecy since within a few months a third of his members were to be idle and output was to plummet. Yet his confidence was shared by his colleagues and indeed based on their reports from the districts. G. W. Cable reported that shipbuilding on the Tyne showed a steady improvement 'while ship-repairing has increased by leaps and bounds and at the end of the year practically every dock on the river was filled.' The same was true over the country as a whole. In the London area, Sam Mason, the district delegate, wrote: 'The conditions of employment are undoubtedly good' and in the North-West 'the year passed out with the majority of our members fully employed.'

Within a few months there was a dramatic change. Westwood described the year 1930 as 'a most anxious and trying time. Throughout the year shipbuilders were hoping against hope that the next month or, at least, the next quarter, would bring with it an improvement in trade and shipping, with resulting benefits to shipbuilding. But instead constant additions were made to the idle shipping fleets and when a vessel left the stocks there was in most cases nothing to take its place.' In fact, it was the near absence of new orders which made 1930 so worrying. Actual output was not much lower than in 1929, which in itself was a comparatively good year. The fact was, however, that this output represented the completion of work booked some time ago and no new orders were forthcoming. The district delegates reported more and more empty berths. Sam Mason said: 'The year 1930 has come to a close and with it probably the blackest year on record as far as this district is concerned. Members quite unaccustomed to unemployment have found it necessary during the year to queue up outside of our Labour Exchanges.' In Bristol there was 'a period of depression in the industry unprecedented for many years.' Westwood urged members not to become despondent. 'The industry has survived many difficulties in the past and is facing its problems today with courage and hopefulness.'

Those qualities were to be needed to the utmost. For no one could then have foreseen that the industry was fast sinking into a depression which would last until the Second World War, would kill off many long-established shipbuilding firms and would create almost permanent unemployment for millions of men, including skilled shipwrights. These were terrible problems and the Government hardly knew how to deal with them.

Before the depression set in, the shipwrights managed to achieve a small increase in wages. They were also parties to an important restructuring scheme. The increase came in 1928 when, following continuous pressure by the Federation of Engineering and Shipbuilding Trades and the six craft unions which did not belong to it, the employers agreed to increase the bonus from 35p to 50p a week for time workers. The employers argued that in giving the increase, the result might be greater unemployment. In fact, wages on the Continent were rising faster than in this country while an outbreak of labour troubles in Continental yards also benefited the United Kingdom.

In July 1929 an important advance was made in the wages structure of the industry—a scheme for national uniform time rates. It was called

'The most important wages development in the history of British shipbuilding'.[9]

The scheme, drawn up by the employers and unions in 1929, came into effect in 1930. It was designed to simplify the wages structure and thereby reduce the many points where friction between groups of workmen could arise. There were to be three broad categories of payment. Fully skilled plain-time workers of twenty-one or over, apart from drillers and other iron workers, would receive £3 a week, made up of £2.50 basic rate and a 50p bonus. Unskilled plain-time workers over twenty-one would receive £2.05. The semi-skilled would receive an advance in each district that would maintain the district margins. Thus each group had a simpler payment system and also had its wages increased by between 5p and 25p a week. The principle of equality was accepted unanimously by all the unions who felt it was constructive and courageous. These changes did not affect pieceworkers or members in those districts, such as the North-East, already receiving higher wages.

A NEW GOVERNMENT

At the same time as he was contesting the General Secretary's position, Westwood was also fighting the Sutton Division of Plymouth in the General Election which was called in the summer of 1929. And a brilliant fight he put up. Standing for the traditional Labour programme of the abolition of poverty and unemployment, for better housing and equal educational opportunities, he mounted an intensive campaign in which he often made ten speeches in a day.

His efforts made great inroads into the Conservative majority of over 5,000 but were not quite enough to produce victory. The count was extremely tense and close in the Plymouth Guildhall, so close indeed that two recounts were called for. In the end the result was:

Lady Astor (Con.)	16,625
William Westwood (Lab.)	16,414
T. H. Aggett (Lib.)	5,430

Lady Astor's majority was therefore 211, a bitter blow to Westwood after his tremendous efforts. But he remained confident of the future. In a speech after the result was announced, he declared: 'Labour has put up a tremendous fight in Sutton against great odds. It has been a hard, thrilling fight and the result is abundant proof that the people of Sutton are determined to have a change. The constituency will go to Labour next time and while we were defeated by a small majority in Sutton, we have been amply compensated by the great victories our Party is securing in the country.'

Labour indeed was doing well. It won 288 seats against 151 in 1924 while the Conservatives won 260 compared with 419 and the Liberals 59 instead of 40. No party had an overall majority but with Labour gaining the largest numbers of seats, Baldwin resigned immediately.

Ramsay MacDonald formed his second Labour Government. Shortly afterwards he wrote to Westwood from No. 10 Downing Street:

'In the rush of business which has followed the General Election I may seem to have forgotten you but indeed I have not. I have often had in my mind that splendid body of men and women who, without the pleasures of success, championed our cause at the recent election. Your efforts must be placed alongside those of the victors in producing the magnificent results which we secured and I am most grateful to you for all you have done. I hope it will not be long before the happiness of triumph is yours.'

But while Westwood was unsuccessful, the union did succeed with its other candidate, J. J. H. Moses, who stood in Plymouth's other division, Drake. He won the seat from the Conservatives with a majority of just over 2,000 and thereby became the first Labour M.P. in the West Country. Moses was better known locally than Westwood and had been a local councillor for a number of years. Indeed he had been the town's first Labour Mayor. Speaking after the result was announced, he said: 'I felt from the very commencement of this fight that I was up against great odds, with little money and the greater portion of the influential people of Plymouth against me..... but during the whole of the campaign I have had behind me a wonderful army of voluntary workers and an enormous volume of self-sacrificing endeavour. My people have provided the whole of my election expenses.' This was not strictly true as the union had provided £125 towards the election expenses in both the Drake and Sutton constituency elections, making £250 in total from the union.

The new Government largely composed of those members who had gained experience of office in the first Labour administration started with high hopes. There were no particular issues or problems confronting the nation. Indeed the election had been fought almost without any issue in contention. Unemployment at over a million seemed to be becoming simply a fact of life. Relations with other countries seemed the most pressing questions. The first few months of the new government were peaceful with conciliation both at home and abroad the key concept. They resumed diplomatic relations with Russia and ratified the Washington Convention on armaments. They sanctioned various small but important improvements in pensions and social services and they offered an extra £120m. for unemployment schemes.

The calm progress was broken in the autumn of 1929 by the economic depression which came in from America and soon settled over the whole world. A collapse of confidence in America—the Wall Street crash—stopped the flow of American money to primary producers of food and raw materials. They ceased to buy goods or to need ships. Export industries saw their markets disappear and went in for retrenchment. Unemployment shot up. In Great Britain alone there were two million unemployed by July 1930 and two and a half million by December. In shipbuilding, a third of all the workers were dismissed. Prices fell. Yet wages remained remarkably stable. For those who were at work therefore things were better than they had been for many years.

But far too many people were not at work. The Labour Government naturally blamed the capitalist system. MacDonald declared: 'We are not on trial; it is the system under which we live..... It has broken down everywhere as it was bound to break down.' The problem was that no one knew how to correct things. Ernest Bevin proposed currency devaluation and George Lansbury wanted earlier retirement. But there was no agreement and no leadership. Britain drifted further and further into the depression which was to have such devastating consequences on the shipbuilding industry.

Westwood was highly critical of the Government's efforts—or lack of them—and caused a sensation in August 1930 by deciding not to contest the Sutton division of Plymouth again. He said in a statement: 'While appreciating the many difficulties the Government encountered in taking office, I think its record of work done shows it to be playing fast and loose with the loyalty of its supporters..... Trade union leaders are not satisfied but they are too loyal to criticize.... The Government should, in my view, have tried to implement at least some of its promises. As a trade union leader I think first, of course, of these regarding unemployment and the amendment of the Trade Disputes Act.... I feel that the solution of the unemployment problem is not a party question. All interested in the welfare of the country should combine to mitigate unemployment. With the army of workless increasing in all the great industrial countries, it would appear that international legislation or agreement on the shortening of the working day and the working week would recommend itself to all countries concerned. Why is the Labour Government not working towards this end?'[10]

By the end of 1930 over 6,600 members of the Shipconstructors and Shipwrights' Association were unemployed, a terrible figure, amounting to 30 per cent of the membership, Such figures were very worrying in personal terms. They also had serious repercussions on the union's finances. Income fell by over £5,000 to £47,600 due in large measure to the increase in unemployment when contributions were not paid. On the other hand, there was an 'alarming' increase in superannuation benefit to £16,300. Had it not been for rigid economies and a reduction in expenditure under all headings particularly sickness benefit, then the year's loss would have been greater than the £1,800 which materialized.

Just as the new leadership was beginning to pull the ailing union along the road it was overtaken by a bigger and wider problem. How it coped in this new situation we must now turn to see.

CHAPTER TWENTY-TWO

The Great Depression stunned the once-great trading nation of Britain. It led to the formation of a coalition government and the shattering of the Labour Party. It brought about the collapse of such important industries as shipbuilding. It made almost four million men unemployed and meant that, with their families, about ten million people were living on the dole.

The nation had to fight for its economic salvation and so did the Shipconstructors and Shipwrights' Association. Membership continued to drift down and financial losses to rise. It would have been very easy for the union to have gone under at this time, so strong were the forces playing upon it. Only a most resolute team of officials using the new constitutional machinery kept the union afloat. Without their admirable work the story might have ended here.

BRITAIN OVERWHELMED

The depression was nothing new. The twenties had hardly been prosperous with unemployment never falling below a million. But the sudden severity of the economic blizzard led to a condition which was identified by capital letters, the Great Depression. Even today, forty years later, the causes are not absolutely clear but the facts remain as awesome to contemplate as they must have been awful to endure. At the peak, in September 1932, about 3¾ millions were unemployed. They were not spread evenly throughout the country but concentrated in certain areas, in Lancashire, Glasgow and Tyneside, and in certain industries, shipbuilding, coal and textiles. These were the industries which had once made Britain great. Now they were humbled. In some of them, half the workforce were out of work. In some towns, virtually everyone was on the streets. A telling description of those days has been handed down to us by J. B. Priestley who in 1933 wrote a book called *English Journey* about his experiences as he toured the country. He wrote of one town in the North-East: 'Wherever we went there were men hanging about, not scores of them but hundreds and thousands of them. The whole town looked as if it had entered a perpetual, penniless bleak Sabbath.' And of another town: 'You felt that there was nothing in the whole place worth a five pound note. It looked as much like an ordinary town of that size as a dustbin looks like a drawing room. Here again, idle men —and not unemployable casual labourers but skilled men—hung about the streets, waiting for Doomsday.' Britain itself, it seemed, was running down: high unemployment, low economic activity, no growth, old patterns of trade disappearing, particularly in export markets. To a considerable extent, the source of the trouble lay in the steadily-deteriorating nature of international trade but Britain, and its governments, had done little to adjust to the new world. Nor had there been any attempt to move beyond the rigid economies of a balanced budget and the need for financial pruning when the economy turned down. Surprisingly perhaps, the most ruthless advocate of this old school was Philip Snowden, Labour's Chancellor of the Exchequer. He believed that only the most rigorous economies could meet the spiralling situation.

When his views were echoed by a national committee headed by a leading industrialist, Sir George May, he felt strong enough to force his views through a confused and divided Cabinet. The main economy was to be on unemployment benefits, which were now costing the country about £300m. a year. The May committee recommended that these benefits should be reduced by 20 per cent. Snowden, in a generous mood, thought a ten per cent reduction would be sufficient. MacDonald as Prime Minister had no clear views. His main interest, after all, was foreign affairs. Other ministers were unhappy but could not immediately focus their discontent. Arthur Henderson, Foreign Secretary, and second only to MacDonald in popularity within the Party, suggested that the General Council of the T.U.C. should be consulted. On 20th August 1930 the meeting was held and Snowden outlined his proposals. The T.U.C.'s reaction was immediate. It was not only against any cuts, it was also opposed to the whole policy of deflation. The T.U.C.'s firmness was enough to convince Henderson and eight other Cabinet colleagues. They refused to accept Snowden's proposals. The Cabinet was split on a major matter of policy. MacDonald felt he could not go on and resigned office on 23rd August.

The following day, the King asked him to try to form a coalition government which he agreed to do. There were three other Labour members, besides himself—Snowden as Chancellor, J. H. Thomas and Lord Sankey—four Conservatives including Baldwin, and two Liberals. Their purpose was to push through the measure which the Labour Cabinet had refused to accept. In doing that, they were not only intensifying the errors of economic policy, they were also making one of the biggest political blunders of the century. For MacDonald and his three Labour colleagues thought they would receive the backing of the Party. They did not.

The formation of a National Government, even though only on a temporary basis and specifically to cure the horrendous economic problem, was regarded as a great betrayal. MacDonald's popularity plummeted. Within two days the T.U.C. General Council and the National Executive of the Labour Party had denounced the new administration. When the Snowden proposals were put to Parliament in September only eleven Labour members, apart from the four in the Cabinet, voted for them. The rest of the party was united in opposition to the new government. But the support of the Conservative and Liberal members gave it a majority of fifty. The measures were carried, increasing taxation by £70m., mainly by raising income tax to 5s in the £, and reducing expenditure by £70m. All those employed by the State, such as teachers, policemen and even judges and Cabinet Ministers, had their wages cut by an average of ten per cent and the unemployed had their benefits similarly reduced.

While the Labour leaders succeeded in the House of Commons, they created a great divide from their supporters which led to a renewal of class bitterness and strife. On 28th September, MacDonald, once the darling of the party, was expelled together with those who supported him in Parliament.

Shorn of his support, MacDonald naturally felt in a very uneasy position. What was more, a most important political step had been taken without consulting the people. For these reasons he felt it was right to hold an election in October. The outcome from Labour's point of view was disastrous. Deserted by its former leaders, facing the combined strength of National Government supporters in the Conservative and Liberal candidates and obliged to explain its refusal to support a national all-party effort to revive the economy, its total vote fell by a quarter. That was bad enough. But because of the peculiar nature of the electoral system, the drop in votes led to the disastrous situation where it won only 52 seats against 288 in 1929 while MacDonald and the National Government supporters, mainly Conservatives, won 556 seats. So the extraordinary position arose of a House of Commons dominated by Conservative members yet led by a coalition cabinet of which a former Labour Prime Minister was the head. But then, MacDonald and certainly Snowden, were so orthodox in economic management that they could be taken for Conservatives.

Certainly the main measures they took, such as tariff protection, were straight from Tory textbooks. In March 1932 the Import Duties Act imposed a ten per cent customs duty on most imports with the explicit exception of goods from the Empire. Later this was extended to a policy of Empire Free Trade with tariffs against non-Commonwealth countries. But this discrimination was modified by trade agreements signed with seventeen countries outside the Commonwealth between 1932 and 1935 which generally agreed quotas of imports in return for concessions to Britain's exports. British farming was helped even further by subsidies and the establishment of specialized marketing boards.

The effect on the unemployment problem was not great. Something more direct and more positive was needed. The Government had little to offer except tinkering with legislation. In 1934 it combined insurance and assistance schemes in the Unemployment Act but the scales of relief were so derisory that they aroused widespread criticism. Another well-meant but ineffective measure was the Special Areas Act of 1934 which was designed to encourage new industries to move to hard-pressed areas or to persuade workers to move to more prosperous regions. The most successful factor in getting the economy going again after the low point of 1932-33 was the boom in house building. Financed by local authorities or the building societies, the boom saw 75,000 council houses a year being built and up to 350,000 private houses. This rising level of construction not only affected a real rise in the standard of living, it also helped to generate employment, first in the building trade, then in furniture-making and many other trades.

The boom was largely a natural development and helped to produce a situation where the depression cured itself. Certainly Government action had proved either wrong, as in the reduction of expenditure, or insufficient as in the Special Areas Act. By 1936 the worst was over. Unemployment was down to around the million mark once more. Production was rising. New industries, such as chemicals and motor manufacture, were beginning to supplant the importance of the old. The cost of living continued to fall and so did the world's commodity prices. The effect was to maintain and in the case of those in employment, actually to improve, the living standards of most people. It was this feeling of relative prosperity amidst unparalleled despair that was the uncanniest feature of the period.

The despair, frustration and anger boiled up in many countries into violence. There was a particular call to strong-armed nationalism. This was true in Italy, for example, where Mussolini, founded the Union of Fascists and in Germany where Hitler became Chancellor in January 1933 and proceeded to establish the National Socialist Party by cruelly crushing all opposition. In England, these movements were mirrored by the British Union of Fascists led by Sir Oswald Mosley, a former junior minister in the second Labour Government. The Communist Party was also growing rapidly at this time and the open physical conflict between the two was a notable characteristic of the period.

Another important characteristic, of course, was the growing political power of the T.U.C. As we have seen, it was the T.U.C.'s opposition to the Labour Government's proposed economy measures in August 1931 that had led to its downfall. For its part in the events of those days, the General Council was accused of the charge of 'dictation', an understandable enough claim but not quite accurate in view of the fact that it had been invited by the Cabinet to give its views and certainly did not wish to press them in any other way but constitutionally.

While dictation may be too strong a claim, the General Council certainly sought to have a positive influence particularly through the efforts of its two dominant personalities, Walter Citrine, its General Secretary, and Ernest Bevin, leader of the transport workers. Following the collapse of the Labour Party after the 1931 General Election, they were largely responsible for recommending the reconstruction of the National Joint Council which would allow the T.U.C. to exercise a continuous influence over the Party. The new council met once a month and had equal representation from the T.U.C. and the Party. It delivered many important statements of policy, particularly concerning unemployment and foreign affairs.

THE ATTITUDE OF THE SHIPWRIGHTS

The attitude of the Shipconstructors and Shipwrights' Association to the turbulent train of events was summed up by Westwood in each year's annual report. No doubt his statements had the full backing of the Executive Committee and of the majority of members. But it is interesting to note that during these years when the union was providing such powerful backing for Labour, it was not actually a member of the Party. It had decided to dis-affiliate in 1927 for financial reasons and had not yet agreed to rejoin. That did not prevent its support in other ways, particularly through Westwood's annual review.

His backing for the Party and his denunciation of the National Government were absolute. In his review for 1931 he wrote: 'We are told that the present Government is a National Government, with a free hand, and not a Conservative Party Government. Ask the leading lights in the Conservative Party how much freedom they, with their big majority in the House, are going to allow the Government if it does not get on with the job very quickly and put into effect the Conservative policy. A non-party Government! The devil can only appear as an angel so long as he keeps out of sight his cloven feet. Even the wilfully blind cannot any longer pretend that these feet are hidden.'

He was particularly scornful of the decision to come off the Gold Standard, as well he and many others might have been considering that this had always been regarded as a sacred cow. A few weeks after the election the cow was happily slaughtered. Or as Westwood put it: 'When the Labour Government resigned, we were told of the terrible havoc to the nation that would take place if there was a flight from the £. Trade would cease, industry would stand still, profits and wages would disappear, starvation would ensue. It would be as though the sun had ceased to shine, the skies had fallen and killed all the larks, the flowers had ceased to bloom and nothing but ruin and desolation everywhere. A few weeks only elapsed and the dreaded thing happened. The Gold Standard had to be given up and the flight from the £ had taken place. Its value for international purposes has fallen by more than 25 per cent. But instead of calamity it was hailed by all the great financial authorities as our salvation. Has the world ever known such a comic anti-climax?'

Westwood was not only a Labour Party supporter, he was also firmly behind the economic line so vehemently argued by Bevin and others and so well justified in logic by J. M. Keynes, the famous economist. The basic argument was that in times of depression, a nation should take the opposite action from an individual. An individual would be advised to reduce his expenditure to match his lower income. But for a country to reduce its expenditure, or more precisely for a Government to cut public expenditure, would lead to an intensification of a depression. In short a country must 'spend its way' out of a depression by creating work.

This important economic precept was but dimly perceived at the time and to be fair even its greatest proponent, J. M. Keynes, did not work out the theory in full until 1936, but even so there were a number of people particularly in the ranks of the unions who saw the essential truth of the argument even in the early 1930's.

Labour's own paper *The Daily Herald* which was largely under Bevin's influence, campaigned on this issue. Westwood quoted extensively from it in his review for 1932.

'Fundamentally,' the paper argued in its issue of 20th December 1932, 'the crisis, both in its internal and external manifestations, is due to a lack of buying.... The world needs more work. More work is only possible if there is more production. More production is only possible if there is more purchasing power.' While the politicians failed to accept this message, the people themselves were to put it into effect, albeit unknowingly. For the housebuilding boom which we have mentioned may have been an attempt, as far as they were concerned, simply to improve their standards of living as was their purchasing of radios and new furniture. But in aggregate these desires spelt out an increase in demand which helped to increase production and reduce unemployment by 1935-6.

But before then, the country had to live through the trough of depression in 1932-33. The Government's answer had been to reduce unemployment benefits in 1931. In 1933 it introduced a Means Test under which the unemployed had to prove their need for subsistence allowance and to prove that they were spending every minute of every day genuinely looking for work. This measure coming on top of the Government's inability to cure the Depression brought out Westwood's strongest invective. In the 1933 review he wrote: 'This gross betrayal of the unemployed is all the more reprehensible in view of the overwhelming medical evidence of the disastrous effect which the Government's cruel "economy" is presently having on the families of the unemployed. The restoration of the cut in unemployment benefit should be the first charge on any available surplus in the national income.'

Widening his attack, he wrote: 'One could go on recording failure after failure of the National Government..... Little, if any, progress has been made in such vital questions as Foreign Policy, Housing, Slum Clearance, Education and Taxation. Unfortunately, the Government is more concerned with attacks on Co-operative Societies, making "cuts" in the name of economy and in degrading still further the unemployed by compelling them and their children to exist on a "fodder" basis..... In every direction we seem to find ourselves in a dilemma. What is to be done about it? We seem to be working on wrong lines. The heart of the world's trade is beating more feebly every year.

'All around you there are masses of people, including perhaps friends, neighbours and even your own families who are plunged in poverty, forced to dwell in slums, driven down by unemployment.... This state of things fills you with indignation. You know that something is wrong somewhere. You want to put things right. You are not prepared to accept, without an effort, a chance to change their conditions, which make life a mockery and a sham.... These inequalities and evils are inherent in the system under which we live: a system that puts profit and private property before the economic security and social well-being of the people.... The enemies we have to conquer are poverty, unemployment, evil housing and the greed of vested interests.'

He ended his attack by calling for the return of a Labour Government as the only Party capable of defeating these 'enemies', a call he made even more strongly in his 1934 review. 'Out of evil cometh good,' he wrote 'and out of the experience of the past three years there should emerge a movement powerful enough to carry Labour's flag to victory.'

When the Election came in 1935, Westwood's prediction, at least in terms of votes, almost proved true. It polled 8.3m. votes, virtually the same as in 1929. But Britain's electoral system again played cruel tricks on the Party, for whereas in 1929 it won 288 seats, in 1935 it won only 154 even though the total vote was about the same. But at least it had secured a hundred more seats than in 1931 and the National Government a hundred less.

Westwood commented: 'In all the circumstances the Party has done very well and its active members have every reason to be proud of their achievements. Let us concern ourselves more with the next General Election than with the one just completed. Victory can be secured if we all do our best from now onwards..... Many seats held by the Government hang on very slender majorities and must be won back, therefore—Victory With Power Next Time.'

He then went on to outline the Party's main policy.

1. Economic and industrial plans to reduce unemployment as quickly as possible.
2. Public ownership of basic industries such as coal, electricity and transport.
3. Increasing social services 'to build up a happy and healthy people.'

Even these policies depended on something more fundamental, the maintenance of international peace. The Labour Party had taken the initiative in calling for peace through the League of Nations. 'The achievement of peace is the most pressing problem of the world today', Westwood wrote in the 1935 review. 'But it is not sufficient to be opposed to war. If we want peace we must plan for it.... The present Government has a terrible responsibility for the present international situation. It did nothing to check the aggression of Japan in the Far East and thus seriously discredited the League of Nations and undermined the Collective Peace System. It encouraged Italy to walk into Abyssinia by its callous indifference to the League of Nations. This war could and should have been prevented.'

By 1936 Westwood could set out in detail the plans which the unions and the Labour Party had been refining over the years. 'No political party has ever devoted such thought to the task which faces it. The Labour Movement can appeal to the country for confidence and for a mandate with the knowledge that Labour is prepared for power.' There would be measures of public ownership of basic industries. Land, too, would be nationalized as a vital asset and so would the Bank of England which would become a public institution. These measures 'will bring full employment and full employment means wages on a rising scale.' Other reforms would then become possible: a shorter working week; holidays with pay; higher school-leaving age; better pensions.

There would be full support for the League of Nations. 'Labour is the Peace Party. It stands for the international rule of law.... It seeks co-operation with all in the maintenance of peace, in the defence of democracy and in the enlargement of the sphere of social justice.'

The union in general and Westwood in particular were thus firmly committed to and open advocates of a Labour Government. In him the Party had found a vigorous, far-sighted and trenchant supporter who had already made and was to continue to make a most important contribution.

THE STATE OF THE INDUSTRY

The Great Depression was particularly severe on export industries like shipbuilding. In fact the industry virtually collapsed. Many firms did not build a single ship for months on end. Some of them went out of existence. Others managed to hang on, despite losses, by living off the profits of previous years. The exciting racket that normally pounds the ears in any shipyard was replaced by a strange and awful silence. In 1920 the industry had turned out over two million tons of shipping. Thirteen years later, it produced only 133,000 tons. The North-East coast which could turn out a million tons produced 37,000.

The shock was even greater than it had been in the 1920's. Then launchings had dropped by a third from one year to the next. Now they were to plummet disastrously. In 1930 U.K. output was 1,409,000 tons. In 1931 it was 500,000 tons, in 1932, 187,000 tons and in 1933 133,000 tons. These were terrible figures and they affected certain areas slightly more than others. In 1931 Hartlepools, an important centre on the North-East coast, did not produce a single ship and Sunderland, 'the greatest shipbuilding town in the world', produced only 9,000 tons. Mr A. L. Ayre, President of the Shipbuilding Employers' Federation, declared: 'The year 1931 will stand in the annals of shipbuilding as the most tragic in its history.' He was to find that there was worse to come although the year was certainly grim enough. There was an almost entire absence of orders. About 60 per cent of the workpeople were unemployed, by far the highest percentage of any basic industry. And these appalling figures were recorded at a time when there had been a large reduction in the number of insured workers in the industry. The number nationally had fallen from 358,790 in November 1921 to 195,390 in November 1931.

William Westwood in his annual review wrote that the 'industry was clouded by a depression of unparalleled severity'. But he tried to find a 'few bright features' such as the continuing technical improvements, for example in electrical propulsion. Such features were hard to find. It was becoming increasingly obvious that the industry had too much capacity in the light of available demand, not only in the short-term but also for the foreseeable future. It was a sad admission but true that British shipbuilding, even when the present depression was over, could not hope to achieve its former output. Other countries, particularly the United States, offered severe competition and British domination would never return.

In these circumstances, the shipbuilders decided on a very controversial move. They set up an organization called The National Shipbuilders Security Limited whose task was to eliminate surplus capacity. Directors were drawn from yards on the Clyde, Tyne, Tees, Wear and the Forth and from Barrow and Belfast so that no area would be presumed to suffer more than another. It was backed by the Bankers' Industrial Development Company, set up by the Bank of England, but its principal source of finance came from the shipbuilders themselves. They agreed to pay a levy of 1 per cent on the price of new vessels laid down. In all the organization would have up to £2½m. at any one time with which to buy redundant or obsolete yards and resell the sites for any other industrial purpose but shipbuilding. While the theory may have been excellent, in practice the work was highly controversial. How much capacity was to be removed and who was to take the ultimate decision? What about the workers of the firms taken over? What was to happen to them? Above all, it was the terrible sense of finality hanging over the organization's work that made it such a dreaded institution. Within a year it had bought up 15 yards with an estimated annual capacity of 600,000 tons with 82 berths and closed them down permanently. In noting these developments, the Federation of Engineering and Shipbuilding Trades stated quite simply: 'Our demand for compensation to displaced workmen has been refused. The difficulty of laying before the directors of this company the rights of our people have been somewhat complicated by the large degree of unemployment prevailing. Towns that depended entirely upon shipbuilding and marine engineering have had their principal industries taken from them and their citizens compelled to seek employment elsewhere.'[1]

The employers argued that there would be no displacement of labour. Rather, the improved efficiency of the industry, resulting from rationalization, would improve employment prospects when trade did arrive. While this might have been true in theory, the fact was that if a firm was bought up and then closed down permanently, its workforce, even if they were unemployed at the time, were displaced. Years of experience of working for one firm were lost. National Shipbuilders Security Limited had to be pressed to provide compensation or the creation of new industries near to the old yards. Local authorities also joined in the controversy. Sunderland Corporation decided to approach the Government over the work of this organization. They were particularly concerned at one of the fundamental conditions, that yards taken over should never be reopened for shipbuilding. This objective was too severe. None of these criticisms had any effect. Shipbuilders Security went on buying companies and refused to offer compensation to the workers. By 1935 it had taken over 150 berths with an annual capacity of over a million tons.

By then things were starting to get better after the terrible trough of 1933 when only 5 per cent of the building berths were occupied. As affairs deteriorated, the call for Government subsidies grew louder. Traditionally, the industry had been opposed to any form of interference. But now it could no longer ignore the fact that the U.S. Government had poured out $1,400m. to help home shipbuilders since 1915; that Italian owners were not allowed to place orders abroad; and that in Germany about 3 million tons of modern shipping had been built virtually without cost to the owners. In his review for 1932 Westwood listed the ways in which various countries were helping their own shipbuilding industries. By 1933 he was pleased to note that British shipowners were being forced to the view that they must adopt some form of retaliation.

But shipbuilders remained unconvinced. Dr G. B. Hunter, chairman of Swan, Hunter and Wigham Richardson, the Tyneside yard, commented: 'I do not advocate subsidies for British industries. I am not aware that British shipowners or shipbuilders desire them. But they do ask for fair play. Should we allow subsidised foreign products and ships into our ports?'

The Government also remained unconvinced, at least until 1935 when a 'scrap and build' scheme was introduced. Under this, the Treasury could advance up to £10m. in loans to British owners for new shipping as long as they scrapped two tons for every ton built. It was estimated that the sum set aside would finance the building of about 600,000 tons of shipping, thus requiring the scrapping of 1,200,000 tons. While successful up to a point, the measure failed to live up to the hopes placed upon it. Theoretically, there should have been no difficulty in finding 1,200,000 tons to be scrapped but owners were reluctant to take action as long as there was the possibility of higher freight rates. They felt that if full scrapping did take place, freights would inevitably improve, thereby providing an income for even the oldest vessels. Everyone waited for someone else to scrap first. Shipbuilders, who had hoped for a lot of work, were therefore disappointed. Only 37 applications, relating to the construction of 50 ships of about 186,000 tons, were approved. The total advances to owners came to just over £3.5m.

Despite this failure, the trend in shipbuilding was now firmly upwards again. Sir Maurice Denny, President of the Employers' Federation, was able to report that there was a rapid and substantial improvement in 1936. There were about five times as many merchant ships being built as during the black period of 1932/33. In fact, tonnage under construction was approaching a million. 'At long last the dark clouds have rolled away,' Sir Maurice commented, 'The barometer registers "fair" and is rising.' Westwood went even further. 'Shipbuilding is booming,' he wrote in his review for 1936. But he had to admit that the better fortune had another side to it for it was based on a big increase in the Navy Estimates for 1936 which called for a good deal of new naval building. Two new battleships were laid down, together with five cruisers and a steady replacement programme for destroyers and submarines. By September 1936 the Tyne alone had seventeen warships under construction or on order. Although such work was welcome from an industrial and employment point of view Westwood added that 'it is by no means a certain sign that sanity is returning to the nations.' But there was no qualification to the pleasure of seeing more men employed. In fact unemployment in shipbuilding was down to 25 per cent and was falling steadily. In that year output went up sharply to 856,000 tons and continued to rise to a million by 1938. Compared with the best years these figures were still worrying but related to what the industry had just been through they were a welcome sign of a return to better times.

WAGES AND CONDITIONS

These were desperate years for the financial health of the shipbuilding companies and for the earnings of the workers. Firms could only obtain the small amount of work that was available by tendering to the tightest of profit margins. Some firms even tendered at a loss in order to maintain some kind of production. S. P. Austin, the Sunderland shipbuilding firm, made a loss every year from 1923 to 1936 with the exception of 1929. In these years its aggregate losses came to £118,000. By 1936 it was able to make a tiny profit of £415 but the following year boosted this to £17,300. This example was not untypical.

Faced with this situation, the employers resorted to the old habit of calling for a reduction in wages, ignoring the fact that there had been no increase for six or seven years except to those men affected by the introduction of national uniform time rates. The Shipwrights' Association again protested against the 'economy bug' arguing that it not only hurt the men and their families but also that it helped to intensify the existing depression. The union in fact refused to accept the reductions of 2s 6d (12½p) called for by the Shipbuilding Employers' Federation from workers earning more than £3 national minimum but they were imposed nevertheless in two instalments. Piece-workers also lost their 7s (35p) a week bonus. The Shipping Federation called for reductions among ratings, including ships' carpenters and carpenters' mates. The reductions were for 18s (90p) for men on monthly pay and 6s (30p) for men in weekly steamers.

An attempt to grapple with the problems of piecework payments was made during 1931 and resulted in a General Wages Agreement being signed in October. The scheme was designed to reduce labour costs and sweep away anomalies, e.g. skilled men on plain time, such as shipwrights, were receiving £3 a week in the North-East for 47 hours while certain classes of piece workers were regularly receiving £7 or £8 for 40 hours. Negotiations between unions and employers lasted from April to August with no serious disagreements. The scheme that materialized involved the withdrawal of time-work bonus of 7s (35p) a week and its replacement by a compensating percentage payment. The scheme also withdrew certain wartime payments. The most important feature, apart from removing anomalies and cutting labour costs, was that it proposed to investigate establishing a general index for automatic regulation of wages when prosperity returned to the industry.

During 1931 the Shipwrights' Association also negotiated on amended Agreement with the Civil Engineering Contractors' Federation governing the conditions of members when working on concrete. Large numbers of members of the union were working in this capacity and it was hoped that more would follow.

The unions did not allow the employers to take all the initiatives. In 1932 and 1933 they strongly urged the introduction of a 40-hour week to increase employment. The Federation of Engineering and Shipbuilding Trades played an important part in this campaign urging members to support it as their forefathers did when they fought for a shortening of the working week from 60 to 56 hours and then from 56 to 47. 'The labour of inventors and scientists should be shared amongst a greater number' the Federation argued in relation to the introduction of new methods. Forty Hour Committees were organized in every large industrial centre. There was a National Committee on which the Federation was represented. But it achieved little and the movement petered out when the Government came down against it.

The interests of the union and its members were meanwhile being threatened by the introduction of electric welding. This new process seriously affected drillers for it superseded much of their work. The employers put forward the view that a new class of workmen was now required, properly trained and highly specialized in this new technique. The Shipwrights' Association and other unions were vigorously opposed. They did not think there was a need for a new or special class of workmen. Even if there were such a need it could be met by extending the training of apprentices in each section of the industry. So firmly did each side put its views that no agreement could be reached at conference after conference. Finally the question was referred to an independent chairman (Mr Graham Robertson, K.C.) under the terms of the Conciliation Machinery Agreement. Even he, however, had to record a 'failure to agree'. The unions reaffirmed their belief that the work to be welded 'should be done by the class hitherto doing the work' while the employers intimated that they were to go ahead with their plans. Westwood hoped that 'in the end commonsense will prevail and that the common and best interests of the industry will be served.' Will Sherwood, president of the Trades Federation, commented: 'No problem in the shipbuilding industry has evoked wilder discussion or revealed greater difficulties and complexities and the need for greater unity amongst all unions in this country.'

The employers enforced their wishes from April 1934 when they stated that the rate for electric welders on new work would be £3 a week. Disputes broke out in various yards and there were attempts to provide 'strenuous opposition' but the efforts were not sufficiently concerted. By 1935 electric welding was largely accepted and discussion centred on particular points such as the need to ensure proper safety and protection not only to welders but also to men standing nearby. Meanwhile the world's largest all-electrically-welded ship was launched and more and more ships were constructed using this technique.

By 1936 trade was reviving, unemployment falling. The unions took this first opportunity to press for an advance in wages. Negotiating through the Federation, of which Westwood had been elected president in 1934, they secured a new agreement with the employers in February 1936. Under this they secured a bonus of 10p a week for timeworkers and 4 per cent for pieceworkers as from April. But the agreement prevented any further demands for an increase until 1937.

The aircraft industry then in its infancy offered 'splendid opportunities' for shipwrights according to Westwood and he continued to urge members to consider the opportunities it had to offer. The work was not only interesting, it was also highly remunerative, with good prospects for the future. Because of the rapid development of this new industry, the unions involved decided to set up a National Council. The primary objects were to secure complete trade union organization and to obtain the best wages and working conditions for those employed in it. Local committees were also set up and were advised to work closely with the local Federation committees. The Shipwrights' Association affiliated to the National Council for the Aircraft Industry and had a representative in the Executive Committee.

One of the first successes of Westwood's reign as President of the Federation and one of the last triumphs of Frank Smith before he retired as the Secretary was to inaugurate the Confederation of Shipbuilding and Engineering Unions. This was done partly by instituting a new constitution and partly by persuading nearly all the unions outside the previous Federation to affiliate. This they did in 1936 with the exception of the Amalgamated Engineering Union and the Foundry Workers. The Confederation now represented 30 unions with an aggregate membership of 1.3m. Westwood was elected the first chairman of the Confederation and the chairman of both the Shipbuilding and Engineering Group Councils.

A spirit of affiliation must have been in the air for it was in 1936 that the Shipwrights decided to re-affiliate to the T.U.C. Westwood commented: 'The T.U.C. is well equipped for all the tasks that confront it, and while there may be grave difficulties and dangers ahead, I am confident, with the revival of the Trade Union spirit and the real unity of purpose which inspires every section of the movement, that the march of progress will continue.'[2]

Britain seemed to have come through the Great Depression at last.

THE EFFECT ON THE ASSOCIATION

These years hit the Shipwrights' Association severely. The reserves continued to fall until 1933 but then rose again while the membership declined every year until 1936 when there was a small increase.

The main problem was on the income side for there was a rigid control of expenditure. In April 1931 it called for a special levy of 2d a week on all employed members and in July the Association event went so far as to suspend superannuation benefit which had started to rise again after the five-year limitation had been imposed in 1927. By 1930 the amount paid out had risen to £16,000 and was climbing steadily.

The suspension which was intended to be temporary, stayed in effect for seven years, so serious was the Association's financial position. By mid-1931 the overdraft at the Co-operative Wholesale Society Bank in Newcastle had risen to £10,303 and was rising monthly. The figure was naturally very serious particularly since the overdraft limit was meant to be £6,000. On 9th July Mr A. Macdonald, the Manager, wrote to the Executive Committee pointing out that 'your indebtedness to us has continually increased' and 'the fact that we have allowed the Account to reach a figure of £10,303 creates a very serious position indeed from our point of view.' The Bank held the deeds of the Eldon Square property which had a nominal value of £11,765. It was the Bank's practice to advance not more than half of the nominal value of such security. This had been exceeded. Macdonald then wrote: 'We desire on our part that you should as a committee face the position immediately in order to avoid your financial position becoming chaotic. It would seem to us essential that you should either take immediate steps to increase the contributions of your members or suspend or drastically reduce your benefits until the financial condition of your Society is once more on a satisfactory basis.' This letter was the final push the Executive needed. It suspended superannuation benefit from 1st August. As a result the amount paid out that year dropped to £10,000. At the same time the salaries of all full-time and branch officials were cut by 10 per cent and district office expenditure was chopped. Westwood's salary was now £8 a week.

Even these measures did not immediately correct matters for income was continuing to decline with the rising unemployment. This factor in itself was aggravating the situation for the Association was still shouldering the responsibility of full liability for benefits to the 6,200 unemployed members although they were exempt from contributions when wholly unemployed. In fact 32 per cent of the membership was not paying contributions. This was a responsibility which few other unions were willing to bear. And by 1932 it felt it could bear it no longer. Reluctantly, the Executive Committee decided to impose a contribution of 3d (7p) a week on unemployed members as it had done up to March 1930 when it had been withdrawn after protest. This was not well received again by members and indeed led to 'criticism of a destructive character' but the Committee felt they had few options left as they watched the reserves continue to fall and the overdraft continue to mount. By the end of 1932 it stood at £11,500. A small reduction in the overdraft was made in 1933 but at the expense of the reserve fund which fell to its lowest point since 1892. It stood at just £27,250 or about £1.50p a member whereas a firm stipulation in the Constitution stated that the reserves should be at least £3 a member.

From now on things started to improve and the run of losses was stopped. In 1934 there was a surplus on the year's working of £3,600 while the overdraft was cut by £3,500 to £6,500. Westwood could end his review for the year with these words: 'These concluding remarks are written in a much happier frame of mind than the closing chapters of the past reviews.... It can truthfully be said that we have had a much better year both as regard to the Association and the industry generally.'

In 1935 there was a surplus of £5,375 and the overdraft was brought down to £1,360. The success was due to the increasing employment of members and their payment of full contributions. Income went up by almost £3,000 over the previous year while expenditure rose only slightly.

This success reflected the very firm control that the full-time Executive Committee kept on expenditure. Frequent audits were carried out on branch accounts; there was continual pressure on members to reduce their arrears; and officials were urged to increase the membership in their area. When a district committee or official failed to make the necessary progress, the Executive acted decisively. In the autumn of 1935 they became concerned that the organization of shipwrights on the Clyde was slipping behind other areas. Of 642 shipwrights employed in 11 yards, only 305 were members of the union. The Executive Committee meeting on 18th September stated quite simply 'that the present condition could no longer be tolerated and that unless an improvement in membership is shown in the next month then steps would be taken to remove officials who were not loyally assisting the Executive Committee.'

Little improvement was made and at the following meeting of the Executive Committee on 21st October it was decided to dismiss John Stewart, the acting district delegate and himself a member of the Executive Committee. His salary would be paid up to the end of the year at the General Secretary's discretion and W. Robertson, the delegate for Ireland, would take over his duties in addition to his own. While the Scottish branches were not sorry to see Stewart go, they were perturbed that no full-time replacement was made. They felt they had been disenfranchised and said so in critical letters to the Executive Committee. This of course was not the case but the Committee in replying to these letters emphasized that as soon as membership started to pick up through the work of Robertson then a full-time official could be appointed again. By December Robertson was able to report that while some yards remained difficult to organize—at Dennys of Dumbarton for example—in others he had been able to achieve 100 per cent organization. The biggest obstacle in signing up members was the 2d a week extra levy and the 3d a week contribution from unemployed members.

The Executive Committee members spent a great deal of time in trying to find employment for members. Every week they were busy visiting employers looking for new openings. In June 1935 Joseph Harrison, the North of England delegate, reported that there was a boom in aircraft work, following Government policy to develop the Air Force, and he had been able to find work for a number of men from his area at Blackburns of Brough. George Burke, the North-West and Bristol Channel delegate, was equally busy following up opportunities in Ferro-Concrete work. He had been able to place 78 men. As the economy started to pick up, new opportunities arose more and more. Every month new work was found. William Westwood referred to the better prospects when he gave his first address as President of the Federation of Engineering and Shipbuilding Trades on 18th May 1935. He said: 'British industry generally has recovered from the prolonged period of depression into which it was plunged in the autumn of 1929 and busier conditions have prevailed in both the engineering and shipbuilding trades. The pace of revival has quickened during the last few months as shown in the reduction of the figures of unemployment.'

The pace continued to quicken in 1936. The level of unemployment in the shipbuilding industry fell from 37 per cent at the beginning of the year to 26 per cent at the end. In Westwood's phrase, 'Great Britain is today the world's busiest shipbuilder'. With this better economic position, union affairs improved. Membership rose to 18,561 which was 1,200 more than in 1935. That increase brought a sharp rise in income while expenditure went up only slightly. This produced an increase to the reserve fund of £9,000. By the end of 1936 it stood at £45,000 or £2.9s a member (£2.45p) The bank overdraft was completely wiped out. The 10 per cent reduction in salaries was restored. Some branches were critical that this should have been done before the reinstatement of superannuation benefit but on the whole members felt the Executive and officials had done well in restoring the Association to financial health.

CHAPTER TWENTY-THREE

As the industry recovered from the Great Depression, unemployment fell and output went up, but never to the same levels as in earlier years. It was not until the advent of the Second World War with its enormous demands for warships that the industry reached full production again. The union too operated on a lower key. Membership certainly continued to rise and with it income but never to the same levels as in the halcyon days just after the First World War. Expenditure rose too but, thanks to careful financial control, at a lower rate than income so that each year produced a rising balance of reserves. The union was once more on a sound financial basis.

THE INDUSTRY RECOVERS

After the traumatic experience of the mid-1930's the industry had only two courses open to it: either complete extinction or recovery. The Government's initiative in 1935 of introducing the 'scrap and build' scheme to act as a powerful trigger towards recovery had not met with great success. Shipowners waited for others to scrap first. But nevertheless a gentle recovery did take place. It was 'gentle' in the sense that not until 1938 did U.K. output reach a million tons a year again, still a long way from the 2m. tons of 1920. Even so it slipped back but in percentage terms it was a dramatic rise, representing an eight-fold increase from 1933. However, as we have seen that was a year of unprecedented and quite inconceivable depression. To rise eight-fold from that low point was hardly a great achievement. If we compare British output with world production, the point becomes absolutely plain. The U.K. percentage of world launchings had been 27 in that dreadful year of 1933 compared with 70 and 80 per cent thirty years earlier. In the subsequent six years the percentage went up but to no more than an average of 36. Foreign yards were taking the place of British ones. And what was more, a third of all the work in these yards was for foreign account. Half of German Shipbuilding in 1936 was for foreign countries. In Sweden, the proportion was over 80 per cent; in this country it was nearer to 10 per cent. Britain's days of undisputed dominance in shipbuilding were over.

After an output of a million tons in 1938 (34 per cent of world output), the industry began to slip back again. It looked as if another slump was on the way.

To counter it, the Government introduced a new aid scheme in March 1939. Under it, the Government granted a subsidy of £2.75 million a year for five years to tramp shipping, a capital grant of £500,000 a year for five years to owners of tramp and cargo lines placing immediate orders in British yards and £10m. for loans to owners on low interest terms for two years to build tramps and cargo liners. No scrapping of old tonnage was now required in this five-year plan before loans would be given. Instead, there was to be a careful laying up programme of 'care and maintenance' under which such ships were not to be brought out for trading except in an emergency. The new measures had an immediate effect. Within six weeks shipowners had placed orders for 144 tramp and cargo liners with an aggregate of over 700,000 gross tons.

In his presidential address to the fourth annual meeting of the Confederation of Shipbuilding and Engineering Unions at Blackpool in May 1939 William Westwood said he thought the Confederation could claim a share of the credit for getting something done. 'A few weeks ago,' he said, 'some shipyards were empty and others were completing their last orders. A black summer and the dole queue lay ahead until the Government announced its proposals which have changed the whole outlook of workpeople in districts where only merchant tonnage was built..... Britain, still the supreme world mercantile marine power, has opened a new chapter in maritime history. The Five-Year Plan is a national policy imperative in the national, commercial and defensive interests.' And it had been forced upon the Government partly by the pressure of the Confederation.

While merchant shipbuilding was struggling out of the depression, warship building became very active as the Government stepped up its naval programme.

In 1937 the Government ordered 98 new vessels of which three were to be battleships of 35,000 ton displacement. In 1938 the Navy Estimates went up a further £20m. to £125m. and in 1939 to £147m. of which £60m. was to be spent on new vessels. Confronted by this rapidly-rising demand, the industry began to face the crisis which many had foreseen in the depression when so many able men were allowed to drift away. There was now an extreme shortage of skilled workers. Between 1929 and 1935 the total labour force in the industry had declined from 350,000 to 157,000. By 1938 it had climbed back slightly to 175,000. But it still was not enough. New machines had been introduced and productivity was a lot higher but there was still a desperate shortage of men in the naval yards. Yet in the areas specializing only in merchant shipbuilding, unemployment among shipyard workers remained at over 20 per cent, a badly unbalanced position for an industry that was still crying out for work.

The Government's Five-Year Plan certainly helped to correct this situation but it was the outbreak of war which produced the real dynamic.

A vast building programme was put in hand. Skilled workers came back to the industry. New machines were installed. By early 1940 the shipyards all over the country were in full swing, every building berth was occupied and there was an exceptionally heavy demand in the fitting-out basins. The basis of the new-found activity was the Government's decision to order a huge tonnage of tramp vessels of a 'simple' type. This meant that almost for the first time in the industry's history it could build 'mass-production models' instead of tailoring each vessel to the whims of the individual owner. This series-production speeded up the work-rate considerably and offered the only hope of being able to build vessels faster than they were being sunk. According to William Westwood: 'It will be the nearest thing to mass production that the industry has ever known. Each yard will build one type of ship only and that type will be the one it can build fastest and most economically.'[11]

The final years of the 1930's thus produced an extraordinary uneven pattern of development. For merchant shipbuilding firms and the towns and areas dependent on them there was a slow and painful struggle out of the Great Depression. By 1938 output had just reached a million tons only to fall back again sharply. Considering that the industry had had its potential capacity cut back to 2m. tons by the rationalization policies of National Shipbuilders Security Limited, only a quarter of this was occupied by the spring of 1939; and considering that 140,000 people had left the industry, there was still an unemployment rate of 23 out of every 100 men still classified as shipyard workers.

On the other hand, the growing threats to international peace stimulated a higher level of naval shipbuilding as early as 1936. Yards involved in this sort of business—and they represented about 18 per cent of the industry's capacity—were very busy. Why the work was not more evenly spread is not clear. Certainly there were calls for it. Writing in the annual report for 1938 Westwood commented: 'Surely it is possible for the Government to divert to these yards some of the smaller naval work, such as sloops, minesweepers, armed-drifters and motor boats of the anti-submarine patrols. Both yards and men are available and this work is necessary for the nation's needs. The Navy is short of the little ships that did more than the big ones to win the last War and no better or cheaper craft have been devised.'[12] But no action was taken along these lines presumably because of the Government's insistence that warship building should be carried out only in approved yards for security reasons.

The slack in the industry was not fully taken up until the outbreak of war. The year 1939 symbolized this transformation with the depression at the beginning of the year giving way to full production and therefore full employment by the end. The industry was at last back at full stretch.

WAGES AND CONDITIONS

The gradual rise in the industry's fortunes was reflected in the successful pressure which the union could bring to bear on employers to concede wage increases and to improve conditions of work. In 1937 it negotiated a long-time ambition of holidays with pay. Westwood said it was a great step forward and one he had advocated for many years. It was gratifying to realize that at long last the worker could enjoy a holiday without the dreaded spectre of poverty. 'It means we shall have to study how to spend our leisure to the best advantage of happiness and health, not only to ourselves but to our dependents.'[3]

In 1937 the Association was also able to complete negotiations with the National Maritime Board for an increase of 25s a month (£1.25) for sea-going carpenters and carpenters' mates. Unfortunately the perennial problem of raising the status of these workers on board ship was again deferred as it had been for year after year but the increase in wages covered at least some of the disappointment.

Dockyard members also received an increase, this time of three shillings (15p) a week while other shipwrights secured an increase of four shillings (20p). Perhaps the most unusual experience in the year was a self-organized strike by 10,000 apprentices on the Clyde for an improvement in wages and conditions. Similar strikes were organized in other districts entirely by the boys themselves. Eventually they came to the unions for help and assistance but it still remained their strike and they stayed out for several weeks. They returned to work only when they were given a specific assurance that their claims would be considered by a conference of employers and trade union representatives. The conference agreed that in future the payment of apprentices should fluctuate with national wages. For every shilling fluctuation in national wages, apprentices' wages should fluctuate by sixpence if the individual was over 18 years of age and by 3d if he was younger. The employers also agreed that the unions could organize the apprentices, something they had hitherto opposed.

By 1938 the average basic wage for time workers was £3 8s a week (3.40p) and for the first time workers in the industry received holidays with pay. Westwood commented: 'This very important concession will go a long way to make a happier and more contented workpeople.'[4] In September 1939 there was another general wage increase of two shillings a week for time workers and 4 per cent for piece-workers. This brought the national bonus to ten shillings a week or 20 per cent for piece-workers on top of the basic wage of £3 a week.

The outbreak of war stimulated the upward pressure of wages still further despite the Chancellor of the Exchequer's warning against the 'vicious spiral' of advancing wages. Shipyard workers received a war bonus of five shillings a week as from 15th February 1940 and the National Maritime Board agreed to increase the monthly rates for all deckhands by £1 a month. The War Risk supplement was also increased to £5 a month.

These increases, relatively large though they were, still did not bring the wage rates in the industry up to the level of 1920. In that year, shipwrights in the Tyneside area had received £4.60. Now they received £3.75. What is more the increases only kept pace with the cost of living. According to the Ministry of Labour statistics, retail prices for such items as food, rent, clothing, fuel and light went up by 77 per cent between

July 1914 and February 1940. In the same period the wages of shipwrights on the Tyne went up from 44s to 78s or by 75 per cent. Despite the increases they were no better off than they had been 26 years before. They were simply keeping pace with inflation.

THE HEALTH OF THE ASSOCIATION

The recovery in the industry, which brought a gradual rise in membership and therefore in income, and the firm control over expenditure allowed the union to build up its financial strength once more. By 1937 income topped the £40,000 mark as it had last done in 1930. Expenditure rose too but at a slower rate and at a considerable distance behind. The result was that in each year from 1937 to 1940 there was a sizeable gain to the reserves ranging from £10,000 to £17,000. By 1938 the union had fulfilled one of its basic constitutional requirements of possessing reserves equal to £3 a member. By 1940 they stood at £95,000 or almost £4 a member.

The renewed financial strength allowed the Executive Committee to look at the possibility of restoring the Superannuation Benefit which had been suspended in August 1931. This benefit had always been regarded as one of the Association's main services to members and its suspension had caused a great deal of criticism and equally had caused the Executive Committee a great deal of concern. Their decision had been severe but it had proved correct. The suspension of that benefit had alone brought the union back to financial health. If it had remained in operation throughout the thirties, the union would have collapsed. No other economy measure could have yielded sufficient savings to keep the union alive. Now, restored to health, it could reconsider the question. The surplus at the end of each year was rising but it was not yet sufficient to allow the full re-introduction of the benefit. In 1938, for example, the surplus was £11,860—a satisfactory figure but in 1930 the Superannuation scheme had cost the Association £16,387. There could be no question of re-introducing the full benefit therefore. That would stop all progress and might indeed begin the slide back down again. But what the Executive Committee did decide to recommend in a fine balance of caution and generosity was a modified payment of £1 per member per quarter. This proposal was carried by a large majority and the first payment was made in time for Christmas 1938. This might not seem much but in view of the potential demand it was as much as could be risked.

There were just over 2,000 claimants, 600 of whom were on the books in 1931 and 1,400 were new claims. Of the 2,000 about three-quarters were idle with 600 at work; 680 were under 65 but over 60 and 1,400 were over 65. At a full benefit of 7s 6d a man per week (37½p) the full cost to the union would have been £39,741 a year.

Even half benefit of 3s 9d a week would have cost £19,870, far beyond the union's reach with an annual surplus of about £10,000. The Committee looked at other options, such as raising the age limit to 65 or imposing a special levy of the members. None of them seemed practical.

If the qualifying age were raised, the cost of half benefit would still be £14,573 while the levy would have to be £2 a member to cover the full cost of half benefit. In the end, therefore, they decided to offer £1 a quarter which still came as a pleasant surprise to many members.

The proposal was dependent on the liability amounting to no more than £8,000 in a full year so that on recent trends there would still be a surplus of income over expenditure at the end of the year. The sum was to be paid to any recipient only for five years, this period including any payment of superannuation benefit prior to 1931.

The Executive Committee, pleased at the reception their proposal received, would have liked to have done more but felt that it was impossible to do so. If more of the younger members had been willing to take out full benefit membership and pay one shilling and sixpence a week rather than simply 8d a week as a trade member then the union's income would have received a tremendous boost. A third of the members were simply on trade benefit. Westwood wrote: 'I cannot help but feel that it is a great pity that the younger members will not recognize their liability to their old and tried brethren; but many are content to be trade members, thereby making it impossible for us to do what we ought to do towards those to whom we owe so much.'[15] The renewal of Superannuation Benefit in its modified form cost the union £465 in 1938 with the amount rising to £3,000 in a full year. The fears as to likely costs did not therefore materialize.

Membership rose gradually in these years picking up from the low point of 17,000 in the mid-1930's to 20,000 by 1937 and 24,000 by 1940. Members of the Executive Committee were each given a particular responsibility to stimulate recruitment and each quarter the figure of new members recruited in each area was given presumably for encouraging competition between the committee members.

The aim was to have 100 per cent membership and to encourage the majority of that membership to join as full benefit members. The Committee was particularly anxious that apprentices for whom they were now empowered to negotiate, should be brought into the fold. They represented the membership of the future and the sooner they were introduced to trade unionism the better.

The advent of war posed a particular problem. For with the tremendous demand for shipping and therefore for labour, many had returned to the craft and without joining the union were reaping all the benefits which had been fought for by members. Westwood thought 'this was not playing the game'. The dockyards were particularly bad in this respect. Officials were continually trying to organize the non-unionists who were prepared to take all the union provided but to make no contribution themselves. The officials were not having great success. To try to overcome the non-unionist's reluctance, the Executive Committee recommended that such people should be admitted on the payment of an entry fee of 2s 6d (12½p) and a weekly contribution of 8d as trade members.

The question was accentuated by the Government's request for a 'dilution of labour'. That is to say, with the tremendous demands for shipping and the severe shortage of labour, members of other trades or even semi-skilled workers were to be allowed to do shipwrights' work. The Executive Committee were prepared to accept dilution schemes but only after a number of conditions had been met. First, complete interchangeability of all the Association's members should be carried out to ensure that all members were fully employed before agreeing to dilution. Secondly any such dilution scheme should be carefully worked out and a written agreement should be made between the Association, the firm and any other unions involved. Above all, any 'dilutees' who were not members of a union and who were taken on to assist shipwrights must join the Association as trade members. This was reasonable since if they were to enjoy the wages, working conditions and privileges of membership they should at least make a minimum contribution to the Association.

In laying down these conditions the Executive Committee were trying to draw a balance between national needs and the interests of their members. Clearly the country needed as much shipping as possible at this critical juncture in its history but at the same time the Committee were only too well aware of the severe times that their members had lived through. They wanted to do all they could to protect their interests and offer them every opportunity for secure, long-term employment before allowing others to move into jobs that they might occupy. The policy that they adopted was an attempt to find a balance between these two considerations.

THE WORK OF THE EXECUTIVE

The Executive Committee was very much the motor of the Association. It provided the impetus for action. It also controlled the direction. It was in fact the main constitutional authority within the Association for all day-to-day matters. The members were consulted from time to time on changes to the rules or alterations in the payments of benefits. And they were polled regularly for the elections of various officials and officers. But the Executive Committee still remained the most concentrated focus of power in the Association. The question of superannuation benefits illustrates this point very well. The Committee sought the opinion of members about the re-introduction of the limited scheme. They had not polled members about stopping the benefit in August 1931. No doubt they felt that on such an emotional issue the members would vote with their hearts rather than with their heads and would thereby block a course of action which the Committee knew was essential. But the fact is that the Committee could assume this degree of power without great heart-searching because they were used to running the affairs of the Association with few restrictions placed upon them.

The five members of the Committee, together with the two senior officials, William Westwood and John Willcocks, the tall, angular, rather lugubrious assistant general secretary, met regularly, usually about every three weeks. Their main purpose was twofold: to decide policy; and to maintain control over the Association's affairs by the receipt of information. For example every member of the Committee, including the General Secretary, reported on his activities since the last meeting: the discussions he had had, the visits he had made, the decisions he had taken. The Committee also received and had to approve the minutes of all the branch meetings. Considering that there were 160 branches this in itself was a formidable task but it was felt to be essential if the Committee was to be the central power that it wished to be. As we have seen, Committee members were also encouraged to take a personal interest in the recruitment of new members or at least to encourage others in their area to recruit vigorously. The sense of competition was increased by publishing the recruitment figures quarterly on an area basis with the name of the responsible Committee member alongside. We can imagine that this would lead to some chaffing of a member who was always bottom of the list and that this in itself would give him an incentive to do better. Recruitment of new members was very much a central issue at this time and its importance was underlined by making each Committee member personally responsible in this way. Each annual report also contained an exhortation to members to do all they could to obtain new entrants. Every negotiated increase in wages or improvement in working conditions was also used for propaganda purposes. In the circumstances, it is surprising that a more powerful direct incentive was not used such as offering a quarterly or annual prize to the person who recruited the highest number of new members.

The Executive Committee were also expected to pay regular visits to the branches in their areas and to inspect the books regularly. Each quarter the members made a report of their visits. Here are some typical reports:

'Preston. I have inspected the books of this branch and find them in good order. Only a small number on the ledger, viz. 7, 6 of whom are Full Benefit. I have suggested to the Secretary the idea of closing the branch and him taking on as collector but as this is a very old branch tradition dies hard. However, it manages to pay its way and I propose to leave it for a little while longer.' G. A. Burke.

'Chester. I have examined the books of this branch and find them in good order. This is a branch that has been hit very hard by the recent activities of the National Shipbuilding Securities Limited and in consequence a loss of membership. The present number on the ledger is 20 and not a single one working at the trade. It is financially holding its own and we can only await the future as to increasing membership. We have a very energetic secretary.' G. A. Burke.

'Glasson Dock. I have inspected the books of the (94) Glasson Dock branch and it is comprised of 11 members—2 Trade, 2 L.F. and 7 Full Benefit. A small branch with a small Dry Dock adjacent but which has suffered from lack of employment but trade is better now and the prospects brighter. A new Secretary has been difficult to get but a good man is now in it. The late Secretary has left and gone to Barrow-in-Furness.' G. A. Burke.

'Birkenhead. I have examined the books of this branch and find room for improvement in the Secretary's book-keeping and I have instructed him in that direction. There are 174 members on the books, of whom no less than 140 are Trade members and only 34 Full Benefit. Practically all new entrants during the last two years being entered up as Trade members.' G. A. Burke.

'Sunderland Drillers. I have inspected the books of this branch on 9th December 1936 and found everything in order. This branch has had a very hard time of it for years but I am pleased to report progress in the port and the branch is in better condition now than it has been for some time.' P. F. Smith.

'Hull C. To say that the books of this, the Hull C. branch, are being kept in accordance with rule would be generous. The Secretary is only just doing the things necessary but I have no doubts as far as the financial side is concerned. There is no question of dishonesty.' S. Ombler.

Occasionally these inspections did reveal small misdemeanours or worse. One check revealed that the Wallsend branch had paid £5 10s out of General Funds to old members as Christmas gifts. This might have been a charitable gesture but it was unconstitutional. The Committee took a serious view of this action and told the Wallsend branch that it must repay the money. There was a good deal of wrangling between the Executive Committee and the branch before the latter finally agreed.

The Committee were also involved in another wrangle, of a much more important nature with John Stewart, the dapper former district delegate for Scotland, who had been dismissed in the autumn of 1935 for general incompetence. Stewart had never accepted his dismissal and in 1937 he began to take out a legal action against the Association. He decided to sue for slander and to claim £500 damages and costs. The case was to be heard in Edinburgh.

The Association instructed its legal agents to try to achieve a settlement outside the courts and by May 1937 it looked as if this would be achieved. Westwood was able to report to the Executive Committee meeting on 5th May that 'the pursuer had agreed to the terms offered by the Association subject to confirmation by his local Legal Agent.' However, although he had intimated his acceptance of the terms, Stewart refused to sign a statement to that effect. His solicitors became 'very much perturbed' by his refusal and threatened to withdraw from the case.

When Stewart continued to refuse to offer his acceptance, his solicitors did withdraw. Stewart now began to write directly to Westwood, who reported to the October meeting of the Executive Committee that the letters were written 'in a slanderous fashion and make statements against officials which, in his opinion, were bordering on blackmail'.

In November 1937 the Association's agents took the issue to court and obtained judgement in the Association's favour with an order for costs against Stewart. At long last it looked as if the matter was over and the Association's position was cleared. In this moment of triumph, the Executive Committee offered the hand of magnanimity towards Stewart who after all had been at one time the President of the Association. They agreed not to press the question of costs unless Stewart 'overstepped the mark or persisted in writing to or maligning any of our officials. If he is prepared to keep quiet and does not in any way interfere with the work of any of our officers, then we will not be vindictive with reference to costs.'

That was the formal resolution of the Executive Committee on 7th December 1937. Unfortunately the dispute was to drag on for a long time yet. For while the Association was prepared to waive its costs which had been assessed by the court at £62 13s 3d, this depended on Stewart's attitude. Considering that his wages at this time were £3 8s a week (£3.40) he was faced with the prospect of a big burden. He was working for Stephens and Company at Linthouse in Glasgow at the time. According to the Association's legal agents 'Stewart was proving very stubborn and was creating unnecessary expense.' When he actually went so far as to repudiate the judgement and the costs, the Association had no alternative but to secure an 'arrestment of his wages' as a means of enforcing the court's verdict.

This process in itself was expensive for the legal expense of recovery costs in this way was 60 per cent of the amount recovered, making Stewart's financial burden even greater. But continuing his path to martyrdom, he now left his employment and became unemployed so that he had no wages which could be 'arrested'. He also stepped up his campaign of vilification by sending open postcards to Westwood and other officials and by seeking the support of colleagues in Glasgow, including the secretary of the Govan branch. By July 1938 the Executive Committee was beginning to lose its patience. It empowered the legal agents to take the necessary steps to force Stewart to meet his financial obligations or to give an undertaking that he would stop the scurrilous and defamatory correspondence. Still little progress was made. By December the legal agents were getting impatient with the attitude adopted by Stewart and suggested that drastic steps should be taken to bring this matter to a head. Again a delay. But in April 1939 the legal agents suggested that the only course to follow was to await his obtaining regular employment and then to repeat the attachment of his wages.

From that point on, the case simply disappears. Whether he gave up his campaign of vilification and paid the costs quietly or whether the war intervened, or whether the union dropped the claim, is not clear. But certainly the union was happy to see the end of an incident which had lasted for four years and which had caused considerable embarrassment and bad feeling.

Once a year the Executive Committee held what was called a Consultative Meeting with the district delegates. These meetings allowed a full exchange of views, helped to keep all fully informed and led to a better understanding of the problems facing the union. These occasions were also the nearest equivalent to an annual general meeting when it was possible to look ahead and to consider wider issues. For example, the rapid development of aircraft manufacture at such places as Brough in Yorkshire and Belfast opened up new job opportunities for members.

The Consultative meetings allowed both the Executive Committee and the District Delegates to consider how best to exploit these potential openings. The Brough factory had been one of the first in the country for aircraft manufacture and shipwrights had been among the first to be employed there. At first they had been employed on the wooden floats and then as the industry developed they had moved over to steel work. They had adapted easily to the use of new machinery and new methods as they were introduced. As a result, they had secured this work for themselves rather than allowing semi-skilled workers to get it. Over a quarter of the Association's members in the Hull area, that is about 200, were now engaged on this sort of work. It was important to see that as new aircraft factories were opened in such areas as Belfast and Dumbarton the members secured equal benefits particularly in the face of competition from other workers and unions.

As the aircraft industry developed and as the demand for planes outstripped supply, the companies were gradually eliminating skilled men and introducing unskilled men, semi-skilled men and women to take their place. One major employer, A. V. Roe, was employing only fifteen skilled men out of every hundred employees. The Shipwrights themselves had suffered very little but the Executive Committee recognized that unless the situation was watched carefully they could find themselves in the same difficulties as other unions. The district delegates were asked to keep in close touch with the developing situation and to report to Head Office.

In contrast to this relatively new situation, the Consultative Meetings also dealt with some of the age-old problems such as demarcation disputes. Such disputes were almost an occupational hazard although the work of the Confederation of Shipbuilding and Engineering Unions had gone a long way to reducing such points of friction. From time to time, however, the Boilermakers would attempt to test their strength. In 1938 they claimed the right to fit armour plating to warships being built in the river Tyne. The dispute never materialized into a full-scale conflict but this was due to the determined attitude of the shipwrights' officials.

While the meetings were very useful in exploring ideas and exchanging information, they were only consultative. Power remained clearly with the Executive Committee. But in the absence of general assemblies or other opportunities to meet the membership at large, they certainly were useful as an extra measure in keeping the Executive Committee fully informed and, in return, giving the district delegates a clear understanding of the latest developments at Head Office and the possible changes of policy that were being considered.

The officials of the union undertook another important function, helping members to reclaim insurance benefits under the Workmen's Compensation Acts. Each month there were reports of monies claimed on behalf of members who had suffered injuries at work. By 1940 well over £600,000 had been successfully claimed, a staggering total, indicative not only of the successful approach by the officials but also of the danger in a shipyard.

The work of the Executive Committee was comprehensive and thorough. To be one of the five members was very demanding, requiring attention to a great deal of detail and the expenditure of a great amount of time and effort. On the other hand, it certainly had its consolations. It must have been a considerable source of satisfaction to appreciate that the Committee's efforts had alone been responsible for restoring the Association's fortunes. If it had not yet returned to its former position, it had at least been saved from extinction. In fact, it was one of the best run small craft unions in the country with excellent management and a sound financial base.

The restoration of the Association's financial position allowed consideration to be given to increasing the wages of staff. They had all accepted a reduction of 10 per cent at the beginning of the depression. The Executive Committee now proposed and the membership agreed by 2:1 to increase wages by 16 per cent from 1st July 1938. The General Secretary's salary went up from approximately £8.50 a week to £9.75 and the Assistant General Secretary from £6 to £7.

THE POLITICAL SITUATION

While unemployment remained the dominant issue in domestic affairs and certainly the paramount issue in the public's mind, a graver threat was beginning to emerge. For by perceptible degrees and quite evident turns of the screw, the world was closing the opportunities for peace. The Disarmament Conference which had begun in February 1932 languished for two years before ending in failure to reconcile the main conflict of interest between Germany and France. Ramsay MacDonald prophesied that this failure would in itself almost automatically lead to war, a safe enough prophecy considering the emergence of the Nazi leader Hitler as Chancellor in January 1933 and Germany's decision not only to pull out of the Conference but also to leave the League of Nations. The screw was turned tighter by the Italian invasion of Abyssinia in 1935 and the German occupation of the Rhineland in 1936.

In the circumstances, re-armament became a real issue. British Governments had consistently put their faith, but not much more, in the League of Nations and had argued that this system of 'collective security', as it was called, was a viable alternative to re-armament. What they did not appreciate was that the League was only as strong as its members but no one argued in favour of arming the League of Nations or in favour of handing over control of national armies to a joint command of the League. The Labour Party was particularly split between the total pacifists such as George Lansbury, the leader of the Party, and those who believed in the collective security of the League of Nations.

A full meeting of the Party and the General Council of the T.U.C. held in 1934 issued a statement entitled 'War and Peace' which disavowed pacificism and declared 'the duty unflinchingly to support our Government in all the risks and consequences of fulfilling its duty to take part in collective action against a peace-breaker'. But it did not quieten the pacifists who continued to press their arguments, even after the Party conference in 1935 had overwhelmingly accepted the statement as official policy.

Nor were the divisions healed by the resignation of Lansbury as party leader and his replacement by Clement Attlee, for he was another pacifist who criticized every demand for arms made by the National Government until war came in 1939.

But there were splits not only in the Labour ranks. There were divisions between the chiefs of staff and the Government. The former were alarmed at the commencement of re-armament in Germany and argued that Britain must take similar steps to protect her interests. The Government did nothing. In fact, the arms estimates for 1934 were lower than they had been ten years earlier in 1924 and in 1935 they were not much higher. But while the Government failed to act, leading civil servants accepted the advice of the chiefs of staff and started to draw up plans for total war, including the conscription of labour, rationing and mass evacuation from large towns.

They also drew up a White Paper which the Government reluctantly agreed to issue, denouncing collective security and advocating rearmament. The White Paper 'Statement Relating to Defence' issued in March 1935 was 'a landmark in British policy'. It announced that the British Government had ceased to rely on collective security and were now going to rely on the older security of armed forces."[6]

It was almost MacDonald's last action as Prime Minister. In June he and Baldwin changed places and Baldwin became Prime Minister. Five months later he called an election where, despite the attempts by the politicians to keep foreign affairs at the forefront, domestic matters such as housing, unemployment and the special areas remained the main concerns of the electors. They returned the National Government, giving it almost 12m. votes and Labour 8.3m. The National Government had 432 seats, the Labour Party gained about a hundred to take their total to 154 and the Liberals won only 20.

The National Government, now given a mandate for rearmament, increased the arms estimates slightly in 1936, still considerably below German expenditure, and appointed a Minister for the Co-ordination of Defence. In fact, the appointment had little meaning for the position carried no weight and was filled by a dull lawyer, Sir Thomas Inskip, who carried less. But behind the scenes a considerable amount of planning was done to prepare for total war.

The Labour Party meanwhile remained divided. Ernest Bevin, leader of the Transport Workers, and a few other trade union leaders, supported rearmament as did Hugh Dalton. They attacked the Government for not doing enough. But Attlee and the majority of Labour M.P.'s were against any kind of rearmament. They attacked the Government for doing too much. But these views became more and more isolated as Germany continued to build up its armaments. When Neville Chamberlain replaced Stanley Baldwin as Prime Minister after the latter's retirement, foreign policy came to the forefront of the national stage and more decisive action was taken on rearmament.

The Labour Party too came out openly in support of such a policy, with the 1937 Conference stating quite simply its commitment. In March 1938 the services were given permission to place what orders they wanted with manufacturers, even if they interfered with 'normal' trade, a relaxation of a previous directive, and T.U.C. was asked to reduce craft restrictions in the engineering industry. By February 1939 Britain was placed even more firmly on a war economy when the Government authorized aircraft production to the limit, that is without worrying about the usual constraints of money.

Some members of the Labour Party continued to regard the arms race as a likely cause of war and they wanted to reduce British armaments in the hope that Germany and other countries would do the same. But generally the Party took a more equivocal view. Officially it argued that some increase in armaments was necessary in order to support the collective security in which the Party still believed. In July 1937 the parliamentary party decided in future to abstain from voting on the armament estimates rather than voting against them. The hope was that this would show that the party had no confidence in the Government yet did not want to oppose its efforts on national defence. This was an unhappy and unclear stance to take and was made even worse by the fact that it had been pushed through the party meeting by trade unionist M.P.'s and opposed by the leader Attlee and two of his principal lieutenants, Herbert Morrison and Arthur Greenwood. The members on the Left, such as Cripps and Bevan, were also opposed. The Labour Party was seen by the public to be still very divided and, if anything, to be against armaments. This confused attitude which was not entirely cleared up by the 1937 Party Conference barred the way to any attempt at national collaboration. It is interesting that no confidential information on military matters was shown to any member of the Labour Party until the outbreak of war, even though the need for national unity on such a vital matter was recognized as early as 1935. The general impression was simply that Labour's deep divisions suggested that it was a party that could not be trusted. On the other hand, the T.U.C. General Council was asked by the Government in 1938 and 1939 to help in plans for war mobilization and air-raid precautions.

William Westwood took a vigorous part in the public debates at this time. Both as President of the Confederation of Shipbuilding and Engineering Unions and as General Secretary of the Shipconstructors' and Shipwrights' Association, he spoke out forcefully. At the annual meeting of the Confederation in May 1938 he declared: 'The danger of war looms over the world. In every field of policy the Government presents a spectacle of moral and political bankruptcy. The present international situation is very ugly and dangerous. During the past two years Europe has been more than once on the very brink of the precipice—and there is a grave risk of a general war in the near future unless sanity prevails. However, if the demands of either Fascist or Nazi dictators are a practical danger, then they cannot be ignored and we shall require to take the necessary steps to ensure that any action they may take will do the minimum amount of damage to life...... Every country has been converted into an arsenal for the manufacture of implements of human destruction with the harnessing of science and of the cleverest brains to invent every conceivable device to destroy the human race. We desire science and brains to preserve life, not destroy it.'

Earlier in his address to the same conference, he mentioned the meeting that had taken place between the Confederation leaders and the Minister for the Co-ordination of Defence, Sir Thomas Inskip on 24th March 1938. The Minister made no definite proposals but he did ask for the unions' co-operation together with that of the employers to accelerate the production of certain armaments. Westwood told the Conference: 'While we may be prepared to do everything possible for the defence of our own country and the defence of democracy, we must not provide arms which will assist either Fascist aggression or dictatorship in any part of the world.' This was a reference to the fact that some aircraft and other armaments were being exported. He went on:

'Any scheme of acceleration of armaments submitted to the unions must contain the necessary safeguards that our members will be fully protected when work slackens off or during the slumps which generally follow periods of abnormal pressure. We cannot forget how the promises both verbal and written to the trade unions who loyally agreed to relax certain rules during the Great War were deliberately broken by the Government.'

In January 1938 President F. D. Roosevelt of the United States of America called for an international conference to discuss world problems and particularly the maintenance of peace. His initiative was brushed aside by Neville Chamberlain, who said that the time was not opportune and it was ignored by Germany and Italy. Westwood told the 1939 Conference of the Confederation at Blackpool: 'Roosevelt's perfectly-timed message has dramatically changed the balance of power and has placed the democratic cause in the ascendant for the first time since Hitler started his career of conquest in Austria a little more than a year ago. The actions of the Dictators have awakened tremendous forces in the democracies which were hitherto unknown. The future must be faced in a spirit of sober optimism and everything done to re-establish confidence between the peace-loving countries. With this accomplished, the year 1940 will, I believe, bring with it the dawn of a new era of peace, prosperity and contentment for the world.'

As a prophecy, that was in the same class as the notorious *Daily Express* headline after the Munich conference: 'Great Britain will not be involved in a European war this year or next year either.' Westwood's forecast was particularly odd in view of the strong words he used in the annual report for 1938 which was written in the spring of 1939. 'While one would like to place confidence in the promises made and the agreement signed by Herr Hitler at Munich, I regret I am unable to place faith in one whose word is not his bond. I believe the Führer has played, in a diplomatic manner, for time and will, during the respite, make his plans for further attacks, by force if necessary, to add to Germany's possession.' In the face of this threat, he felt there was no alternative but to support the Government's expenditure of £580m. on defence although regretting it as 'the tragedy of universal waste—wasted money, wasted effort and squandered happiness.' But he wanted to see the problem of defence at least tied to that of unemployment so that this enormous sum of money could alleviate the latter as well as provide for the former. Air raid precautions provided a specific case. There was a tremendous demand for shelters which could be built by unskilled labour. 'But in this instance the Government, which is spending money like water in other directions, runs no risk of "going broke" to pay for a cure. On the contrary, large scale air raid precaution work would certainly prove the cheapest form of national defence.' He pointed out that labour could be had for almost next to nothing or at most for the difference between unemployment benefit and a standard wage. In addition, new roads, car parks and storage spaces were needed and there were many other ways of using idle men and idle money. Although this was an appealing argument, it did not seem part of the stern stuff of rearmament politics. Nor did his plea for better old-age pensions which followed in the next paragraph of his review. And he ended again with a note of misplaced optimism: 'We might well ask—"what sort of a world will it be for our children?" It is certainly going to be a sterner one but not a less happy one for us in Britain. It is a pity that we could not have been without threats from over the seas so that we might have devoted our energies solely to the conquest of poverty and disease. In the new age we can be happier than before, not solely owing to the keenness of the struggle itself but through the knowledge that the great resources which have been built up, and the great qualities that we ourselves fundamentally possess, will bring victory to our ideals.'[7]

TEN YEARS AS GENERAL SECRETARY

William Westwood had now been General Secretary for ten years. And those years had been the most dramatic—and traumatic—in the Association's history. They had seen the membership fall to the lowest point since the nineteenth century and unemployment rise to its highest point by far. They had seen the workforce in the industry slump from over 350,000 to 150,000, of whom over half were unemployed at one time. Many shipyards had disappeared and others had been idle for years on end. The great skills of a proud craft had lain wasted and wasting.

The Association had seen its income ebbing away, to a figure of just £25,000 in 1933—a level that it had not known since 1895. Expenditure too fell, but not fast enough and for twelve consecutive years, from 1921 to 1933, with the exception of 1927, the union made a loss. In this time its reserve funds were reduced from £268,000 (giving a balance per member of £5.65) to £27,000 (with a balance per member of £1.50). A powerful union was humbled and with less resolute management could have passed out of existence. It was William Westwood who above all provided that resolute management. He was forty-nine years of age when he got the top job and he had plenty of solid experience behind him. His own personal circumstances had made him a fighter for he was born of a poor family. He had had four part-time jobs before he was ten years of age and had worked hard for all he had achieved. He had been in the union all his adult life and as well as taking an official position as a branch secretary while he was still an apprentice and working his way through every position in the branch, he had also studied hard and turned himself into an expert on the complexities of national insurance. It was this studying that gave him the break for in 1913, at the age of thirty-three, he was made the Union's National Supervisor on National Industrial Insurance. But his energy and political commitment gave him a further dimension still as a political figure, first as an agent and then as a candidate himself in two elections.

He was ideally suited, personally and professionally, to lead the union through this demanding and testing time. And he succeeded. He sharpened the Executive Committee to a small, semi-permanent body of five, reorganized the work of the district delegates, reduced the costs of running the head office, recommended the temporary stoppage of the highly emotive superannuation benefit and even accepted, along with other full-time officials, a 10 per cent reduction in his own salary. Even these measures took four years to produce results, largely because the union was working in such adverse conditions with the Great Depression deepening and intensifying all the time. But by 1934, with the first slight lifting of the Depression, the union made its first surplus in twelve years and from then on its recovery was steady, if not spectacular.

Into this task, he threw a tremendous amount of personal energy. He worked long and hard. He travelled great distances and attended frequent meetings. He also developed a great talent for negotiation, for bargaining with employers intelligently for recognizing when to press a claim and when to withdraw and try again at a more opportune time. This skill particularly came to the fore during his three years as President of the Engineering and Shipbuilding Trades Federation followed by his three years as President of its successor body, the Confederation of Shipbuilding and Engineering Unions. Indeed, his skill contributed not only to winning concessions from the employers over wage awards or holidays with pay, it also brought more unions into the Confederation's fold. By the time he retired as President it embraced thirty unions representing 1.5m. workers.

Yet although he was recognized as a powerful and honourable leader in his own industry, he never achieved a national platform. He was never elected to the General Council of the T.U.C. which would have given him national status independent of his own union. And he shut himself off from national politics by refusing to stand again for Parliament although he was offered at least one constituency and presumably could have had other opportunities if he had wanted them.

Within his own sphere, he had no shortage of work and indeed seemed to thrive on committees. Besides his own union and the Confederation, both of which were onerous, he was a magistrate, a county councillor, a vice president of the North-East Development Board, a member of the Unemployment Assistance Advisory Board, a member of the Board of Trade Advisory Council, a member of the National Maritime Board, a director of the Co-operative Printing Society and so on and so on.

As a man, he was ebullient, forceful and gregarious. He had a great gift of the gab, was a powerful speaker and had a fund of stories. In fact, when he was fighting the Sutton Division of Plymouth in the 1929 Election, the local reporters kept a book of all his jokes and quips and printed many of them in their articles about him.

He was also a great optimist, a born believer that things would get better. This quality had probably been the making of him as a man and as a union leader. It probably also explains some of the gaffes he made in his forecasts of the future. We have already noted his prediction in the spring of 1939 that 1940 would see the beginning of better times. He made a similar, although less serious, mistake in 1937 when he talked of the 'boom conditions' in British shipbuilding. He told the annual meeting of the Confederation: 'The position in general gives grounds for asserting that the depression is over and that the shipbuilding trade of the world is emerging from the deep depression which caused such unparalleled hardships for many years. British shipyards are producing on an average one large cargo vessel a day. They cannot turn out this type of vessel fast enough to keep pace with the orders that are pouring in.'

By 1938 he had to admit that 'for those yards which do not build naval craft, the outlook is unfortunately causing much anxiety..... The shipbuilding industry must not be allowed to drift again into the sloughs of despond but, as berths become vacant through launchings, it is morally obligatory on the Government so to assist that other keels are laid.'[8]

When the war began, he was invited by Winston Churchill, then First Lord of the Admiralty, to join him as principal labour adviser. Two years later he was made Director of Contract Labour. While he was involved in this work, he remained General Secretary of the Shipwrights in a consultative capacity and John Willcocks took over as Acting General Secretary. As soon as the war ended, Westwood retired from the Union. He was by that time sixty-five and probably felt he had lived a full life in trade unionism. However, it certainly was not the end of his working life for he built a new career in industry and commerce. He became the director of numerous well-known public and private companies including several cinemas in the North-East. He was a director of the Government-backed Finance Corporation for Industry and Vice-President of the Building Societies Association. He also had a great interest in sport and became a director of a number of sports clubs or organizations including Newcastle United Football Club.

For his work at the Admiralty during the war he was created a Baron, Lord Westwood of Gosforth, thus becoming the first trade union leader elevated to the peerage.

This second career opened him up to a good deal of controversy. How could a socialist become such a dedicated exponent of capitalism? Did he really believe in a fairer Britain if he was only too ready to 'operate' within the present system for his own financial benefit? Such questions are not easy to answer although one can certainly put forward a number of points. Firstly, it is worth stressing that he was past retirement age before he took to his new career. By that time he had already served his union for almost fifty years with devotion and energy. There was never any question of the vigour and imagination he displayed as a union leader. And considering the directorships he picked up in his retirement, his loyalty to the union must have been a considerable financial sacrifice. Secondly he always claimed that his main loyalty was to his family and if his membership of the Party conflicted with that basic loyalty it was the Party that would have to go. Equally, it could be argued that he was serving the working man by representing his interests on company boards. To put forward their views within the framework of the present system was an honourable thing to do and to work for change from within rather than revolution from without was to follow one of the historic aims of the Labour Party as distinct from more radical views of other groups on the Left.

It is a pity that his later life was surrounded by a controversy that called into question his earlier commitment for there can be little doubt that he was a prime example of the vigorous, moderate, capable union leader from the mainstream of British trade unionism.

CHAPTER TWENTY-FOUR

Considering the privations suffered by so many workers in the 1930's, the response to the demands of war-time was staggering. The threat of invasion and of national defeat brought forth an overwhelming degree of co-operation and support. Output soared. Productivity per manshift jumped to new levels. Timekeeping improved, absenteeism declined almost to nil. Disputes were reduced to a minimum. In fact the year 1940 saw fewer working days lost by strikes than in any other year since records were first kept in 1893. So whole-hearted indeed was the response to the war effort that 'the problem was not how to get the workers to work longer hours but how to prevent them from overworking.'[1]

But despite this magnificent response, industrial production remained a key problem throughout the war. In fact, victory was seen to depend not only on military success and bravery but also on the output of the factories, particularly in armaments, aircraft manufacture and shipbuilding. The efforts of shipyard workers, including the shipwrights, were therefore vital. It was the task of the union to inspire these efforts while safeguarding the interests of the members in terms of current wages and future conditions.

THE WAR AIMS OF THE UNIONS

This balance between the nation's needs and the interests of individual workers was described at length in a brilliant speech made by Mr J. W. Stephenson, president of the Confederation of Shipbuilding and Engineering Unions at the annual conference at Morecambe in May 1941. Mr Stephenson, of the Plumbers, Glaziers and Domestic Engineers Union, had succeeded William Westwood as the president in 1938. After three years in the top position, this was to be his final address before handing over to Mr H. M. Harrison, of the General Workers. He made it a memorable occasion. Speaking with remarkable warmth, understanding and foresight, he sketched a vivid picture of industrial Britain, and particularly industrial workers, at war.

'In my mind at this moment,' he said, 'there is a moving picture of the shipyards and engineering shops.... I see our members at their jobs. I see them labouring amid all the complex conditions of the yards; the repairing sheds, the engineering shops; the foundries. I see them swarming the ships.... They know that ships mean food for our people, arms for our soldiers, sailors, airmen, the essential raw materials for the trade and commerce on which alone the country can live, the nation fight.... They know the fate of Britain—the fate of the world—largely depends on what they can accomplish.... We hear much talk about the need for greater and still greater production. Shipyard workers are as entirely aware of that as any. No complaint can be made against them..... Any cause for complaint.... is due to faulty organization or lack of organization. It is due to lack of means or facilities. ... At the moment I am thinking of the manner in which our shipping was mishandled and our great heritage of shipbuilding was left to decay and rot. It is common knowledge that long before the war the Imperial General Staff were of the opinion that Britain was likely to be faced with a major war.... The Government and those gentlemen controlling and directing shipping knew how desperate would be the need of ships. Yet National Shipbuilders Securities Limited bought up shipbuilding yards, closed them and rendered them legally sterile for forty years. The armies of skilled shipbuilding workers were thrown into hopeless wretchedness and despair.'

Turning his full wrath on to the wasteful policies of the 1930's, Mr Stephenson declared: 'I think back. I think of the labour wasted, the skill wasted, the wonderful machinery and plant wasted, the opportunities wasted. I think of the waste of human values; the shocking impoverishment of human values, the shocking impoverishment of thousands of families—their hunger, worry, frustration in regard to everything that gives joy and savour to life—the ruin of their homes.... What labour, what mental misery, what shortages of food and other necessities, what gallant lives of seamen, could have been saved but for the folly of letting the shipbuilding industry crumble largely into dissolution?

'I want to make certain—and Confederation wants to make certain—that such a state of affairs should not occur again. We will win the war. That is a settled conviction and determination. Shipyard workers will, come weal or woe, play their laborious part in winning it.

'The war will end.... and will find this country, Europe and the world generally in a state of economic and social disruption.... There is however one thing we have most to fear. It is that statesmen and others in power and control will fall into a state of torpor and stupidity and spinelessness.... The particular concern and endeavour of the Confederation must be to bridge the transitional period from war to peace in regard to the shipyards. The war effort has accustomed them and conditioned them to the work to the highest degree. They can engage upon the tasks of peacetime. It is the set determination of the Confederation that they shall do so without checks, delays, hindrances, without muddles, confusions, without unemployment or hideous slumps.... I have said that the men the Confederation represents are unbeatable, unvanquishable, that they can mould the future given the will and understanding. It is now that they should fixedly resolve to become the masters of their destinies. They are conquering the future! Let them conquer it for themselves!'

The speech, quoted here at length, was a masterly mixture of analysis, forward-thinking and emotion. It was also remarkably prophetic. The war was won. The shipyards did play a key role. And the men did conquer the future for themselves, at least in the immediate objective of seeing the return of a Government sympathetic to their needs which maintained full employment and introduced a revolution in social security.

John Willcocks, the Acting General Secretary of the Shipwrights, shared the trade unions' general concern for the future of Britain. He wrote: 'One thing is certain: that those who have fought for their country in this terrible war must have a larger stake in the country itself. The country which is worth fighting for must be worth living in.... We must see that our own resources are developed to a far greater extent than hitherto and these great monopolies such as land, railways, mines and shipping should be used for the interests of the community as a whole and not for the benefit of the few. To maintain our industrial and economic position we must have no patched up system of reconstruction but a deliberate, thought-out system and comprehensive plan of social and industrial re-building, but all these plans for the re-building of our social, industrial and economic life of this country depend on one condition and that is winning the war. Without that essential condition, all such schemes will be so much waste paper.'[2]

But while they were striving to win the war, the workers were to be paid the proper rate. Hours of work became longer and longer and the conditions more and more trying—restrictions on lighting were a particular source of inconvenience and often of accidents—but there was one way in which the men could receive immediate rewards, through the pay packet. As we shall see later, the unions kept up a constant pressure on employers for higher wages and, where the latter refused, they used the national arbitration service set up by the Government to get their way.

SHORTAGES OF MANPOWER

After the Chamberlain era when Government and unions had a somewhat strained relationship, the war brought about a much closer alliance. This was perhaps natural considering that Labour members were in the Government and that trade unionists were in Government service and that industrial production was, throughout the period, of vital concern and that this depended largely on manpower. In the early years, immediate manpower demands could be supplied from the pool of unemployed but by 1940 the slack had largely been taken up. Now it became much more difficult. Throughout these years it was the central problem facing Ernest Bevin, the former Transport Workers' leader, who was now Minister of Labour, and other unionists such as William Westwood who were working for the Government. The shipbuilding unions played an active part in trying to recruit every possible individual.

In this they worked very closely with the Ministry of Labour. In March 1940 there was a high level meeting between the Minister, Ernest Bevin, the employers and the unions to discuss the supply of workers, the level of unemployment and the shipbuilding programme. The aim was to find ways of getting still more workers into the industry. It was agreed that while it would be possible to find some extra men by combing the unemployment registers, the most likely source was from among the 8,000 shipyard workers who had enlisted for the Services and of whom only 800 had been released to return to the yards. (The Services were unwilling to release more.) The Shipwrights' Executive met at Westwood's office in the Admiralty on 30th April 1940 when various suggestions were put forward, including proposals to speed up the design and construction methods of shipbuilding. But while they were ready to consider and implement many suggestions, the unions were opposed to the greater use of women. They felt it was 'a drastic departure from custom and practice.' The situation was to become so desperate, however, that women had to undertake heavy work normally reserved for men and a union conference only a month later accepted the new situation 'subject to adequate safeguards being inserted.'

On 25th May 1940 Ernest Bevin addressed a national conference called by the T.U.C. and announced new initiatives including the setting up of a Labour Supply Board. John Willcocks, acting general secretary of the Shipwrights, attended the conference and subsequently called a special meeting of his Executive Committee to discuss the Minister's proposals. The Committee recognized the need for such a scheme and agreed that if any officials were offered positions they should be encouraged to accept them and would be offered leave of absence. In fact three district delegates became Labour Supply Officers. They were G. W. Cable, Tyne and Blyth; W. H. Ford, Bristol Channel and H.M. Dockyards; and J. McMillan, Scotland and Ireland Drillers. Two members of the Executive Committee, G. A. Burke and A. C. Allen, were similarly appointed.

A few days after the T.U.C. conference, Bevin called a meeting in London to discuss another serious development arising from the capitulation of Holland, Belgium and France. Germany now controlled the whole coastline opposite the British Isles. This constituted a very real danger to ports on the east and south coasts. Severe bombardment was already taking place and shipyard work in Southampton and London was being critically disrupted. Men were becoming unemployed day by day. To cope with this emergency, Bevin told the union leaders he was introducing a Voluntary Transfer Scheme to encourage men to move to the North and East coasts where future work would be concentrated.

The scheme provided free fares. It also carried with it the rate of pay operative in the district. For most of the men from the south, this meant an increase but in addition they would receive £1.22½ a week subsistence allowance. The scheme was to be run by a Central Committee in London, of which John Willcocks was appointed a member. But a great deal of the detailed work would be done by local committees. They would be responsible for the transfer of the men or, on the other hand, for their reception, housing and welfare whilst they were away from home. The Shipwrights agreed to provide every assistance to the operation of the scheme even though it would entail a considerable extra burden on their officials.

Writing in the annual report for 1940, John Willcocks commented on 'the wholehearted manner in which the Government, Employers and Trade Unions have co-operated to ensure the greatest output being achieved.' The evidence provided by the way labour supply problems were tackled certainly justified that comment. A great deal of the credit must go to Ernest Bevin for his forceful but sympathetic leadership. In particular, he pleased the unions by allowing them to carry out his schemes rather than imposing them from above. In other words, he relied on a voluntary spirit rather than on compulsion. On the other hand, the unions deserve the highest commendation for the ready way that they accepted new ideas and new schemes. Particularly, this was the case with the Shipwrights' Association. In September 1939, the very first month of the war, the Executive Committee drew up a voluntary scheme for the dilution of labour. It was put into immediate effect and loyally accepted by the members. John Willcocks commented: 'In this process we can feel proud of the part we have played to ensure the fullest use of the available labour of our crafts in the interests of the nation. We feel that maximum production has not yet been reached although we have managed to meet the current demands.'[3]

Of course there were occasional difficulties. In May 1940 G. A. Burke, the North-East of England and Bristol Channel Executive member, reported that in Barrow-in-Furness the question of dilution 'had been one of great difficulty owing to the stubborn action of a certain section of our Barrow members.' In Aberdeen members even placed an embargo upon overtime working in pursuance of a pay claim. The Executive Committee felt very strongly about this action and were even prepared to expel the men involved for what they called 'a national calamity'. Indeed the Committee were so incensed they sent a telegram to the Minister appealing for his help under the Emergency Powers Act. The men soon dropped their embargo. The incident did have an odd sequel however, for it led to some friction between the union and Bevin. For two months later, on 13th February 1941 at a meeting with representatives of the Shipbuilding Employers' Federation, Bevin criticized the Shipwrights' Association for not having control over its members and quoted the Aberdeen case as an example.

The Executive Committee were annoyed at these aspersions by the Minister. They were also annoyed at the employers whom, they felt, had misled the Minister by not presenting him with all the facts.

At a meeting with the employers two days later in Carlisle, John Willcocks went out of his way to rebut the criticism and to show that his union had sufficient control over its members. He pointed out they had been able to achieve unlimited dilution on a voluntary basis since the beginning of the war. The employers agreed that they had not set out the full position and agreed to write to the Minister accordingly. John

Willcocks also wrote on behalf of his Executive.

Bevin immediately agreed to have his remarks expunged from the record and he apologized for any misunderstanding. As often happens, the apology was more than gratefully received and Bevin's stock rose even higher.

Incidents such as those at Aberdeen and Barrow were rare. By and large there was an overwhelming desire to co-operate.

Despite this high degree of co-operation, manpower remained a critical problem. In March 1941 Bevin felt compelled to introduce the Essential Work Order. Under this regulation, work in certain factories could be designated as essential. Skilled workers had to register and could be directed into employment which fell within this category. It represented a serious reduction in personal freedom and Bevin sought to modify its impact by ruling that all undertakings classified as 'essential' should satisfy basic standards of working conditions and wages. They were also to have adequate provision for the welfare of employees, including the right to permanent employment for the duration of the emergency regulation. In other words while an employee was forbidden to leave a classified establishment, an employer was forbidden to dismiss him, except for misconduct.

Again the details were to be left to district committees and even yard committees to work out.

In the preliminary discussions over these radical proposals within the Confederation, the Shipwrights opposed the principles of control, interchangeability and the creation of a Dilution Officer. But they supported the questions of registration, transfers, payments by results and the introduction of labour-saving machinery. They also argued in favour of compulsory trade union membership for those drafted into shipbuilding work and particularly into shipwrights' work. And they suggested that union contributions should be collected within the premises of the firms concerned.

John Willcocks put forward these views at a meeting of the Shipyard Group Council of the Confederation in York at the end of February. He found that he was in a minority on the central question of control of employment. The other members thought that although it was a drastic step, it was essential in the national interest. But they were opposed to complete interchangeability and to the creation of a Dilution Officer.

The meeting between the Confederation and the Employers on 24th February in Carlisle showed 'a wide difference of opinion', so wide in fact that two sets of opinions were presented to the Minister. It was left to him to decide on all the points raised. Bevin again showed his sympathetic touch by leaving the details to the local committees. For example, on interchangeability, he directed that where this was felt to be necessary the District Shipyard Controller should refer such questions to the Yard Committees. He also set up Local Appeal Boards to hear any disputed cases. But he made no reference to compulsory membership of a union. However, the unions found that the Order did allow them what amounted to the opportunity to impose compulsory membership. There was a test case on the Clyde. A man who had refused to pay his contributions had been dismissed for 'misconduct' under the Order. In the first instance, this would have meant that he lost three days' pay but if he persisted in non-payment, he would lose his accreditation under the Order and would have to seek work elsewhere. With regard to union dues, this was left to the unions and the employers to sort out between themselves. As Mr J. W. Stephenson, president of the Confederation, said at the annual meeting in May 1941: 'Definite lines are not always easy to lay down on various questions and we are satisfied that yard committees will, generally speaking, find their own lines of procedure. Discipline, absenteeism, non-union cases for Tribunal should all be the subject of discussion within the yard. The maintenance of harmony is of first importance: non-unionism must be put down in such an effort. Local committees should make it their business to closely watch the Yard Committees.'

These sacrifices made by the unions under the intense pressure of war were really very remarkable. They gave up, largely without question, many of their hard-won benefits. But, as Willcocks said, 'we have the satisfaction of knowing that what we are doing is appreciated by the Government and by all concerned.'[4] As in the First World War, the unions were given assurances that any practices abandoned during the emergency would be restored if they so wished at the end of the war. These assurances were embodied in the Restoration of Pre-War Practices Act of 1942.

But the unions went further still in their attempts to help the war effort. In October 1941 the Engineering Shop Stewards' National Council called a conference to discuss ways of improving output. It was agreed that there should be joint workshop production committees where men and managers could exchange ideas for boosting production. There was already a Central Production Advisory Committee but the Conference emphasized the need for something much more local and particular. This idea was taken up by the Confederation and in March 1942 an agreement was reached with the engineering employers to set up these committees. Later the system was absorbed into the shipbuilding industry where the existing yard committees undertook this extra function. The success of the committees varied from one factory to another but at their best they led to remarkable improvements in output. At the top, their efforts were given greater impetus by the creation of a Ministry of War Production first under Lord Beaverbrook and then under Oliver Lyttelton.

By the direction and allocation of labour and the widespread use of women, Britain was thus able to overcome the critical shortage of manpower. By the end of 1941 half of the labour force in the whole country was employed upon Government work of one sort or another. But because of Bevin's determination that the control of labour should not preclude the normal collective bargaining system over wages, there was little resentment. Indeed, the opposite. According to one historian: 'Workers wanted to be told what to do and welcomed their mobilization for war production.'[5]

The benefits of the production committees, the more flexible working arrangements and the physical exertions of the men themselves all played a part in securing a vast output of new ships and of repaired vessels. Despite the heavy losses at sea, the country's naval strength by 1942-43 was greater than it had been in 1939. Indeed so high was the output that the target figure set by the Admiralty at the beginning of 1942 was exceeded by tens of thousands of tons. The Rt. Hon. George Hall, Financial Secretary of the Admiralty, told the 1943 Conference of the Confederation: 'All this has been done with fewer shipyards than there were in 1918 and with many thousands fewer workmen so that it can truly be said that output in relation to labour and industrial capacity has been very fine indeed.'

But, despite the achievements, it was not enough. Still more was needed. The war had now reached a critical stage. Hitler was offsetting his losses on land by an intensification of the U-Boat war. An even greater burden was now thrown on to the Navy, who needed yet more ships. Vice Admiral Sir W. F. Wake-Walker, Controller of the Navy, emphasized the same point to the same Conference. The particular need, he urged, was for more escort vessels which alone could protect convoys in mid-ocean and which alone could defeat the U-boats. The Navy had therefore embarked on a programme of building frigates and corvettes in a larger number than ever before. These vessels were to a large extent pre-fabricated in engineering workshops and transported by rail to the yards where they were assembled. The Admiral appealed to the Conference delegates to use their influence to secure co-operation in the introduction of this new system of working. He also wanted to see a relaxation on the rules of interchangeability in order that ships could be built as quickly as possible.

While the delegates accepted the need for the new method of construction, they refused to accept the point about interchangeability. Mr J. W. Stephenson, chairman of the Shipyard Group Council, said that the Group Council had not been unmindful of the importance of interchangeability in war time but they reaffirmed the previous decision that this was to be left to individual unions. Mr Stephenson declared: 'The Executive Committee have laid down very firmly and strongly the policy that they will not interfere as between unions and the industry but they will seek to support on every occasion unions' policy.'

This note of truculence was not something exceptional. It was becoming more widespread. It is interesting to notice that from 1942 onwards the original attitude of total co-operation became somewhat modified. The number of working days lost in strikes for example rose from the low point in 1940 to 1.5m. in 1942 and 3.7m. in 1944, which was worse than in many peacetime years. Absenteeism rose. A stronger attitude was taken in wage negotiations.

At the 1943 Conference of the Confederation there were sharp attacks on the employers, for example over their refusal to consolidate war bonuses into standard rates of pay. One speaker said: 'There is nothing more disgusting than having to record that we have got war bonuses with us still that were contracted in the last war. This complicated system has been continued because the employers have got certain advantages out of it.' And they attacked the Government for paying lip-service to what would happen once the war was over. 'We see vested interests pegging out their claims at every turn.'

There was a good deal of agitation over the transfer schemes for although the original intention was that individuals should not lose by being moved from one area to another, in fact there were many cases of men finding themselves £1 or even £2 worse off through extra living costs. A new subsistence allowance of 50p a week was introduced but it did not provide sufficient recompense.

The Shipwrights' officials found themselves involved in an increasing number of disputes. In October 1942 over 300 members at Barrow went on strike for six days because of their dissatisfaction with the contract system. John Willcocks was called in by the Admiralty and after persuading the men to return to work, he was able to negotiate a new agreement which satisfied all sides.

There was a more serious dispute in the Tyne area involving all trades. For eight days the men came out on unofficial strike because of a change in the working hours. Although the various union officials tried to persuade them to stay at work, the men preferred to listen to their shop stewards who had urged them to come out. The strike was unofficial and was clearly condemned by the unions but nevertheless many man hours were lost. When the strike was over and the men went back to work, some of the branches tried to claim dispute pay. This was really rubbing salt in the wounds. The Executive Committee of the Shipwrights turned down the requests out of hand.

It is possible to overdo these signs of disgruntlement and certainly compared with peace-time they were no more than pinpricks. But there was a noticeable difference in collective attitudes by 1942-43. And perhaps this was not unnatural. The war had been going on for three years. There was no end in sight. The physical strain and the social privations were beginning to take their toll. The men were beginning to ask how long it was all going on. It could be expected that their pent-up feelings should be released in minor disputes and harsh words.

On the other hand, it was still possible to see signs of new initiatives in boosting production: new ideas for interchangeability among craftsmen were introduced all the time and there was a willingness by traditional time trades to consider piecework. The Association also agreed to the Minister of Labour's request to send a delegation to the United States to investigate the use of electric welding. The delegation consisted of three boilermakers, a plumber, an electrician and two shipwrights, Luke Mitchell, district delegate for Wear and Tees, and George Cook, district secretary in the Portsmouth area. And the Association supported an Admiralty scheme for the creation of local Tribunals to investigate disputes. They consisted of an employer and a trade unionist not directly involved under the chairmanship of the Conciliation Officer for the area.

These local Tribunals were able to operate quickly before there was too much interruption of production. So in these ways new efforts were added to those already in operation and the impetus was kept up for more ships and faster repairs.

But the pace and the pressure were certainly taking their toll in frayed nerves, stronger words and hasty actions.

This was especially true of the relationships between various unions. By the summer of 1943 the Shipwrights' Association was very concerned about the attitude of members of the Amalgamated Society of Woodworkers. They had been brought in under the dilution scheme to help shipwrights. But, according to John Willcocks, they 'were becoming rather arrogant in their attitude and appeared to be forgetting that they were only dilutees and, to make matters worse, some managers were aiding and abetting this attitude.' The result was that an increasing number of demarcation questions were being raised. The Executive Committee twice placed the matter before the Shipbuilding Employers' Federation at its Central Conference. The employers agreed that such disputes were undesirable but they still went on. Willcocks also raised the question at the annual consultative meeting between the Executive Committee and the district delegates. He asked them to watch this development very carefully and wherever possible to avoid definite decisions on demarcation, but to ensure that work continued.

T. H. Evans said he had had a great deal of trouble with the Woodworkers in the Bristol area. In Tyneside, some shipwrights were suffering because employers preferred to use dilutees rather than craftsmen even though there was no scarcity of shipwrights. In the London area, the problem was more with other unions. W. E. Edwards, the district delegate, reported that he had recently reached an agreement with the employers and five out of ten unions. This was a step forward and he hoped that he could reach a measure of understanding with other unions in the near future.

The major problem in demarcation arose, however, with the boilermakers over pre-fabrication and welding. The boilermakers were increasingly claiming that this was their work while the shipwrights felt it was their 'birthright'. Willcocks thought this was going to create 'very serious trouble in the near future.' At Haverton Hill in Teesside the boilermakers had actually terminated the existing Demarcation Agreement and had refused to meet the shipwrights' district delegate, Luke Mitchell, to discuss questions in dispute. He thought that a 'crisis was developing'. In the Vickers yard at Barrow, platers were doing this work but it had been clearly recorded as a war-time measure while the shipwrights were busy on contract work. At Hill's yard in Bristol, the boilermakers had tried to take a hard line but the Admiralty had intervened and the firm had clearly come down in favour of the shipwrights.

By November 1943, after a number of abortive meetings, the Executive Committees of the Shipwrights' Association and the Boilermakers' Society, were able to come together and reach an agreement. Under this, they recognized that it was impossible to specify who should do the work in every case. Practices varied from yard to yard and in some instances there were no past practices at all. 'In these circumstances, and having in mind particularly the national need and the necessity for continuous production, we recommend that earnest local efforts should be made to overcome the present difficulties and thus allow work to proceed. Past practices relating to erection of built sections as far as they exist should be a guiding principle during the deliberations.'

The agreement was signed by Syd Ombler, chairman, and John Willcocks, acting General Secretary, for the Shipwrights, and by Thomas McKinney, chairman, and Mark Hodgson, General Secretary, for the Boilermakers' Society. Neither the employers nor the Admiralty were altogether happy with it for they wanted to retain control of the allocation of work.

LOOKING FORWARD TO THE END

As the war continued and defeat became less and less likely, the unions turned their attention increasingly to the post-war situation. They were determined to avoid if at all possible the unemployment and disorganization that had occurred in the 1920's and 1930's. They continually pressed the Board of Trade for its policy on the post-war reconstruction of the industry. The Board of Trade replied that it had delegated the question to the Admiralty Central Consultative Committee. The latter said they had the question under consideration and when they had reached some conclusions they would call a conference. Unfortunately they never reached any conclusions. For two years they considered the question but they never called a conference. One cannot help feeling that either they had no ideas or that they wanted the industry to return to its old ways, a course which they knew would upset the unions and could therefore interrupt the war effort. Better to keep quiet and play the unions along. The unions also asked the employers for their policy for the planned future of the industry. They too were very vague. It was too early to say. It depended on the world's shipping position.

At the end of 1944 the Admiralty did call a conference with the Employers and the Confederation but only to seek the views of both sides of the industry on its future. The meeting was chaired by the Rt. Hon. A. V. Alexander, First Lord of the Admiralty, with Lord Leathers, Minister of War Transport, in attendance. Both the unions and the employers expressed surprise. They had been told eighteen months previously that the Admiralty and the Ministry of War Transport were giving the question detailed consideration. They had expected a memorandum by now, setting out the considered view of the Government. But now the Government was simply asking them for their views. If this memorandum was not ready then they must accuse the Admiralty and the Ministry of inactivity. Stung by this criticism, Lord Leathers replied that of course he had had discussions with the employers and 'while no definite scheme had yet accrued he was of the opinion that the industry would be reasonably busy in the immediate post-war years....' But he did agree that unless a plan was devised, then, once the rush was over, there would unquestionably be a decline in orders and a reduction in employment. The members present could have been excused for saying that that was a masterly statement of the obvious. However, some weeks later the First Lord announced that he was setting up a Shipbuilding Committee to advise on all matters relating to priorities of building work. Sir Mark Hodgson, now knighted in the 1945 New Year's Honours List, and Mr Stephenson sat as trade union representatives on the committee. They found its work 'not only interesting but also extremely important.' Unfortunately much of it was confidential so that they were unable to report to the Confederation or to their individual unions on the progress that was being made 'in achieving a proper and well-planned shipping and shipbuilding and shiprepairing industry for this country.'

John Willcocks put forward his own solution at the 1944 annual conference of the Confederation held in Newcastle. He moved a resolution, 'That we consider the time is opportune for the introduction of a shorter working week of 40 hours, without reduction of wages, as an essential contribution to post-war reconstruction, together with an extension of holidays with pay to 12 days, together with payment of all statutory holidays.'

In moving the resolution, he argued that this 'will be one of the principal solutions of the problem to prevent mass unemployment in the post-war years.' With the introduction of labour-saving machinery greater output could be achieved for less physical effort. There was need therefore for a better distribution of leisure without impairing living standards.

As for longer holidays, he thought this was long overdue. He thought it was something 'not only desirable but necessary' which would be reflected in better standards of health and greater efficiency at work.

The resolution was accepted unanimously and was to remain the cornerstone of the Confederation's policy but it was to be some years before it was implemented.

Meanwhile the Shipwrights' Association was facing increasing pressure from the members to put its own house in order. For the war had meant that many officials were acting only in a temporary and certainly in an unconfirmed capacity. Elections had been suspended for the duration of the war. Officials had been nominated by the Executive Committee. The rank and file were growing restive and there was an increasingly powerful shop stewards' movement, backed by the direct power of the members. At a meeting of the Executive on 4th December 1944, James Spiers, the member for Scotland, said that the persistent requests from the branches could not be ignored. The drillers' delegate, Arthur Williams, agreed. At every meeting he attended, the members were demanding their constitutional rights to elect their own officers. The Executive had managed to put this off but he did not think they could do so much longer.

The Executive Committee agreed that there should be elections in 1945 but they did not move very quickly in arranging them. In fact, it was to be October before the elections were actually held. Of course, there were a number of questions to be considered first but even so, progress was not exactly rapid. The two most important questions were the position of the General Secretary and the rearrangement of boundaries on the South Coast to allow a separate delegate for the London and Kent area. On the former, Westwood would be retiring at the end of 1945 when he reached the age of 65. John Willcocks, who had been acting General Secretary during the war, was 63. He would therefore retire in 1947. The Committee decided to appoint Willcocks to the General Secretary's position without an election but to call for nominations for Assistant General Secretary. The members approved this action when it was put to them. They also agreed to new boundaries to provide for a separate delegate for the London area and a rearrangement in Scotland.

There were seven positions up for election: Assistant General Secretary, Executive Committee members for Scotland, and Ireland, South Coast and Dockyards and North-West and Bristol Channel; and district delegates for Tyne and Blyth, North-West, and Scotland and Ireland (drillers).

More than 60 nominations were received for these positions, a clear indication of the unrest felt by members about the lack of elections. Of these, half, were turned down by the Investigation Committee because they did not possess the necessary qualifications on the score of length or scale of membership but it was still a substantive election. By the time the Investigation Committee had carried out its work and the members had agreed on a change in the areas to be covered by district delegates on the South Coast and in Scotland, it was October. The elections that month produced James Spiers as the Executive Committee member for Scotland and Ireland, Fred King as the Executive Committee member for South Coast and Dockyard, Joseph Shaw as the Executive Committee member for North-West and Bristol Channel, and John Hall as the district delegate for Tyne and Blyth. Voting for the district delegates for the North-West and Scotland and Ireland (drillers) did not produce an overall majority for any candidate. The two with the highest votes were subject to a second election. The same was true of the position of Assistant General Secretary. Sydney Ombler and John McMillan went to a second vote. Ombler finally won by the very small margin of 95 votes: 2,600 for McMillan, 2,695 for Ombler. John Taylor was elected district delegate for the North-West and Ronald McDonald as the drillers' delegate for Scotland and Ireland.

THE WAR AND THE ASSOCIATION

Despite the heavy burden of the war, the Association remained healthy. It lost members to war service but gained others through the dilutee scheme. It also had fewer officials and each of them had to do more than their predecessors. There were more regulations to carry out, more committees to sit on. But they coped. And the Association came through the war stronger than it had been at the start.

Membership went up from 20,000 in 1938 to 29,250 in 1944. It slipped back to 28,500 in 1945 with the retirement of some members and the return of dilutees to their former jobs. But it was still substantially higher than it had been and represented over 90 per cent of all shipwrights and apprentices.

Largely as a result of the increase, income rose from £42,000 in 1938 to £71,000 in 1944, a very creditable jump. Expenditure also rose but not so steeply in either actual or percentage terms. In 1938 it was £31,000. By 1944 it was £47,000. Each year there was a reasonable surplus, generally amounting to 50 per cent of expenditure. There was thus considerable leeway in the operation of the Association's affairs. The result was that by 1944 there was a balance in the reserves of £183,000 and by the end of 1945 this had risen to just over £200,000 or £7 a member. This was well in excess of the constitutional requirement of £3 a member.

The major expenditure was on sickness and accident benefits. It averaged £12,000 a year throughout the war. This was considerably less than during those years at the beginning of the century or in the late 1920's when the membership was comparable in size. Superannuation averaged £3,000 until it dropped to about £2,500 in the last two years of the war. By contrast, expenditure on salaries, printing, hall rents and other administrative overheads averaged £25,000 and thereby accounted for 60 per cent of all expenditure whereas during the Association's history it had generally accounted for about 35 per cent of all expenditure. The main reason for the change was the rapidly rising costs of running the head office, district and branch offices, particularly with the salaries of officials being linked to wage-rates. As the latter went up so did the salaries of officials. Considering the rapid rise in wages and therefore salaries, it was no surprise that expenditure under this heading should have jumped up by a quarter and should assume a larger proportion of the whole with income fixed at the same level of contributions as before. Let us take one example which sets the pattern for the rest. In 1940 the Acting General Secretary received a salary of £512 and his fares and other expenses came to £227, making a total of £739. In 1945 he received a salary of £702 and his fares and other expenses came to £302, making a total of £1,004.

WAGES AND WORKING CONDITIONS

Throughout the war the unions continually pressed for wage increases. This was the only recompense they could hope for to offset the greater burdens. It was also just about the only area of industrial relations outside Government control. The unions were naturally in a strong position for with full—indeed overfull—demand, they could press for substantial increases and, where the employers refused, they could automatically refer the dispute to a National Arbitration Tribunal which equally automatically provided them with a large proportion of their claim.

Yet despite this power, it was not abused. One observer has commented that by the spring of 1944 the level of wage rates had not risen by more than 11 per cent above the cost of living.[6] 'It is true that wage rates do not give a clear indication of the improvement in average earnings: a large proportion of the money in the workers' pay packets was overtime and piece-work payment. But if higher total wages were offset by higher production the Government had no reason to cavil', he wrote. Another historian commented that in 1944 the cost of living was 50 per cent higher than in 1938 while average weekly earnings (the full take-home pay) was 81 per cent higher.[7] Most of the population was thus better off.

The Shipwrights shared in this general pattern. Working through the Confederation, they saw their basic wages rise steadily but never by spectacular amounts. There was usually only one rise per year and in some years no rise at all, for example in 1943. The usual increase was between 20p and 30p a week for a basic 47-hour week. This brought the total in most areas to £4.80 for old or repair work in April 1944 compared to £3.40 in 1938, an increase of about 30 per cent. In May 1945 the rates went up to £4.90 for new work and £5 for old or repair work. But by working an average of 10-12 hours overtime a week, and this was by no means uncommon, they could augment those basic earnings by another £2 or more. By 1944 the average take-home pay came to about £6.50, a rise of over 90 per cent compared with 1938 when there was no overtime available and the basic rate was the wage packet.

Apprentices also benefited. In 1941 they received war bonuses to add to their basic rates, depending on their age. A first year apprentice, for example, received a basic rate of 70p, plus a bonus of 25p making a total of 95p. A fifth-year apprentice received a basic rate of £1.65, a bonus of 70p, making a total of £2.35. It was also agreed in 1941 that the wages of boys and youths should fluctuate in accordance with the wages of adult workers on time rates. For boys aged 15 and 16, they would receive just under 1p for each 5p fluctuation in adult rates, while boys of 20 would receive 2½p increase for each 5p of adult workers.

The wages paid to shipwrights for a standard 47-hour week were composed of two parts, the basic rate and a bonus which was added to it. As we have seen nearly all the increases that shipwrights received were to the bonus element while the basic rate remained the same. This meant that in most cases the men were receiving more in bonuses than they were in the basic rates. Overtime payments were separate. The unions continually pressed for consolidation of the bonuses into the basic rates but the employers prevaricated. Some bonuses agreed in the First World War had still not been consolidated. Sydney Ombler of the Shipwrights always took a particular interest in this question and at meeting after meeting of the Confederation he pressed for progress. There was usually little to report. First the employers raised the difficulty of men working in oil ships; when the unions answered that one, they said that the position of pieceworkers needed examination. It was less easy to consolidate their wages than it was for time workers. By 1946 no consolidation had taken place.

The industry turned out an extraordinary amount of shipping during the war, despite the initial shortage of steel and the almost constant shortage of labour. In the six years of war the men and women in the industry produced six and a quarter million tons of merchant shipping. In addition there was a similar amount of naval work and a large range of conversions and repairs.

The Clyde was a major centre. In the six years from 2nd September 1939 to 15th August 1945 it built, repaired and converted a total of 25,731 naval and merchant vessels. This total would have been even higher if peak production had been achieved before 1944 but the industry took time to get over the depression of the 1930's and the steel and labour shortages. This can be seen from the fact that in 1944 the area built 504 vessels compared with 79 in the first year of the war. In the country as a whole output rose from 600,000 tons in 1939 to 1.2m. tons in 1942 then tapered off slightly.

This was in contrast to the world position. In 1940 world output was 1.7m. tons and Britain was responsible for 48 per cent of it. By 1943 world output was 13.8m. and Britain produced only 8 per cent. The main difference was the impact of American shipbuilding. Under the leadership of Henry Kaiser, it went in for mass shipbuilding in new yards using new machinery such as welding equipment. Equally it did not suffer from the interruptions to production that Britain faced through air raids or black-outs. As a result enormous quantities of ships poured out of American yards.

British shipbuilding, on the other hand, was concentrated in its traditional centres. It was not easy to expand the yards, nor to protect them from air-raids. It relied still on riveting. And although it did produce more standard ships than before, such as the 3 Twelves cargo liner, it still had a degree of specialization unknown in American yards. Nevertheless despite these inherent difficulties, productivity in Britain, i.e. output per manshift, was as good as in the U.S.A.

The 54,000 shipyard workers in the North-East produced 500 merchant ships of 3.5m. tons. The output of the river Wear at almost 2m. tons was greater than that of any other centre of comparable size. Swan Hunter and Wigham Richardson built eighty-three warships of all kinds at their Tyne and Clyde yards and seventy-five merchant ships.

The Shipbuilder magazine commented: 'No one will wish to minimize the superlative contributions of our Allies to the victory which has crowned our united exertions and sacrifices; but our admiration and gratitude for their magnificent achievements need not blind us to the magnitude of our own immense efforts, nor to the fact that, at the most critical period, we saved ourselves, and them, from a tyranny unsurpassed in its terror and violence in human history.'[8]

CHAPTER TWENTY-FIVE

The immediate post-war years were relatively good for shipbuilding and for its workers. Demand remained high and unemployment was almost non-existent. There were few disputes and such as there were lasted for only a short time and were largely unofficial. Wages continued to rise in line with the cost of living. Unfortunately, the industry failed to take the opportunity presented by these conditions to modernize itself, to invest in new machinery, to reconstruct the yards and generally to prepare for the competition which foreign countries had shown they could provide.

In the country as a whole, these were good years for labour. Their party unexpectedly won the 1945 General Election and by a large majority. Tried and tested through those early, rather unhappy years in power, through the cataclysmic economic depression and now through the rigours of war, it was ready to provide firm, radical government. It faced grave economic problems—the reconstruction of a peace-time economy, the balance of payments and incipient inflation—but it still managed to be true to itself in carrying out a full-blooded programme of nationalization. In the period, the mines, the railways, gas and electricity, the Bank of England and the iron and steel industry were all taken into public ownership. In addition, the National Health Service was set up to provide free medical care for all. This massive programme carried out in six years under adverse economic conditions represented one of the finest achievements of any government. It formed a revolution in English life carried out under the mantle of Parliamentary democracy.

POST WAR BRITAIN

The 1945 Election, it was thought, would produce an overwhelming victory for the Tories in gratitude for the war-time leadership of Winston Churchill. Instead, there was a solid Labour victory based on the proposition that the conditions of the 1930's must not be allowed to return. As John Willcocks had put it during the war: 'The country that is worth fighting for must be worth living in.' Or as he now put it: 'Democracy has triumphed and for the first time a Labour Government equipped with power for action has been returned by the people to govern the destinies of the nation.'

There were 393 Labour M.P.'s of whom 120 were sponsored by the unions. Six of these union-sponsored M.P.'s were given posts in Attlee's Cabinet of 20. Ernest Bevin, the most powerful of them all, was made Foreign Secretary.

One of the first measures of the new Government was to repeal the Trade Disputes Act of 1927, which had been passed by Stanley Baldwin in the wake of the General Strike. The Act had made illegal sympathy strikes or strikes 'designed or calculated to coerce the government.' This might have been justified in the aftermath of the General Strike and the unions might almost have accepted it. But the Act had contained other clauses which they thoroughly disliked. Civil servants, for example, were forbidden to join a union affiliated to the T.U.C. while members of unions who wished to pay the political levy had to 'contract in', i.e. make a definite decision to do so, rather than 'contract out'.

The new Labour Government repealed this Act within weeks of coming to power. The effect was that certain unions, like the Civil Service Clerical Association, immediately joined the T.U.C. The other main effect was that the Labour Party's trade union membership rose by over a half. As one historian put it: 'The Labour Party thus received a considerable accretion to its funds from the members of unions with political funds who had not previously taken steps to contract in and who now with equal passivity failed to contract out.'[1] The contributions from the shipwrights rose from an average of £13-£16 to £300 a year. Only 37 branches had returned contracting-in forms.

For while the contributions jumped substantially they should have been much higher. By 1948 for example, when the Political Fund income rose to £345, only 1,597 members had claimed exemption. But the proceeds resulted from payments by only 6,902. So, 21, 226 members who should have paid in fact failed to do so. The income for the political account should have been £1,137. The annual report commented: 'Are we to believe that less than one third of our members are willing to give financial support to the Labour Party to the extent of one farthing per week? Surely that cannot be the truth.... We urge our members to work for the Party, vote for the Party and support the Party by paying the contribution of one shilling per annum as required by our Political Fund Rules.'

The transition from war to peace involved a massive transfer of men and women from the forces or war industries back to civilian employment. There were 4½ million in the services and as many in war-time occupations, causing a massive problem of redeployment. Yet by and large it was carried through quickly and smoothly and without any transitional unemployment. The success can be attributed partly to the Government's careful planning but, more particularly, to the high level of potential demand throughout the economy.

But while the transition in employment worked smoothly, the country as a whole was facing serious difficulties. The end of the war saw Britain with a substantial balance of payments problem and it was clear that there would have to be a massive export drive, combined with minimal consumption at home, to produce a favourable balance. In the circumstances, George Isaacs, of the Operative Printers and Assistants, who had taken over Ernest Bevin's former position as Minister of Labour, persuaded the General Council of the T.U.C. to agree that Order 1305, which made strikes illegal, should remain in force while the Restoration of Pre-War Practices Act of 1942 should be deferred in its implementation. It became law on 1st January 1949 while Order 1305 was not repealed until 1950.

In 1947 the situation deteriorated further under the harshness of a hard winter, a fuel crisis and a foreign exchange panic which forced the Government to abandon the convertibility of sterling. Again the Government sought the co-operation of the General Council. It wanted the re-introduction of a Control of Engagement Order and the re-establishment of joint production committees in the factories. The General Council agreed. It also agreed to a policy of wage restraint which was not easy at a time of full employment. This policy allowed wages to rise in line with prices but not ahead of them. The co-operation of the unions was imperative for the pressure of demand 'would have made any Government policy of holding down prices impossible had it not been for the deliberate restraint practised by the unions.'[2] Between 1946 and 1950 average weekly earnings went up virtually in line with the cost of living or were only fractionally ahead.

By early 1948 the Government felt impelled to produce a White Paper on prices, profits and wages even before consulting the unions. But it took good care to woo them towards the new restraint. The Chancellor of the Exchequer, Sir Stafford Cripps, attended the 1948 annual conference of the Confederation and spoke at length on the White Paper. He said: 'We want our wages and salaries to buy more and not less of the things we want. That means bringing down and keeping down prices. But we can't have rising wages and falling prices. That's just impossible unless we have increased efficiency to more than counteract the disparity between the two.'

The Government did not want to end free collective bargaining on wages. 'So we haven't put a ceiling on wages or frozen them. What we have done is to ask the negotiators to observe the fact that this country is sunk if at this moment in our history we indulge in a general rise of wages.'

To prove their desire to achieve an equal sacrifice and a much greater equality of incomes, the Government raised the top rate of income tax and surtax to 19s 6d in the £. That meant there were only 70 people in the whole country with more than £6,000 they could spend out of income. Equally severe taxation was applied to company profits.

The unions were willing to accept these restraints and to co-operate with the Government partly because of their sense of loyalty to the country, partly because of the Government's overt political sympathy with them but mainly because of these deliberate attempts to secure a sense of equal sacrifice through these high taxes on the rich. John Willcocks, president of the Confederation as well as General Secretary of the Shipwrights foreshadowed the union's attitude when he said at the 1946 annual conference of the Confederation: 'After ten months of power the Labour Government is facing up to and resolving the problems affecting the country. It is tackling them in a manner more equitable to all the people in this country than was ever done under Tory rule. These steps towards a more equitable life are what we have stood for in these unions as long as they have been in existence. The future belongs to the people.'

THE FUTURE OF SHIPBUILDING

As we have seen in the previous chapter union leaders in shipbuilding and engineering were anxious to ensure that the industry which had contributed so much to the war effort should be allowed to play an equal part in peace-time. Willcocks said at the 1946 conference of the Confederation: 'We want to emphasize this point: that in the industries for which we cater, peace-time needs are of equal importance to those of war. The saving of the national economy has still to be done. The men who can do it must have an adequate wage, proper hours and better conditions and our industries must become more efficient, more up to date and modern in every aspect.... If the plans of the Government for export trade, which are absolutely vital to success, are to be achieved, the first essential is that Great Britain shall have a powerful mercantile marine backed by a strong shipbuilding industry with which no other country can compare.'

Willcocks saw three main objectives in front of the Confederation: normal negotiations with employers over such issues as wages and working conditions; strengthening individual unions and relations between them; and helping to plan the future of the industry. On the first question, the Confederation wanted to see a simpler wage structure and wage rates that would rise with the cost of living or with improvements in productivity. On relations with other unions, the Foundry Workers' Union and the Amalgamated Engineering Union which had previously stayed aloof from the Confederation were now willing to join, so that a co-ordinated, all embracing front could be presented to employers. The Confederation now covered 2½m. workers and, according to Willcocks, was the 'greatest industrial trade union movement in the country if not in the world.'

As for planning the future, the Confederation aimed for a properly-planned industry, with manpower budgets set out, with proper distribution of plants, with greater thought on the location of industry and with the greater involvement of the unions and workers. The Government's answer was to set up a Shipbuilding Advisory Committee and an Engineering Advisory Council with representatives of unions and management. Union leaders were also invited to sit on many other Government Committees.

The Shipbuilding Advisory Committee, set up early in 1946, was to advise the Government on all questions concerning the efficiency or stability of the industry. It consisted of 18 members, of whom four represented management and four represented trade unions. The latter were Sir Mark Hodgson, General Secretary of the Boilermakers' Society, J. W. Stephenson, of the Plumbers, Glaziers and Domestic Engineers' Union, H. N. Harrison, of the General and Municipal Workers' Union, and Gavin Martin, General Secretary of the Confederation.

The Advisory Committee had to face the problems of greater international competition, particularly from the United States which had built up a large mercantile marine during the war and wanted to expand it further. By contrast, this country which owned 17.4m. tons of shipping in 1938-9 was down to 13.9m. tons in 1946.

In these circumstances, the Government called for greater output. It also announced that it was to purchase 139 ships of 1,125,000 gross tons from the United States for resale to British shipping interests. In addition, owners would be offered 250,000 tons of German prize ships. The unions were highly alarmed by this announcement for it followed the policy adopted after the 1914-18 war which they thought had led to high levels of unemployment within a couple of years. The Confederation took the view that these ships should not be sold to shipping companies but should be chartered to them until they 'ordered and secured new and up to date tonnage built in the shipbuilding industry and thereafter all chartered vessels to be withdrawn by the Government and to be placed in a reserve pool and to be well maintained for any emergency which this country may meet in peace or war.'

There were 190,000 employed in the industry, of whom 85,000 were involved in new construction. The unions feared that their jobs could be at risk in two years' time when the current construction for orders for three million tons were completed. On the other hand, 105,000 were employed on repairs and reconversion of naval and merchant vessels. This figure compared with 25,000-30,000 pre-war. When the reconversion work was completed by 1948-49, about 70,000 of these people could be made redundant unless there was careful planning.

The Government gave consideration to the point made by the unions but in July 1947 the Minister of Transport replied that he felt the fears were groundless. The Government owned a good deal of tonnage already which was on charter to British owners while it also had a good deal of Canadian-owned tonnage on charter. 'If in a few years' time a surplus of dry cargo tonnage under the British flag were to emerge, the Government would still not be without means of influencing the situation.... The disposal of these ships thereafter will be considered in the light of our shipping prospects at that time.... Thus on the present view of the position it can reasonably be expected that the fears of the shipbuilding unions will not be realized.'[3] The unions were not convinced and combined to express disapproval when the Government went ahead with its plan to buy 900,000 gross tons of American shipping and re-sell it to British owners. The Government pointed out that this still left a gap of over two million tons of dry cargo tonnage alone to return to 1939 levels. But in addition Britain was behind in replacing old ships. Almost 32 per cent of dry cargo tonnage was over 20 years old as against 22 per cent in 1939. In tankers a third of the fleet was already over 16 years old, about the normal life of a tanker, and some was over 25 years old. And with the world increase in the transport of oil, the country had to cater for a great expansion in the demand for tankers.

With all these factors in mind the Government calculated that there would be an annual requirement of about 900,000 gross tons for the next ten years just to restore and maintain the 1939 fleet. But this did not take into account the rising demand for oil tankers and other shipping. 'Whether orders are placed on the scale indicated depends of course upon the competitive efficiency of the shipbuilding industry and the success of the shipping industry in re-establishing its interests,' the letter from the Minister concluded.

In fact, the industry soon faced a more immediate problem than the purchase of American ships, namely a critical shortage of raw material and particularly of steel supplies. The fuel crisis and the shortage of raw materials led to a situation of allocations by the Government. Because of the severe short-fall, shipbuilding, like many other industries, was not provided with all it required. After strong representations by the Advisory Committee which foresaw rising unemployment, the Government increased the allocation of steel for the third quarter of 1947 to 190,000 which was about 47,000 tons more than in the previous quarter. This shortage prevented the industry from increasing its output above 1.1m. tons but with similar problems world-wide this was still enough to account for over 50 per cent of world production. In very difficult circumstances, the industry had made a reasonable return to peace-time activity.

CONDITIONS IN THE INDUSTRY

The ending of the war, when enormous exertions had been called for from the workers, and the full employment situation naturally prompted the unions to press for certain improvements in wages and working conditions, the first claim was for higher wages. In April 1946 the employers agreed to a war bonus of 6s (30p) a week as from 9th April. The unions then went for better holidays demanding a 12-day summer holiday with pay plus payment for six other statutory holidays per year. The employers agreed on the last point but did not increase the annual holidays.

The most serious claim, presented at a conference with the Employers' Federation in October 1945, was for a five-day working week of 40 hours without loss of earnings. The unions, represented by the Confederation, argued that the reduction from the current 47 hours would help to improve the standard of living of the workers and the efficiency of the industry. More work would be done in less time. Or as the Confederation put it: 'Our members in shipbuilding and shiprepairing establishments would be prepared to use their initiative to help to develop efficiency if, and only if, they were convinced that their wages, conditions and hours of work were improved as a result.'

The employers gave their answer in January 1946. They said that in their view the end of a great world war was one of the 'strangest times' to put forward a claim for increased leisure, 'when the portents so clearly proved that even the maintenance of existing standards was going to be a colossal struggle.' The employers added that the increase in costs as far as time-workers were concerned was likely to be 20 per cent. In the circumstances they could not agree to a reduction.

The employers had an unusual ally in the person of the Rt. Hon. George Isaacs, the former trade union leader and now Minister of Labour. Speaking to the 1946 annual conference of the Confederation, he said he appreciated the desire for a shorter working week. But 'present circumstances demand that this desire must be considered by all concerned in the light of the paramount need to speed up and increase production.' Perhaps there could be a reduction of the working week in progressive stages.

The Confederation was not prepared to give up its case however, although some members felt that Isaac's suggestion of a phased reduction might prove more acceptable to the employers. The unions continued to press their views on the employers and when a failure to agree was recorded they asked the Minister to set up a Court of Enquiry rather than referring the matter to a National Arbitration Tribunal. The Court, presided over by Sir John Forster, heard representations from both sides and then toured various shipyards to see conditions for themselves. Their recommendation was that a five-day week of 44 hours should be introduced except for the months of November, December, January and February when the 44-hours would need to be spread over five and a half days because of the darkness. The recommendation was accepted by the Minister, the employers and the unions. The pieceworking unions, such as the Boilermakers, had serious reservations, however. For while the time-working trades, such as shipwrights, would receive 47 hours' pay for a 44-hour week, the pieceworkers would lose three hours of earning power. It was agreed that individual unions who were involved should be permitted to pursue these questions directly with the Employers' Federation. The employers naturally pointed out that the reduction in hours had been agreed on the basis that production would not suffer. This was the basis of the unions' case—were they now going back on that? The average time worked by a pieceworker was 42 hours per week. He should therefore be able to maintain his output and thereby his earning power. In short, he should not be affected by the reduction in hours for time-workers.

UNOFFICIAL SHOP STEWARDS MOVEMENT

The extra burdens of wartime when there were not quite as many officials as before and the lack of elections which had led to a reduction in the personal authority of officials produced the ideal climate for the growth of a popular, grass-roots, anti-establishment movement led by local leaders, namely shop stewards. By 1945 this movement began to cause serious concern for it was undermining the work and the authority of the union itself and its officials.

At the annual Consultative Meeting between the Executive Committee and the District Delegates held in June 1945 there was a lengthy discussion on this subject. John Willcocks reported that the movement was particularly strong on the Clyde. Shop Stewards there had taken 'a very active part' in a recent dispute on the river and had created trouble for the Association. J. McMillan, one of the district delegates, endorsed these views and said that the position would become worse still unless precautions were taken. Arthur Williams, chairman of the Executive Committee, outlined the Association's view that the shop stewards movement could play a positive role in the development of the union as long as it was brought within the ambit of the union. Shop stewards' meetings should be held under the guidance and authority of district officials. In other words, this movement should be encouraged to put its energies into the positive development of the union rather than creating a kind of fifth column within the union. Williams and another member of the Executive travelled to Scotland to put forward this view at a meeting of shop stewards. If this positive approach did not work, the Executive Committee could see the need for tougher action to discredit the shop stewards. In fact, the positive approach turned out to be the right one.

It was an approach followed by the Confederation of Shipbuilding and Engineering Unions. In February 1947 the quarterly meeting of the Executive Council of the Confederation drew up a constitution which integrated shop stewards into the general framework of the unions. Shop stewards were to be elected by their own unions but would come together to act as a Joint Shop Stewards Works Committee over matters of common interest. The chairman and secretary of a joint committee would be 'Confederation shop stewards and shall act on behalf of and be responsible to the Confederation District Committee in their area.' The District Committee would convene regular meetings of the Works Committees in their area at which reports would be received and Confederation policy outlined. In this way the power of this new movement was harnessed effectively to the work of the unions and the Confederation rather than acting as a counter-force.

UNOFFICIAL DISPUTES

While the post-war period was a relatively quiet one in industrial relations, there was a particular problem with unofficial disputes. The increased power of the shop stewards caused considerable concern to union officials. In 1946 there was a spate of unofficial strikes in shipbuilding, often involving shipwrights. The men were encouraged to strike without the backing of the union and then to turn a deaf ear to the district delegates who tried to resolve the difficulties. The Executive Committee felt that such action undermined their authority as well as that of the officials. They worked hard at preventing these disputes and they resolutely refused to pay dispute benefit. They hoped that this financial penalty would check the recalcitrant members. But the real solution did not arrive until the shop stewards movement was integrated into the union structure.

Meanwhile, there were equal problems over demarcation disputes. These clashes, although localized, were highly annoying to the men involved, to the officials who had to try to resolve them and to the employers who more or less stood to one side as innocent but injured bystanders. The essence of the problem lay in the introduction of new machinery, such as welding apparatus, and the difficulty of fitting these new processes into union structures which remained as entrenched as ever. The eye welding process was a particular case in point with both shipwrights and boilermakers claiming it as their responsibility. Both could see that it was going to have an important effect on the nature of shipbuilding and that if they failed to secure it as their own responsibility, their members could be vitally affected in the future.

A POSSIBLE AMALGAMATION

It was this sort of example which led the boilermakers to propose to the shipwrights that they should follow the T.U.C.'s general directive to unions to find ways of amalgamating. On 18th April 1947 the Executive Committee of the Shipconstructors' and Shipwrights' Association met the Executive Council of the United Society of Boilermakers, Iron and Steel Shipbuilders to discuss the question. The Boilermakers made their position very clear. They wanted a complete amalgamation of the two unions including a pooling of all resources. The two executive committees should decide in principle and then take the view of members. All details should be worked out after a successful vote in favour rather than before. In suggesting this method of procedure, the boilermakers no doubt had in mind the ill-fated discussions which had taken place at the turn of the century. The initial high hopes of amalgamation then had foundered on the rocks of detail.

The shipwrights were much more cautious. They were not ready to commit themselves to such a course of action immediately. They wanted time to think about it. When they met separately on 2nd May they had a long discussion which ended with two settled views: that the principle of amalgamation was a good one but that the practical arrangements 'bristled with difficulties'; and that they should take no further action until they had discussed the whole question with the district delegates at the annual consultative meeting.

This was held on Thursday, 5th July. There were four members of the Executive Committee present, including the chairman James Spiers, ten district delegates and John Willcocks and Syd Ombler, the Assistant General Secretary.

Willcocks gave a long review of the current position. He had no axe to grind, he said, and could speak without bias for he was on the point of retirement and had nothing personally to gain one way or the other.

Shipbuilding was changing. New methods of construction were coming in. Some of these changes were quite radical, such as the use of welding techniques and the development of pre-fabrication. The craftsmen—and none had a greater pride than the shipwrights—needed to protect their interests in this new situation and this could be done only by greater unity with other unions. This unity among craft unions was even more necessary following the decision by the Amalgamated Engineering Union to join the Confederation and their appeal for a single union for the whole of the engineering industry. By amalgamating with the boilermakers, the shipwrights could ensure that the craft unions rather than the labouring unions remained dominant in shipbuilding.

The effect of amalgamation would be to increase inter-changeability between jobs and to reduce demarcation disputes when new techniques were introduced. The development of prefabrication techniques had already brought the loftsman, the plater and the shipwright closer together but their membership of different unions was causing friction. This could be overcome only by amalgamation.

On the other hand, there were problems. There would need to be a vote of all members. At least half of them must take part in the voting and there would need to be a 20 per cent majority. This in itself would be no small task for the officials to organize. Willcocks also pointed out that the constitutions of the two unions were different on many points. For example, he was a strong believer in national elections for all official positions but the boilermakers voted on a regional basis. There was the question of the residence of the Executive Committee members. The Boilermakers' representatives all resided in Newcastle. The Shipwrights' officials resided in their own areas carrying out their executive duties there and only coming to Newcastle for meetings. As to finance, there was no problem. Both unions were strong. The Shipwrights' Association had reserves which equalled £7 13s 4d (£7.66) a member while the Boilermakers' Society had reserves of £10 a member.

The delegates and Committee members then expressed their own views in turn. The principle was considered sound but they were nearly all concerned about safeguards for their own positions and those of members. The Shipwrights' Association had only 27,000 members and they feared they would be swallowed up by the much bigger Boilermakers' Society with three times as many members. It was agreed that the Executive Committee should have another meeting with the Boilermakers' Executive Council to express these fears. That meeting was held on 20th August 1947. From that moment onwards 'we have heard nothing more from the Boilermakers.' The line of communication went dead. The talks stopped as suddenly as they had started. The sceptical shipwrights were not inclined to reactivate the initiative. But it seems odd that the Boilermakers, who had appeared so enthusiastic, should have let the question drop, even if the shipwrights were proving difficult. The result was that demarcation disputes continued. A particularly insoluble and long drawn out dispute involving the use of welding apparatus at Cammell Lairds at Birkenhead had to be referred to the T.U.C.'s Disputes

Committee in October 1948. It found in favour of the Boilermakers.

REVISION OF THE RULES

The end of the amalgamation talks allowed the shipwrights to go ahead with the revision of their rule book which had been deferred. Seventeen representatives of the main shipbuilding areas chosen by special ballot of members, plus the Executive Committee, spent almost three weeks in November 1948 amending the rules. According to the annual report: 'They addressed themselves to this very onerous and exacting duty in a most businesslike and praiseworthy fashion.' Every proposal from a member or branch was discussed with considerable thoroughness until a majority decision was reached. In the main, the proposals could be classed under four main headings:
(a) a desire for greater communication between branches;
(b) annual meetings;
(c) area elections;
(d) increased benefits.

The Executive Committee, who had discussed the proposals before the Conference, were against greater communication between branches for they thought it would lead to 'disorganization and chaos and a complete undermining of Executive authority'. They were also against annual meetings which would only prove an opportunity for 'refractory gatherings'. On area elections, they thought that they would limit the independence of the officials, make their positions less secure and prevent them from taking unpopular action even when they knew this was necessary from the Association's point of view. As for benefits, they could go up only if contributions also went up. They did in fact recommend that trade membership should go up from 8d a week (about 3p) to a shilling (5p) except for Dockyards where it should be 10d and that apprentices should pay 6d (2½p) a week irrespective of age. In fact, the Conference agreed to increase all contributions. Trade benefit contributions went up to a shilling as proposed by the Executive Committee and Full Benefit contributions to 1s 9d (about 9p) from 1s 6d with intermediate scale rising proportionately.

The Conference spent a great deal of time discussing these major issues. It had to face the fact that many branches wanted to see area elections rather than national elections for all full-time officials with the exception of the General Secretary and the Assistant General Secretary. There clearly was a good deal of pressure for this change and it was favoured by a number of the conference delegates. The full-time officials, however, were unanimously against. They all felt that they should be given more security of tenure, not less, that the probationary period should be extended to two years and that once re-elected, they should not have to go to the vote again unless their positions were challenged on the grounds of unsatisfactory behaviour. They also threw out the suggestion from the Dumbarton branch that district delegates should be superseded by shop stewards.

Another important discussion took place on the subject of benefits. With the introduction of better social security payments by the Labour Government, some conference members queried the continuation of unemployment benefits and even of superannuation and all other friendly benefits. Unemployment benefit at three shillings a week had been re-introduced in 1946 after an interval of 20 years, particularly to help drillers who were suffering from redundancies. As for superannuation benefit this had been increased to £3 a quarter from 1st April 1946. While the suggestion of eliminating these benefits was tempting, in the end the Conference decided to leave things as they were—a wise decision. Members would not have looked kindly at increased contributions and reduced benefits. They might even have wondered whether membership was worthwhile if one of the central services, namely the provision of benefits, was removed.

A NEW GENERAL SECRETARY

John Willcocks retired in March 1948 at the age of 65. He had been General Secretary in his own right for just over two years although acting as general secretary since 1939 when William Westwood joined the Admiralty. He and Westwood had been very close not only in the union but also in private life. They had been elected to the top positions —Westwood as General Secretary, Willcocks as his assistant—in 1929 when the union was in a perilous state. It had been losing money for years and by 1929 its reserves were down to only £41,000. They had acted with speed and determination to stop the drain, only to find their labours undone by the Depression of the 1930's. But by 1934 their reward started to appear as, with the easing of the Depression, the measures they had put into effect started to pay off.

Now the Association had reserves of £230,000 or about £8.50 a member, an efficient administration and a high reputation throughout industry. Willcocks himself had held one of the highest positions in the trade union world as President of the Confederation of Shipbuilding and Engineering Unions and had sat on many Government committees.

Now he was going. At his last Executive Committee meeting in February 1948 his colleagues laid on a special lunch and paid glowing tributes to his work. The official minutes then record: 'Responding to the Toast, J. Willcocks gave a very interesting and delightful resume of his career from his apprenticeship days up to the present time and there is no doubt that his record of technical and trade union achievements came as a surprise to the listeners, especially to the younger delegates who were very much impressed and there and then decided that it would be very fitting to have such a notable record printed and made available to the whole of the Association's membership.'

Within three months, Willcocks was dead. He had hardly had time to enjoy his retirement. His obituary notice said: 'No man worked harder for the interest of the members and the Association in general .... and Mr Willcocks by his tact, ability and fairmindedness won the respect not only of the men but of the employers whom he had to meet so often in pursuance of his duty.' The Association opened a Testimonial Fund for him which raised £171. This was presented to his widow.

His successor as General Secretary was Sydney Ombler, formerly the Assistant. Ombler was elected unopposed in the autumn of 1947. In his mid-50's, he had been a member of the Association for almost 40 years. Belonging to the Hull area he had been branch secretary there for 18 years and a member of the Executive Committee for nine years before narrowly beating John McMillan for the position of Assistant General Secretary. He was highly regarded by his colleagues who spoke of his work with 'utmost satisfaction'. He was only the fourth General Secretary in the Association's 66 years and being a relatively young man, the members could look forward to him guiding their fortunes for twelve years.

While Ombler was elected unopposed, there were no fewer than eleven candidates for the position of Assistant General Secretary. They included two members of the Executive Committee: Arthur Williams and Fred King. They polled the highest votes and on a second election Williams won by a small majority. A driller from Wallsend, he had served on the Executive Committee for eight years as the Drillers' Representative.

DECLINING MEMBERSHIP

One of the first problems with which they had to deal was a slow but steady decline of membership. After reaching a post-Depression peak of 29,251 in 1944, it had steadily fallen away each year and now stood at just under 27,000. Ombler commented that there were 'thousands' who were gaining the fruits of the Association's work and not paying a penny towards its upkeep. He appealed to members to 'leave no stone unturned' to recruit new members. He was particularly concerned with the situation on Clydeside and in the Dockyards.

There was also an associated problem which caused him a good deal of worry. The income for the year 1948 was £61,000 whereas according to membership figures it should have been £69,000. 'We must ascertain the cause of this unsatisfactory state of affairs', he noted in his first review as General Secretary. 'Is it due to an incorrect record of membership or to the failure of a large proportion of the members to pay the full contributions?' The recorded arrears did not provide the answer and he asked all branch officials to check their figures carefully.

A GROWING ECONOMY

The British economy, which some economists had viewed with such alarm, put up a surprisingly good performance after the war. In particular, there was a much lower degree of unemployment and a much higher level of output than many had expected. According to one observer: 'The employment policy was successful beyond all hope.... Capital investment was also at a rate higher than many had believed possible.'[4]

Unemployment remained below 2 per cent except during the fuel crisis in the spring of 1947 while capital investment topped 10 per cent of net national product compared with 7 per cent in the late 1930's. As a result both production and productivity showed most satisfactory increases despite reductions in the length of the working week. The increase in manufacturing output was 8 per cent and the per capita increase in all industry was 3 per cent 'which compared well with any previous period in British history and with other countries including those of Western Europe and North America. It was also bound to make the most effective contribution to the solution of the other major problems including the foreign trade gap and inflation.'[5]

Unfortunately the highly impressive increases in production and productivity were not uniform throughout the economy. There was good progress in many branches of engineering, particularly motor car manufacturing and aircraft production. 'The shipbuilders and marine engineers, by contrast, failed to make use of the sellers' market in 1945-50 to modernize the yards and works and were soon to be driven out of neutral markets by builders in Germany, Japan, Sweden, Holland and elsewhere.'[6] The nub of the problem was that British output failed to rise or did so only very slowly from 1.1m. gross tons in the years 1945 and 1946 to 1.3m. tons in 1950. While British output remained steady, world production expanded quickly. In 1947 output of 1.1m. tons gave the United Kingdom 57 per cent of world output. In 1950 production of 1.3m. tons accounted for only 38 per cent of world launchings. And every year the situation got worse as British output hovered around the million mark and world output went up to higher and higher levels.

Even union leaders failed to see the writing on the wall. In his review for 1950 Syd Ombler commented: 'From every aspect regarding the present position of British shipbuilding, only one conclusion can be drawn and it is that the industry is in an exceptionally healthy condition. Apart from the output during 1950 which even surpassed that remarkable achievement of 1949 the industry took on a new lease of life by way of substantial replenishment of the order book, thus clearing the gloom which prevailed in many quarters.' Certainly there was full employment and the prospect of it remaining for at least three years but the industry was not doing as well as in overseas countries or as well as other industries in this country. And most people in the industry knew it.

In October the Executive Committee of the Confederation, of which Ombler was a member, had severely criticized a Government document on the future of the shipbuilding industry. The document which had Cabinet approval had been drawn up by a working party and made 'optimistic deductions ... regarding the volume of orders for the next ten years.' The Confederation leaders felt these deductions had little basis in fact and spelt a complacent attitude on the part of the Cabinet.

The First Lord of the Admiralty, Viscount Hall, pointed out that the industry had orders for over a million tons which would provide enough work for two years. This of course was not a figure to boast about—it spelt a poor performance. Hall denied complacency. The Cabinet were keeping a close watch on the situation and would consider alternative forms of employment even of introducing a scrap and build scheme if necessary. Having taken part in this lively discussion, Ombler's comments about a healthy industry seem even more remarkable.

The full employment throughout the economy, the rising cost of living (it went up 23 per cent between 1946 and 1950) and the retention of the principle of collective bargaining between union and employer all put pressure behind wage-push inflation. Attlee had called for wage restraint in February 1948 which was fully endorsed by the General Council of the T.U.C. and by a special conference of trade union senior officials held in March 1948. The General Council reiterated its call for wage restraint after devaluation in September 1949 unless the retail price index rose by more than 5 per cent. By 1950 the trading position of the country had improved considerably, partly due to the assistance offered by the American Government under the Marshall Plan. The General Council felt it was safe to call for 'greater flexibility in the future'. But Congress went even further, approving a motion that there was now 'no basis for a restraint on wage applications'.

Prices, profits and wages now began to rise rapidly under the stimulus of the Korean War which broke out in the summer of 1950. But although the wage restraint policy came to an end, together incidentally with many other controls over life in Britain, it had been at least partially successful. 'At least a definite degree of voluntary discipline was successfully imposed and this gave industry a breathing space and set an example to other sections of the community.'[7]

WAGE CLAIMS

Shipbuilding employers took a stronger line than their counterparts in other industries. Even moderate claims were turned down. It took the Confederation many months to secure an increase of five shillings a week for both time workers and piece-workers. The agreement was signed on 8th October 1948 and represented an increase of about 4 per cent. It would not have been signed but for the findings of a special Court of Enquiry set up by the Ministry of Labour after the Engineering and Allied Employers' National Federation had refused to concede any part of the claim submitted by the union. The Court recommended an increase of five shillings. The shipbuilding unions used that precedent to press their claim afresh and were now successful.

By 1950 the unions were no longer willing to put in a moderate demand or to accept refusal on the part of the employers. They wanted more money and they were prepared to take industrial action to secure it. The Confederation of Shipbuilding and Engineering Unions now demanded an increase of £1 a week (about 17 per cent increase) and specified that the increase should be paid for out of the profits of the industry. The Shipwrights for one were not wholly sympathetic to such a big demand and they also doubted the 'practicability' of the increase being found out of profits. As the Executive Committee told the members:

'We had in mind the competitive aspect of the Shipbuilding Industry and the possible effects upon future orders if the cost of a wage increase was passed to the consumer, in this case, the shipowner. Shipbuilding costs are at such a level that, having regard to foreign competition, any further substantial increase may speed a decline in the industry and run counter to the Government's policy of full employment.' The Shipwrights thus urged caution on their colleagues in the Confederation. They suggested an examination of the profits position to see if they could bear such an increase.

The suggestion was turned down, even though it did receive a fair measure of support. Instead a recommendation submitted by the Amalgamated Engineering Union was carried by a narrow majority. This recommendation was that members of all affiliated unions should be balloted on the choice of two courses of action:

1. Are you in favour of strike action to enforce the £1 per week claim?
2. Are you in favour of submitting the claim for £1 per week increase to National Arbitration Tribunal?

Most of the union representatives at the meeting of the Confederation in York on 9th March 1950 were against this course of action. They thought the question should go to arbitration and that their members should not be offered the option of a strike. In fact 27 of the 34 unions at the meeting voted in favour of arbitration but the 7 who voted for balloting the members had the majority of votes.

The Executive Committee of the Shipwrights wanted arbitration. 'If the case has merit in it then it should stand the test of arbitration and should be pursued constitutionally', they said. Besides if the ballot did achieve the necessary two-thirds majority in favour of strike action, the Executive would still be unable to call for a strike because the Employment and National Arbitration Order 1940, forbidding strikes, was still in operation. The Committee counselled shipwrights to consider two questions:

1. What would be the prospects of securing £1 per week increase by strike action and would not a widespread strike retard the economic recovery of the country upon which the living standards of the workers so closely depended?
2. Would the doubtful prospect of securing an increase of £1 per week (a glittering prize on the surface) justify accepting the risks and hardships which are invariably a consequence of strike action and would it not be better policy to rely upon the outcome of a National Arbitration hearing?

In putting these questions to members, the Executive Committee were leaving no doubt as to their own feelings on the question. And the members supported them. Just over 1,000 voted in favour of strike action; well over 4,000 voted for arbitration. From the Committee's point of view the only dissatisfying thing was that less than a quarter of the members had bothered to vote. Members throughout the Confederation took the same view by a majority of 3 : 1 and the claim was referred to the National Arbitration Tribunal. The Tribunal provided a very satisfactory result as far as the shipbuilding workers were concerned. It recommended an increase of 11s (55p) a week for time-workers, which of course was less than the claim. But since that was a very big claim, it was not surprising that it was not met in full. The finding of the Tribunal then went further and solved one of the union's long-standing grievances by consolidating the increase, the basic wage and the national war bonus payments into new inclusive plain time rates. The new rate was £6 a week for new work and £6 3s (£6.15) for repair work. This was an excellent result. It did, however, have one important drawback. It did not apply to pieceworkers. That problem was felt to be so intricate that it had to be the subject of a separate investigation which the employers said they would carry out. The employers also agreed to consider a claim for two weeks' holiday with pay and for a five-day week throughout the year.

In November 1951 the Confederation secured another increase of eleven shillings a week for all workers making a Consolidated Time Rate of £6 11s for shipwrights. What was even more important, the employers agreed to an additional week's holiday with pay.

In 1952 when the unions came back for another wage increase they were faced with 'a long and to some extent bitter struggle' with the employers. The claim for a flat rate increase of 7s 6d (37½p) per week was first presented to the employers on 27th June. It was not settled until 10th November and even then had been wished on the employers by the Minister of Labour to prevent what might have been a major disturbance. The employers were also pushed into conceding a five-day week throughout the year. They at first turned down the demand at national level. But later they agreed that the question was one which might be resolved by district or even yard discussions. The Tyne and Wear areas were the first to move. By the end of 1952 local employers and union officials had agreed on a five-day week and discussions had started in other parts of the country.

MEMBERS' MORTGAGES

The scheme to help members to buy their own houses which had been started many years previously was now well developed. In effect, the Association operated as a Building Society except that the rate of interest at 4 per cent was slightly more favourable than most building societies offered. Mortgages could range from £100 to a maximum of £1,500. They were repayable over 20 years by instalments of 12s 6d a month for £100 to £9 2s 6d for a mortgage of £1,500. By 1952 the Association had advanced £23,000 to members under this scheme.

A HOUSE FOR THE GENERAL SECRETARY

In March 1949 Syd Ombler, who came from Hull, reported to the Executive Committee that he had found it impossible to find a house to rent. For the previous two years he and his wife had lived in furnished rooms which they found unsatisfactory. He suggested that the Association should buy a house for the General Secretary. The Committee considered his suggestion both from the investment point of view and from a feeling of having an obligation to house its General Secretary. In the end they authorized Ombler to acquire a house on behalf of the Association. The purchase price should be about £2,000 and he would be charged a rent equal to 3 per cent of its purchase price.

A month later he reported back that he had been unable to find a house because the figure of £2,000 was 'too restrictive'. The prospect of getting a house for £2,000 was 'very remote'. He was empowered to go up to £3,000. This time he was successful in buying 7 Beverley Road, Monkseaton, at the coast, about eight miles from Newcastle, for £2,600. There were some repairs needed but even so the total expenditure was not more than £2,800. He was authorized to go ahead and purchase which he duly did.

A few months later, the Assistant General Secretary, Arthur Williams, suggested to the Executive Committee that 'an obligation lay upon the Association' to provide him with a house as long as he held an official position. He was buying a property at 2 Cedarwood Avenue, Walkerville in Newcastle for £1,800. He was willing to sell this to the Association for that sum and to pay 3 per cent per annum of the purchase price by way of rent, i.e. £54. The Committee agreed.

NATIONAL DELEGATE CONFERENCES

The Rules Revision Committee which met in 1948 conceded a demand which went back many years and was put with particular force at the end of the war. This was for an annual delegate conference. It was something to which we drew attention in earlier chapters as an important omission in the union's system of government if it wished to be considered a democratic body.

The Rules Revision Committee proposed and the membership agreed that there should be an annual delegate conference. It would consist of eight full-time officials and seventeen elected members of the Association from each of the seventeen main areas of production. Candidates were to be members of the branches within the respective area and were to be voted upon within the area. This was in contrast to the voting procedure for the full-time officials. When this suggestion had come up for their positions, the Executive Committee had insisted upon national elections.

The first conference was held at the Tyne Hotel, Hood Street, in Newcastle on Wednesday and Thursday, 26th and 27th July 1950. It discussed the current financial situation of the Association, wage claims that were pending and methods of increasing union membership. All in all it was felt to be an excellent opportunity to stand back from day to day work and look at the long-term developments. It also gave the officials a chance to discuss in detail their work and problems.

The General Secretary spent some time describing the Association's financial situation for it was causing him some concern. He also raised it at the annual meetings between the Executive Committee and the twelve district delegates. With a declining membership, income from members' contributions was falling. In 1946 there had been 28,200 members and they paid £62,000 in subscriptions. By 1949 there were 25,900 members and they paid £60,700. Meanwhile expenditure was going the other way; it was rising from £54,000 in 1946 to £61,500 in 1949. If the trend continued, the Association would soon be making a loss again and would start to eat into its reserves which had been brought back to £250,000.

The Rules Revision Committee had provided the solution to this problem by recommending an increase in subscriptions. The immediate effect was to increase contributions to £68,000 in 1950 but, because of a continuing decline in membership, this became £66,000 in 1951. In 1952 membership rose slightly and income from this source was £67,000.

But all the time expenditure rose and by 1951 it had become £67,000. The Association was once more expending more than it was receiving from members and was only saved from making a loss by its investment income from fixed interest securities. In these years its income from this source was around £4,000. In 1952 there was a reduction in expenditure of about £3,000, thanks largely to reduced claims on benefits. Even so, that year saw the following benefits paid out:

Funeral Benefit	£2,856
Superannuation Benefit	£7,530
Sickness Benefit	£8,728
Disablement Benefit	£1,242
Unemployment Benefit	£634
Tool Compensation Benefit	£13
Trade and Dispute Benefit	£1,112
Legal Charges	£770

A reduction in benefit payments made 1952 an unusual year. Expenditure had a habit of going up remorselessly. That certainly was the case with operating costs, i.e. all expenditure other than on benefits. They had doubled in the past ten years and were now the equivalent of £1 14s 5d (£1.72p) per member or 8d a week while benefit payments was half that amount. According to the annual report for 1952: 'Without pushing the mercenary aspect too far, we are still to urge the need for pruning and prudence in all matters of expenditure to avert the need for an increase in contribution rates.'

On the other hand, the Association might have queried a policy whereby contributions had gone up only twice in its history. A full benefit member paid 1s 9d a week compared with 1s in 1882. Wages, on the other hand, had gone up from £2 to over £6. It would have been reasonable to have suggested that the contributions should have been linked to wages. This would have prevented the need for special consideration to be given to increases in contributions, would have avoided the inevitable antagonism that accompanied such considerations, would have produced an automatic increase in income and would have prevented a situation where administration costs rose but benefit payments had to be severely scrutinized and held within check. For two thirds of expenditure to go on administration and one third on benefit payments was surely a situation members would have wished to rectify and wage-linked contributions would have provided one answer.

A NEW RETIRING AGE?

In 1952 the Executive Committee asked the members to consider altering the age of retirement for full-time officials. They did so following a report issued by the National Joint Advisory Committee which represented the T.U.C., the British Employers' Confederation and the Government. This body produced a review of the present position showing that a rising percentage of the population was over sixty-five. In 1911 two and a half million people, or one in fifteen of the population, were over sixty-five. By 1947 the figure had risen to six and a half million, or approximately two in every fifteen. The report concluded that there was a need to encourage the employment of elderly people.

The Shipwrights' Executive Committee took a very sympathetic view of this report. They felt it was wrong to compel retirement against a person's will and particularly when the means of enjoying that retirement namely by an adequate pension, had not been provided. The question of providing proper pensions for officials had come up frequently in the past but no positive outcome had been achieved. The Committee saw the extension of the working age as a posssible way out. A former General Secretary, William Westwood, was still as active as ever after he left the union. On the other hand, there were distant memories of Alex Wilkie who stayed in office until he died at the age of seventy-eight. The Committee therefore proposed that a full-time official should be allowed to hold office up to the age of seventy, when he must retire. What was more he had to submit himself for re-election once he had reached the age of sixty-five and would be eligible only if he provided a medical certificate of fitness. These were somewhat tiresome restrictions which cast doubt upon the Committee's enthusiasm. But they were concerned about a principle. 'The date of his birth should not debar him from continuing in office providing he otherwise gives satisfaction.'

The Committee put their proposal before the National Delegate Conference of 1952 which supported it unanimously. The members were less enthusiastic. By the narrowest of margins, 1,700 to 1,629, they turned it down. Officials must retire at sixty-five.

DEATH OF THOMAS HILL

The Association lost one of its oldest supporters in 1952 with the death of Thomas Hill, aged eighty-one. He had joined the Association in 1890, eight years after its formation, and had served as secretary of the West Govan branch from 1899 to 1907 when he was elected full-time technical adviser for Scotland and Ireland. He held that position until 1918 when he returned to his trade as a shipwright. In 1921 he was appointed secretary of the Ardrossan branch and held that position until shortly before his death. He was also chairman of the Scottish District Committee from 1930 to 1946. The obituary notice in the 1952 annual report of the Association said: 'The present generation owes much to the activities of T. H. Hill, a worthy fighter in the cause of Trade Unionism and an able exponent of the principles of the Labour and Socialist Movement in the days when the foundations were being laid. The Movement has lost a stalwart. May the memory of his life and activities act as an inspiration to those to come.'

CHAPTER TWENTY-SIX

The 1950's and early 1960's were a difficult time both for the union and for the country. The country's reputation and prestige which had stood so high at the end of the war and were further enhanced by the radical programme of the first Labour Government were allowed to decline and slip away. Victory in the military conflict was not complemented by success in the economic and industrial battle. It is true that the economy did better than it had done historically. But it is also true that its performance trailed behind that of other countries.

In this regard, shipbuilding was more typical of the economy as a whole than some of the fast-growing sectors such as agriculture, chemicals, motor manufacture or even coal mining to take an example of an old-established industry. These showed growths, often spectacular, in either output or productivity. Shipbuilding, by contrast, put up a poor performance.

Some critics blamed the unions and their failure to modernize. Certainly there was a feeling that there were too many unions in shipbuilding and disputes between them were a constant element in industrial relations. But on the other hand the two most important disputes of the period—in 1953 and 1957—were with the employers. They were criticized for showing a remarkable unwillingness to invest in new machinery, yards, men or ideas. Britain had for decades been the world's greatest shipbuilder. By 1962 Japan was building twice the output of this country and Germany about the same.

Within the Shipwrights' Association the years were ones of continual financial concern as expenditure kept bumping up against the limits of income. They were also years when the relations with employers deteriorated to such an extent that a fifteen-day national strike was called. And, above all, they were years when working with other unions involved continuous care and application.

BRITAIN CONTINUES TO DECLINE

Perhaps the country was expecting too much. Success in the war still coloured the views of many people and made them think that this country was a great power, as great as any other. Certainly that was true in the sense of national prestige. The country was seen throughout the world as the saviour of democracy and the champion of individual freedom. But it had to pay a high price for victory. International debts had risen alarmingly. Essential reconstruction and modernization had been deferred. There was a great feeling of being over-strained and of desiring an easy and quick life. Most people, and most companies, wanted to return to their former ways.

It is true that industrial output increased by a greater amount than it had ever done before. Unfortunately the increase did not match the rate in other countries who slowly but surely overhauled the United Kingdom. This country certainly had its successes both in the new industries, like chemicals and motor manufacturing, or among the older industries like agriculture and coal-mining. But these successes did not counterbalance the low growth areas such as cotton manufacturing or shipbuilding. And above all the general average was too low.

The reasons for this overall failure have been analysed by many commentators. Some say that the fault lay with the traditional conservatism of the British worker and boss. And this conservatism was heightened by a lack of absolute need to scrap old ideas or machinery. Other countries which had suffered invasion or destruction during the war had no alternative but to rebuild, using the latest techniques and processes. Britain was, in this analysis, unlucky to have won the war. Unquestionably, the victory had been highly expensive in monetary terms and in terms of sapping national strength.

Another line of attack tends to put the blame at the door of the Government. One critic has written: 'Thus, on the face of it, British economic policy, the attempt to control the economy as a whole, proved to be astonishingly unsuccessful between 1950 and 1967, particularly by comparison with other countries similarly placed. It failed to maintain stability or the value of the currency. It led to lower rates of growth than technological improvements would have warranted. It demoralized employers and workers by periodic squeezes, discouragements to expansion and enforcements of breaches of collective agreements.'[1]

A third avenue of criticism was the capitalist system itself or at least the people who were operating it, namely the employers. They failed to show sufficient drive. They did not invest enough in new plant and machinery. They did not make the best use of the talents and energies of their work people. They did not pursue the essential tasks of selling, marketing and servicing with conviction. The age of the supremacy of the engineer was over. The day of the salesman and the accountant was slow to arrive.

Finally another area of criticism was the trade unions. One writer commented: 'By the late 1950's the T.U.C. had lost much of that popular repute and was widely felt to be unable to adapt itself to the changed social conditions of the time.' Yet the beginning of this period had augured well. The General Council of the T.U.C. had offered to work as closely with the new Conservative Government, elected in 1951, as they had done with the previous Labour Government. The Council issued a statement which said in part: 'We expect of this Government that they will maintain to the full this practice of consultation. On our part we shall continue to examine every question solely in the light of its industrial and economic implications.' And they had sympathetic ministers to deal with, firstly Sir Walter Monkton and then Ian MacLeod as Minister of Labour. The T.U.C. for their part 'saw to it that the cautious and moderate policy which they had pursued under the Labour Government was maintained under the Conservatives. This was particularly true in wages policies where restraint remained the order of the day.'

The first few years of the 1950's saw a continuation of the peaceful period of industrial relations. The ending of the Korean War boom brought a reduction in commodity prices and an easing of inflation. Wage increases were not so vital to the workers. But from 1955 onwards conditions began to deteriorate. By 1957 about 8.4m. working days were lost in strikes, the worst figure since 1926. There were strikes over demarcation disputes, strikes over union recognition, strikes over pay and working conditions. And these strikes had a marked impact upon the public reputation of trade unions as a whole. There were widespread calls for firm Government action but Monkton refused to be stampeded. Industrial relations were and are a notoriously difficult area for Government legislation and he felt, probably correctly, that the suggested remedies—such as banning unofficial strikes—would not make matters better and might conceivably make them worse. There is, however, common ground among commentators that the sheer number of unions was militating against successful industrial relations and that fewer unions, even if they were stronger as they probably would be, could lead to a greater degree of industrial harmony and at the same time improve the conditions of the workers. Indeed the first would be achieved by the satisfaction of the second. It is this course which the Shipwrights were to take.

THE SHIPBUILDING INDUSTRY

In the years 1952 to 1962 U.K. merchant shipbuilding output averaged 1.3m. gross tons a year. In 1954, 1955 and again in 1957, 1958 the output exceeded 1.4m. tons but by the early 1960's a decline had set in and by 1962 production was just over a million tons. In 1963 it was to be even worse. Meanwhile, world output continued to rise steadily and by 1958 had reached well over nine million tons. There was a world-wide decline in the early 1960's but it did not last long and production then shot up even more spectacularly than before. The result was that the United Kingdom's share of this total tonnage steadily declined. In 1952 the country was responsible for 29 per cent of world output as against 57 per cent in 1947. By 1962 the proportion was down to 12 per cent and was to continue falling until the U.K. occupied the fourth or fifth position in the world league which she had dominated for so many years.

Trade union leaders followed these gloomy statistics with great interest. At first Syd Ombler, general secretary of the Shipwrights, was inclined to think that the pessimistic forecasts were a plot by the employers to prevent the granting of wage increases. In the annual report for 1953 he said as much: 'The shipbuilding employers in particular have been anxious to paint a very gloomy picture of the future, an attitude closely connected with their efforts to resist wage claims and also to seek tax relief from the Chancellor.'

In 1954 there was a considerable reduction in the order book and thirty-two ships of 300,000 tons which had been on order were cancelled. But Ombler saw this as not necessarily bad. 'This reduced order book should mean a healthier state of affairs in the industry. It should make earlier deliveries possible, thus giving better opportunities to secure new orders in the face of the much talked-of foreign competition.'

There was a pick up in ordering during 1955 and 1956 but unfortunately production now slumped due to labour disputes and stoppages, particularly in the second half of 1955, while steel supplies were still not as adequate as the industry required. So critical was the problem of output becoming that the annual reports of the Shipwrights' Association started to reproduce numerous tables from the statistics compiled by Lloyd's Register of Shipping. These showed the orders booked by various countries, the types of ship, the launch figures and other relevant data. The members could thereby see for themselves how this country's performance compared with that of foreign countries. They could also see how the immediate output potential of 1¾m. tons was never reached. Even in 1957 and 1958 when demand was high, U.K. output stubbornly refused to exceed 1.5m. tons. The new General Secretary of the Shipwrights, Arthur Williams, put the failure down to limited manpower and the limited number of berths available.

At the same time, Williams maintained that international comparisons should be based on value rather than weight, quality rather than quantity, in order to take account of the great variety of shipping produced in this country. He felt that the Swedish, Japanese and German output was comprised mainly of the simpler types of vessels, particularly the oil tankers. Only 46 per cent of U.K. output in 1960 consisted of tankers; the rest was made up of passenger liners, cargo liners, barges, trawlers, tugs and some Admiralty work carried out in private yards. He thought that international comparisons should take account of this diversity and reflect the extent of Britain's output. The recession in world output in 1959 and 1960 affected other countries rather more than the U.K. Japanese production which had topped 2.4m. tons in 1957 slumped to 1.6m. in 1960 whereas U.K. output came down from 1.4m. tons in 1957 to 1.3m. in 1960.

When boom conditions returned in the 1960's however, Japan, Germany and Sweden all moved ahead smartly while the U.K. stagnated. In 1962 Japanese output again exceeded two million tons while the U.K. declined to a million. In that year this country was one of the few to decline—nearly all other countries expanded their production. With the decline, employment also went down. By 1962 there were 50,000 employed on merchant work construction, 14 per cent less than in the previous year, while the total number employed in shipbuilding and ship-repairing was now 85,000 as against 125,000 a few years previously.

Williams commented in his annual report: '1962! That was the year that was. With shipbuilding in the doldrums, shipyards and mines closing, the steel industry working below capacity and the axe poised over railway workshops, 1962 presented a picture of unrelieved gloom.... Unemployment figures for the year were on a progressively ascending scale until they got very near the million mark at the end of the year. Much of the blame for this stagnation can be attributed to the policies and the ineptitude of the Tory Government. As regards the shipbuilding industry, it is well known that our Continental and Japanese competitors receive some form of State aid, whether by direct or indirect subsidies, or the provision of attractive credit facilities to such an extent as to place them in an extremely advantageous position over British shipbuilders.' He also saw the need for a workers' charter to remove the fear of unemployment at short notice and to offer rewards for co-operating in the introduction of new equipment. He himself took part in the discussions arranged by the Ministry of Labour between representatives of the employers and the unions to find a way of improving labour relations. Although the talks were useful, little emerged of a concrete nature.

A few years after our period closes the Government set up the Shipbuilding Inquiry Committee to examine the industry. The Committee, headed by Mr Reay Geddes, reported in March 1966. The report called for the grouping of individual yards to provide stronger management and the amalgamation of unions to provide more harmony. In a section on industrial and human relations in the industry, the report had this to say: 'The joint failure of both management and unions to tackle the problems of bad industrial relations resulting in the wasteful use of labour has cost the industry dear in money and reputation. The present state of affairs has hampered the work of managers, planners and individual workers alike; has kept costs up and deliveries late; and has in consequence tied the industry's right hand behind its back. We were therefore encouraged in our contacts at all levels in management and trade unions to find there were so many who were, at last, fed up with the situation. ... Both sides of the industry must resist the temptation to seek short term gains at the expense of the long-term interests of all. During 1965 signs of a new mood began to appear in agreements.... A start has been made and we are confident that the climate within the industry can be transformed in a relatively short period of time.' On the basis of this new spirit, the report called for Government support of £68m. in credit or compensation for losses to bring about the amalgamation of the sixty-two independent yards into three or four large combines. The report also hoped that the fifteen unions then concerned in the industry would amalgamate into five. In this way, the industry would be able to turn back the sad decline and regain something of its lost place although the report did not see the old glory returning.

Although the industry failed to grow, it did maintain a relatively stable level of output throughout the 1950's and with one or two exceptions there was reasonably full employment. In these circumstances, the Confederation of Shipbuilding and Engineering Unions, prompted by its members, kept up powerful pressure for regular wage increases. To this extent it differed from the T.U.C. which, at least at the beginning of the fifties, continually urged the unions to restrain their wage demands in line with Government policy. The Confederation took a more militant line because of the sharply rising level of profits recorded by the shipbuilding firms. One of the largest companies, Swan Hunter and Wigham Richardson of Tyneside, saw profits rise from £422,000 in 1949 to £601,000 in 1952. Another Newcastle company, R. and W. Hawthorn Leslie, recorded an increase from £202,000 to £275,000 in the same period. The unions could hardly be expected to exercise wage restraint in the face of such dramatic rises. Labour costs amount to 15-20 per cent of the cost of building a ship. The unions felt they could increase their share without having a serious impact on total costs.

The first people to show dissatisfaction were the apprentices. They went on strike because of the employers' delay in replying to their demands. The employers retorted that they would be unwilling to consider the demands at all unless there was a return to work. The Confederation also urged the apprentices to go back, which they did. On 17th April Sir Alexander Ramsay for the employers, put forward what he called 'a fair, just and reasonable proposition'. The unions turned it down but after further negotiation they did accept a schedule which offered boys of fifteen an increase of 5s 6d (27½p) a week and those aged twenty an increase of 11s (55p) a week. This brought an apprentice in his fifth year up to about £5 a week.

On the same evening of these successful negotiations with the employers, the Executive Committee of the Confederation agreed to recommend an immediate application for a substantial increase in the wages of all male manual workers in engineering and shipbuilding. Thus, the first step was taken in what was to prove one of the Confederation's toughest fights. The unions deferred until just before their meeting with the employers in June the precise amount to be claimed. They then decided to ask for an extra £2 a week on top of the £6.55 basic rate. This was a very big increase to ask for and the employers turned it down. The unions then set to one side a specific figure and asked for 'a substantial increase'. This too was turned down and according to Syd Ombler's report to his Executive Committee the employers had no alternative offer to put forward. The same replies were received from the engineering and railway employers. Flat rejection of any increase. The Confederation expressed its 'profound dissatisfaction with these refusals' and prepared for further action. But first the Confederation asked to meet engineering employers and shipbuilding employers rather than their national federations which had represented them in the discussions up to that time. At the meeting with the shipbuilding employers, Mr Ted Hill, the new General Secretary of the Boilermakers, hinted that an increase of 12½ per cent, about 15s (75p) would be given favourable consideration by the unions. The employers made no immediate response but said they would consider the question carefully. The same suggestion was put to the engineering employers.

They were the first to reply. They reaffirmed their earlier view that the claim was unjustified, would inflict grave damage on the industry, would increase costs and unemployment and would therefore be against the national interest. The lead offered by the engineering employers was gladly followed by the shipbuilders. There was to be no increase of any kind. The Confederation reacted by calling for a ban on overtime. This was against the wishes of the Shipwrights' Association whose Executive Committee preferred that the issue should be referred to a Court of Enquiry. The news of the Confederation's decision brought the Ministry of Labour into action anyway. The Industrial Relations Commissioner, Sir Robert Gould, asked if he could help. The unions and employers both accepted his offer and as a result of his mediation new talks were opened before the overtime ban was put into effect. The separate meetings with engineering and shipbuilding employers were very sticky but eventually an increase of 7s 6d (37½p) a week was offered. The unions were unhappy about such a small rise compared to their initial request for £2 but in the end they reluctantly accepted the offer which came into effect in November 1952.

Within five months, the unions returned with new demands. The Shipwrights' Association expressed the general view when the Executive Committee said that 'the wage increases of recent years have done little or nothing towards improving, or even maintaining, the standard of living of the workers in the industry due to prices and unrestricted profits outstripping the increases.' The Executive Committee also went on to say: 'If the Government of the day refuses to interfere with prices and profits, then the unions are reluctantly left with no alternative but to pursue claims for wage increases as a matter of necessity rather than advantage.' Other unions were of a like mind and the Confederation called for an increase of 15 per cent on consolidated rates, about £1 15s (£1.75p) at its meeting in May. The employers took longer than usual to consider their replies but by November they were ready to say that no increase could be offered. The unions had been expecting this reply. The Shipwrights' Association indeed had already started to ballot members on the action they wanted to take: whether it should be a ban on overtime or a reference to a Court of Enquiry. The members voted overwhelmingly for the latter and since this coincided with the views of other unions, the Minister, Sir Walter Monkton, was asked to set this up.

This he did under the chairmanship of Lord Justice Morris. The Court heard ten days of evidence from the shipbuilding and engineering employers and unions in January 1954 and then had to sift through a mass of written evidence. It finally reported at the beginning of March.

The outcome was unsatisfactory from the union's point of view. An increase of 5 per cent, a third only of their claim, was suggested. The employers 'showed a very rigid determination to comply as barely as possible with the recommendation of the Court.' The unions replied that the 5 per cent increase 'did not provide a basis for negotiations.' The employers relented a little and made an offer of about 7 per cent, i.e. an increase of 8s 6d (42½p) a week for fully skilled men, 7s 6d for semi-skilled and 6s 6d for the unskilled. The unions haggled over this concession—the boilermakers in particular were still unhappy—but in the end it was just enough to secure their argument. The new rates came into effect in April 1954. They were £7 7s (£7·35p) a week for shipwrights doing new work and £7 10s for repair work.

Again, the unions quickly came to feel that the increase was not enough. The Confederation's annual conference called for another claim and for a better wage structure. On 18th October a claim was submitted to both engineering and shipbuilding employers for a weekly increase of 10s for unskilled workers and 15s for skilled men. In March 1955 both sets of employers offered increases of 11s a week for skilled men, 9s 6d for intermediate grades and 8s for unskilled. These increases were accepted without demur by the unions. For once the claim had been settled reasonably quickly and without conflict.

In July 1954 workers in the Dockyards also received increases. They ranged from 6s 6d for unskilled grades to 8s 6d for craftsmen. Craftsmen in the London area now received £7·50 a week and those elsewhere £7·35.

In the space of five years, wages had gone up by about a third and earnings, including overtime, even faster. But then retail prices went up by 30 per cent between 1950 and 1955 so that few shipyard workers would be much better off. On the other hand, they were not losing. As one commentator put it: 'The power of organized labour was now greater than ever before and substantial increases in earnings in general kept ahead of price rises.'[2] The same author also commented: 'Already by the early 1950's inflation was coming to be recognized as an outstanding economic problem but the means of curbing it while maintaining full employment continued to elude successive governments.'

OTHER WORKING CONDITIONS

The level of wages was so critical and resulted in such protracted negotiations with the employers that few other items were ever raised seriously. The unions were anxious to reduce the constant threat of immediate redundancy and unemployment that constantly hung over their members. They wanted to see a guaranteed week of not less than forty-two hours. The employers were unwilling to offer such a guarantee and with more pressing questions in front of them the unions were not able to press the case.

The unions wanted to have uniform pay dockets throughout the industry so that it would be easier to compare wages in different districts or companies. The employers thought it was unreasonable to compel firms to adopt a uniform system and again it was not pressed by the unions.

Equally, the introduction of a five-day week was sporadic and haphazard. Some companies had introduced it more or less at once. Others felt it was necessary to work on a Saturday morning during the four dark winter months. But gradually the adoption of the five-day basic week became universal.

THE DEATHS OF VARIOUS MEMBERS

A number of notable servants of the Association died in the middle 1950's. The most notable was Lord Westwood, the former General Secretary, who died on 13th September 1953 aged 73. He had been a member of the Association for almost 50 years. Mr Frank Savage, the district delegate for Wear, Tees, Hartlepool and Humber, died in February 1954 aged 49, and Mr Peter Smith, a member of the Executive Committee from 1929 to 1939, died a month later. He was aged 80 and had been a Sunderland councillor since 1936. A few months later, in September 1954, Mr James Spiers died. He had been a member of the Executive Committee from 1938 to 1951. Another district delegate, Mr Norman Dunlop, the delegate for Tyne and Blyth, died at his home in Jarrow in August 1954 aged 57.

During 1954, the General Office had a visit from Mr William Wilkie, who was almost 80 years of age, the son of the late Alex Wilkie, the first General Secretary. William Wilkie visited the office to present to the Association the medallion of the Companion of Honour bestowed upon his father by King George V. The Association's annual report recorded: 'The Executive Committee acknowledge with grateful thanks the kindly gesture of Mr Wilkie and have accepted the medallion which will be preserved at our General Office as a token of esteem and remembrance to a man who so firmly established the Association of which we are proud to be members.'

THE FINANCIAL POSITION OF THE ASSOCIATION

Finance caused continual concern to the officials of the union. Expenditure now invariably exceeded the income from contributions and it was only the income from investments that allowed the Association to produce a net gain at the end of the year. The officials were also conscious of the fact that expenditure on benefits, such as superannuation or sickness, amounted to only a third of the total outlay, the rest going on overheads. In fact, the balance was slowly swinging more and more towards administrative expenses. In 1943, expenditure worked out at 40 per cent on benefits and 60 per cent on operating costs. But by 1953 the proportion was 33 per cent on benefits and 66 per cent on administration. The changing balance was caused by the increase in costs, particularly salaries, which simply had to be met. Benefits on the other hand were felt to be tied to contributions. As long as there was resistance to increasing contributions the Executive Committee felt that there could be no rise in benefits. But as long as benefits remained fixed while other costs increased inescapably, then the proportion of outlay would move more and more towards administration. This subject was raised at every consultative meeting between the Executive Committee and the district delegates but without any firm resolve to take action.

The consultative meeting held on 2nd June 1954 included a discussion on this topic. Syd Ombler, the General Secretary, again stressed how difficult it was to keep expenditure within income limits. Each national wage increase resulted in an increase in administrative costs and the time was coming when it would be imperative to call for increased contributions. Meanwhile he thought that income might be boosted by a recruitment drive to bring all apprentices into membership. He felt there was ample scope here. It was not so long ago that apprentices were receiving between 4s and 12s a week. Now, largely due to the union's efforts, the senior ones were receiving over £5 a week. They should be urged to recognize their obligations to the Association by becoming members and paying something back. These efforts produced results. The number of apprentice members went up from just over 2,000 in 1954 to 2,300 by 1956.

Contributions did not go up until 1956 and even then by only small amounts. Full benefit was increased to 2s a week from 1s 9d and trade benefit from 1s to 1s 3d. All other classes stayed as they were, including apprenticeship rates which remained at 6d a week. The rates were to go up only once more, again by 3d for certain categories, before amalgamation. These rates of contribution represented good value. In the 80-year history of the Association, they had slightly more than doubled while wages went up from about £2 a week to £10, a five-fold increase. The result of these small increases in contributions was that the financial health of the union remained a constant worry. Expenditure continued to exceed income from contributions—except in 1956 immediately following the introduction of new rates. But income from other sources, particularly investments, just helped to cover expenditure during most years. But the margins were getting smaller and smaller, falling from an average of about £10,000 a year to about £3,000. In 1959 and 1961 the balance at the end of the year was only just over £1,000. In two years there were losses. In 1957 there was a loss of £36,000 because of the 15-day strike in the industry which cost the Association over £45,000. But in 1962 the loss resulted simply from the inadequate income produced by contributions. With falling membership the income generated from contributions was more unsatisfactory than ever. But before action could be taken it was decided to amalgamate with the boilermakers and other unions.

There can be no doubt that during all these years the members were receiving the benefits of the Association very cheaply. Indeed by the 1960's full membership cost them only 1 per cent of their wages, a small enough amount for all the services and benefits that the union provided. But moves to increase contributions always met with resistance and could only be for small amounts, generally 3d a time. A recommendation for an increase in 1958 was thrown out by the members. Arthur

Williams, the General Secretary, commented that it was 'a great disappointment to me and the Executive Committee.... Whilst the financial position of the Association is not in jeopardy, it would be folly to allow it to sink to an irremediable position.' Even so, it was 1960 before the members would allow the increase to go through and then only for an extra 3d. A second proposal that the increase should be 6d a week was defeated with 2,200 voting for the smaller increase and 1,700 for the larger. Arthur Williams reported: 'The increase of contributions which became effective on 1st January 1960 has produced welcome results and has helped to make good some of the reverses of recent years.' The improvement did not last long for both 1962 and 1963 produced losses. But when the amalgamation took place the Association was able to take with it reserves of £282,190 which considering the trials they had laboured under, internally or externally, during all these years was a very creditable achievement on the part of the officials.

A DECLINE IN MEMBERSHIP

Part of the financial problem arose from the steady decline in membership. From a peak post-Depression membership of 29,251 in 1944 (the all-time high was 47,000 in 1920), the numbers slowly fell away. They steadied around the 24,000 mark during the 1950's but then the recession in the early 1960's saw them drop more suddenly. In 1963 there were just over 20,000. Of these 11,000 were paying full benefit of 2s 3d a week, 7,000 were paying for trade benefit at 1s 6d a week and there were 1,500 apprentices paying 6d. Arthur Williams put the fall-off down to the depressed state of the industry and to the effect of modernization. In his report for 1962 he commented: 'It is both disappointing and disturbing to record this further reduction in membership as this setback is also reflected in our income for 1962. One can only hope that we have now reached saturation point and that there will soon be a turn in the tide for the better.' His point about income can be illustrated by the fact that although contributions now stood at their highest level, income from this source produced £71,000 whereas in 1955 it had been £81,000 with contributions at a maximum of 1s 9d. In other words, the level of contributions had gone up almost 30 per cent in eight years but the income they produced had gone down by 12½ per cent because of a reduction in membership of 3,000 in eight years.

Williams was particularly scornful of the relatively small number of apprentice members. He wrote in the annual report for 1960: 'I ask myself how much longer are our journeymen members prepared to carry these non-union apprentices on their backs. Gone are the days of wages ranging from 5s to 18s for a 54-hour week; apprentices' wages now range from £3 11s to £7 11s for a 42-hour week. It is high time that they were all made to toe the line in the matter of membership.' But the opposite was the case. In 1960 there were 2,209 apprentice members. By 1963 there were only 1,519.

The members were fairly evenly spread throughout the country: about a fifth in Scotland, a quarter in North-East England, another quarter in H.M. Dockyards along the South Coast and the rest spread through London and the South-East, the Bristol Channel area, the North-West and in Ireland.

THE UNION GOES ON STRIKE

As we have noted above, wage negotiations became more and more difficult in the mid-1950's. In 1957 the unions affiliated to the Confederation of Shipbuilding and Engineering Unions came out on strike as 'the only measure, unfortunately, open to us in face of the Employers' adamant attitude.' It was the first industry-wide strike for many years and lasted 15 days.

The unions first applied for a wage increase in October 1956, six months after their previous increase of 12s 6d (62½p) had come into effect. The employers rejected both the initial and subsequent approach. A conference of all affiliated unions of the Confederation held in York on 7th March recommended the withdrawal of labour as from 16th March.

The recommendation was approved and implemented. A similar motion for the gradual withdrawal of labour in the engineering industry from 23rd March was also agreed. The response to the strike call 'gave cause for very great satisfaction as indeed it was almost 100 per cent response', according to the shipwrights' annual report for 1956. The overwhelming response had another result. It brought the Ministry of Labour into action to bring the two parties together for further negotiations.

The shipbuilding employers took a very tough line. They said they were fed up with the current state of industrial relations in the industry; the constant disputes, particularly over demarcation questions; the frequent recourse to unofficial stoppages; the go-slow tactics; the unwillingness to accept new machines and techniques; the general failure to improve production and productivity. For their part, the unions laid much of the blame at the door of the employers. They pointed to the very high profits in the industry—Swan Hunter and Wigham Richardson on Tyneside saw profits rise from £1m. in 1956 to almost £1.5m. in 1957. Those profits arose from the work of men who were not properly rewarded and whose working conditions were far from satisfactory.

After further discussions, the employers offered increases of up to 8s 6d for skilled men if the unions agreed to rectify the points they had made. The unions found this offer unacceptable. The engineering employers made an even smaller offer which the unions turned down even more quickly. The Minister of Labour decided that in the circumstances the best course of action was to set up Courts of Enquiry into the Shipyard and Engineering disputes. He also said that it would be 'of the greatest assistance to the Courts of Enquiry if the strikes in the industry were now to be ended.' The Confederation considered the Minister's request. There was a powerful minority in favour of continuing the dispute until an acceptable cash offer was made. But by 710,000 votes to 449,000 it was decided to call off the strike until the findings of the

Courts of Enquiry were known when the position would be reviewed.

The Courts spent about a month listening to oral evidence or examining written submissions and other data. The findings were issued early in May and in essence suggested that the unions and employers had a choice between two pay schemes; a 5 per cent increase (amounting to 8s 6d for craftsmen, the employers' original offer) without any commitments; or a 6½ per cent increase, which would mean an extra 11s for craftsmen. Attached to this alternative offer was a condition that the unions would make no new wage claims for 12 months, abide by agreements and settle disputes through procedure, stop unofficial strikes, overtime bans and restrictions on output, facilitate use of new machines and techniques and insist on workers doing a full day's work without interruptions.

New meetings were now held between the unions and the two sets of employers on the basis of the Courts of Enquiry reports. The engineering unions were prepared to accept the conditions and go for an increase of 6½ per cent. The shipbuilding side were strongly opposed to any 'strings' whatever and decided to press for increases of at least 8s 6d without conditions. After two more meetings between unions and shipbuiding employers, agreement was finally reached on 11th June. This was on the basis of a compromise. The unions were offered a 6½ per cent increase in wages—11s a week for craftsmen, 10s a week for semi-skilled and 9s for unskilled. In return, they agreed to accept one of the conditions, that there should be no fresh wage claims for at least a year unless special factors required a reconsideration of this position. The unions also agreed to meet the employers in special conferences to discuss and, hopefully, resolve the difficulties referred to at the hearings before the court. As the Annexe to the Agreement signed on 11th June 1957 put it: 'It is in the best interests of the well-being of the industry that there should be goodwill on the part of employer and employee alike.' The first meeting was held on 10th July but as 'nothing concrete was decided upon' a sub-committee was set up to try to make progress. Little more was ever heard. Demarcation disputes continued—there was a particularly sharp clash between boilermakers and shipwrights over pre-fabrication work at Alex Stephens of Linthouse which was finally resolved only by the T.U.C. Unofficial stoppages also went on. So, little changed in the industry.

The cost to the Association was heavy. About £45,500 was paid out in dispute benefit, resulting in a loss on the year's working of £36,000. But even so many members were critical of the amounts paid out compared with other unions. The Executive Committee had made an ex gratia payment of 10s a week to supplement the normal dispute benefit of 10s a week but even so many members felt it was too low. It certainly represented a very big drop in income for them. But it also underlined the point the Executive Committee had been making for a long time, that there should be an increase in contributions to pay for higher benefits. The Consultative meeting between the Executive Committee and the district delegates held on 22nd May heard that there were 'Manifestations of discontent by our members due to the disparity in the dispute benefit paid by our Association as compared with benefits paid by other shipbuilding unions.' The delegates agreed that the Association's finances could not stand up to a prolonged major strike and that there must be an increase in contributions. An increase was not agreed until 1960, however, and then only of 3d a week.

It is worth speculating on whether the poor dispute benefits and the Association's financial vulnerability were still in members' minds five years later when they voted to amalgamate with the boilermakers and gain security from the increased size of their organization. Shipwrights in the Admiralty Dockyards also received increases of 11s, 10s and 9s according to grades at about the same time.

ARTHUR WILLIAMS—GENERAL SECRETARY

Sydney Ombler retired at the end of 1957 after ten years as General Secretary and was succeeded by the man who had been his Assistant during that time, Arthur Williams. He was the second driller to become General Secretary and won the position in a five-cornered election. The other four nominees polled only 1,000 votes between them, whereas he received 3,997 votes. Three of his opponents stood in the contest for Assistant General Secretary, together with another six candidates, making nine in all. One of them, John Dennett, was a member of the Executive Committee and he too had an easy victory, securing, 2,811 of the 5,405 votes cast. Aged 48, he was ten years younger than Arthur Williams. He had been a member of the Executive Committee for a number of years, during which he had served as chairman of the Association, and he had also been district delegate for the Clydeside area. The General Secretary's salary was now £1,340 and the Assistant £963.

One point that arose with the retirement of Sydney Ombler was the Association's property at Beverley Road, Monkseaton. This had been bought by Ombler on behalf of the Association and he was to be the tenant during his period as General Secretary. Now he was about to retire he wished to stay on. After consideration, the Executive Committee agreed that 'Sydney Ombler shall have the option of retaining the tenancy during his lifetime.' Arthur Williams requested permission to stay on at Cedarwood Avenue, Walkerville, and this too was agreed. John Dennett was to look for suitable property for the Association to buy when he would become the tenant. The Association's solicitors, however, questioned the legality of providing residences for retired officials. They pointed out that the Rules made no provision for such a course and that the Executive Committee might be in difficulties if any member challenged the right of Mr Ombler to remain in the Association's property after his retirement. The solicitors suggested that the best course of action was to offer the house for sale to Mr Ombler under the Association's scheme for advancing money to members on mortgage of property.

The Committee readily agreed to accept this advice and decided to offer the house to Mr Ombler at the purchase price of £2,600 less 10 per cent for depreciation. When this was put to Mr Ombler he accepted the offer. The new General Secretary, Arthur Williams, requested that he too be given the option to buy the property he rented. He also recommended that his rent should be increased from 3 per cent to 4 per cent of the purchase price per year.

DEMARCATION DISCUSSIONS WITH THE BOILERMAKERS

Although the joint conferences between employers and unions over the industry's problems proved largely abortive, the shipwrights and boilermakers held a number of meetings to try to settle their differences. Both unions agreed that there should be better relations between them and that any differences should be disposed of quickly and amicably. The question was how to do it. The shipwrights felt that the answer lay in local arbitration where a failure to agree was recorded. The boilermakers on the other hand were traditionally against compulsory arbitration. They felt that the 1956 Joint Procedure Agreement should be scrapped and demarcation questions should be settled in the districts. After further discussions, it was decided to retain the 1956 Agreement but to add a clause calling for local arbitration where both sides agreed. In other words, there should be voluntary rather than compulsory arbitration. The boilermakers' and shipwrights' officials signed a document agreeing to this extra clause. But despite the hopes for its success, it seemed to make little difference. At a consultative meeting between the Executive Committee and the district delegates on 3rd December 1958 there was a thorough discussion of the working of the new Agreement.

The delegates 'overwhelmingly indicated that they were not satisfied with the working of the Agreement in its present state.'

At the same time Arthur Williams, for one, tried to fend off the criticisms over demarcation disputes. Writing in the annual report for 1959 he commented: 'I am not prepared to accept the assertion that demarcation disputes—much as they are to be deplored—are irresponsible 'tug o' war' affairs. Employers can by no means be absolved from blame. I could cite many instances where such disputes have been caused by managerial errors or managerial inclinations without due consideration being given to the rightful claims of the contending parties. At the same time I do feel that it should not be above the competence of the unions to dispose of their differences without recourse to internecine warfare.'

It might not have been above their competence but it certainly took some achieving. A particular dispute about the operation of certain equipment at Cammell, Laird of Birkenhead brought matters to a head. The shipwrights were very dissatisfied with the attitudes of the boilermakers and decided to withdraw from the 1956 Agreement. At the same time they realized that some new machinery for settling disputes had to be put in its place. There could not be a vacuum. They therefore submitted fresh proposals to the boilermakers for a new agreement. The nub of their plan was the clear need for compulsory arbitration. The boilermakers did not make a speedy reply. Indeed it was, according to the shipwrights, only pressure from the T.U.C. and possibly from public opinion that brought them to the negotiating table to consider the proposals. Three meetings were needed in all before the details were finalized.

The new Agreement which was to come into force on 12th October 1959 offered something to both sides. The boilermakers agreed to compulsory arbitration if, first, the relevant shop stewards or, secondly, district delegates had failed to solve the difficulties. On the other hand, the shipwrights' executive accepted a clause, No. 9, which aroused a good deal of opposition within the union. This clause stated: 'It is clearly understood that this agreement shall not be invoked to interfere with established practices on prefabrication work.' Some shipwrights were concerned that if the amount of prefabrication work carried out in the Platers' Shed increased, the amount of work done on the building berths by shipwrights would necessarily contract. The General Secretary made it absolutely clear that this was not the interpretation he gave to Clause 9. The Clause only referred to present practices, he said. If prefabricated work was extended, then shipwrights would not be precluded from the right of entry into the Platers' Shed.

This clarification stilled the criticisms for a while. As for the Agreement as a whole, it was welcomed as a necessary piece of mechanism. Similar agreements were sought with the Amalgamated Engineering Union, the Woodworkers, Electricians, Sheet Metal Workers, Plumbers and Blacksmiths.

Unfortunately the hopes that rested on the new Agreement with the boilermakers were confounded. And Clause 9 was the source of the trouble. Within a few months the Shipwrights were to charge the Boilermakers with violating Clause 9 in three instances—Fairfield at Govan, Cammell, Lairds at Birkenhead and the East Coast of Scotland. As a result two meetings were held between the senior officials of both unions but, according to the shipwrights, they proved abortive. At a consultative meeting between the Executive Committee and district delegates held on 17th May 1960 Arthur Williams declared that he could understand the resentment felt by the delegates and members. He was no longer prepared to restrain the members from resorting to whatever action they considered effective to safeguard their trade rights. At the same time action should be kept to a minimum—it was not necessary to use an army where a platoon would do—and the consent of Head Office should be sought first. The Executive Committee agreed that a request should be made to the T.U.C. Finance and General Purposes Committee to help to settle the issue. This was done and Sir Thomas Yates prepared a report which the T.U.C. accepted. It recommended that 'where ... there is any transfer of shipwrights' work from the berth or elsewhere in the yard into the prefabrication or assembly bay, that work shall continue to be shipwrights' work.' It also recommended that shipwrights should not make a claim to boilermakers' work simply because it had been enlarged in size. The report finally recommended that there should be a fixed ratio of platers to shipwrights on ship erection work.

The Shipwrights were prepared to accept this report in its entirety. The Boilermakers on the other hand, were not prepared to do so unless the Shipwrights agreed to the principle of amalgamation of the two societies. The Shipwrights were at first reluctant to agree to this but later agreed to discuss amalgamation if the Boilermakers would accept local arbitration in the current disputes between them.

A SHORTER WORKING WEEK

For some years, the Confederation had been pressing for a phased reduction in the working week from 44 hours to 40. In early 1960 they succeeded in reaching the half-way point. From 28th March 1960 the normal hours in the shipbuilding and ship-repairing industries were reduced to 42 per week for both day-shift and night-shift workers. A similar reduction was made in the engineering industry.

In return for the reduction, they agreed there was 'an obligation' on them, on all workpeople as well as on management 'to co-operate to the fullest extent towards the avoidance of demarcation and similar difficulties and towards the achievement and maintenance of maximum production based on the most efficient use of manpower and equipment without restrictions.'

A DIFFICULT DECADE

A difficult decade had come to an end; a decade when foreign competition had increased alarmingly, when relations with employers had grown stickier as evidenced by the national strike; when the fellow-feeling with the boilermakers had become very strained. It was not at all a happy period for the shipwrights and the feeling of apprehension must have been increased by the steadily dwindling membership and the tight financial situation. It had even led to an economy drive when such items as telephone calls from head office were to be restricted as much as possible. The Association seemed to be fighting a rearguard action within an industry which itself was in retreat.

LABOUR RELATIONS

Labour relations, between unions and management and also between individual unions, continued to be a source of concern. Almost every day disputes, official or unofficial, were breaking out in one yard or another, disrupting production and the smooth flow of output which was essential in an industry involved in fierce international competition. So critical was the position becoming that the Shipbuilding Advisory Committee set up a sub-committee to examine the prospects for the industry and to make recommendations. Arthur Williams was a member. The sub-committee presented its report in March 1961. Half of its recommendations were concerned with labour relations. They were that:

(a) Management and trade union leaders should make the most strenuous efforts to improve their labour relations;
(b) Trade union leaders should warn their members of the serious prospects facing the industry and should call for the maximum possible co-operation to achieve the most efficient methods of production;
(c) Employers and trade unions should together review their arrangements for avoiding and settling disputes;
(d) Joint yard consultative committees should be set up for free consultation about ways and means of improving efficiency and welfare;
(e) Employers and trade unions should form a national joint consultative committee to deal with matters of national interest relating to ways and means of improving efficiency.

The Report called for further discussions between the Employers' Federation and the Confederation but although numerous meetings were held little of a concrete nature emerged. Arthur Williams was anxious to see the introduction of a workers' charter covering terms of service, welfare facilities, pensions and related matters. And he continually held up Swedish practice as a model to follow. He had visited that country as a member of the British Shipbuilding Productivity team and he wrote in the annual report of 1961: 'Unquestionably labour relations in that country are superior. So are conditions of employment and therein lies the explanation. Good labour relations emanate from good conditions of employment. The two things are synonomous. Swedish shipyard workers have, through the medium of their enterprise councils (works committees) a considerable say in the running of their yards. They maintain regular contact between the employers and employees and information is conveyed to the latter on the technical and financial situation of the establishment; thus is confidence generated. The fear of redundancy which is the main cause of demarcation disputes in British yards, does not trouble the Swedish workers. They are not, as is the case in the U.K., subject to only two hours' notice of termination of employment.' He also went on to describe, with a good deal of justifiable envy, the excellent canteens, washing and changing facilities and other arrangements which put the Swedish worker in a different category from his U.K. counterpart.

AMALGAMATION WITH THE BOILERMAKERS

Considering the bad feeling that existed between the two unions, particularly over a demarcation dispute at Cammell, Lairds of Birkenhead, it may seem surprising that amalgamation was ever achieved. Remember that merger proposals had been broached twice before but had failed to win support. Now the officials themselves felt a considerable sense of suspicion and mistrust. Could they really be expected to continue talks which would lead to a favourable response by the members? And yet it was done. The vote for amalgamation was overwhelming. Why?

Paradoxically the very difficulties which bogged down the talks probably proved the biggest factor in favour of amalgamation. The members appreciated that their work was so closely allied to that of the platers—indeed in many respects was identical—that the only solution to demarcation disputes lay in amalgamation. In their work, they were already as one. They might as well come together under a single union banner.

As early as November 1960 the Executive Committee of the Shipwrights had set down their attitude quite clearly. They were 'prepared to agree to discuss with our full-time officials the possibility of making a declaration for amalgamation subject to the Boilermakers' Society giving an undertaking that the Cammell, Laird's dispute, and any other which may arise in the interim, would be referred to local arbitration.' But there was a good deal of suspicion. John Dennett, the Assistant General Secretary, at a special meeting of the Executive Committee on 17th January 1961 said that although he thought amalgamation was inevitable he could raise no enthusiasm for it when there was such a pronounced feeling of distrust. Arthur Williams went even further. He said he was against amalgamation but the trend of events might force it upon them. But he would never willingly accept it until he had definite confirmation that the rights of members were guaranteed.

The situation was not made easier by the resort to independent arbitration, as the Shipwrights had hoped, at Cammell Laird's for the award by Dr Nicholson itself led to a difference of interpretation by the two unions. As a result, platers took over the work done by shipwrights and the latter blacked their work and then went on strike.

The Shipwrights' Executive felt that Dr Nicholson's summing up—'what has to be done and how it is to be done is more important than where it is done'—was exactly in line with their own views but the detailed interpretration of the award by the company and by the Boilermakers was not to their liking. They wanted the arbitrator recalled, a step which the Boilermakers refused to accept.

But while the sniping went on, the National Delegate Conference called by the Executive Committee to consider amalgamation, took a longer-term view. By a majority of 14 to 5 it urged the Executive Committee to continue the talks with the Boilermakers' Executive with the object of reaching agreement on acceptable terms for amalgamation. The Delegate Conference resolution added: 'The basic requirements of the terms must provide for the employment of shipwrights in any part of a particular establishment on the work which was performed by them at or since October 1959. Adequate safeguards should also be secured regarding the administration of the resources of the amalgamation.'

From this point, a new atmosphere seemed to emerge in the discussions between the two executive committees. Where before there had been 'suspicion and mistrust' now in Arthur Williams' words there was 'mutual goodwill and understanding, together with a genuine belief that amalgamation would be in the best interests of the members of both organizations.' A sub-committee consisting of the two general secretaries, Arthur Williams of the Shipwrights and Ted Hill of the Boilermakers, and the two assistant general secretaries, John Dennett of the Shipwrights and John Chalmers of the Boilermakers, was set up to discuss the details. They quickly reached agreement on many matters: administration, benefits and contributions, pension funds, the number of full-time officials, general funds and mortgages to members. Even the vital question of work-sharing between platers and shipwrights was resolved. It was also agreed that all disputes must go to local arbitration. By early 1962 the terms for amalgamation were put up to both Executive Committees and agreed at a special joint meeting held on 21st February 1962 under the chairmanship of Sir Thomas Yates of the T.U.C. The proposals were basically for a kind of tightly-knit federation of unions, each carrying out its own work for its members but adding the greater strength from a unified General Executive headed by a President and a representative of the various interests. The headquarters would be at Lifton House, the home of the Boilermakers' Society, and the Shipwrights would therefore give up their premises in Eldon Square. The name of the new organization would be the Amalgamated Society of Boilermakers, Shipwrights, Blacksmiths and Structural Workers. It would be the biggest union in shipbuilding with 128,000 members, of whom 96,000 were boilermakers, 10,000 blacksmiths and 22,000 shipwrights.

Arthur Williams was invited to attend the annual meeting of the Boilermakers' Society in Worthing at the end of May as a fraternal delegate and to speak about the proposed amalgamation. He said that the objective was to put an end to the warfare between the two societies and he felt that the agreed proposals constituted a fair and equitable basis for amalgamation. The two unions had been made scapegoats for the shortcomings of the industry—well, they could not be used as scapegoats any longer. He added that when discussions started no one had been more reluctant or sceptical than himself but he was now convinced that amalgamation would be in the best interests of their members and of the industry as a whole.

Williams' speech was well received by the Boilermakers' delegates who presented him with a pocket wallet, a plaque, a book of their history and a copy of their original rules. Mrs Williams was presented with a handbag. In return, John Chalmers, assistant general secretary of the Boilermakers' Society, attended the Shipwrights' annual conference.

By the summer, copies of the proposed rules were ready for despatch to branches and the two executive committees had agreed on the ballot procedures. Officials of both organizations were to attend meetings to propagate the proposals. Voting took place throughout November and December. The result was declared on 30th January 1963:

For Amalgamation 11,933
Against " 2,579

Only nine branches voted against: Walker, Dumbarton, Howdon, Blyth, Liverpool 'A', Grimsby, Hendon, Liverpool 'B' and Hylton. But in each case the total number of votes was very low. By contrast, there were 24 branches where not a single vote was cast against. Arthur Williams commented that the result was 'most impressive'. The requisite number of more than 50 per cent of the membership had voted in exceptionally quick time and there was clearly the statutory 20 per cent majority in favour. In fact the voting was approximately 5:1 in favour, virtually the same as among the boilermakers and blacksmiths. They voted:

For Amalgamation 54,588
Against „ 11,853

And so it was done at the third and least promising attempt. But whereas before the proposal had seemed attractive but not vital, now amalgamation seemed to many members to be absolutely imperative. Not only did the nature of the work confirm this attitude but so did the continually-worrying financial position. The union was too small to carry the necessary overheads while the members were clearly reluctant to increase the contributions to provide a higher level of income. In the circumstances, amalgamation seemed the best way out. The discussion had been going on irregularly since 1955. To have brought them to a successful conclusion was a fine achievement for the officials of the unions and particularly for the two general secretaries, Arthur Williams and Ted Hill, both of whom were 63 and therefore near to retirement. Ted Hill became the first President of the amalgamated unions until he stepped down in 1965 in favour of Dan McGarvey. The officials felt that one of the greatest benefits of the new structure would be the elimination of many disputes which could now be resolved within one union rather than between rival unions. Compulsory local arbitration would also help to prevent disputes escalating into strikes or other forms of industrial action. The amalgamation also allowed a greater interchangeability of jobs which would help to reduce bottlenecks in production during busy periods.

The new rules laid down the principal objects of the Society. They were defined as the regulation of the relations between workmen and employers and also between workmen and workmen; the provision of benefits to members; and the organization of all qualified workers.

As a condition of amalgamation and with a view to reducing trade disputes between shipwrights and platers it was agreed that a ratio on a yard-by-yard basis was to be maintained on assembly, erection and fairing as determined in October 1959.

The rules covered 42 different tradesmen from angle-iron smiths to yacht-builders. The traditional shipwrights' trades were naturally included: shipwrights, shipconstructors, carpenters, eye-arc operators, profile machine cutters, modellers, constructional workers, blacksmiths, sailmakers and ship-riggers.

The 'motor' of the amalgamation was to be a General Executive Council responsible for all general and financial matters and for ensuring that the terms of the amalgamation were adhered to. It was to consist of a President, seven Boilermakers' Executive members, three Shipwrights' Executive members and two Blacksmiths' Executive members. The blacksmiths thus had one representative for each 5,000 members, the shipwrights one for each 7,000 members and the boilermakers one for each 14,000 members. Although the boilermakers had the most 'diluted' representation they had an overall majority in the Council. The Rule Book contained 56 clauses dealing with the functions of the Executive Council.

Above this body was to be a General Council consisting of 12 lay members (seven boilermakers, three shipwrights and two blacksmiths) in addition to the General Secretary from each Section, the President and two representatives from the General Executive. The General Council was to be the custodian of the Society's constitution. It could set aside any acts committed or documents issued by the General Executive that did not accord with Rule and was to consider all matters referred to it by the General Executive. It was also to be responsible for putting all major propositions for a change of rules to the members.

After the amalgamation took place detailed consideration was given to benefits and contributions. Full benefit contributions were to be five shillings a fortnight plus levies, a small increase on what the shipwrights had been paying. Sick benefit section was four shillings a fortnight plus levies and trade benefit section was to be three shillings a fortnight plus levies. For apprentices contributions were 3d a week for those under 18, 6d a week for those between 18 and 20 and 9d a week for those over 20.

In return the Society was to pay the following benefits:

Superannuation: 5s a week to members of the full benefit section on reaching 60 and having 40 years' continuous membership.

Sickness or Injury: payment for 26 weeks on the basis of 16s for those joining when aged 25, falling by stages to only 2s for those joining when aged 60.

Funeral Benefit: this also depended on the age when the member joined the union and ranged from £20 for those who joined at 25 to £4 for those who joined after the age of 60.

Dispute Benefit: 30s a week provided that the Special Defence Fund was in a position to afford the same.

These benefits were to be common to all members of the amalgamated Society. Within this general structure each of the three former unions—boilermakers, blacksmiths, and shipwrights—were to be governed by their own rules administered by their own officials. These officials were to be elected only by their own members. The senior one would continue to be the General Secretary who would be paid £31 a week compared with £37 for the President of the amalgamation and £26 for Councilmen.

The motto 'Unity and Strength' was chosen. The preface to the new Rule Book declared: 'The Amalgamated Society of Boilermakers, Shipwrights, Blacksmiths and Structural Workers is instituted to protect and guard the interests of those who follow the trade and to raise the standards of its members.' And it ended with the words: 'We can remove from the minds of our members the constant dread of bad trade with all its consequences and create a commonwealth in which the misfortune of one shall be the concern of all with due provision for every vicissitude of life. It is with this great end in view that these Rules have been drafted. If they only help us along this road, our work shall not have been in vain.'

And so the work of the independent Shipconstructors' and Shipwrights' Association came to an end. It had been in existence for 82 years and in that time had provided great service to its members in improving their wages and working conditions and buttressing them against the accidents or misfortunes of life through its benefit schemes.

It had had five general secretaries. Each of them had played a prominent part in the affairs of shipbuilding and trade unionism, generally, while two of them—Wilkie and Westwood—had also had distinguished political careers, doing a great deal to forward the cause of democratic socialism.

In terms of wages and working conditions, the Association had played its part either independently or through the Confederation in securing improvements against reluctant employers. In the 1880's shipwrights received a basic wage of £1.75 for a 54-hour week. By 1962 they received £10.17 for a 42-hour week. They also received two weeks holiday with pay. In other respects, however, the advances were very slow. Security of employment was little better than it had been in the 1880's. Working conditions were not much improved while the work itself, for all the introduction of new machinery and techniques, remained as arduous and demanding as ever. The men who built luxury liners or sophisticated Admiralty vessels were offered few comforts themselves.

As a friendly society, the Association was supremely successful considering the continual shortage of funds arising from the small contributions. In its time it paid out:

Trade and Dispute Benefit	£236,212
Tool Benefit	£ 10,186
Unemployment Benefit	£398,374
Sickness and Accident Benefit	£909,848
Superannuation	£433,952
Funeral Benefit	£203,963

During its history it raised £3,644,186 in contributions and earned £263,020 in dividend payments on its investments. Together with other small sources, its total income was £3,752,171. In 18 of its 82 years it made a loss yet it still managed a final balance of £282,190 to take into the amalgamation.

The financial strength and the benefits it provided for members, the years of struggle to improve wages and working conditions overlaid a deeper reality. For what was really achieved was a brotherhood, a community, a sharing of troubles and triumphs, a preservation of high standards of craftsmanship and a search for the just rewards for those standards. The aim itself was a dignified one and in many respects it was largely achieved. But the work, like life itself, goes on unremittingly. It is continuous and never-ending. But the example of those 80 years provides inspiration for the present and the future.

NOTES AND REFERENCES

CHAPTER ONE

1. Trevelyan, G. M. *English Social History*. London 1944, page 39.
2. Quoted by T. Sowler in *A History of the Town and Borough of Stockton upon Tees*. Teesside 1972.
3. Trevelyan, G. M. *English Social History*. Page 190.
4. Ibid. Page 191.
5. Young, Rev. George. *A History of Whitby*, Vol. II. Whitby 1817.
6. Hyde, Francis. *Liverpool and the Mersey*. 1971. Page 39.
7. Little, Brian. *The City and County of Bristol*. 1954. Pages 142-3.
8. Hodgson, G. H. *The Borough of South Shields*. Newcastle 1903.
9. Ibid.
10. Picton, Sir J. A. *Memorials of Liverpool*. 1875.
11. White, George. *A Few Remarks on the State of the Laws at Present in Existence for Regulating Masters and Workpeople*. 1883. Page 84.
12. Pelling, H. *A History of British Trade Unionism*. London 1963, page 33.
13. Mitchell, W. C. *A History of Sunderland*. Sunderland 1919.
14. Pelling, H. Ibid. Page 55.
15. Webb, B. & S., *Industrial Democracy*. 1897.
16. Pelling, H. *A History of British Trade Unionism*. Page 69.
17. Clegg, Fox and Thompson. *A History of British Trade Unions since 1889*. Oxford 1964.
18. Ibid. Page 8.
19. Mortimer, J. E. *History of the Boilermakers' Society*. Vol. I London 1973, page 83.

CHAPTER SIX

1. Clegg, Fox and Thompson. *A History of British Trade Unions Since 1889*. Page 128.
2. Phelps Brown, E. H. *The Growth of British Industrial Relations*. 1959. Page 160.
3. Webb, B. & S. *Industrial Democracy*. 1897, page 512.
4. *Shipwrights' Statement to the Joint Committee of Shipwrights and Joiners*. Glasgow 1893.

CHAPTER SEVEN

1. Shipwrights Quarterly Report January-March. 1892.

CHAPTER TEN

1. Sharp, Dr I. G. *Industrial Conciliation and Arbitration in Great Britain*. 1950, ch. 3.
2. Clark, J. F. *Industrial Relations in the North East 1850-1914*. M. A. Thesis, Newcastle University 1966.
3. Clegg, Fox and Thompson. Ibid, page 129.

CHAPTER ELEVEN

1. Jenkins, Roy. *Sir Charles Dilke*. 1958, page 391.
2. Pelling, H. Ibid. Page 124.
3. Webb, B. & S. *History of Trade Unions*. 1889, page 568.

CHAPTER TWELVE

1. Layton & Crowther. *An Introduction to the Study of Prices*. 1938. Appendix E, table 1.
2. Ibid.

CHAPTER THIRTEEN

1. Scott, J. D. *Vickers, A History*. London 1963. Page 53.
2. *Shipbuilder Magazine*, Vol. I. Page 61.
3. Thomson, D. *England in the Nineteenth Century*. Page 201.

CHAPTER FOURTEEN

1. Clegg, Fox and Thompson. Ibid, page 438.
2. Ibid, page 405.

CHAPTER SEVENTEEN

1. James and Smith. *Shiprepairing on the North East Coast During the War*. N.E. Coast Institution of Shipbuilders & Engineers. July 1919.
2. *Shipbuilder Magazine*. April 1918. Pages 142-3.

CHAPTER EIGHTEEN

1. Taylor, A. J. P. *English History 1914-1945*. 1973, page 188.
2. *Shipbuilder Magazine*. Sept. 1918. Page 69.
3. *Shipbuilder Magazine*. March 1919. Page 111.
4. Shipwrights Annual Report. 1919. Page 97.

CHAPTER NINETEEN

1. T.U.C. Annual Report, 1923. Page 92.
2. Shipwrights Half Yearly Report January-June 1923. Page 6.
3. T.U.C. Annual Report 1924. Page 115.
4. T.U.C. Annual Report 1924. Page 67.

CHAPTER TWENTY

1. *Shipbuilder Magazine*. July 1926.
2. Shipwrights Quarterly Reports June-Sept. 1925. Page 5.
3. Shipwrights Quarterly Reports June-Sept. 1926. Page 6.
4. *Syren and Shipping Magazine*. May 1926.
5. Shipwrights Quarterly Reports.

CHAPTER TWENTY-ONE

1. *Newcastle Daily Journal*, 3rd Sept. 1928.
2. Shipwrights Quarterly Reports June-Sept. 1925. Page 5.
3. Shipwrights Quarterly Reports June-Sept. 1926. Page 6.
4. *Evening World*, 7th July 1929.
5. Executive Committee Minutes, 5th June 1929.
6. *Syren and Shipping Magazine*, 7th May 1930.
7. Shipwrights Annual Report 1929, page 4.
8. Ibid, page 9.
9. *Shipbuilder Magazine*, January 1930.
10. *Evening World*, 14th August 1930.

CHAPTER TWENTY-TWO

1. Federation of Engineering & Shipbuilding Trades Annual Report 1932, page 15.
2. Shipwrights Annual Report 1936, page 16.

CHAPTER TWENTY-THREE

1. Shipwrights Annual Report 1939, page 9.
2. Shipwrights Annual Report 1940, page 12.
3. Shipwrights Annual Report 1937, page 13.
4. Shipwrights Annual Report 1938, page 15.
5. Shipwrights Annual Report 1938, page 19.
6. Taylor, A. J. P. *English History 1914-1945*, page 464.
7. Shipwrights Annual Report 1938, page 21.
8. *North Mail*, 28th October 1938.

CHAPTER TWENTY-FOUR

1. Pelling, H. *A History of British Trade Unionism*, page 214.
2. Shipwrights Annual Report 1940, page 12.
3. Shipwrights Annual Report 1940, page 8.
4. Shipwrights Annual Report 1941, page 7.
5. Taylor, A. J. P. Ibid, page 623.
6. Pelling, H. Ibid, page 217.
7. Taylor, A. J. P. Ibid, page 668.
8. *Shipbuilder Magazine* June 1945, page 276.

CHAPTER TWENTY-FIVE

1. Pelling, H. Ibid, page 222.
2. Pollard, S. *Development of British Economy 1914-1967*, page 393.
3. Quoted in the Report of the Confederation of Shipbuilding and Engineering Unions 1948, pages 167-8.
4. Pollard, S. Ibid, page 375.
5. Pollard, S. Ibid, page 375.
6. Pollard, S. Ibid, page 382.
7. Pelling, H. Ibid, page 226.

CHAPTER TWENTY-SIX

1. Pollard, S. Ibid.
2. Burnett, J. *A History of the Cost of Living*. Page 314.

FURTHER READING

Ashworth, W. *Economic History of England 1870-1939*, London 1960.

Clegg, H. A. and Others *History of British Trade Unions Since 1889*, Vol. 1. 1964.

Jones, L. *Shipbuilding in Britain*. Cardiff 1957.

Parkinson, J. R. *The Economics of Shipbuilding in the United Kingdom*. Cambridge 1960.

Pollard, S. *Economic History of Shipbuilding*. Ph.D Thesis, London University.

Pollard, S. *The Development of the British Economy 1914-1967*.

Dougan, D. J. *History of North East Shipbuilding*. London 1968.

Trevelyan, G. M. *English Social History*. London 1944.

Shipwrights, Associated Society. Reports and Papers. Boilermakers Head Office, Newcastle.

Shipwrights, Shipconstructors and—Association Reports and Papers. Boilermakers Head Office, Newcastle.

Brown, K. *Labour and Unemployment 1900-1914*. London 1971.

Shipbuilding Enquiry Committee 1965-1966. Cmnd. 2957. Chairman Mr R. M. Geddes.

Mortimer J. E. *History of the Boilermakers Society Vol. I. 1884-1907*. London 1973.

Pelling, H. *A History of British Trade Unionism*. 1963.

Webb, S. and B. *Industrial Democracy 1897*.

Webb, S. and B. *History of Trade Unionism 1894*.

Taylor, A. J. P. *English History 1914-1945*.

Burnett, H. J. *A History of the Cost of Living*.

Tuckett, Angela. *The Blacksmiths' History*. London 1975.

APPENDIX

WEEKLY WAGES OF SOCIETY MEMBERS ON TYNESIDE

	OLD WORK		NEW WORK	
1881	38s	£1.90	35s	£1.75
1882	40s	£2.00	37s	£1.85
1883	40s	£2.00	37s	£1.85
1884	38s	£1.90	35s	£1.75
1885	37s	£1.85	34s	£1.70
1886	37s	£1.85	34s	£1.70
1887	36s	£1.80	33s	£1.65
1888	37s 6d	£1.87½	34s 6d	£1.72½
1889	40s	£2.00	37s	£1.85
1890	41s 6d	£2.07½	38s 6d	£1.92½
1891	41s 6d	£2.07½	38s 6d	£1.92½
1892	40s 6d	£2.02½	37s 6d	£1.87½
1893	39s	£1.95	36s	£1.80
1894	39s	£1.95	36s	£1.80
1895	39s	£1.95	36s	£1.80
1896	40s 6d	£2.02½	37s 6d	£1.87½
1897	42s	£2.10	39s	£1.95
1898	43s 6d	£2.17½	40s 6d	£2.02½
1899	43s 6d	£2.17½	40s 6d	£2.02½
1900	43s 6d	£2.17½	40s 6d	£2.02½
1901	43s 6d	£2.17½	40s 6d	£2.02½
1902	42s	£2.10	39s	£1.95
1903	42s	£2.10	39s	£1.95
1904	40s 6d	£2.02½	37s 6d	£1.87½
1905	42s	£2.10	39s	£1.95
1906	42s	£2.10	39s	£1.95
1907	42s	£2.10	39s	£1.95
1908	40s 6d	£2.02½	37s 6d	£1.87½
1909	40s 6d	£2.02½	37s 6d	£1.87½
1910	40s 6d	£2.02½	37s 6d	£1.87½
1911	42s 6d	£2.12½	39s 6d	£1.97½
1912	43s 6d	£2.17½	40s 6d	£2.02½
1913	44s 6d	£2.22½	41s 6d	£2.07½
1914	44s 6d	£2.22½	41s 6d	£2.07½
1915	48s 6d	£2.42½	45s 6d	£2.27½
1916	51s 6d	£2.57½	48s 6d	£2.42½
1917	72s 6d	£3.63	69s 6d	£3.47½

1918	81s 0d	£4.05	78s 0d	£3.90
1919	87s	£4.35	84s	£4.20
1920	92s	£4.60	89s	£4.45
1921	87s	£4.35	84s	£4.20
1922	63s	£3.15	60s	£3.00
1923	60s	£3.00	57s	£2.85
1924	67s	£3.35	64s	£3.20
1925	67s	£3.35	64s	£3.20
1926	67s	£3.35	64s	£3.20
1927	67s	£3.35	64s	£3.20
1928	70s	£3.50	67s	£3.35
1929	70s	£3.50	67s	£3.35
1930	69s	£3.40	65s	£3.25
1931	63s	£3.15	60s	£3.00
1932	63s	£3.15	60s	£3.00
1933	63s	£3.15	60s	£3.00
1934	63s	£3.15	60s	£3.00
1935	63s	£3.15	60s	£3.00
1936	65s	£3.25	62s	£3.10
1937	69s	£3.45	66s	£3.30
1938	71s	£3.55	68s	£3.40
1939	73s	£3.65	70s	£3.50
1940	78s	£3.90	75s	£3.75
1941	81s 6d	£4.12½	78s 6d	£3.92½
1942	86s 6d	£4.32½	83s 6d	£4.17½
1943	92s 6d	£4.62½	89s 6d	£4.47½
1944	96s 6d	£4.82½	93s 6d	£4.67½
1945	101s	£5.05	98s	£4.90
1946	107s	£5.35	104s	£5.20
1947	107s	£5.35	104s	£5.20
1948	112s	£5.60	109s	£5.45
1949	112s	£5.60	109s	£5.45
1950	£6 3s 0d	£6.15	£6	£6.00
1951	£6 14s 0d	£6.70	£6 11s 0d	£6.55
1952	£7 1s 6d	£7.07½	£6 18s 6d	£6.87½
1953	£7 1s 6d	£7.07½	£6 18s 6d	£6.87½
1954	£7 10s	£7.50	£7 7s	£7.35
1955	£8 1s	£8.05	£7 18s	£7.90
1956	£8 13s 6d	£8.67½	£8 10s	£8.50
1957	£9 4s 6d	£9.22½	£9 1s 6d	£9.07½
1958	£9 12s	£9.60	£9 9s 0d	£9.45
1959	£9 12s	£9.60	£9 9s 0d	£9.45
1960	£9 12s	£9.60	£9 9s 0d	£9.45
1961	£10 0s 0d	£10.00	£9 17s 4d	£9.88
1962	£10 0s 0d	£10.30	£10 3s 4d	£10.17

INDEX